RIFLES AND AMMUNITION

THE EMPIRE'S RIFLEMEN IN SPORT AND WAR

Photo: Sport and General
THE 1,000 YARDS RANGE AT BISLEY
The Australian team finishing their victorious shoot for the Mackinnon Cup, 1914

Photo: Newspaper Illustrations
SOMEWHERE IN BELGIUM
An open trench in Belgium in the early days of 1915. One man is using the front of the trench as an arm-rest, and the other is steadying his body against the back wall.

RIFLES AND AMMUNITION
and Rifle Shooting
By H. OMMUNDSEN, G.M., G.C.
and ERNEST H. ROBINSON

The Naval & Military Press Ltd

In reprinting in facsimile from the original, any imperfections are inevitably reproduced and the quality may fall short of modern type and cartographic standards.

To

B. O. and M. R.

Whose encouragement and enthusiasm have much helped in the making of this book

PREFACE

STARTED when the Great War was yet a few months more than a year away, and finished when it has run eleven months, this book can at least claim that it appears when the minds of men are more concerned with rifles and ammunition than ever before in the history of the world. That this is altogether an advantage we are inclined to doubt. The touchstone of war has proved some things to be gold that we counted dross, and some to be dross that we cherished as gold, so that it is not always possible to determine exactly where we stand as regards our theories and our facts. Maybe there are some who will tell us that in the circumstances it might have been well to postpone the publication of the book. Such a course did, indeed, appeal to us with some insistence; but the ordinary rules which govern the "expectation of life" are now no guide to one's chances of being able to take up again a job once put on one side. No man can contemplate with equanimity a risk of not being able to complete that work to which he has put his hand; and so the book sees the light of day whilst Bisley expert and Hythe instructor are united in teaching Britain's new armies to shoot, and whilst comrades, friends, and fellow competitors of many beflagged and wind-swept ranges are risking and laying down their lives with rifle in hand.

We feel that an apology is needed from us for venturing on fields where others more able have so skilfully trod before. But it is difficult to apologise for a thing one loves; and the writing of these pages, the gathering together of the illustrations, the making of the book, the proving and polishing of all its parts, as far as our abilities would allow, has indeed been a labour of love. If our readers get but half the pleasure in reading our chapters that we have had in the writing them, they will need no apology from us. In any case, we hope that the somewhat novel arrangement of the chapters in Part I. where the histories of the rifle and the ammunition run alternately, and our endeavour in Part II. to present the practical side of rifle shooting in a clear and concise manner, will be acceptable to rifle lovers, and that matters of interest will be found in more just relation to the wealth of words we have expended than was Falstaff's "half-pennyworth of bread to this intolerable deal of sack."

Not the least pleasurable part of undertaking a work of this kind is that one finds a number of good friends who are only too glad to help in any way within their power. We are under obligation to many, and cannot thank them all here; but we feel we must not let this opportunity pass without mentioning our indebtedness to Lieut.-Colonel C. R. Crosse (Secretary to the N.R.A.), to Captain J. H. Hardcastle, to Mr. Max Baker (Editor of *Arms and Explosives*), to Mr. F. W. Jones, to Mr. H. W. R. Tarrant (of the Birmingham Small Arms Company, Limited), and to Messrs. the Remington Arms Union Metallic Cartridge Company. From all of these we have received many kindnesses and just the help wanted at the moment when it was needed.

H. O.
E. H. R.

June, 1915.

CONTENTS

Part I
HISTORICAL AND GENERAL

CHAPTER		PAGE
1.	The Origin and Theory of Rotatory Projectiles and the Early History of Rifled Arms	1
2.	The Early History of Propellants and Projectiles	27
3.	The Perfecting of the Muzzle-loader and the Development of the Military Breech-loader	54
4.	The History of the Cartridge up to the Adoption of the Solid-drawn Case for Military Arms	78
5.	The Development of the Bolt-action and Magazine	90
6.	The Demand for Higher Velocities and How it was Met by Reduction in Bullet Diameter and the Invention of Smokeless Rifle Powder	102
7.	Modern Military Rifles Critically Examined	121
8.	Military Rifle Ammunition of To-day	149
9.	The Sporting Rifle—Its History and Development	171
10.	Sporting Rifle Ammunition	179
11.	The .220-in. Calibre Rifle	186
12.	The .220 Cartridge	200
13.	Simple Ballistics	205

CONTENTS

Part II
PRACTICAL RIFLE SHOOTING

CHAPTER	PAGE
1. Shooting in War, in the Field and on the Range	219
2. Physical Condition in Relation to Rifle Shooting in War and Peace	226
3. Trigger Pulling or "Let Off"	234
4. Eye Training and Aiming	238
5. Judging Distance	244
6. Time Occupied in Aiming	250
7. Wind Allowance	252
8. The Trajectory Curve and the Part it Plays in Practical Shooting	264
9. The Effect of Cant	271
10. A Summary of the Conditions necessary to Accurate Rifle Fire	274
11. The Care of the Rifle	282
12. Team Selection and Team Shooting	290
13. The National Rifle Association	300
14. Some Foreign and Colonial Rifle Associations—British Teams Abroad	316
Index	325

LIST OF PLATES

The Empire's Riflemen in Sport and War . . . . . . *Frontispiece*

PLATE	FACING PAGE
I.—Three Early Rifles in the Tower Collection	4
II.—(a) An Early Matchlock. (b) The Last British Service Matchlock	12
III.—(a) A Wheel-lock. (b) A "Snaphance" or Flint-lock	16
IV.—(a) A Breech Action of 1537. (b) Another of Henry VIII's. Breech-loaders	22
V.—(a) A German Flint-lock Magazine Rifle. (b) An American Percussion Rifle	26
VI.—(a) An Ancient "Peep Sight." (b) An American Under-Hammer Rifle	30
VII.—Early British Service Rifles	36
VIII.—(a) An Early Percussion Carbine. (b) Sharp's Capping Carbine	40
IX.—(a) Whitworth's Hexagonal Bullets. (b) Cartridges for a Muzzle-loader	46
X.—Three Military Percussion Rifles	50
XI.—Three Muzzle-loading Percussion Military Rifles	56
XII.—Three Match Rifles	60
XIII.—(a) Prussian "Needle-Gun." (b) French Chassepot (Zouave). (c) Single Shot Mauser Rifle	66

LIST OF PLATES

PLATE		FACING PAGE
XIV.—(a) Kerr's Bolt Action Rifle. (b) The Spencer Repeating Rifle		70
XV.—(a) Prince's Breech-loading Carbine. (b) The Mont Storm Cavalry Carbine. (c) The Westley Richards Military Rifle		74
XVI.—Three Specimens from the N.R.A. Museum		80
XVII.—(a) An Early Pattern Remington. (a) The French Tabatière Rifle		82
XVIII.—Types of Early Cartridges		86
XIX.—(a) Kerr's Rifle. (b) The French Gras Rifle		92
XX.—(a) The Hotchkiss Magazine Rifle. (b) The Lee-Burton Magazine Rifle		96
XXI.—The Action of the Lee-Enfield		100
XXII.—Three Modern Military Rifles		104
XXIII.—The Canadian Ross Rifle Action		110
XXIV.—The Ross Rifle Military Back-sight		114
XXV.—Rolling the Barrel "Mould" or Blank		118
XXVI.—A Drop Forging Hammer		122
XXVII.—(a) Testing for Straightness. (b) Barrel Setting		128
XXVIII.—Inspecting the Barrel in the Rifled State		132
XXIX.—Gauging Bolt Bodies		138
XXX.—The Mechanical Rest Used in Testing Service Rifles		142
XXXI.—The First Shooting Test at 100 Feet		146
XXXII.—The Range Test at 600 Yards		150
XXXIII.—Washing and Cleaning after Testing		154
XXXIV.—Types of Cartridges Used in the Balkan War Compared with British Cartridges		158
XXXV.—Three Types of Chargers		162

LIST OF PLATES

PLATE	FACING PAGE
XXXVI.—Types of Clips and Chargers	164
XXXVII.—A British Service Bullet in Flight	168
Folding Plate—A Nomograph of Rifle Elevation	170
XXXVIII.—Professor Boys' Photographs	174
XXXIX.—(a) An Ogival-Headed Projectile in Flight. (b) A Pointed Bullet in Flight	180
XL.—(a) Bullets Fired Base First. (b) French "Balle D" in Flight	188
XLI.—Types of High-Velocity Ammunition for Target Shooting	198
XLII.—Types of Sporting and Target Bullets (Actual Size)	206
XLIII.—The Off-hand or Standing Position	222
XLIV.—(a) The Kneeling Position. (b) The Prone Position	228
XLV.—War Shooting in the Open	236
XLVI.—War Shooting in the Open: An Ideal Position	240
XLVII.—(a) The Loading Position. (b) The Best Grip	242
XLVIII.—The Back Position	246
XLIX.—Colonel J. D. Hopton	254
L.—The School of Musketry, Bisley, 1914-5	258
LI.—A Winter Fighting Expedient	262
LII.—A Long-Range Score Sheet	266
LIII.—(a) The Pull-Through in Use. (b) The Boiling Water Method of Cleaning	272
LIV.—The Bazaar Lines, Bisley	278
LV.—The Stickledown Butt, Bisley	284
LVI.—The First Stage of "The King's"	288
LVII.—(a) The "Running Deer" Firing Point. (b) The "Running Deer" Butt	292

LIST OF PLATES

PLATE	FACING PAGE
LVIII.—The Target Pits at Bisley	296
LIX.—(a) A Short-Range Target. (b) Repairing the Frames	302
LX.—(a) The Scoring Panel. (b) The Long-Range Bisley Target	306
LXI.—The Century Butt, Bisley	312
LXII.—(a) The Short-Range Firing Point, Camp Perry, U.S.A. (b) American Firing Point Arrangements	318
LXIII.—(a) The Shooting House, Camp Perry, U.S.A. (b) The 300 Yards Firing Point, Camp Perry, U.S.A.	322

ERRATA

Plate IV., *read* "in fact, a cartridge, when loaded ready for insertion."
Plates XXXVII. and XXXVIII., *read* "Professor Boys."

LIST OF ILLUSTRATIONS

FIG.		PAGE
1.	Gas escaping past loose ball	5
2.	Gas escaping in bent barrel	6
3.	The trajectory of a spherical bullet	9
4.	Hardcastle's pressure curve of air resistance to a bullet	10
5.	Robins's ballistic pendulum	32
6.	A Patch tube	36
7.	The Brunswick ball	39
8.	Jacob's two-flanged ball	42
9.	Sections through Pritchett bullets	49
10.	Whitworth's bullet	50
11.	Boucher's disc bullet	51
12.	Whitworth's rifling	57
13.	Boucher's rifling	62
14.	The Remington action	67
15.	Gilbert Smith's breech-loader	69
16.	Prince's sporting rifle	70
17.	Double-set trigger	75
18.	Terry's rifle	81
19.	Colt's revolving rifle	92
20.	The Winchester repeating rifle	95
21.	The development of the ·303 case	103
22.	The development of the ·303 bullet	117
23.	The Mauser bolt	127
24.	The Mauser action (section)	129
25.	The straight-pull Mannlicher (section)	135

LIST OF ILLUSTRATIONS

FIG.		PAGE
26.	The Lebel rifle	141
27.	Trajectory compared with unimpeded flight	159
28.	Flatness of trajectory due to speed	159
29.	Line of sight and line of trajectory	241
30.	The fixed relation of the trajectory to the rifle	241
31.	The fall of the trajectory after crossing line of sight	268
32.	A sporting rifle trajectory	269
33.	Stag target	270
34.	The effect of cant	272
35.	The effect of cant when the sight is adjusted for wind	273
36.	The effect of cant against wind with sight adjusted	273
37.	The Bisley marking panels	305

Part I
HISTORICAL AND GENERAL

RIFLES AND AMMUNITION
AND RIFLE SHOOTING

Part I
HISTORICAL AND GENERAL

CHAPTER I

The Origin and Theory of Rotatory Projectiles and the Early History of Rifled Arms

MODERN rifles and ammunition are the outcome of centuries of evolution, and are not entirely the result of recent scientific experiments, therefore no consideration of them can be complete without an account of the slow processes that have led up to their present comparative perfection. Before it is possible to appreciate properly the difficulties which lie in the path of rifle and ammunition users and makers to-day, it is necessary to have some knowledge of those difficulties which already have been overcome either wholly or in part.

The man who first succeeded in providing himself with a weapon with which he could kill, from a safe distance, either his necessary animal food or his enemy, was the originator of all missile weapons. It is easy for the imagination to trace in a brief period of time the main steps that have led slowly to the very efficient thermo-dynamic instrument with which man arms himself to-day, and throws a projectile over many thousands of feet in a few seconds. The ultimate development of missile-throwing weapons may be as great an advance on the rifle as the rifle is upon the hand-thrown stone; but the rifle as we have it in these early years of the twentieth century is at least an accurate engine of destruction.

A rifle is a tube closed at one end, having grooves cut screw-wise upon its interior surface. These grooves are the "rifling," and are the one essential of a rifled arm. The propellant, placed in the closed end of the tube with the projectile lying between it and the open end, is ignited and turns very rapidly into gases which must escape or burst the tube. The projectile offers less resistance than the walls of the tube, and is driven forward in front of the escaping gases until it is thrown from the open end. Besides this forward motion imparted by the expanding products of combustion, the projectile is given another motion. It is caused to spin rapidly by its efforts to escape through the retarding grip of the twisted grooves.

This spinning of a projectile upon an axis coincident with its line of progress along the bore of the rifle has the effect of very greatly increasing the accuracy of its delivery. The spinning does not add to the ranging power of the projectile, as was imagined by early experimenters with firearms, but merely tends to keep it travelling along the path in which it was originally projected. Any missile, whether thrown by hand or by a mechanical appliance, has its direction very greatly influenced by the distribution of weight within its mass, and the only means of counteracting the tendency to inaccurate flight, due to an unequal distribution of weight, is to cause the missile to spin. The inequalities of weight are then acting with equal force in all directions around the axis of spin.

When a spherical projectile is spun by the grooves of a rifle, its revolutions are about an axis roughly coincident with the line of departure. That is to say, its axis of spin is an imaginary line which is, throughout the whole flight of the bullet, more or less parallel to the line of original projection (see Fig. 3). With rifled arms firing spherical bullets this would be a decided disadvantage at the longer ranges, for at the end of the sharp drop from a high trajectory the axis of spin might be nearly at right angles to the line of flight. Consequently, the lateral drift of the ball due to its spin would be very great. As a matter of fact, rifles firing spherical bullets were never sufficiently accurate to fire at ranges where drift could be appreciated.

Some degree of knowledge of the peculiar attributes of spin when applied to missiles has belonged to mankind since very early times. The Zulu of to-day, when throwing his assegai, imparts to it a sharp rotary motion by spinning it between the thumb and fingers of his throwing hand. Some savage tribes twist round the end of their spears or throwing sticks a long thong of leather, which is used to impart this necessary spinning motion. There can be no reason for supposing that barbaric peoples of earlier times had not similarly discovered the virtues of spin as an aid to straightness. Feathers set at an angle to the long axis of an arrow have been used for centuries to impart a spinning motion about that long axis whilst the arrow is in flight.

It is one of the curiosities of human thought and the development of ideas that though archers, javelin throwers, and spearmen went to considerable trouble to spin their weapons, and therefore must have had an inkling of what they were effecting, it was not until some hundreds of years after projectiles had first been thrown from guns that the idea of spinning those projectiles was evolved. It is probable that the reason for this delay lay chiefly in the fact that nearly all the early projectiles were roughly spherical. Slings and the catapult-like crossbows, which were used before the days of firearms, obtained their effects without any conscious effort on the part of the user to impart a spin; there thus arose in the minds of early users of "hand gonnes" no apparent analogy between a round bullet and a long arrow. It should be noted, however, that in very early guns a short "bolt," like that of the crossbow, was used for some purposes.

The date of the invention of rifling is not known with any certainty. It has been claimed by some writers that a date between 1470 and 1500 marked this important step in the art of dealing death at a distance; but this approximation is arrived at by the examination of weapons collected in museums, and therefore only tells us the date of the earliest examples of rifling now existing.

It is difficult to judge from any available material whether rifling of gun barrels was in the first place due to a deliberate attempt to spin the bullet, or whether it resulted from the accidental cutting of twisted grooves in place of straight grooves designed to minimise the ever-present nuisance caused by the accumulation of fouling within the bore. The great improvement in accuracy that could be obtained by using a well-fitting bullet must have been very early discovered by the discerning target shot or sportsman, but this knowledge was discounted by the fact that to get a well-fitting bullet down the bore necessitated cleaning after every shot. It is possible that some ingenious soul thought of cutting grooves straight down the barrel, into which the fouling would be pushed by the new bullet in its passage down the barrel of the muzzle-loader, and it may be possible that these grooves might some time have been cut twisted with the very inefficient tools then available, but it hardly seems likely that such an error led to the discovery of the merits of spinning the bullet. Straight-grooved rifles are known in collections of early arms, and they have led to the propounding of the above hypothesis. There is, however, no evidence that these straight grooves preceded the proper twisted ones.

It is far more likely that some observant gunsmith, anxious to improve the shooting of his weapons, recognised the analogy between the bullet and the arrow, and sought to spin his bullet as the arrow was spun. If this were the case, it is possible that many devices for imparting spin were tried before the simple expedient of spirally grooving the interior of the bore was hit upon. More recent experimenters, desiring to spin bullets projected from shot-gun barrels, have tried vanes on the bullet, spiral holes in the bullet, and have even suggested revolving the whole barrel at a high speed whilst the bullet is passing through it. As lately as 1894 this idea of a revolving barrel was mooted, but it was suggested many times before that date.

There are extant some early German crossbows the missiles from which were delivered through guiding tubes having spiral slots or grooves cut upon their interior surfaces. Unfortunately, the makers of crossbows did not habitually date

PLATE I

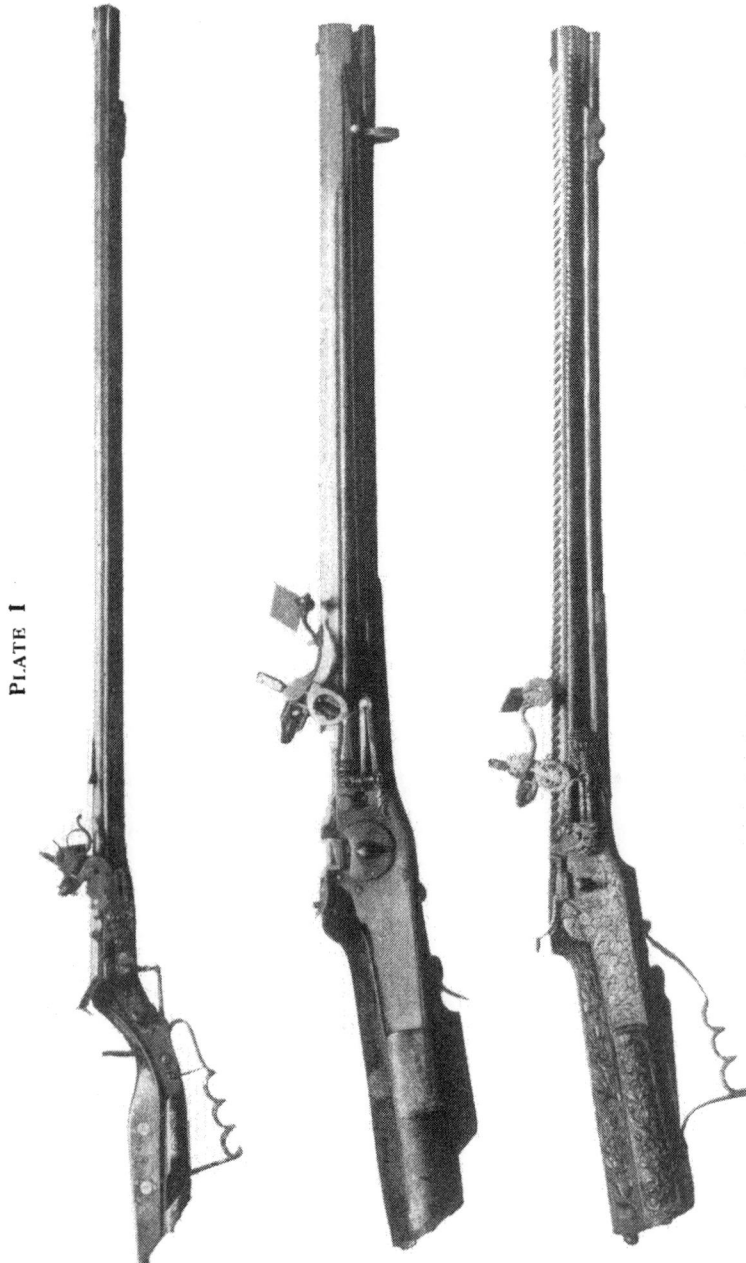

THREE EARLY RIFLES IN THE TOWER COLLECTION

The upper of these three rifles has a tricker-lock and an eight-grooved barrel. The stock is inlaid with ivory and mother-of-pearl. The middle piece is a carbine with tricker-lock, and is dated 1669. The bore is hexagonal with grooves at the angles. The bottom rifle is dated 1675. It has a wheel-lock and is very richly ornamented. The barrel has a bore of about .60 inch and is cut with seven circular grooves

their pieces, and there is no evidence to show whether the use of the rifled crossbow ante-dated or was subsequent to the adoption of rifling in firearms.

When the rifling of firearms was first carried out it would naturally seem to experimenters that a very large percentage of the added accuracy must be due, not to the rifling itself, which was rough and very elementary in its form, but to the fact that, in order that the bullet should be revolved, it had to fit the bore more or less tightly. This fact would be obvious even to the unscientifically-minded gunners of early days, and was indeed so apparent that it helped theorists to obscure for centuries the real virtues of the rifled barrel.

The amount of fouling that was left in the barrel after each shot in the early days of gunpowder was very great; rapidity of fire was then,

Fig. 1.—Gas escaping past one side of a loose ball and rolling it along the side of the bore. MD indicates the path the ball so rolled may be expected to take

as it is now, very necessary for military purposes, and the projectiles fired from the musket and its forerunners fitted the barrel very loosely, so that they could easily be dropped down a badly fouled barrel. As a consequence, there was an enormous escape of gas round the bullet, which escape usually took place past one side of the bullet. The bullet was therefore jammed against the other side of the barrel and rolled along to the muzzle, and so every ball projected from an unrifled barrel must leave the muzzle with a spin imparted by this rolling progression. It should be noted that the spin of a ball from an unrifled barrel can never be round the axis of the bore. There is no possible means of determining past which side the gases will escape, and as a consequence the axis of spin and the curve of the bullet's path (drift) is in this case an unknown quantity. It may operate to throw the ball in any direction; if it throws the ball up, it will operate against gravity and give it longer range; if the ball is thrown down, the range may be much reduced.

Early firearms were so inaccurate that an ordinary expert user of the longbow could outshoot the musket both in distance and accuracy. But for the moral effect of noise the firearm must have been longer than it was in coming to its own. In 1585 Montaigne criticised firearms as being of little use in war save for their noise, "to which it is not easy to become accustomed."

With the adoption of rifling, though loading was of necessity slower, as the bullet, made of sufficient size to take the grooves of the rifling, had to be forced down the barrel from the muzzle with a heavy ramrod or a ramrod and mallet, the wobbling of the bullet was practically done away with, together with the escape of gas. In this the theorists found further means of confusing their thoughts and hiding the true virtues of the rifled barrel.

Fig. 2.—By bending the last inch or two of an unrifled barrel the direction of the drift can be controlled. With a barrel bent as shown at M, the drift will always be in the direction M D

Benjamin Robins, an experimenter of the middle of the eighteenth century, who was gifted with true scientific insight, was the first to publish the important discovery that the virtues of rifling lay not in the better fitting bullet it was necessary to use, nor in the resistance of the rifling, nor in any of the other reasons that had been advanced to account for the straight shooting of a rifled arm, but simply and solely that it was a means of determining the axis of the spin of the round ball then used at the moment of leaving the barrel, and as a consequence throughout its flight. He showed that by bending the last inch or two of the barrel of a smooth-bore he could determine the direction which the ball would take. If, for instance, he bent the barrel to the left, so that the ball was travelling along the right side of the bore as it left the muzzle, it would curve to the right in its flight.

BENJAMIN ROBINS

The following extract from the "Mathematical Tracts of the late Benjamin Robins, Esq., containing his New Principles of Gunnery, etc.," published in 1761, gives a very clear statement of the knowledge of the principles of rifling as he understood them, and summed up the matter in a manner which satisfied experimenters for a good many years after he had finished his work:

"When the piece is fired, the indented zone of the bullet follows the sweep of the rifle; and thereby, besides its progressive motion, acquires a circular motion round the axis of the piece, which circular motion will be continued to the bullet after its separation from the piece; by which means a bullet discharged from a rifled barrel is constantly made to whirl round an axis which is coincident with its line of flight. And hence it follows that the resistance of the foremost end of the bullet is equally distributed round the pole of its circular motion, and acts with an equal effect on every side of the line of direction, so that this resistance can produce no deviation from that line. And (which is of still more importance) if, by the casual irregularity of the foremost surface of the bullet, or by any other accident, the resistance should be stronger on one side of the pole of circular motion than on the other; yet, as the place where this greater resistance acts must perpetually shift its position round the line in which the bullet flies, the deflection which this inequality would occasion, if it acted constantly with the same given tendency, is now continually rectified by the various and contrary tendencies of that disturbing force during the course of one revolution."

The well-known sporting writer, "Stonehenge," discussing this very paragraph in 1859, adds some observations on the flight of a long, cylindrical-shaped bullet which show that with the use of these bullets the virtues of rotation were found to be even greater than Robins had imagined.

Starting with a statement that Robins's conclusions are admitted to be correct and require no support, he continues:

"A ball from a smooth-bore (that is, from a barrel not rifled in any way) will have a greater velocity and range than a similar ball projected from a rifled barrel, on account of the friction caused by the rifling absorbing some portion of the original force of the explosion. Hence, neither increased range, nor its synonym, velocity, is gained by rifling, but only truth or correctness of flight; so that, though the ball does not really go further, it will be of service at a greater range, because it will hit the object at which it is aimed. At the same time, the introduction of rifling may be said to increase our range—not, it is true, in the use of spherical balls, the flight of which it retards, but because, from the spinning motion given to it, a more elongated ball may be used than from a smooth-bore; and hence, the weight being increased in a greater proportion than the area to which the atmosphere offers resistance in its passage, the flight is greatly extended. In a smooth-bore a slightly oval ball can be relied on, if one end is slightly thicker than the other (or egg-shaped), for that end being heavier will always fly forward; but a pointed cylinder soon 'upsets,' as it is termed, and is then at once rendered useless as a projectile. By 'upsetting' is to be understood the turning sideways of an elongated ball, and it is this accident which forms the chief impediment to rifle shooting. The impetus being given to the hind end of the ball, while the resistance of the air is offered to the front, there is a constant tendency to the one overtaking the other, in doing which the ball must necessarily offer its side to the point at which it is aimed. The greater the spin the more this tendency is checked, for no sooner does the base begin to turn over to the right than it is forced round to the left, and so on in succession to every point in the circle of which its line of flight is the centre."

Having given these two quotations, one from the posthumous "tracts" of an early scientist, and the other from a book by a sporting journalist and practical shot of great repute, whose active lives were separated by nearly a century, it will be well to jump another fifty-five years and quote from a modern "gunner" the most up-to-date views on the effect of spin on the bullet. The two quotations refer to the action of spin in keeping an elongated projectile point foremost. The quotation that is about to be made deals with the drift of the

THE THEORY OF DRIFT 9

bullet from a straight line of flight due to the gyroscopic effects given rise to in the bullet by the rapid spin.

It is found that a bullet always swerves in its flight; to the left if the rotation is left-handed, and to the right if the rotation is clockwise. This swerve, which may be regarded as a constant for a given rifle and given range, is known as drift. Sir George Greenhill describes it as a "side issue" of the gravity curve, by which is meant that if there were no drop due to gravity there would be no drift of the bullet, because the turning of the point of the bullet is due to the resistance caused by the falling of the bullet, as will be explained.

Captain J. H. Hardcastle, R.A., an experimentalist whose name needs no introduction to the student of rifle-shooting

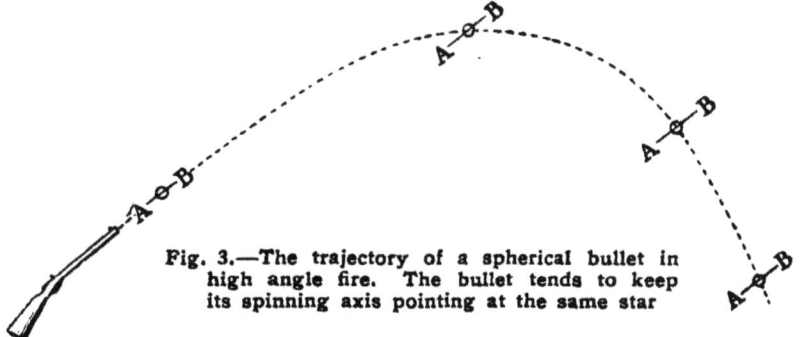

Fig. 3.—The trajectory of a spherical bullet in high angle fire. The bullet tends to keep its spinning axis pointing at the same star

science, may be quoted as giving the clearest exposition of our knowledge as it is to-day. In a private letter dated May 6, 1914, to a young enthusiast in technical difficulties as to the effect of spin on spherical and elongated bullets, Captain Hardcastle explains the matter with illuminating clarity:

"The spherical rifle-bullet tends to keep its spinning axis pointing at the same *star*, just like the elongated bullet, and any force tending to twist it out of this line actually sends it out of it at right angles. If you press upwards at the top of a Lee-Enfield bullet (left spin), the axis does not go *up*, but to the *left*, like any other top.

"A force tending to put the nose to the left sends it down.

"A force tending to put the nose down sends it to the right.

"A force tending to put the nose to the right puts it up.

RIFLES AND AMMUNITION

"When the bullet emerges from the muzzle, truly centred, the air resistance acts dead along the axis. But the bullet immediately begins to fall, and the resistance is then acting to lift the nose slightly, as all the resistance is at the nose portion. Thus the cycle of events just mentioned is started, and the bullet progresses on a minute corkscrew path, with diameter about .01 in. and pitch of about 14 ft. for a bullet 1.25 in. long.

$$\frac{1.25}{.303} = 4 \text{ (about)}. \quad 4^2 + 1 = 17.$$

17×10 in. spiral = 170 in. = 14 ft. 2 in.

"The *first* movement is to the left always, and hence the drift is to the left; and that is *all that is known*. We cannot get a numerical expression for the drift."

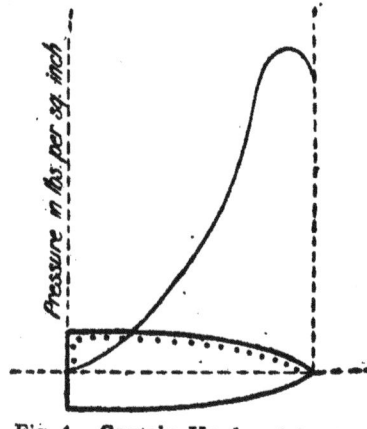

Fig. 4.—Captain Hardcastle's diagram of the pressure curve of the resistance offered by the air to a modern bullet

The figures given by Captain Hardcastle are based on the following law:

"In the steady motion of a shot, the centre describes a helix, of which the axial advance is the square of the length of the shot in calibre plus one, multiplied by the length of one turn of the rifling." (Hardcastle on "The Rifle: A Weapon of Precision," read before the Royal United Services Institution, July, 1912.)

As regards the resistance which the air offers to a modern bullet, Captain Hardcastle writes as follows:

"The pressure curve of the resistance has a shape like this: Very intense at the top, and coming off to little or nothing (possibly slight vacuum) at the sides and base. If you had a lot of recording barometers inside connected to minute holes, my curve would show their respective readings."

In these quotations we have, first, a clear understanding that a spinning bullet drifts, and that for accurate shooting

THE PROPER RIFLING TWIST

the drift must be governed; second, that a long bullet must be spun to give it the necessary gyroscopic stability to keep it point foremost in its flight; and, third, a clear statement of Mr. Metford's discovery that spinning tends to keep the spinning axis pointing at the same *star* during its flight—an enunciation of the laws governing drift and a clear explanation of pressure on the bullet.

There is every reason for supposing that many early riflemakers adjusted the degree of twist given to the rifling with regard almost entirely to the amount of resistance that could be given to the powder gases without the bullet "stripping." On the other hand, more than one gunsmith arrived at the conclusion that the nearer the rifling could be got to a straight line the better was the accuracy and ranging power. "Stripping" means that the lands of the rifling do not get sufficient grip of the bullet to prevent it being driven over them. With the lead bullets of the muzzle-loading era this "stripping," or jumping the rifling, was a very real trouble. With breech-loaders firing a bullet which expands to fit the bore, any danger of stripping absolutely disappears.

The paragraph from "The Shot-Gun and Sporting Rifle," by "Stonehenge," indicates another difficulty which was thought of great importance for many years. The resistance which the rifling offered to the free progress of the bullet along the bore seemed a great waste of energy, and there were sportsmen as late as the middle of the nineteenth century who could not be persuaded that rifling could possibly give advantages which would make up for the loss of velocity caused by the resistance of the lands of the rifling. This was another reason why the rifling of many early weapons was of a very slow twist.

As regards the proper amount of twist necessary to give the bullet proper gyroscopic stability, all that was known until Professor Greenhill began his classic experiments in 1879 was that "the longer the bullet the greater the spin required." Up to the time when Greenhill's formula and the tables based on it were published, the only way of finding the correct spin was by "trial and error," though, of course, certain empirical rules and traditions had been collected by gunmakers and experimentalists.

Since Professor Greenhill's solution of the twist problem has been public property his formula has been blindly followed by all nations without a word of acknowledgment. Gunmakers say that they arrive at their twist by experiment, but the evidence that they follow Greenhill is to be found in the fact that (again we quote Captain Hardcastle) "the moment you begin to experiment you find that the calculated twist is 25 per cent. quicker than necessary!"

We must now leave the consideration of rifling and continue the history of the weapon itself.

In 1563 the Swiss Government found it necessary to legislate against the use of rifled arms in competition with unrifled arms for target-shooting purposes. Special prizes were instituted for rifles, and the Swiss was given permission to rifle his military weapon and use it in competition for these special prizes. This edict is the earliest known mention of target-shooting with rifles, and it is interesting to note that even so far back—three and a half centuries ago—the ingenious and thoughtful target-shot had to be prevented from gaining an undue advantage over his fellow-competitors who were less well supplied with time and means to improve on the standard weapon and ammunition. All through the history of target shooting the necessity for holding back the expert shot with experimental tendencies has shown itself, though it is almost entirely to these men that we owe the development of the rifle.

As lately as the year 1800, though by that time the principle of rifling had been known and applied to small arms and occasionally to bigger pieces for nearly two centuries and a half, the unrifled musket was generally regarded as a superior weapon to the rifle for military purposes. During that two hundred or so years the rifle was developed almost entirely for sporting purposes and for target shooting. This slow development of the rifle must be attributed in some measure to troubles inherent in the ammunition and the methods of loading the weapon, which troubles and difficulties will be discussed in the next chapter; and to the elementary systems of ignition which obtained. The

PLATE II

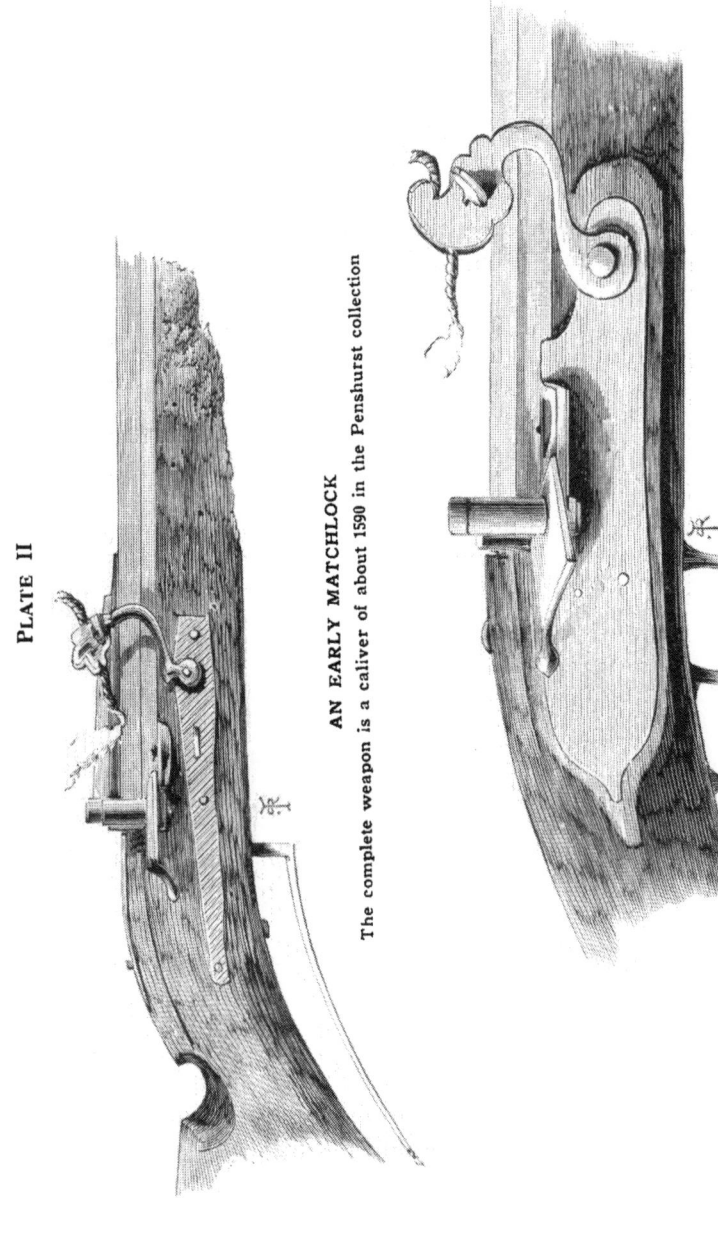

AN EARLY MATCHLOCK

The complete weapon is a caliver of about 1590 in the Penshurst collection

THE LAST BRITISH SERVICE MATCHLOCK

This drawing is from a matchlock musket of the time of William III. The specimen is in the Tower

IGNITION MECHANISMS

rifle did not begin thoroughly to demonstrate its immense superiority over the smooth-bore until some measure of regularity in the load and charge and the firing of the charge had been obtained, and the modern high-velocity weapon did not come into the field of possibilities until the successful adaptation of the breech-loading principle to small arms.

The simplest method of igniting the charge in the chamber of a gun is by applying a light to a hole bored through the wall of the chamber, the hole being filled with powder to convey the flame from the light to the charge. Such a touch-hole or flash-hole was necessary to all muzzle-loading weapons. In the earlier examples of small arms the light was applied to the touch-hole by means of a "match" held in the fingers of the firer. The first touch-holes were on top of the barrels, but an early development was the provision of a flash-pan to hold a quantity of firing powder, and the touch-hole was moved to the side, the flash-pan being immediately under it.

The disadvantage of holding the burning match in the hand led to the invention of the matchlock. In its most elementary form this consisted simply of a holder for the match, which was attached to the weapon; but it was developed into a very ingenious piece of mechanism, by which a light could be taken from a slow match burning on top of the barrel, and transferred to the powder in the flash-pan at the moment it was required to fire the piece. This mechanism, known as the "serpentine" from its shape, was in appearance very like the hammer and trigger of later date, though "hammer" and "trigger" were in one piece. A later development of the matchlock had a real trigger, pressure upon which released a spring and allowed the serpentine to fall upon the flash-pan.

Another early development was a flash-pan cover to keep the powder dry and in place until it was required. This flash-pan cover was a necessary part of the action of all small arms until flash-pan and all were displaced by the invention of the percussion cap.

The wheel-lock, which is the next step in the progress of means of igniting the charge, is said with some authority to be of German origin. It was on the "flint-and-steel" principle, sparks being thrown into the flash-pan by the rapid revolution of a steel wheel with a roughened edge against a flint held in the "cock." The wheel was actuated by a simple piece of clockwork, the motive power being a spring which was wound up with a key. A modification of this idea has recently been adopted for cigar-lighters, the priming powder in the flash-pan being replaced by a petrol-soaked wick.

The late W. W. Greener, in that classic volume, "The Book of the Gun," stated with conviction that, "As a sporting weapon, the gun dates from the invention of the wheel-lock." There is no reason at all to doubt that assertion, for the burning match must have been a grave drawback in hunting, especially when it is remembered that the range for an effective shot with these old weapons was an extremely short one. The smell of the burning match would warn the game, and by night the burning coal would be an additional terror to the inhabitants of the wild. The invention of the wheel-lock dates somewhere between 1510 and 1520, but, though the wheel-lock was largely adopted for sporting rifles—and many beautiful examples are extant—there is no record that wheel-lock rifles were ever made in large quantities for military purposes. Rifled matchlocks were in use for military purposes in Bavaria in 1641.

The expense of manufacturing the wheel-lock soon directed the attention of inventive minds to the necessity of producing a cheaper action which would combine the good points of the wheel-lock with simplicity and ease in making. The result was the flint-lock, which made its appearance early in the seventeenth century.

There are one or two romantic tales of the invention of the flint-lock, but as they have many times been told at length we need not here consider them. Like most other inventions connected with small arms, the flint-lock had a long fight before it established itself as a satisfactory means of igniting the charge. Its early imperfections, combined with the prejudice of those who were used to the matchlock, led to a curious combination of match- and flint-lock, in which the old lighted match could be used when concealment was not necessary, the flint-lock being brought into play when the burning "coal" of the

EARLY REPEATERS

match would have been disadvantageous. The flint-lock triumphed over all opposition in the end, however, and remained the standard method of ignition for close on two centuries.

In the flint-lock the cover-plate of the flash-pan—known as the "hammer"—was so arranged that the descending flint held in the "cock" knocked it upwards, uncovering the priming powder and causing, by the impact of the flint against the steel hammer face, a shower of sparks which fired the priming powder. There was no means of directing the sparks so that they were sure to fall on the priming, and even in the best made models miss-fires would occur from the sparks falling to the side of the flash-pan. The arranging of the flint so that a thick stream of sparks would fall in the right direction was a constant source of study to the flint-lock users.

Having thus briefly summarised the means employed to ignite the charge, up to the adoption of the flint-lock, it is now necessary to consider the development of the "repeating" or magazine idea.

Very early in the history of firearms it must have become sufficiently apparent that the length of time required to load the musket—and later and more particularly the rifle—was a grave disadvantage. The musketeer, having discharged his piece, was at the mercy of the enemy whilst he reloaded, unless he was protected by a pikeman. One method of coping with this very considerable disability in the firearm was by fitting the firearm with a bayonet, and thus turning it into a pike. This was the "line of least resistance," so to speak. The more difficult problems were those of speeding up the loading, or, as an alternative, providing means whereby one arm could be made to fire several shots without reloading.

The provision of several barrels was the first effort in the direction of providing a repeating arm, and evidence that a magazine weapon was an ideal that came into being almost at the birth of the firearm is provided by the fact that multi-barrelled hand guns with the most primitive match ignition are still in existence in collections of old arms. The earliest known example of a true magazine gun is the repeating matchlock, which was provided with a sliding serpentine and a series of flash-pans on one barrel. 'A number of charges, equal to the number of flash-pans, were loaded one on top of the other down the barrel, the charges being separated by thick wads. They would then be fired in rotation, beginning with the one nearest the muzzle—unless by some unlucky chance several of the charges exploded together. The disadvantages of this system are sufficiently obvious.

The butt magazine, with a lever-actuated breech-block, was experimented with somewhere about the same time that the flint-lock was evolved. The powder was loose in the butt, and fell into the chamber by gravity, the bullet having first been placed in the opening made for the purpose in the breech-block. It is interesting to note that the movement of the lever performed all the operations of loading and cocking the piece except the placing in position of the bullet. With separate cartridges this action might have been successful, but as it was it failed because it was considerably ahead of its time. The presence of loose powder in the butt constituted a grave danger that workmen of the time were not able to overcome by the accurate fitting of the breech-block.

The repeating system that was developed with most success before the breech-loading rifle proper came into being was the revolver, either in the shape of revolving barrels, or with revolving chambers fitted to a single barrel. The latter of these two revolver systems seems to have been the earlier thought of. Both systems were used to some extent during the sixteenth century for sporting purposes, and seem to have very much preceded in popularity the double-barrelled weapon, which is only to be expected when the great expenditure of time in loading is remembered.

Early forms of repeating arms certainly made possible the discharge of several successive shots without reloading, but they did not do away with the labour of loading, nor with the great amount of time expended in loading operations, and concurrently with their development the breech-loading principle was being experimented with. For the smooth-bore a system of loading from the breech was a great convenience; with the adoption of the rifled barrel it became a necessity.

PLATE III

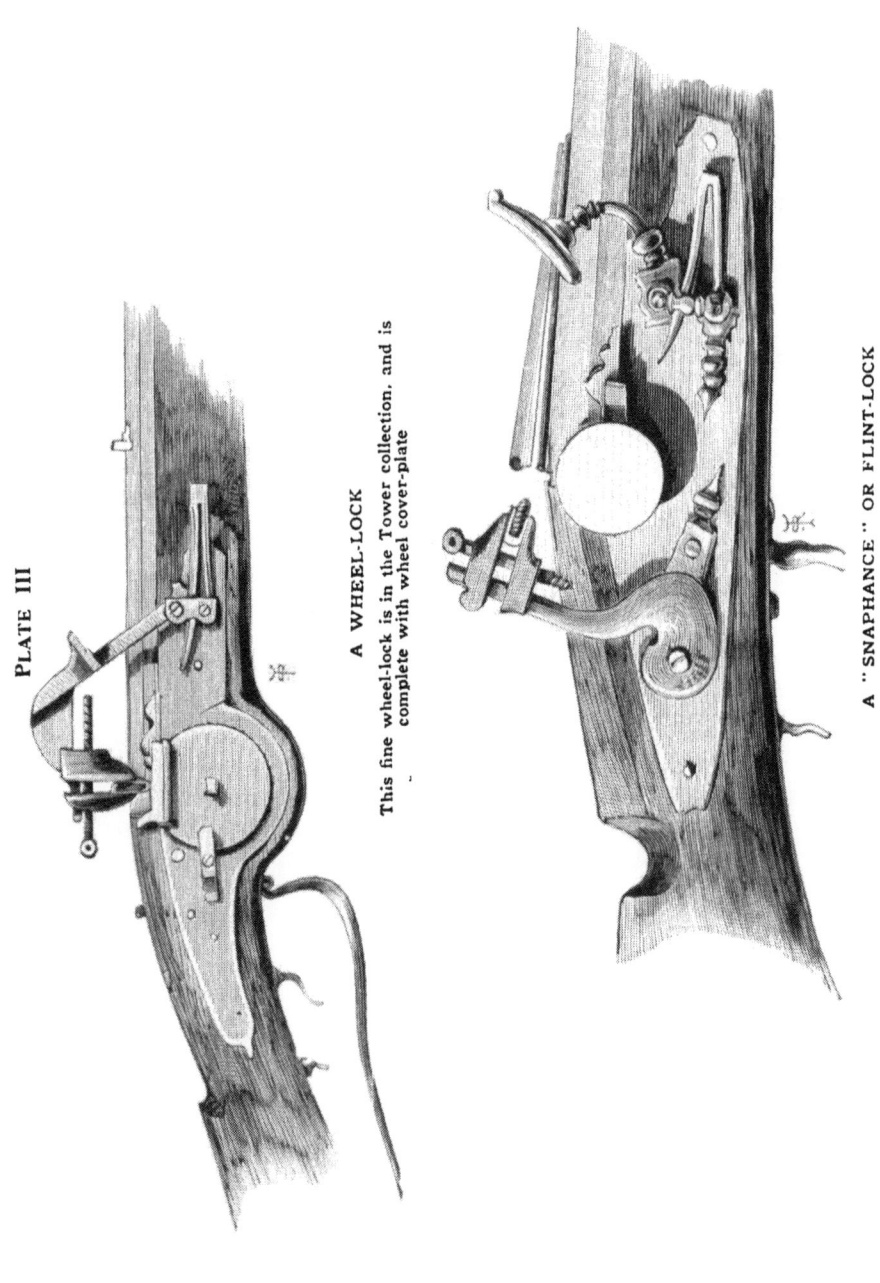

A WHEEL-LOCK

This fine wheel-lock is in the Tower collection, and is complete with wheel cover-plate

A "SNAPHANCE" OR FLINT-LOCK

This specimen is from Haddon Hall. The date is about 1620

DANGEROUS BREECH-LOADERS

It is impossible to give a date to the invention of breech-loading. Breech-loading firearms were certainly known in the days of Henry VIII., and the finish of the workmanship that has been lavished on those examples which are still in existence suggests to the inquirer that breech-loading was then not a very new thing, though perhaps regarded as a refinement that was not a necessity for the ordinary weapon. The development of the breech-loader was held back by the difficulty of efficiently closing the breech against the backward escape of gas and flame. We shall see that the breech-loader did not really become possible until the invention of the metal or metal-based cartridge-case.

The breech-loading devices that were experimented with in gradually increasing numbers during the two and a half centuries which were necessary to demonstrate the superiority of the rifled barrel over the smooth-bore for both sport and war, were many and various. In their earliest form they consisted of a movable breech-piece or chamber, which was wedged into position behind the barrel. This movable chamber was, in fact, a cartridge which was loaded as it was required. The "break-open" idea, which is seen to perfection in a modern double-barrelled sporting gun, was very soon hit upon as a possible way out of the difficulty of loading the weapon from the muzzle. The barrel was made to break down in some patterns and sideways in others; and the soundness of the principle is evident in its persistence through centuries.

The difficulties which early experimenters found in the effective closing of the breech against escape of gas is emphasised in the history of military arms. Again and again the breech action was adopted, to be quickly discarded as "too dangerous." This grave disability had not been got over as lately as 1871, for it was a grave defect in both the French chassepot and the Prussian needle rifle.

We have now considered the invention of rifling, by which the projectile can be spun and kept travelling to nearly the limit of its energy in a steady path, the development of the means of igniting the charge from the touch-hole and lighted match to the highly developed flint-lock mechanism, the early attempts to provide a means whereby two or more shots could be discharged without the painfully slow processes of reloading intervening, and the efforts of early mechanics and inventors to provide a means of loading the weapon from the breech and at the same time prevent the gases of the explosion in the chamber from escaping through the breech. All these developments proceeded more or less together. They were interdependent inasmuch as improvements in one department helped towards improvements in another; and so with action and reaction, zig-zagging slowly up the hill of progress, we come to the last years of the eighteenth century and the beginning of the nineteenth.

The year 1800 is a very important one in the history of the rifle, and particularly so in regard to the rifle in the British Army. It was towards the end of the eighteenth century that the Government began to awaken to the fact that, despite the difficulty of loading it, the superior accuracy and range of the rifle made it a most efficient weapon. The Americans, against whom we were fighting, were largely armed with sporting rifles—and they knew how to use them. Officers and men of the British Army were picked off when they considered themselves well out of range—and their muskets gave them no chance of replying in kind. The American, in fact, often played a game similar to that which proved so disastrous to us in the Boer Wars. Known ranges, hunter's knowledge of cover and stalking, and highly developed individual skill in marksmanship were too much for ordinary military weapons and military methods to get the better of. In the American War we tried the "thief to catch a thief" plan of engaging skilled German and Swiss rifle-shots to come over to North America and help us; and it was this undignified seeking for help from foreigners which set our people thinking.

We may take it that up to the end of the eighteenth century the rifle had not been very seriously regarded as a military weapon by any nation. As early as 1611 some small portion of the Danish army was armed with the rifle, and from that date until about 1795, when Napoleon ordered a regiment of his light infantry to discard as useless the rifles with which

THE RIFLE BRIGADE

they had been armed but a year or so before, we find chronicled the sporadic appearance of the rifle as a military arm, now here, now there, now in greater quantities, now in lesser, but always as an experiment that was to prove abortive.

The rifled barrel had been conceived before its time; neither the right ammunition nor the right action for it had been evolved, but as the eighteenth century came to a close the slow processes of mechanical evolution were bringing about a condition of affairs more favourable to the production of an accurate firearm. In 1800 the actual available knowledge of the principles of rifling was very small. It had been developed almost solely in the sporting weapon, and, as we have seen, it was the use of the sporting rifle in the hands of the American backwoodsmen that decided the British War Office to investigate its claim as a military weapon. Once the rifle was adopted for fighting, its improvement was all along the direct outcome of a desire to make it more efficient as a manslayer.

In 1800, then, we have a committee appointed to find the best rifle with which to arm the newly-formed Rifle Brigade, the 95th Foot. In that same year the rest of the Army was being supplied with the famous "Brown Bess" musket, the weapon which carried us triumphantly through the Peninsular War and that memorable campaign which terminated so gloriously for us and our allies on the field of Waterloo. "Brown Bess" was the third of the firearms of our Army. The first was the Matchlock Musket, which had a barrel about 42 inches long, and weighed, with its bayonet, about 20 lb. This was the weapon that was used by Marlborough's troops at Blenheim and Ramillies. Next came the Army Musket, introduced about 1750. It had a bore of over three-quarters of an inch in diameter. The length of the barrel was 42 inches, the action was flint-lock, and the weight was $11\frac{1}{4}$ lb., with its bayonet. This weapon, sighted up to 200 yards, but wonderfully inaccurate even at that short distance, was the one with which we tried to subdue the Americans in the War of Independence, their riflemen being able to pick off a man with a fair certainty at 200 yards, and sometimes at longer distances. This digression is to negative the often-repeated statement that the musket used at Blenheim was the same as that used at Waterloo.

The 1800 committee could call in the service of many makers of sporting rifles in this country, on the Continent, and in America. Invitations were sent out, and as a result the committee had the pick of the best specimens of the rifle-maker's art to choose from. In the end the committee decided on the adoption of the Baker Rifle, made by Ezekiel Baker, a London gunsmith. This rifle, which was the arm of the Rifle Brigade up to the year after Queen Victoria came to the throne, had seven grooves, turning once in 10 feet— that is, one-quarter turn in its 2-ft. 6-in. barrel. It was sighted up to 200 yards, and could do fair shooting at that distance, though, if report spoke truly, there was already in existence in America rifles that would do as good work at twice the range. At 100 yards the Baker Rifle was capable of making groups about 1 foot 6 inches wide by 2 feet 6 inches deep. This, however, was only for the first ten shots. A thirty-shot group fired as continuously as the accumulation of fouling would allow, deepened the group to about 3 feet 6 inches, though it did not much affect the lateral deviation. As a comparison it may be noted that the modern "small-bore" or miniature rifle, fired at 100 yards, from the shoulder, is capable of putting an almost indefinite number of shots inside a 4-inch circle, the great majority of them being inside a 2-inch circle.

Inaccurate as these early military rifles seem to us in these days, the achievement of worthy Ezekiel Baker in producing as the first rifled arm of the British Army a weapon that could be depended upon to hit a man at 100 yards was a great one. A few years later another London maker brought out a rifle which, at 200 yards, from a fixed rest, would put the greater number of its shots over a long series into 2 feet 6 inches, both lateral and horizontal deviation remaining fairly constant.

Subsequent improvements up to the date of the adoption of breech-loading were directed towards reducing the fouling, and so adjusting weight of bullet, twist of rifling and power of explosion as to give the longest and most accurate range to the bullet. These improvements properly belong to the next

THE PERCUSSION CAP

chapter, in which the evolution of ammunition will be dealt with in so far as it has progressed during the period we are now covering with the rifle itself.

The most noteworthy improvement, apart from those affecting the bullet or the charge, was the invention, in 1807, of the percussion system of ignition. Though fulminates, which on ignition by percussion give an instantaneous hot, strong flame, had been known for a century, the credit for applying them to the ignition of the charge, in firearms, belongs to a Scottish clergyman, by name Alexander J. Forsyth, of Belhelvie. Percussion ignition was first applied by means of a plunger working in a "percussion chamber" communicating with the charge. The fulminate was placed in the bottom of the chamber, and the descending hammer forced the plunger sharply upon it and caused detonation.

This invention is the direct parent of our modern method of ignition. Improvements on Forsyth's invention came fairly rapidly. But a year had elapsed since the clergyman's patent rights were granted when a French gunmaker invented a paper cartridge, to the base of which a paper fulminate cap was attached. The firing of the charge was brought about by piercing the cap with a needle, which was impelled forward by a spring when the scear was released from the bent. This system was combined with a breech-loading action, and in it we have a very definite step toward the breech-loader as we now know it. It was subsequently developed into a very effective breech-loading sporting gun.

The skill and ingenuity devoted to the improvement of percussion ignition led in less than a decade to the evolution of the copper percussion cap, which was placed over a nipple. The flame from the detonating fulminate passed through a hole in the nipple and ignited the charge. This was the final form of the cap until, to cope with new conditions brought about by the general adoption of the breech-loading action, it was incorporated in the cartridge.

Percussion ignition was adopted for the Brunswick rifle, which was issued to the Rifle Brigade in 1835, and is found in all subsequent army rifles which were muzzle-loaded.

The Brunswick two-grooved rifle, though it was easier to load than the Baker rifle, had nothing like the accuracy of the latter, so that in 1846 our Army had the distinction of being the worst armed of any as regards its rifle except the Russian, which had adopted the British two-groove weapon for its rifle regiments. It will be interesting to here review the principal Continental muzzle-loading rifles in use immediately before the adoption of the first military breech-loader. In 1845 the French were making a large number of experiments with the Delvigne breech-loading rifle, which was a kind of early hint of the straight-pull principle, though the sliding plunger which fitted into the barrel was worked by an under lever. The French rifle of the period was, however, an .8-in. muzzle-loader, firing a round ball approximating to $1\frac{1}{2}$ oz. in weight. It had six shallow grooves, making one turn in 18 ft. The French had at this period been making a considerable number of experiments with regard to the correct degree of pitch for the rifling, and though their rifle had only one turn in 18 ft., they had arrived at the conclusion that a slightly quicker twist of about one turn in 15 ft. was the best.

The Austrian rifle or carbine was a short weapon with a 2-ft. 6-in. barrel, 20-bore, and with rather deep grooves somewhat steeply pitched. This carbine was, however, discredited in the Austrian army, the musket outshooting it at almost all ranges. The Prussian carbine was even shorter, the barrel being only 2 ft. 2 in. long. The rifling was unevenly cut, and the spiral very quick (as pitch went in those days), being usually about one turn in 3 ft. Though the rifling was so rough and so far behind that of some of the other nations as regards its principles of construction, the appearance of the carbine gives evidence that a considerable amount of care had been given to its outward appearance and finishing. The Belgian rifle of the time was an 18-bore weapon with a 3-ft. barrel. The twist of the rifling was one in 15 ft., and contemporary accounts give it a range of 1,200 yards, with a charge of $3\frac{1}{2}$ drms. of powder.

It will be noted that these early twists in rifling were very slow compared with those made necessary by present-day

Plate IV

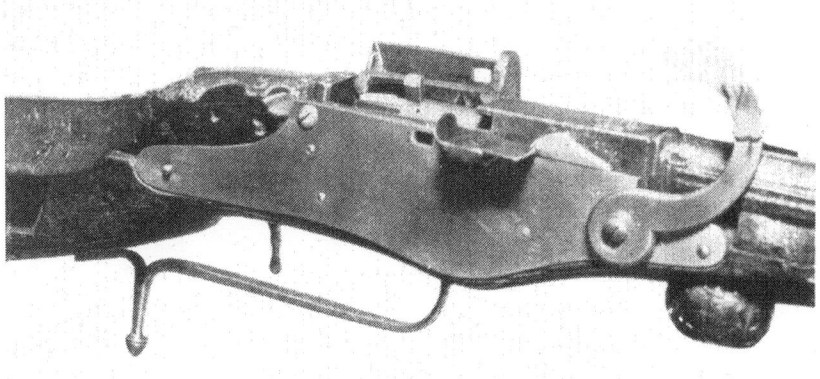

A BREECH ACTION OF 1537

The breech-closing arrangement of this Harquebus, which belonged to Henry VIII, and is now in the Tower, closely resembles the Snider. In the breech can be seen the movable chamber made of metal—in front, a cartridge when loaded ready for insertion

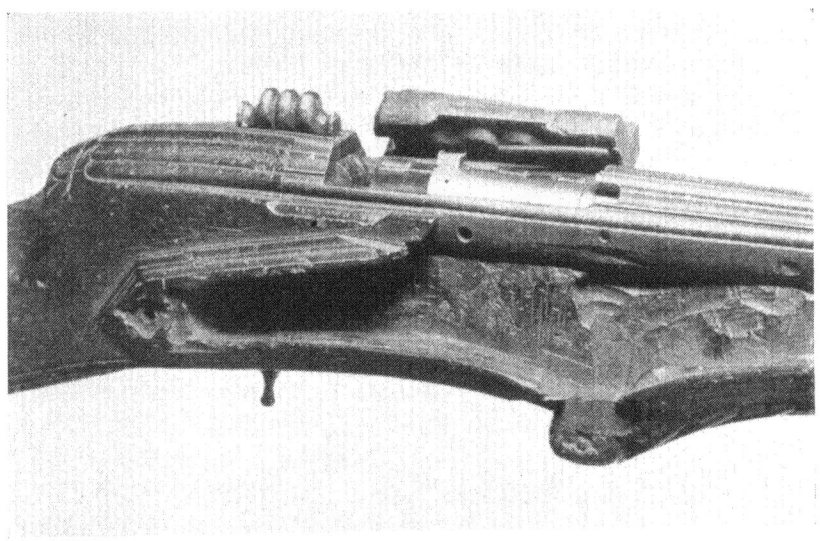

ANOTHER OF HENRY VIII.'S BREECH-LOADERS

This Harquebus is in the Tower collection. From the photograph can be seen the way the movable chamber was held in position so that the touch-hole of the chamber came in line with the touch-hole of the lock. The lock was probably a wheel-lock, but is lost

requirements, but they were found sufficient to ensure stability in the flight of spherical projectiles.

Activity in rifle-making was already very great in America, so much so that certain old-established British firms were already evidencing their disgust of American methods, and starting to decry what they termed "machine-made rifles and guns." It is curious to notice how quickly the American rifle began to evolve along special lines. The vast plains and woodlands of the North American continent being filled with small or smallish wild creatures, the American marksman desired a weapon throwing a light ball with considerable velocity and accuracy over a short range; and it was along these lines that the American rifle developed and made a very big reputation. In the 1846 edition of W. Greener's "Science of Gunnery" there is evidence that at that date machinery was being used at Liége and in the American factories to an extent undreamed of in this country. As regards Liége, Mr. Greener says:

"The government have lately instituted a small but compact manufactory for the construction of their military arms, where the barrels are welded and every stage completed within the walls. Their arrangements in machinery for various parts and purposes about the construction of the gun are admirable. Much that is done in this country by hand is here done by machinery. The barrels are squared, and the part where the nipple is inserted all shaped and fashioned by aid of the engine. The rifling of their barrels is also done by steam, and is an invention of extreme simplicity. The workmen are drafted from the ranks of the army, taught a branch of the trade, and by their engagements as military men become a description of workmen divested of that discontented nature so frequently met with in the gun trade, and at the same time enabling the government to secure their services at a moderate expense. The perfection of the machinery and the great division of labour leave but little for an active mind to master, for a young man may be soon taught one operation; but if two or more are attempted to be added, he fails in all; and in this light the Belgian Government views the matter, for one defection is of no importance."

In describing American methods, Mr. Greener quoted the following extract from a description written by a gentleman who had, on the publication of his book, just returned from America:

"It must be interesting, where the manufacture of firearms is carried on to some extent, to know that our Transatlantic brethren have perfected machinery for this purpose of the most admirable description. We regret that we have been unable to procure any definite idea of its details, or even of its mode of working. By it, however, the metal is wrought into the most eccentric shapes without any further intervention of human hands than is requisite for superintending the machine. Owing to this skilful arrangement of machinery, only thirty-five men are required to carry on the works, turning out nearly 3,000 rifles a year, worth about thirteen dollars apiece. In the manufacture of these about 50,000 lb. of iron, 6,000 lb. of copper, and from 4,000 to 5,000 lb. of steel are annually consumed. The steel is worked up into ramrods, springs, and portions of the lock. The iron costs about one hundred and forty dollars per ton, and is obtained from Salisbury, Connecticut, that procured there being found of a superior quality to either the English or Pennsylvanian iron. The stocks are made of black walnut, which is brought from Pennsylvania. The rifles, when finished, weigh $10\frac{1}{2}$ lb. each. A striking advantage gained by the extended use of machinery in making the different parts of the rifle is the perfect uniformity of the work. So accurately, and in so many different ways, is every part—even the most minute—gauged, that in putting together the whole no delay is occasioned from trifling inaccuracies in fitting. Each screw, spring, sight, topboard, or any other piece whatever, is so nicely wrought that it may be applied to and will fit any of the 3,000 rifles made in the course of the year as exactly as it does the one of which it finally forms a part. The rifles are made on contract for the government, and are not offered for sale."

This quotation is particularly interesting because it shows clearly that the Americans had in 1846 progressed very considerably in the development of repetition machinery and accurate gauging. No move in this direction was made in Great Britain until fifteen years later.

In order properly to trace the evolution of the various parts of the rifle in its early form, it has been necessary to write this chapter in a series of more or less disjointed histories, the development of one portion or principle being taken some distance and then dropped whilst another was reviewed. It is very necessary that, in reading a history so presented, the mind should free itself of any impression of individual and disjointed evolution.

The development of the various parts of the rifle have taken place in so interdependent a manner that really we have been considering the growth of the weapon as a whole whilst apparently considering its parts only. This history has few definite landmarks such as the one the Rev. J. Forsyth erected when he applied the percussion system to a gun, and therefore it is all the more necessary that we should force ourselves to consider it as a whole, and not as a series of detached episodes. Usually we find the growth of an idea or principle to be a very slow thing. Slowly it reaches maturity, and slowly it declines before some more advanced idea or newer principle.

How slowly a superseded principle in rifle manufacture reaches oblivion may be illustrated by the following quotation from "Arms and Explosives" for February, 1895, nearly ninety years after Forsyth's great idea had been made public:

THE MANUFACTURE OF FLINTS FOR GUN-LOCKS.—Our discursive and brilliant contemporary, the *Pall Mall Gazette,* turned its attention recently to the question of manufacture of flints for the old-fashioned type of gun-locks. It appears that there is still a community of persons whose sole industry is the obtaining and shaping of these antiquarian adjuncts to firearms. Bad times seem at last, however, to have come on them, and the demand is almost extinguished. Our contemporary seems to imagine that South Africa is the only market for these wares, but we might ourselves add the names of several countries where the demand for them is comparatively brisk, but we will satisfy ourselves with naming Canada, where, in the remoter parts, the flint-lock is the rule rather than the exception.

Despite failure upon failure, and the sarcastic pessimism of the conservatively minded sportsmen and gunmakers, the more imaginative of those who worked in that fascinating field of possibilities presented by firearms, hoped for the perfecting of the breech-loading rifle and the consequent dismissing of the loading difficulties which stood so definitely in the way of the progress of the grooved barrel weapon. And not only did these men hope, they worked. Each fresh invention for overcoming the loading difficulty by some tinkering with the projectile itself only made it more apparent that, despite large sums awarded by governments for such devices, the solution of the difficulties did not lie in such a direction.

Early attempts to produce a breech-loading gun had only resulted in producing and fostering a great and grave distrust of any and all systems of loading from the breech end. This prejudice had to be combated and lived down, and, like most prejudices which are founded on experience, it was a long time dying.

We have already glanced at the early attempts to produce a breech-loader, and must now follow this branch of our story to that most important period in the history of the rifle when breech-loading mechanism had been so far improved that the system was recognised as being absolutely necessary for army rifles. Before this state of affairs came about there was still to be done a very considerable amount of necessary work, not only in the improvement of the ammunition and breech action, but in the barrel itself. The muzzle-loading rifle had by no means reached the perfection of which it was capable, and it remained for British investigators to show how great this perfection could be. Though the work that was done in this direction in England held back for some years the adoption of the breech-loader into British military practice, because the results that were being obtained with the muzzle-loader showed an accuracy that did not seem possible with the breech-loaded weapon, in the end they were productive of far-reaching improvements to which experimenters and manufacturers all over the world are indebted.

PLATE V

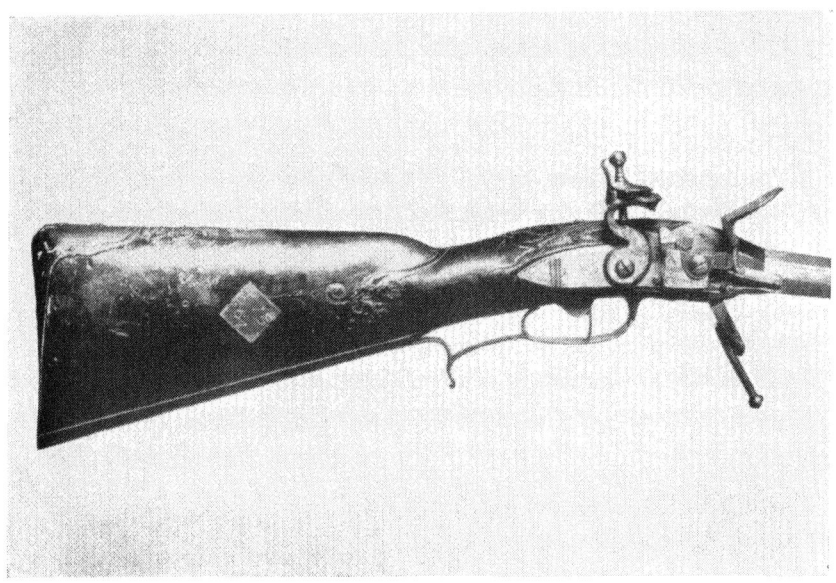

A GERMAN FLINT-LOCK MAGAZINE RIFLE
There is no date on this rifle, which is in the Tower collection. The barrel has seven grooves

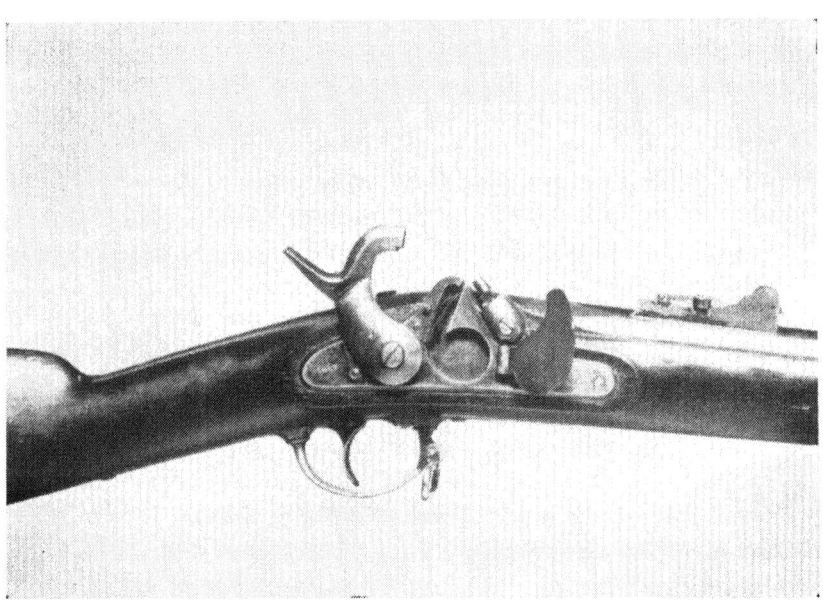

AN AMERICAN PERCUSSION RIFLE
A self-priming rifle in the Tower collection. There is no date; the lock plate is stamped " W. S., Harpers Ferry "

CHAPTER II

The Early History of Propellants and Projectiles

THE lay mind, seizing on salient facts to the exclusion of those of more detailed exactness, ascribes the invention of gunpowder to the Chinese. Gunpowder, to the popular mind, promptly suggesting guns, cannon, and similar instruments for the propulsion of missiles, the Chinese are, by process of thought which can easily be followed, credited also with the use of explosives for throwing destructive missiles to a distance. There can be little doubt that both these popular impressions are wrong in so far as they refer to guns and gunpowder as we know them to-day; though the beginnings of the science of explosives undoubtedly came from the East.

The "Text-Book of Service Explosives," in a remarkably succinct account of the historical knowledge on the subject of the invention of explosive mixtures and compounds, follows Henry Wilkinson in suggesting that we can find the beginnings of the human understanding of disruptives and propellants in "the accidental discovery of the peculiar properties of the nitre so plentifully found mixed with the soil upon the vast plains of India and China. By means of the charred embers of wood fires, used for cooking, the two most important ingredients of gunpowder might easily be brought into contact, and, under the action of heat, considerable deflagration would ensue; in fact, the accidental dropping of some of the crude saltpetre into the coals would show its remarkable power of supporting and accelerating combustion. The combination of saltpetre and charcoal into a more or less powerful mixture can therefore be easily conceived, the sulphur being an after addition, and not necessary to explosion. Our present gunpowder is only an improvement of such a mixture."

In this paragraph we have the progress of many decades, probably centuries, stated in one fact; but, whatever the origin of gunpowder, it seems probable that the use of the crude compositions at first invented was either incendiary or disruptive rather than propellent.

Indulging a little more in probabilities before we reach the realm of known fact, we may surmise that the first use of propellants was in some firework-like instrument of the nature of a "Roman candle." Classical references lead one to suppose that fireworks of some such nature have been known in the East for twenty centuries or so, and it is reasonable to suppose that other classical references to "fire from a distance" and "war thunder" have regard to fireworks rather than to the actual use of explosive propellants.

Having indicated that our knowledge of explosives probably began with observations of the results which were obtained when saltpetre and charcoal are mixed, it would be absurd to seek for an actual inventor of gunpowder within historical times. Credit for the invention of gunpowder in a somewhat similar form to that in which we now know it is claimed for a German monk named Bertholdus Schwartz, and the date of this discovery is usually stated to be about A.D. 1320. Now, in a treatise which he published about A.D. 1265, Roger Bacon refers to an explosive which contains saltpetre and other ingredients; and in another chapter of the same work indicates what these other ingredients may be, disguising their name by an anagram, an artifice to the use of which writers of that time were much addicted. He mentions "salis-petræ" and "sulphuris," and also "lura nope cum ubre." These last four words, of course, mean absolutely nothing in Latin or any other tongue, but by a rearrangement of the letters we have "carbonum pulvere," and so arrive at the ingredients of gunpowder—saltpetre, sulphur, and charcoal.

Benjamin Robins, writing five centuries after the publication of Roger Bacon's treatise, suggests that Bacon probably knew of the manuscript of Marcus Græcus, which was then in the French National Library. This manuscript, which dates from the end of the eighth century or the beginning of the

THE SIEGE OF BAZA

ninth, mentions fireworks of the rocket or Roman candle order, and speaks of sulphur, charcoal, and saltpetre, reduced to a fine powder and mixed together, as a filling of a long, narrow cover which forms a firework.

The early years of the fourteenth century saw the use of gunpowder as a propellant, for in 1326 authority was given for the appointment of certain persons in Florence to superintend the making of brass cannon and iron balls to be used in the defence of the Republic of Florence. A year previously the Moors had used cannon in the siege of Baza, in Spain. This date marks our first authentic record of guns.

In the later years of the fourteenth century we begin to find fairly frequent references to guns and gunpowder in literature, and often used in such a way as makes it evident that the properties of gunpowder as a propellant were quite well known to the majority of people. From Chaucer's reference in "The House of Fame" it is evident that the "pillet" which was fired out of the "gonne" by the explosion of the "pouder" was a single projectile, though it seems fairly certain that, at the very first, short "quarrells," similar to those used for cross-bows, were used, though they were quickly followed by shot of stone or iron.

At this time the three ingredients of gunpowder were mixed roughly together in about equal proportions, with the consequence that the powder produced was comparatively weak.

From the end of the thirteenth century, for two or three hundred years, very few improvements were made either in gunpowder or in projectiles. Gradually, as the weapons themselves improved in construction, the strength of the powder was increased by adding more and more saltpetre to the mixture, until in 1546, in the middle of the sixteenth century, we find that though, for use in cannon, four parts of saltpetre and one part each of charcoal and sulphur were considered correct proportions, for use in muskets forty-eight parts of saltpetre were used to eight parts of charcoal and seven of sulphur; and these proportions were adhered to, with slight alterations, for about 200 years, for in 1740, when Benjamin Robins was conducting his experiments with guns, bullets and powders, he definitely states that the proportions mentioned by Tartaglia, the Venetian, in 1546 were almost the same as those used in his own time.

It is curious that knowledge of the best proportions for the ingredients in the mixing of gunpowder had for a very considerable time preceded weapons capable of using gunpowder of the then maximum strength. Nearly a hundred years before Robins's time Baptista Porta, an investigator with leanings towards accuracy which were rather remarkable in his time, had recommended a mixture which is practically identical with that indicated by the best modern practice.

Benjamin Robins was not content to know that if you mix saltpetre, charcoal, and sulphur together, and thoroughly grind them up so that they make a mealy powder, the mixture could be used for propelling a ball with considerable velocity from a tube by applying a light to the mixture. He wanted to know the why and wherefor of this phenomenon, and he set out to investigate matters on lines which were quite in accordance with his genius for painstaking accuracy in scientific investigation. During the course of these experiments Robins arrived at the conclusion that gunpowder, when exploded, produced a permanently elastic fluid. He arrived at this conclusion in the following ingenious manner: From a receiver, to which was connected a mercurial gauge on the barometer principle, the air was exhausted, and in the vacuum gunpowder was caused to fall on to a red-hot plate which had previously been placed in the receiver. The powder, of course, took fire, and Robins chronicles the fact that the mercury in the gauge descends on the explosion, though it ascends immediately again, though never to the height it stood before the explosion, but will continue depressed in proportion to the quantity of powder which was burnt in the explosion. When the gases produced by the burning powder have cooled to the temperature of the surrounding air they cease to contract, and in Robins's words "remain a permanently elastic fluid."

Robins also went to a very considerable amount of trouble to determine the quantity of "elastic fluid" produced from the explosion of a given quantity of gunpowder. Though his

PLATE VI

AN ANCIENT "PEEP SIGHT"

This curious backsight, which is on a stone bow in the Tower collection, represents a mermaid holding her tails—the old arms of Nuremberg. It is pierced with five orthoptic holes for different elevations

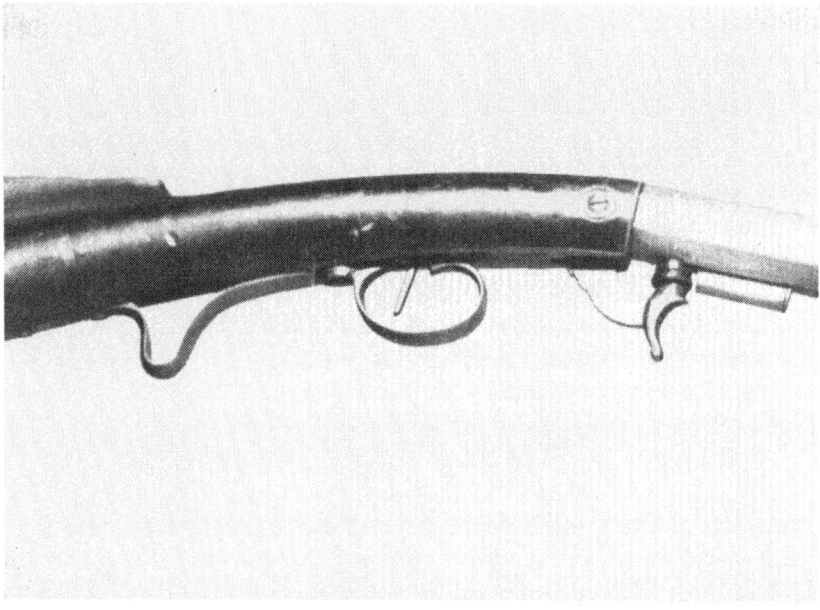

AN AMERICAN UNDER-HAMMER RIFLE

Smith and Kendal's patent rifle with the hammer underneath. It was so placed in order that the face might not be endangered by the detonation of the cap and to keep the hammer out of the way of the sights

THE BALLISTIC PENDULUM 31

figures, dealing as they do with a comparatively weak form of powder, are of no practical interest to-day, his conclusion that 2 cubic inches of powder, which was the space occupied by 17 drms., would give rise upon explosion to 274 cubic inches of "elastic fluid" at least put upon record the enormous force which it was possible to generate by burning powder in a confined space.

Robins stated definitely his opinion that the action of the powder on the projectile ceases as soon as the latter escapes from the barrel, but he also arrived at the conclusion that the whole of the powder was converted into gas, or, as he calls it, "elastic fluid," before the projectile moved from its place and started to travel up the barrel. This assertion of the great Robins was not allowed to go long unchallenged. In 1742 the Royal Society made some experiments on the subject of burning of powders, and laid down the fact, which has never since been controverted, that not only is the burning of a charge of powder not instantaneous, but that the coarser the grains of powder the more slowly it burns. The first statement mentioned in this paragraph was not so easily disposed of, for it is only within recent years that we have arrived at any exact conclusions with regard to the action of the gases following the bullet from the muzzle.

In the course of his experiments Benjamin Robins was continually faced with the difficulty of arriving at any definite data as to the amount of work done by the powder when exploded in the chamber. Seeking to solve this problem, he evolved the apparatus known as the "ballistic pendulum," which is used to measure the velocity of a bullet at the moment of impact. The ballistic pendulum was the basis of all experiments in exterior ballistics until the chronograph or time-measuring apparatus was invented by Boulangé and used by Bashforth for his historic experiments in 1865-1870.

Robins's pendulum was a wood-faced iron plate suspended from a tripod so that it could swing like a pendulum. To the front two legs of the tripod a cross-bar was attached, and through a brass catch on this bar a piece of tape fastened to the iron plate was drawn when the pendulum was swung by a shot hitting it. The extent of the tape drawn through the notch measured the extent of the swing.

Robins's own description of his invention is of considerable historical interest, and as we are not aware that it has been published in any modern work, we make no apology for letting the ingenious mathematician tell his own story.

"If the weight of the pendulum be known," says Robins, "and likewise the respective distances of its centre of gravity and of its centre of oscillation from its axis of suspension, it will thence be known what motion will be communicated to this pendulum by the percussion of a body of a known weight moving with a known degree of celerity and striking it at a given point; that is, if the pendulum be supposed at rest before the percussion, it will be known what vibration it ought to make in consequence of such a determined blow; and, on the contrary, if the pendulum, being at rest, is struck by a body of a known weight, and the vibration which the pendulum makes after the blow is known, the velocity of the striking body may from thence be determined." Describing the pendulum itself and his method of

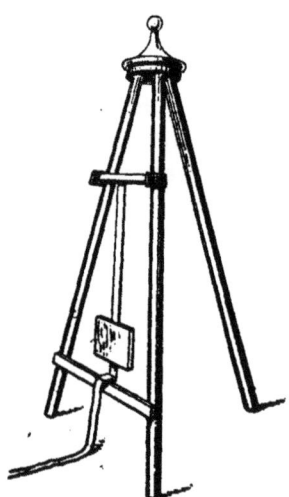

Fig. 5.—Robins's Ballistic Pendulum

calculation with it, Robins says: "The weight of the whole pendulum was 56 lb. 3 oz.; its centre of gravity was 52 in. distant from its axis of suspension, and 200 of its small swings were performed in the time of 253 seconds; whence its centre of oscillation is $62\tfrac{2}{3}$ in. distant from that axis. In the compound ratio of 66 to $66\tfrac{2}{3}$ and 66 to 52, take the quantity of matter of the pendulum to a fourth quantity, which will be 42 lb. ½ oz. Now, geometers will know that, if the blow be struck in the centre of the plate, the pendulum will resent the stroke, as if this last quantity of matter only were concentrated in that point, and the rest of the pendulum was taken away; whence, supposing the weight of the bullet impinging on that point to be the twelfth of a pound, or the $\frac{1}{504}$ of this quantity of matter nearly, the velocity of the point of oscillation after the stroke will, by the laws observed in the congress of such bodies as rebound not from each other, be the $\frac{1}{505}$ of the velocity the bullet moved with before the stroke; whence the velocity of this point of oscillation being ascertained, that, multiplied by 505, will give the velocity with which the ball impinged.

"But the velocity of the point of oscillation after the stroke is easily deduced from the chord of the arch through which it ascends by the blow; for it is a well-known proposition that all pendulous bodies ascend to the same height by their vibratory motion as they would do if they were projected directly upwards from their lowest point with the same velocity they have in that point; wherefore, if the versed sine of the ascending arch be found (which is easily determined from the chord and radius being given), this versed sine is the perpendicular height to which a body projected upwards with the velocity of the point of oscillation would arise, and consequently what that velocity is can be easily computed by the common theory of falling bodies.

"To determine the velocity with which the bullet impinged on the centre of the wood, when the chord of the arch described by the ascent of the pendulum, in consequence of the blow, was 17¼ in., as measured on the ribbon, no more is necessary than to multiply 3¼ by 505, and the resulting number (1641) will be the feet which the bullet would describe in 1 in. if it moved with the velocity it had at the moment of percussion. The velocity of the foot of the pendulum on which the bullet struck is determined to be 3¼ ft. in 1, by the following calculation: The distance of the ribbon from the axis of suspension being 71⅛ in., reduce 17¼ in the ratio of 71⅛ to 66; the resulting number, which is nearly 16 in., will be the chord of the arch through which the centre of the plate ascended after the strike. Now, the versed sine of an arch whose chord is 16 in. and its radius 66 in. is 1.93939, and the velocity which would carry a body to this height, or what a body would acquire by descending through this space, is nearly that of 3¼ ft. in 1 in."

It will be seen that the actual basis of these calculations is the height to which the pendulum is swung by the blow of the bullet. As the distance from the point of impact of the centre of gravity had to come into the calculations, these were rather complicated.

The history of projectiles can be divided into a number of periods, each period representing some advance in thought and practice. These periods are not, of course, to be thought of as being divided from one another at distinct intervals. They ran into and overlapped each other, and are only distinguishable now by the predominant characteristic of the progress that was made. The first period may be said to comprehend all progress up to the general adoption of rifling. The second to contain the years which were given to more or less futile endeavours to get good results with spherical projectiles fired from rifled barrels. The third begins with the first hint that experimenters had begun to realise the necessity of making the bullet expand into the rifling. The fourth is the modern period, and dates from the adoption of the solid cartridge-case used with the breech-loader.

When guns first came into use there can be little doubt that missiles of the same nature as those used in the crossbow, or others projected from throwing instruments, would suggest themselves as the only form that could be used. Very quickly it would be found that the long-shaped crossbow quarrell quickly took a whirling motion on its short axis, which would seriously interfere with its straight progression towards the desired mark; so we then have the slow but sure ousting of every other kind of projectile by the spherical ball, at first made of stone, iron, or any other convenient metal, but eventually manufactured solely of lead.

With the acceptance of the principle of rifling as a necessity for accurate delivery of projectiles to a distance, which may be put down at about the beginning of the nineteenth century as far as military rifles were concerned, there came the beginning of another period. Gunners had become increasingly aware of the inaccuracy brought about by the fact that the ball they used was really considerably smaller than the bore from which it was fired, and as a consequence could never be got to leave the muzzle truly centred on a line coincident with the axis of the bore of the gun. The "windage," as it was called from the fact that the gases of explosion escaped round the bullet as it travelled up the bore, was a serious defect in the musket, though it could not be remedied owing to the fact that the weapon was loaded from the muzzle, and the bullet had to be so made that it could be got down on to the powder even when a succession of discharges had made a thick deposit of powder fouling on the interior of the barrel. The rifle presented a new difficulty. If the rifling was to be of any use it must grip the bullet, which meant that the ball itself had to be a little bigger than the smallest diameter of the bore over the lands. Picture to yourself, then, the difficulties of the early strivers after accuracy in rifle-firing. They had to ram the bullet down the barrel—an operation which required time and force in the best circumstances, but which became a truly heroic operation when the barrel was fouled by many discharges. Unless they were very careful the ball would be pushed over the grooving whilst going down and be badly deformed. They had also other difficulties connected with bad powder and faulty ignition.

Benjamin Robins, who saw how essential the rifle was for military purposes more than a century before science and mechanics had made the really efficient rifle a possibility, had already indicated a way of getting over the difficulty of muzzle-loading.

"The most usual (method of loading) is doubtless what I have described," he says—"that of forcing a leaden bullet down the piece by a strong rammer driven by a mallet. But in some parts of Germany and Switzerland an improvement is added to this practice, especially in the large pieces which are used for shooting at great distances. This is done by cutting a piece of very thin leather or of thin fustian in a circular shape, somewhat larger than the bore of the barrel. This circle, being greased on one side, is laid upon the muzzle with its greasy part downwards, and, the bullet being placed upon it, is then forced down the barrel with it, by which means the leather or fustian encloses the lower half of the bullet, and by its interposition between the bullet and the rifles prevents the lead from being cut by them. But it must be remembered that, in those barrels where this is practised, the rifles are generally shallow, and the bullet ought not to be too large."

This system of patching the bullet continued in use until the breech-loader superseded the muzzle-loader, though many practical shots gradually came to the conclusion that the patches, which were a continual nuisance, could be dispensed with if certain conditions were observed. Patches were used for the Baker rifle adopted by the newly-formed Rifle Brigade in 1800, and the bullet was forced down the bore by a ramrod and mallet, exactly as Robins had described sixty years or so before. Nearly sixty years after the Baker rifle came into being, and twenty years after it had been abandoned (in 1857, to be exact), a correspondent to whom the editor of the *Field* lent the hospitality of his columns says: "The inconvenience is known to all rifle shooters of handling patches and balls separately in the field, picking the former with difficulty out of the box, and adjusting them with the ball at the mouth of the rifle." He then goes on to describe a kind of "false muzzle" which he loaded with ball and patch before going out. All he had then to do in the field was to place the "false muzzle" containing the patch and ball over the bore, press the bullet lightly into the muzzle, pluck off the tin "false muzzle," and continue the ramming with the ramrod.

Despite the continuance of patching the bullets as a palliative to the evils of muzzle-loading for a number of years after the need of patching might be held to have disappeared, the patch was not a cure, but only an expedient made necessary by lack of real knowledge of the simplest facts of interior ballistics. The real solution of all the difficulties which rifle-shots were in those days contending with lay in the simple fact that a long-shaped bullet would expand under the influence of the explosion of the charge and fill the bore and grooves,

Fig. 6.—A Tube or False Muzzle to carry the patch and ball in the field

PLATE VII

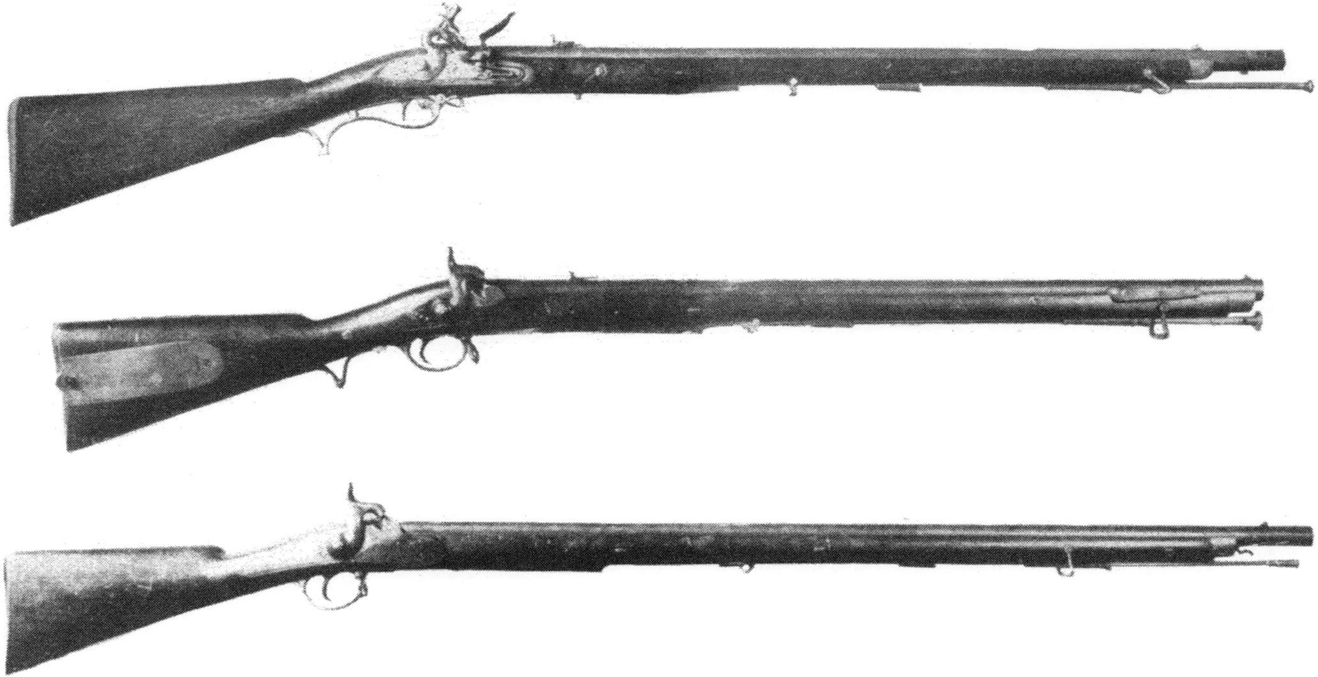

EARLY BRITISH SERVICE RIFLES

At the top is the Baker, the first British Service rifle; it was issued to the newly formed Rifle Brigade in 1800. In the middle is the Brunswick, which was issued to the 2nd Batt. Rifle Brigade about 1840. At the bottom is a muzzle-loader issued to the City of London Rifles in 1850

THE ELONGATED BULLET 37

sealing the bore against all possibility of "windage," and being gripped so firmly by the rifling that it rotated with certainty and with no possibility of "stripping."

This phenomenon is capable of a simple explanation. The bullet before the explosion of the charge is in a state of rest. When the charge is exploded, the inertia of the whole mass of the bullet has to be overcome by the force generated by the explosion before the bullet can start on its passage up the barrel. The impulse of this force acts first on the base of the bullet nearest the explosion. The metal of the base starts to move forward, but the inertia of the front part of the bullet is not yet overcome; the impulse has not yet been passed on to it. In the brief moment of time during which the forward impulse is being transmitted to the whole mass of the bullet the inert front of the bullet offers sufficient resistance to the moving base for the sides to be pressed outwards until they meet the resistance of the walls of the bore and take the impression of the rifling. It should be here noted that the procedure is somewhat different with the high-power rifles of the present day. In these the bullet in its original state is bigger, and not smaller, than the bore of the rifle. The force of explosion drives the bullet against the rifling, which cuts into its surface instead of driving the walls outwards, as was the case with the lead bullets.

Before the virtues of the long bullet were recognised it had become very evident to practical rifle-shots that some method of making them bigger when they started up the bore than they were when they were passed down was absolutely necessary. Setting aside the patching of the bullet, which our quotation from Robins has shown us to have been in his day an alternative to the hard work of ramming a tightly fitting ball, which had already commended itself to the experienced riflemen of some parts of the Continent, the only possible way out of the difficulty seemed to lie in the direction of expanding the bullet at the bottom of the bore. In order to give ease and speed in loading, particularly after the bore had become foul by repeated firing, the musket was loaded with a ball about two sizes smaller than the bore. This expedient commended itself to riflemen who were constantly confronted with the criticism that, though the rifle might indeed be expected to deliver its projectile with better directness than the musket, the time taken to load the rifle negatived the gain in straight shooting. Granted, then, that a ball smaller than the bore was a necessity, how was it to be made to take the grooves of the rifling and get its spin?

The first attempt to solve the problem, whilst clinging to the round ball, was made by a Monsieur Delvigne, a French infantry officer, who caused to be manufactured, in 1826, a rifle with a powder-chamber smaller than the bore. The powder lay in the chamber, and the ball was dropped down the muzzle just as easily as in the musket. The soft lead bullet now rested on the edge of the powder-chamber, and a stroke or two with a heavy ramrod had the effect of forcing a portion of the metal of the bullet outwards into the rifling. The ball was, of course, now elongated; but it was elongated the wrong way, for its long axis was at right angles to the axis of the barrel. Though Delvigne's chamber caused the ball to take the rifling, the effect was not so good as when the balls were made the same size as the bore and forced down the barrel.

The failure of Delvigne's breech did not deter those who were working with him to solve the loading problem from experimenting further with it. Lieut.-Colonel Poncharra, in 1833, set to work with a bullet more nearly the size of the bore, so that it should not be so badly deformed by the ramrod, which expanded it. Of course, immediately he did this the old difficulty of getting the ball down the bore obtruded itself. To get over this the colonel adopted the old idea of the greased patch, which more or less cleared the bore in its passage and materially assisted the downward travel of the ball. A year or so later, continuing his experiments, Poncharra added a wooden shoe, or "sabot," to the round bullet. The sabot rested on the shoulders of the chamber of Delvigne's rifle, and prevented the bullet from being very greatly deformed when it was expanded by the rammer.

By fastening the patch to the sabot, and so connecting it to the ball, Poncharra got a kind of compound elongated bullet,

CARABINE-À-TIGE

with a flat base and a hemispherical head; but, of course, the wooden shoe parted company with the ball soon after it left the rifle, and in any case the wood was not capable of expanding into the grooves. It only acted as a protection for the ball. The Delvigne rifle with Poncharra's saboted ball was considered good enough to be adopted in 1838 by the Chasseurs-à-pied, the French Rifle Brigade. The shooting of the rifle was not improved when a metal sabot was substituted for the wooden one, for this adaptation gave the effect of loading with two projectiles, with consequent loss of direction and velocity.

Colonel Thouvenin, another French officer, of the artillery this time, working along similar lines to those on which his brother officers were travelling, invented the Carabine-à-tige. This rifle had a pillar projecting from the base of the chamber in a line with the axis of the barrel. The purpose was exactly the same as the shoulders of the reduced chamber in Delvigne's invention. The top of the pillar acted as a "tige," or anvil, on which the ball could be slightly flattened to take the grooves of the rifling. It was no more successful in its original form than was the method of Delvigne.

In 1836 the British Government, as the result of inquiry, adopted the Brunswick rifle, in which the difficulty of loading was sought to be overcome by the provision of two deep grooves. A collar to fit these grooves was cast round the spherical ball, and guided the ball both in and out of the barrel. The fouling was still, however, a nuisance difficult to overcome, and, besides, the belted ball was very inaccurate in its flight. The Brunswick weapon did little to enhance the reputation of the rifle with military gentlemen, who still clung to the belief that the musket could not be surpassed for war purposes (see Plate VII.).

Fig. 7.—The Belted Ball for the Brunswick rifle

There were not wanting, even in those days, those who saw the defects of the Brunswick rifle. Amongst them was that "grand old man of gunnery," William Greener, who, in his own characteristic fashion, belaboured it in print, and with it all who were connected with it. In December of 1841 he wrote a long letter to the *Times* on the subject of military arms. This letter he reproduced in an appendix to the 1846 edition of his "Science of Gunnery," and it is certainly worth reproducing again, for it is now of considerable historical value. Not only does it explain the view point of the sponsors of the two-grooved rifle, but it gives the considered opinion of a practical gunmaker, who was certainly one of the best of his day, on the subject of rifles in general and the utility of rifling.

After some caustic remarks on the subject of military muskets, Mr. Greener proceeded as follows, still dipping his pen in the ink of irony:

"Another scientific (*sic*) arrangement of the last two years is the manufacture for the Army of the two-grooved rifle, an invention bearing date as early as 1646. The acumen of our ancestors was sufficiently keen, even at that early period, to perceive the defects of this gun, and as soon to discard it as unfit for even their generation. . . . Novelty is the ruling passion of many men, more especially if it be advanced with a specious gilded specification of many apparent advantages and a careful concealment of defects. The advocates of this novelty—this two-grooved rifle—lose sight of one most essential point. Dr. Ure says, 'The intention of all rifles is to impart to the ball a rotatory motion round its axis as it passes out of the barrel,' etc.; and after a lengthened description of loading, he thus proceeds: 'But instead of this laborious and insecure process, the barrel being now cut with only two opposite grooves, and the ball being framed with a projecting belt, or zone, round its equator of the same form as the two grooves, it enters so easily into their hollows that little or no force is required to put it down upon the powder, yet so much more hold of the barrel is at the same time obtained that, instead of one-quarter of a turn, which was the utmost that could safely be given in the old way without danger of stripping the ball, a whole turn in its length can be given to the two-grooved rifle. The result is that better practice has been performed at 300 yards than with the best old military rifles at 150 yards; and it is, when skilfully used, of unerring aim even

Plate VIII

AN EARLY PERCUSSION CARBINE
A Prussian percussion action of the transitional period

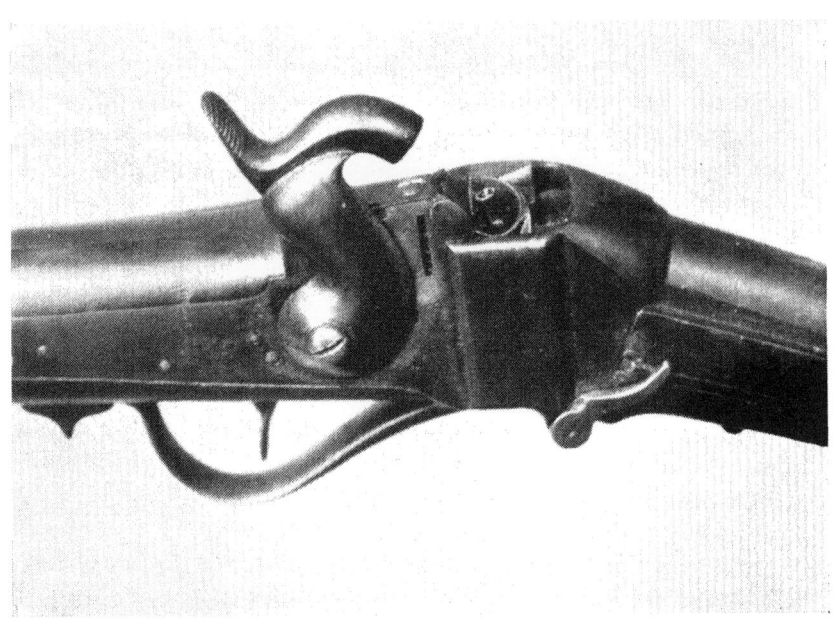

SHARP'S CAPPING CARBINE
This American carbine was issued to a few British regiments for experimental purposes in 1857

THE BRUNSWICK RIFLE 41

at the prodigious distance of 700 yards.' Now, it is such palpable mystification as this that leads astray unpractical men, and enables a schemer to obtain a footing for, at best, very doubtful plans. The matter stands thus: There was in reality no rifle in the British service; for what individual would for a moment maintain that a quarter of a turn in their length (2 ft. 9 in.) constitutes a spiral at all, since it can but thus cause a ball to turn on its own axis once in every 11 ft. during its flight? There is not sufficient spiral motion to counteract the contending influence; therefore, it is very easy for Dr. Ure to say the other excels them at double the distance. The one certainty approaches nearer to what a rifle ought to be than the other, which is no rifle at all, but a barrel grooved in seven places, and those equal in space or area to the projections. The defects of the two-grooved are twofold—first, the excessive spiral (a turn and a quarter in 2 ft. 9 in. long) creates an immense degree of friction in the barrel; secondly, the projections upon the ball create such a 'sawing upon the air' as to change the axis of a spiral motion from that coincident with the line of flight to an axis perpendicular to, or the reverse of, that intended. This extreme spinning motion is obtained at a sacrifice of velocity, force and range. For what is the fact? Why, that instead of a weapon 'of unerring aim at 700 yards,' it will only range at that distance. So much for puff! Now, a well-made rifle under the same circumstances will range above 900 yards, or 25 per cent. farther than this abortion of science; and because we had formerly very imperfect arms we are now to be content with any, if they but excel the old. I contend that national weapons should be the most perfect that can be produced, and not be adopted because they are the greatest novelty of the day."

Mr. Greener then goes on to say that those acquainted with gunmakers know them to be a scheming race, always discovering some great improvement, even though they dig up what has been interred for years. In making this statement the great gunmaker's honesty of intention is undoubted, but it is difficult to understand why the whole race of gunmakers should be included in a sweeping statement because one of their number had recurred to an old idea in an endeavour to produce a good military weapon.

"I would suggest to the Government," continues Mr. Greener, "that rifles are at best but weapons of doubtful excellence. I may truly say I have tried more experiments than most individuals of the present day, and have ever found that the supposed advantages of the rifle exist more in imagination than in reality. A well constructed, cylindrically bored barrel will project a ball farther than the best rifle under the same circumstances fully 100 yards farther, and that with only a very trifling addition of elevation. The disadvantages of the rifle as a military arm are very numerous, and it can only become useful in the hands of a man well skilled in its use; and it is for this reason unfit to be put into the hands of a body of men of indiscriminate ability. So convinced am I of this, that I would undertake to teach any number of men, taken promiscuously from a regiment, to contend, with a well-constructed musket, against any similar number armed with the best made rifle yet produced, quickness and accuracy combined. Therefore, I think it behoves any government to study well the subject before more rifles are manufactured, for they at all times involve a considerable increase of cost."

It might, of course, be contended that Mr. Greener was prejudiced against anything official—as, indeed, he had some cause to be—but it must be remembered that, whatever mistakes he made in his judgments, he was a supremely honest man, and one who was not above owning to his mistakes. In subsequent publications he showed a very clear perception of the utility of rifling; and it must not be laid against him that, at a time when the friends of the rifle were very few, he had some doubts as to the usefulness of the grooved barrel.

Fig. 8.—Jacob's Two-flanged Ball for his four-groove rifle

That truly remarkable gunner, mathematician, and practical scientist, Colonel (afterwards General) Jacob, was evidently also amongst those who were dissatisfied with the Brunswick rifle, for he experimented with the idea of bettering its very inefficient shooting, and developed a four-groove rifle to shoot

JACOB'S FOUR-GROOVE RIFLE

a round ball with two bands cast on it. This rifle must have had very considerable advantages over the ordinary Brunswick, or Jacob, who was an investigator of no ordinary attainments, would not, in 1846, have thought it worth offering to the Honourable East India Company. He might have saved himself the trouble, for his rifle and ball were rejected on the ground that if the Brunswick was good enough for Her Majesty's Army, it was good enough for the East India Company—a modesty which the Company did not always display in other directions.

With Colonel Jacob's rebuff we may leave the history of the spherical projectile. It was at that time nearing the end of its long and inefficient life. The long-shaped bullet which would expand to fill the grooves had been, so to speak, knocking at the gates for many years, and could not much longer be kept from the recognition that was its right. There was not, of course, any immediate understanding of the fact that a long bullet would expand without any aid other than that given by the blow of the powder gases on its base. For many years inventors and experimenters sought to help its expansion by various aids; but very early it cleared the most vexatious of the rifleman's difficulties from his path.

Many columns of matter have been written to prove that this or that person was the inventor of the expanding bullet, and rival claimants had each many adherents. At this length of time after the event we may set ourselves to sift the evidence without heat and without bias. In 1823 a Captain Norton introduced a long-shaped bullet which had a length of about one and three-quarter times its diameter. It had within it a thimble-shaped cavity, which was designed to hold the charge of powder the explosion of which would effect the expanding of the thin walls so that they would fit the bore with reasonable tightness. There were many objections to such a system, the most important undoubtedly being that such a projectile must be very liable to become badly malformed from the force of discharge. This bullet was refused by the Committee of Firearms in 1824, the reason given being that "the spherical ball was the only shape of projectile adapted for military purposes"!

In 1835, twelve years later, Mr. W. Greener made known to the authorities the results of his experiments with an elongated bullet of oval shape, which was manufactured in two parts. The greater portion was of lead, in which was a thimble-shaped cavity. Into this cavity was fitted an iron plug with a broad, button-shaped base. Upon the ignition of the charge, the force of the explosion drove this plug into the lead, expanding it to fit the bore. Mr. Greener, writing five years after his projectile had been rejected, thus describes it:

"The end of the plug being slightly inserted into the perforation, the ball is put into the rifle or musket with either end foremost. When the explosion takes place the plug is driven home into the lead, expanding the outer surface, and thus either filling the grooves of the rifle or destroying the windage of the musket, as the case may be. The result of this experiment was beyond calculation; and for musketry, where the stupid regulations of the service require three and a half sizes of ball difference for windage, it is most excellent, as remedying this considerable drawback upon the usefulness of the arm. And the facility of loading is as great, if not greater, than by the present. As regards its application to rifles, there can be no question of its advantage, if there exist any requirement for a ball to be acted upon by the grooves at all, which we do not think is advantageous; in fact there exists no question."

This last sentence is of great interest, as it shows that there still remained in the mind of Mr. Greener a prejudice against rifling. He regarded his invention as a means of making a musket-ball expand to fit the barrel. He describes the test of his invention in the following way:

"A round of experiments took place, consisting of about 120 shots, fired by a party of the 60th Rifles, commanded by a major of the artillery. The result was most satisfactory as compared with the same number of rounds on the old plan. A man was able to load three times while by the old system he loaded once; and the accuracy of range at 350 yards was as one to three. A considerable anxiety seemed to have taken possession of the officer in question, and, not heeding the

THE HOLLOW BASE BULLET   45

concealment of the matter, we explained the plan, and the consequence was that the excellent shooting, the rapidity of loading, were all at once lost sight of—the talisman was broken. The only further notice we ever received from the Board was, ' It being a compound, rendered it objectionable.' "

Meanwhile, the necessity for a long-shaped bullet for rifle work was gradually coming to be understood. At first these bullets did not have sufficient bearing surface. They were more or less thimble-shaped, and as a consequence were difficult to deliver from the muzzle truly centred.

Somewhere about 1831 M. Delvigne suggested that a long-shaped bullet might give better results than the round ball. Apparently he did not do much in this direction personally at that time, doubtless having in mind the very keen liking of the military authorities of his country for the round ball to which they were used. He mentioned the matter to one Thierry, however, who made long bullets, and used them with some little success in the Delvigne rifle.

The next record of experiments with long bullets comes from India. In 1832 a Colonel Davidson used a bullet the long axis of which was about one and three-quarter times the short axis. Like most long bullets of these early years, the Davidson bullet was nearly all point, what little bearing surface there might have been towards the tail being sacrificed in favour of a wide cannelure and a curve inwards to the base.

Delvigne was still experimenting, and in about 1835 or 1836 seems to have satisfied himself that the solution of the rifleman's difficulties lay in the direction of the long bullet. He tried many variations of the then prevalent form, his variants being mostly in the amount of cup, or hollow, he had in the base. During the course of these experiments he arrived at the truth that an elongated bullet, with its centre of gravity well forward and a hollow in its base, could be expanded to fit the grooves of the rifling without being battered down and outwards by a ramrod, as was necessary in his own and the Thouvenin rifle. He published this discovery and patented his bullet in 1841.

The French authorities had by this time apparently given

up their uncompromising objection to long-shaped projectiles, for the following interesting extract from the *Times* of October 28, 1844, undoubtedly describes a test of Delvigne's bullet against the round ball commonly used:

"The formation of a rifle corps in France, under the title of Chasseurs d'Afrique, at present called Chasseurs d'Orléans, was viewed at first with jealousy, because that body was regarded in the light of a Garde Royale. Whatever the views of the Government in respect of it, the training of the corps has proceeded with much activity. The soldiers of it are now said to equal the best in Europe. 'Of their pretensions to the rank of riflemen,' says one of our Paris letters, 'your military readers will at least be able to judge from the following account of their practice, published in the *Journal des Débats*:

"'An experiment was made at Vincennes on Wednesday, the 19th inst., in the presence of the Duke de Montpensier and of General Rostolan, as to the relative merits of the common musket used by the infantry of the line and the improved carbine of the Chasseurs. The musket was fired by some of the best marksmen of the 68th Regiment of the line, but their address was impotent against the great superiority of the carbine. In a series of experiments, which lasted six hours, the men of the 68th placed seven balls out of 200 shots in the target, at 400 yards' distance, while the Chasseurs placed ten times the number of balls in the same number of shots. The Chasseurs afterwards placed thirty-three balls out of 200 in the target at 500 yards' distance, and twenty-five at 600 yards'. When it is considered that 500 yards is the usual distance at which field-pieces are placed from the object to be reached, and 600 yards that of a 24-pounder, it cannot be denied but that a complete revolution is about to be made in infantry muskets in consequence of the adoption of M. Delvigne's invention.'

"A month or five weeks since," continues our correspondent, "I went to Vincennes to see the new works in progress for completing the fortress. I am not qualified to decide upon their claim to perfection—for they will, it is said, be perfect—but I was astonished by their extent.

"I returned to town on foot through the wood, and found

PLATE IX

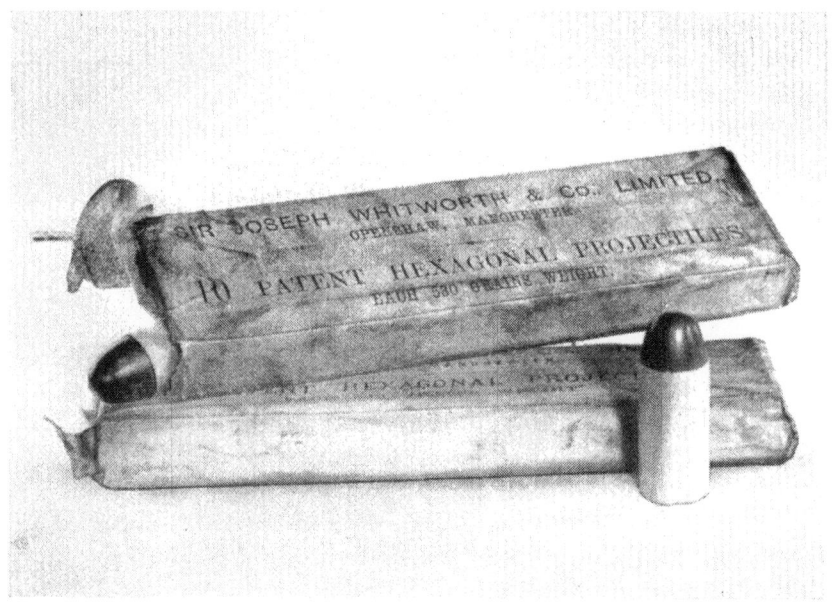

WHITWORTH'S HEXAGONAL BULLETS
A broken and an unbroken packet of the special bullets made for the Whitworth rifle

CARTRIDGES FOR A MUZZLE-LOADER
A packet of Enfield cartridges and the original wrapper preserved in the N.R.A. Museum at Bisley

CAPTAIN MINIÉ   47

a battalion of the new rifle corps at exercise in the alleys and thickets. They were occupied in a way quite new to me, who am, I confess, unlearned in these matters. If it be new, a word or two respecting it may not be uninteresting to some classes of your readers.

"A soldier bearing a target ran ahead from his section (for the body was divided into many) to a distance of, it would seem, as many hundred yards as he pleased. Having planted it, his comrades of the section were then in rotation called up to the point from which he with the target had started and asked the distance to it. Having replied, his guess was entered opposite to his name, and so on with the rest.

"Although this was evidently exercise, and with a view peculiarly applicable to the rifle service, and done, too, in the presence of an officer, it combined with it amusement, which the soldiers appeared to relish exceedingly. There was first a laugh at those who guessed widely, and then the fun of a race to take a new start; but I could perceive by the gravity with which the presiding sergeant inspected the entries that he entered warmly into the system of training for that branch of the army."

This contemporary account is valuable, not only because it shows the degree of accuracy which was expected of rifles at the time, and also contains the first mention of "distance judging" as a military exercise, but because it indicates the advantages which Captain Minié possessed when he began experimenting.

Captain Minié was an officer in the Chasseurs d'Orléans, and must therefore have been closely acquainted with the work of other rifle experimenters. He first tried expanding the Delvigne flat-based bullet on the steel pillar of the Thouvenin rifle, and got results far in advance of those obtained with the round ball. But Minié, like all other riflemen of the time, was hampered and hindered at every turn by the imperfections of the powder he had to use. He could never be certain that the powder would explode with sufficient force to expand the bullet properly. To get over this difficulty he placed in the hollow base of an elongated bullet of the usual shape used at the time an iron cup which, being driven into the base, effectively expanded it to fill the grooves.

When Minié brought out this bullet in 1849, the merits of his discovery were quickly recognised. His bullet really did expand, and the expansion did not necessitate the use of any contrivance in the breech, nor any battering with the ramrod. France and Belgium adopted it quickly, and Great Britain followed in 1851, the arm being officially known as "The Regulation Minié Musquet" (see Plates X. and XI.).

One can imagine the delight of the enthusiastic believer in the rifle when he first handled the Minié Musquet. Here, by a simple little contrivance in the base of the bullet, all his troubles seemed solved. The bullet was so well expanded, that its passage up the bore when fired removed nearly all the fouling of the previous shot. Fouling had been the bugbear of riflemen ever since grooves had been cut in barrels; now the bugbear had vanished! No wonder Captain Minié's name rang throughout those countries where his invention was used.

The English Minié had a bore of .702 in. diameter, rifled with four grooves, making one turn in 6 ft. Before discharge, the bullet, which weighed 680 grains, had a diameter of .69 in. Though a tremendous fuss was made about the Minié, and some muskets were rifled to take Minié's ball, the weapon was never generally issued. A few of the converted muskets were used in the Crimea.* The reason that the Minié rifle was held back can be found in the shape of the bullet which the War Office adopted. It differed considerably from Minié's pattern, and had no cylindrical part at the base to keep it properly centred up the barrel. Considerable trouble was also caused by the fact that the hollow at the base was so large, that the expanding cup cut off and left behind in the barrel a ring of lead from the base of the bullet.

The powder and ball for the Minié was made up into cartridges. A tube of paper was wrapped round the bullet, which

---

* The "Text-Book of Small Arms" (1909) states that the Minié "was used by some of the troops in the Crimea," but we incline to the opinion that the Minié ball was fired in this campaign from the converted musket rifled with three grooves and known as "The Sea Service Rifle."

MR. METFORD AND MR. PRITCHETT 49

lay with its point in the tube. The powder charge was put in the tube and the whole closed up, the paper round the bullet being lubricated with a mixture of tallow and beeswax. When the rifle had to be loaded the top of the tube was opened and the charge poured down the bore. Then the paper above the bullet was torn off, and the bullet, base first, was rammed home.

With the adoption of the Enfield rifle in 1853, we have the first influence of a man who has possibly done more for the rifle than any other. It was Mr. Metford who suggested to Mr. Pritchett the form and dimensions of the projectile which was adopted for the Enfield rifle, and became known as the Pritchett bullet. This bullet had a length of very nearly twice its diameter, and was provided with a hollow base with no base plug. This abandonment of the base plug was quite in accordance with the most advanced opinion of the day, for in the same year which saw the adoption of the Pritchett ball, Mr. Boucher, in "The Volunteer Rifleman and the Rifle," restated and emphasised the truth which Delvigne had dimly seen a dozen years before—that a leaden projectile will expand at the impact of the powder gases. "All will expand, from the simple cylindrical solid plug to the most elaborate hollow conoidal bullet, and the expansion will be more or less according as the bullets are longer or shorter." Despite this, the base plug was soon restored in the shape of a tapered plug of boxwood, and later of clay. The reason was that the powder used in the Army was still incapable of always effectively expanding the bullet.

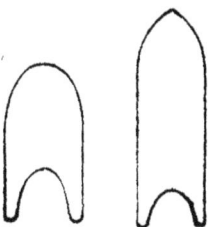

Fig. 9.—Section through two types of Pritchett Bullet. On the left is the Enfield type, and on the right a modification used by Whitworth in his hexagonal bore rifle

About this time General Jacob, who had been experimenting more or less continuously, despite his disappointment at the way his rifle had been treated by the East India Company, produced a bullet of .5 in. calibre, with a length of 1.25 in. The head was ogival, and the point was considerably sharper than that of any bullet made up to that time. General Jacob

E

still kept to his four flanges cast on the bullet, but with its new shape he succeeded very well with it. It is said that he made good practice at 2,000 yards with the double-barrelled rifle he had designed. Jacob also invented an exploding bullet. In the nose of the bullet a hole was cast, and in the hole a copper tube containing a bursting charge was inserted. In 1856 this rifle was again tried by the Indian Government, and the following report was made:

"At ranges from 300 to 1,200 yards the flight of the shell (used with this rifle) was always point foremost, and the elevation at extreme range inconsiderable. The shells which struck the butt invariably burst with full effect; and practice was made by the many officers who attended at distances which could not have been attained with any other missile."

The Jacob shell would have probably been taken over by the Government had not Mr. Metford turned his attention to the question, and manufactured an explosive variety of the Pritchett ball which was adopted, after much hesitation, in 1863.

The influence of Whitworth, who had been experimenting since 1854, now began to make itself felt. By reducing the bore of the rifle and keeping his bullet the same weight as the Enfield, he at once gained a big advance in ballistic efficiency. By making his rifle-bore hexagonal, and casting his projectile to the same figure, he did away with any necessity of expanding his ball into the grooves. All he had to make sure of was that the bullet would expand to fit the corners of his hexagon. This he could do with a hard lead bullet. His many experiments in the amount of spin necessary to give gyroscopic stability to a bullet of a certain length were of the utmost value in settling points previously held to be hopelessly obscure; and though his mechanically fitting bullet was eventually found to be unnecessary to accurate shooting, it set so high a standard for many years, that the competition it encouraged was of the utmost value to rifle shooting and rifle manufacturing.

Fig. 10. — Whitworth Hexagonal Bullet

Though successful trials of the Whitworth rifle were made in 1857, the principle of adopting a mechanically fitting bullet

PLATE X

THREE MILITARY PERCUSSION RIFLES

At the top of the plate is the British Minié Rifle issued in 1851; in the middle is the original model Enfield, with three grooves, issued in 1855; at the bottom is the Dutch pattern of the Snider breech-loader

BOUCHER'S DISC BULLET

did not commend itself greatly to practical rifle-shots, who were most of them seeking for accuracy in other directions. How far in the right direction practical experience was leading thoughtful riflemen can be judged from a letter written by Mr. Boucher to the *Field,* and published in the issue of May 14, 1859. This letter dealt with two matters which at that time were beginning to occupy a good deal of attention. One was the efficacy of the base plug, and the other the necessity for the patch.

Fig. 11.—Mr. Boucher's Disc Bullet in section and viewed from the base

"My 'disc' bullet . . . is what is commonly called 'cylindro-conoidal' in its outward form," says Mr. Boucher. "That which I generally use is about $1\frac{1}{16}$ in. in length, as represented by the diagram, though it may be made longer if the rifleman desires a heavier one for particular purposes.

"In the end of the bullet, which is a *fair* cylinder for half its length, I have a cavity formed as shown at *a*, which extends a little more than half the length of the bullet. Upon the edge of the cavity *b b* I place the round disc *c*, which is cut out of thin iron to fit exactly, so that it will not drop out after it has been pressed in by the thumb or gently on a table. When the explosion takes place the disc becomes so firmly fixed by the contraction of the lead around it that it never falls out, nor is it driven, or intended to be driven, further in than the rest of the lead at the base of the bullet.

"Experience shows that the 'disc' bullet rifles itself as distinctly as if it had been cast in the grooves of the barrel—a complete answer to the *supposed* effects of all such nonsense as the 'expanding' cups and plugs which many who ought to know better still believe in. It may also be called a *safe* bullet, for any number may be fired at a distant object over the heads of bodies of men employed or moving in the intermediate space without any fear of the discs leaving the bullets, like the cups of the 'Minié,' and injuring the men. I have fired thousands of these bullets, and, though not a first-rate marksman, I have repeatedly placed 70 per cent. of them in a space 2 ft.

broad by 4 ft. high at 600 yards' distance. This can be corroborated by unquestionable authority."

It is interesting to read at this time of the actual experience of a practical rifleman who used the Minié, and to realise how far we have advanced in a little more than half a century. Mr. Boucher generously placed his discovery at the disposal of fellow rifle-shots, and told them that a Mr. Greenfield, of Broad Street, Golden Square, had been in the habit of making his bullet-moulds, and "as my object is to encourage rifle-shooting, he has full permission from me to make moulds of this pattern for any gentleman applying for the same. In giving the order, however, I would recommend the barrel to be given to him, with instructions to make the bullet large enough just to touch its sides, but to fall to the bottom by its own weight. My reason for advising this is that I never use paper or patch, but simply dip the bullet half-way in a *very hot* mixture of two parts beeswax, one part soft soap, and one part tallow or hog's lard, the refuse being previously carefully skimmed off. I generally mix a few pounds of these ingredients together at once, as it has then only to be made thoroughly hot and liquid for use at any time afterwards.

"Some years ago, when carrying on an extensive course of experiments with bullets of various sizes and forms—some with paper wrapped round them like the Service ammunition, some with patches, and others in a *naked* state—I became so satisfied of the superiority of the 'naked' bullet, and its simplicity in loading over other methods, that I have continued ever since to use such for my own private shooting. Our most scientific military authorities have also lately declared themselves in favour of this system. One says: 'The employment of a naked bullet, thus doing away with that interfering medium, the paper, will be a matter of great importance, if we can succeed.' Another says: 'I entirely concur in what has been said as to the advantages to be derived from the naked bullet in preference to one with paper; it is evident that the naked bullet, properly supplied with grease, will fill the grooves of the rifle better than one which has the intervening substance of paper

THE DISADVANTAGE OF PATCHES 53

around it.' A third adds: 'In my opinion it is to the paper alone the defects in fouling and accuracy are attributable; bullets have lately been constructed and used without paper, and the result has been that these bullets have not only shown themselves superior to the plug, but barrels which would have been rejected with the latter as bad barrels have produced greater accuracy than has ever been obtained with the plug ammunition.' These are the opinions of officers of high standing who have devoted much time to the study of rifled arms, and are therefore worthy of every consideration."

With this quotation from Mr. Boucher's letter, which will be referred to again, we leave rifle ammunition in a fairly advanced state, and ready to be improved out of all knowledge within the next dozen years.

CHAPTER III

The Perfecting of the Muzzle-loader and the Development of the Military Breech-loader

THE younger generation of rifle-shots often have great difficulty in realising how modern a thing is the military breech-loader. It is younger than the electric telegraph, and much younger than the railway. Practically its whole history is within living memory, and there are men alive to-day who shot with the muzzle-loaded weapon at Wimbledon and other important ranges. The period during which the breech-loader was most energetically developed corresponds with the younger and, may one say, the more vigorous days of the National Rifle Association. From its first prize meeting held at Wimbledon in 1860, the meetings of the Association attracted all that was best in rifle and ammunition design. Wimbledon saw the perfecting of the muzzle-loader and its decline before the manifold advantages of the breech-loader for military purposes.

That "the hour produced the men" is a truism with regard to that most vital period in rifle history, the years between 1860 and 1872. Engineers and scientists of skill and ability were turning their attention to rifle problems, with the result that, once it was started, the transformation of the rifle from a muzzle-loading to a breech-loading weapon proceeded rapidly. At the same time, so many important improvements were made, both in breech actions and in less apparent but none the less important parts of the weapon, that we have the impression given us, as we look back on those years, that the nations were tumbling over one another in their efforts to get hold of the latest and most deadly weapon.

Rifles and rifle-shooting were in the public eye in this as

THE ENFIELD RIFLE 55

well as in other countries. On July 2, 1860, Queen Victoria had fired the first shot at Wimbledon. The shot was fired from a muzzle-loading Whitworth rifle, the product of the skill of that great engineer, Sir Joseph Whitworth; but the majority of the competitions took place with the "long Enfield" muzzle-loader with which the Volunteers were then armed (see Plate XI.).

The Enfield rifle, which was issued in 1855 and was used in the Crimea, was rifled at first with three grooves having a depth of .012 in. at the breech, decreasing to .005 in. at the muzzle; and the pitch was one turn in 78 in., the twist being right-handed, or clockwise. The bore was .577 in. In 1858 a short Enfield with a barrel only 2 ft. 5 in. long, instead of the 3 ft. 3 in. of the long Enfield, was made and issued to the Navy, being known as the "Sea Service Rifle." The rifling was progressive, just as in the first model, but had a much more rapid twist, making one turn in 4 ft. Previously to this a short rifle had been experimented with by the rifle regiments. Both these short Enfields had five grooves (see Plates X. and XI.).

The Enfield rifle, though it was only five years old, was already considered far from satisfactory; sporting rifles could be produced to give far greater accuracy. Even with the expanding bullet the old troubles did not disappear, and with each step in advance the ideals of the rifle-shot advanced as well. The truth of the matter is, that with the rising of the Volunteer movement shooting had again become, as it had been in the past, the pastime of the people. The Volunteer wanted an accurate weapon, and in the ranks of the Volunteers there were many men who could help to produce one, and thousands who could appreciate it when it came.

The line of least resistance in overcoming the troubles of muzzle-loading had been thought by many experimenters to lie in the direction of providing a rifle to fire a bullet which had cast on it flanges to fit the rifling. The first important example of a rifle grooved to fire a mechanically fitting projectile was the two-grooved Brunswick issued to the Rifle Brigade in 1836. The Brunswick rifling was very rapid, as ideas went in those days, the pitch being one turn in 30 in., which was the length of the barrel; so rapid a twist was possible only because the flanges on the ball fitted the grooves more or less, and so had a good hold and could not jump the lands. As has already been mentioned, the Brunswick was not a success. Purdey's rifle, a sporting weapon which was of considerable repute in the middle of the nineteenth century, was on the same two-groove principle, the grooves being about one-sixteenth of an inch deep and made to fit flanges cast on a cylindro-conical bullet. The pitch was one turn in 6 ft. By decreasing the twist Purdey obtained an increase in velocity, and gave his bullet sufficient spin to keep it point first up to about three hundred yards, which was considered quite sufficient for a sporting rifle. The rifle for firing a mechanically fitting bullet reached its climax in that produced by Whitworth (see Plate IX.).

The Jacob rifle was another example of a weapon made to fire a bullet with flanges cast upon it. In this case the grooves were four in number and had a twist of one turn in 3 ft. General Jacob thought about and experimented with rifles for close upon forty years. The height of his ambition was to produce an accurate muzzle-loading rifle that would not be difficult to load. In this he succeeded; but his weapon was never adopted by the Government, though when he had abandoned his experiments with the round projectile and turned his attention to long bullets, the Indian Government, in 1856, reported very favourably on his finished product. Most of his work dealt with bullets rather than with rifles, and a short account of his experiments has already been given.

At its first meeting the National Rifle Association, in accordance with its avowed policy of furthering the interests of rifle-shooting, decided that the long-range competition for the Queen's Prize should be shot with the best military weapon that could be obtained. Trials were therefore held, with a result that only emphasised the conclusions come to by experts in the trials of 1857, and the Whitworth rifle was chosen for the 800 yards', 900 yards', and 1,000 yards' competition for the Queen's Prize, the "Blue Ribbon" of the meeting.

PLATE XI

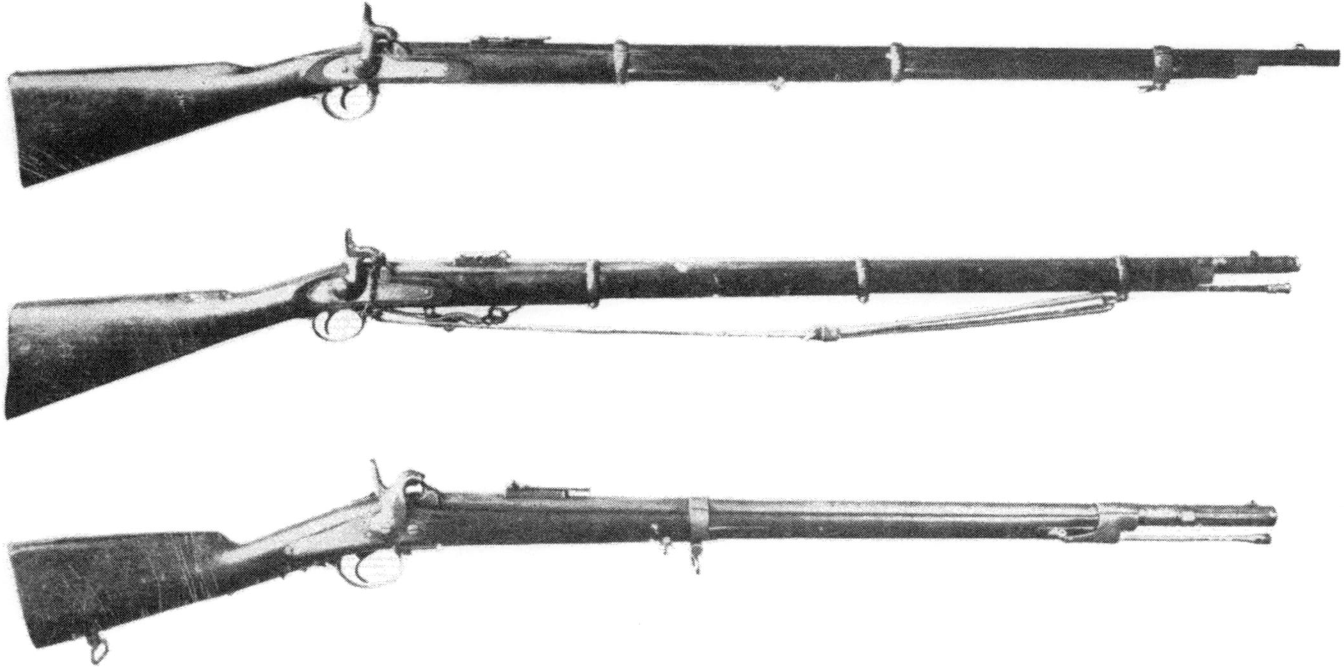

THREE MUZZLE-LOADING PERCUSSION MILITARY RIFLES

At the top is the Whitworth such as was used to shoot with in the final of "The Queen's" during the first years of that competition. In the middle is the Service Enfield (5 grooves). At the bottom is the French Minié

SIR JOSEPH WHITWORTH

For over ten years this system of providing for the second, or long range, stage of the "Queen's" a better weapon than the official one of the Volunteers was followed, and the rivalry amongst inventors and manufacturers to produce a rifle that would be judged fitting to be used in this important match resulted in a wonderful improvement in the weapon and in knowledge of its capabilities.

Sir Joseph Whitworth's work, as has already been told, was principally in the direction of finding the best form of rifling and the correct twist for that rifling. All the weapons he produced were percussion-cap ignition, muzzle-loaders with hexagonal rifling, the hard lead bullet being cast in the correct form to fit the rifling, though he conducted some experiments with the Pritchett bullets in his rifles. Whitworth had little or no knowledge of the rifle when he began experimenting at the invitation of the Government in 1854; but he had great engineering and scientific skill and knowledge, with the wealth of the nation behind him. It was said at the time that his first successful rifle cost £1,000 to build, when experiments and trials had been paid for. It is likely that the sum was considerably greater.

The rifle which Sir Joseph Whitworth produced was of .450-in. bore, as against the Enfield .577-in. It had a twist of one turn in 20 in. It was in all ways a very great advance on any rifle that had been produced up to 1857, when it was officially tried against the Enfield rifle. The great advantage that the Whitworth rifle had over the Enfield was particularly noticeable at long ranges. At 500 yards the mean deviation of the shots from the Enfield was 2.24 ft., whilst that of the Whitworth was only .37 ft. At 1,100 yards the Enfield bullets showed a mean deviation of 8 ft., whilst the Whitworth figures were only 2.62 ft., or very little more than

Fig. 12.—The figure of Whitworth's hexagonal rifling

those of the Enfield at 500 yards! At 1,400 yards the Enfield gave up the struggle and retired, but the Whitworth went on triumphantly to 1,800 yards, where its mean deviation was 11.62 ft.

Broadly speaking, inquiry and experiment as regards rifles in these years proceeded along two lines. One was directed towards the elimination of the still prevalent fouling and other troubles of the muzzle-loader by improving the system of rifling. The other concerned itself with the improvement of the breech-loading system.

Already a very considerable amount of knowledge on the subject of rifling had been accumulated, and a brief recapitulation of the principal points that had been decided may here prove of advantage. The French and Belgian Governments, as has been told in the first chapter of this book, had many years before conducted experiments to find out the proper pitch of rifling for their army rifles. And Whitworth had more recently given his attention to the matter. Everything was in train for the great improvements which were soon to come.

The generally accepted idea was that, whatever the grooving adopted, the grooves should be rather on the deep side, to allow fouling to accumulate to some extent without preventing the bullet from being forced down the muzzle; and though this difficulty did not have to be overcome in the breech-loader, the breech-loading rifles of this time, with a few notable exceptions, followed the plan accepted as correct for the muzzle-loading rifle. With the general adoption of rifling in military and other arms it had been seen that the rifling must diminish the muzzle velocity of the bullet, on account of the friction caused by the lands gripping the bullet absorbing some of the original force of the explosion. Of course, the greater the twist of the rifling the more friction must be developed, which with deep grooving was very considerable indeed. Then there was the tendency for the somewhat loosely fitting spherical bullet to be driven across the lands instead of following the rifling. This fault was not likely to occur with the expanding bullet, but it was still feared; and this again encouraged the making of deep grooves, with the very obvious intention of giving the bullet more to catch hold of. The consequence was a great increase of friction. To try to get over these difficulties several devices were resorted to. One of these, which was probably originated in America, was to gradually increase the twist of

VARYING THE TWIST

the rifling from breech to muzzle. It was thought that by starting the bullet revolving with less twist than was necessary to give it proper gyroscopic stability, and letting the proper number of turns be given just as the bullet left the muzzle, the friction would be lessened, and the soft lead bullet, being gradually made to acquire the necessary revolution, would not have so great a tendency to "strip" or jump the lands. A variation of this notion was that propounded by a gentleman who proposed to decrease the twist from breech to muzzle so that friction would be lessened towards the muzzle, and the bullet would leave with something like the velocity it would have acquired had the barrel not been rifled at all.

Another arrangement, which is usually attributed to Captain Tamisier, was to make the grooves deeper at the breech than at the muzzle. The principle was adopted for the Enfield and retained in the Martini-Henry.

Of those days of almost feverish endeavour it might truly be said, "Of the making of grooves there was no end," for not only were depth and twist altered in hundreds of ways, but the varieties of shape were legion. Whitworth's experiments had shown experimenters what might be done by definitely shaping the bore, and many men sought to adapt Whitworth's bore to fire an expanding bullet. A rifle having ratchet-shaped grooves was made by a Glasgow gunsmith, and in 1861 Mr. Henry, an Edinburgh gunmaker who had already made a good reputation, entered in the trials a rifle with a curiously shaped figure which had apparently been arrived at after a deep consideration of Whitworth's figure. At the junction of the sides of the hexagon, the rifling was so cut as to leave small sharp projections, with the idea of making this style of boring suitable to an expanding bullet.

When the 1852 trials were made, one of the rifles which had been unsuccessfully entered against the Government-designed Enfield was the "oval-bore" Lancaster. The figure of the rifling was as though an oval tube had been twisted upon itself with an increasing twist. The Lancaster carbine was adopted for the Sappers and Miners in 1856, and proved itself an efficient weapon. In 1862 the report of the

Ordnance Committee which condemned the Enfield was very complimentary to the Lancaster rifle "on all points connected with military efficiency." It was this same report which, whilst praising the Whitworth rifle and acknowledging its superiority, stated that the Committee, "although they do not at present feel warranted in recommending the introduction of a rifle of so small a bore as .450 in. for the entire army, they think the employment of arms having such superior precision would be attended with advantage, and is not inexpedient."

The battle of the grooves was fought out with a degree of keenness that is remarkable even when we take into consideration the ability and energy of the men who were experimenting, and this despite the fact that Whitworth's rifle won the N.R.A. trials repeatedly. John Rigby—a name still great in the shooting world—was experimenting, like many others, with a ratchet-shaped grooving; but, despairing of getting over the many difficulties that he had to contend with, he abandoned the idea, and in 1864 he produced a rifle firing a mechanically fitting bullet on Whitworth's principle, and succeeded in beating the all-conquering Whitworth "on its own ground," so to speak.

The chief difficulty that had to be contended with was still and always the fouling that accumulated after each shot. This fouling not only made the firing of a number of shots without cleaning out impossible, because of the difficulty of ramming the bullet down the barrel whilst the fouling was in it, but it also destroyed the accuracy of the rifle as long as it remained in the bore. Now that tight-fitting bullets had been found to be a necessity for accurate shooting, the trouble with the sooty residue became even greater than it had yet been. Whitworth, with his very accurately fitting bullets, was so much troubled by the fouling that he went to considerable trouble to find a better variety of black powder than that ordinarily used; but not getting satisfaction even here, introduced for the benefit of users of his rifle a scraper which fitted the bore and could be relied on to remove the last traces of the hard deposit.

It was surely an irony of fate that Whitworth should have found his greatest trouble because of his insistence on the

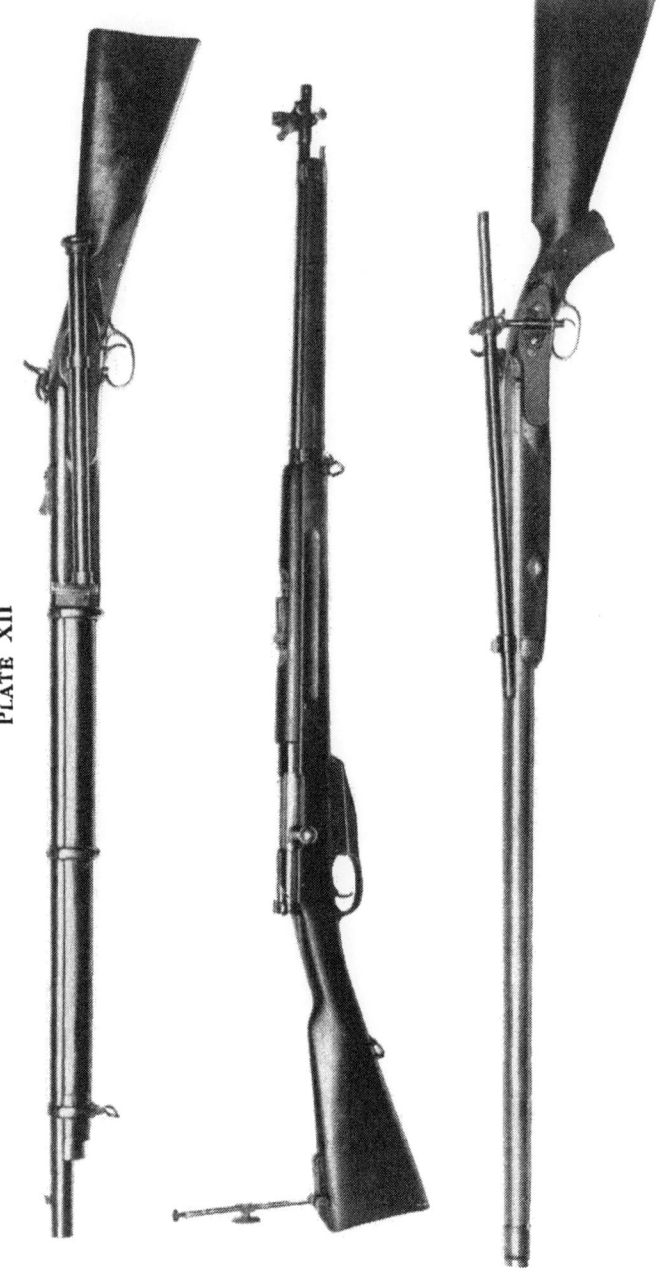

PLATE XII

THREE MATCH RIFLES

The rifle at the top is one made by Sir Joseph Whitworth. The middle one is a Mannlicher fitted with "optical" sights for firing in the back position, and used by Major Richardson in the match Ulster Rifle Association v. U.S.A. The third rifle was made by Mr. Metford and used by Sir Henry Halford in the 2,000 yards competition in 1865-6. The rifle has a false muzzle. The Whitworth and Metford rifles have telescopic sights

METFORD AND HALFORD

greatest possible accuracy of measurement in the making of rifle barrels and casting of projectiles to fit them. He was the first to introduce that supreme accuracy which now makes it necessary for first-class rifle manufacturers to provide themselves with instruments that will measure to the one ten-thousandth part of an inch. In 1860 Whitworth recommended the Government to introduce into the Enfield and Woolwich factories a system of accurately gauging all parts of the rifle during manufacture, and making them all to exact scale. This, the beginning of modern repetition methods in this country, was soon adopted.

Despite the careful and painstaking work of other experimenters in those fruitful years, that of Mr. W. E. Metford stands out with a prominence that is the direct result of his almost inspired genius for rifle work, and with it must be coupled that of Sir Henry Halford, to whose friendship and encouragement he owed so much. Mr. Metford's early hints as to bullet shape have already been spoken of; but it is for his work on the bore of the rifle that we owe him the greatest debt of gratitude. How far-reaching and important were his discoveries may be judged from the fact that in 1914 a very large proportion of the winning rifles in the Match Rifle Class at Bisley were rifled on the Metford system, slightly modified, whilst very many Territorial target shots, having the choice between the Metford and the Enfield systems of rifling, have for years chosen the former. As a matter of fact, both systems were of Metford's devising, that known by his name being the later development.

Metford's idea was that the system of deep grooving then in vogue was wrong. He proved conclusively by experiment that a very shallow grooving was all that was necessary to spin the bullet, and also that with shallow grooves, which did not trap and hold the fouling, the fouling trouble practically disappeared. The form of grooving which he first adopted for his muzzle-loading rifles was exactly similar to that subsequently known as the "Enfield system," when it was used for the breech-loader of the Royal Small Arms Factory.

It is another of those ironies of fate which pursue inventors that Metford should have brought out his perfected muzzle-loader in 1865, the very year that saw the adoption of the breech-loading principle by the British Government. The perfect muzzle-loader came too late on the field to be of any service as a military muzzle-loader; but the work was by no means wasted, for Metford's system was scientifically right, whether the weapon was loaded from the breech or from the muzzle. For the next five years muzzle-loaders on the Metford system, or copies of them, won most of the long range and match rifle prizes at Wimbledon. In 1871 we find Mr. Metford's rifles continuing their triumphs in the breech-loader class.

Though the honour of having demonstrated the value of shallow grooving undoubtedly belongs to Mr. Metford, it is interesting to note that his ideas on the subject had been anticipated in 1859 by Mr. Boucher, who later wrote an excellent little book on "The Volunteer Rifleman and the Rifle." On May 14, 1859, he wrote a letter to the *Field,* a portion of which has already been quoted and which we now complete.

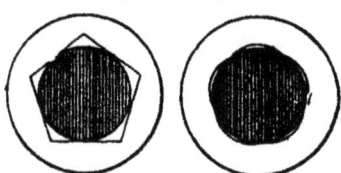

Fig. 13.—Mr. Boucher's five-groove rifling based on the pentagon

"I am an advocate for a somewhat heavy rifle," says Mr. Boucher, "as the shooting with such a weapon is always more steady, with less recoil, particularly if the weight of the metal is judiciously accumulated behind and immediately surrounding the breech. The barrel of the one I am now about to describe is 2 ft. 6 in. in length; weight, 5½ lb. The bore is exactly half an inch in diameter—a size which a great majority of our practical marksmen agree now in recommending. I am not favourable to four grooves, for this reason: When the bullet leaves the muzzle of the piece it is made, by the force of the explosion, nearly *square,* or four-sided, especially if the grooves are deep, causing a considerable amount of extra friction, and consequently retardation, by its grinding motion whilst passing through the air. I have therefore fixed on five, though, from my style of grooving, many have supposed the barrel to be a smooth-bore.

BOUCHER'S SHALLOW GROOVES 63

"In order to understand the mode of grooving thoroughly, I must ask the reader to draw for himself, on as large a scale as he pleases, for the sake of distinctness, the geometrical figure called a pentagon. Then in the centre let him draw a circle, so that the edges may just touch the sides of the figure. This circle is to represent the end of the bullet. The next process is to round off the angles of the figure to rather less than a third of their original depth, when they will appear to be *broad, shallow grooves,* somewhat like the second diagram above, the first diagram representing the figure before the angles were rounded off.

"The twist of the spiral is at the rate of one turn in 5 ft., which generates a rotary motion quite sufficient for a range of one mile; for as there is little friction, comparatively speaking, to retard the progress of the bullet in the barrel, it proceeds with greater velocity after leaving the muzzle, thus rendering a less amount of twist necessary than in a barrel having more friction.

"Taking into consideration all the experiments I have made myself, all I have witnessed in other quarters, and all the experimental reports I have read on the subject, this is the mode of grooving which I still prefer, and which I recommended to our authorities in the autumn of 1853, and again in 1855. I have loaded and fired hundreds of rounds from such a barrel without the slightest trouble, the last bullet going down as easily as the first; in fact, a glance at the diagram will show any man conversant with the subject that there can be no friction that cannot be overcome by merely *pressing* the ramrod gently and steadily down, so that the shape of the bullet cannot be destroyed, nor the powder caked, by the bullet being jammed down upon it.

"This mode of grooving requires only *attention* on the part of the workman, without which any sort of grooving becomes worse than useless, disappointing and deceiving the man who pays a high price for a showy and *said to be* superior weapon. The cutter should be just a fifth of the circumference of the bore, and very shallow, and care taken not to go so deep as to affect the five points of the original surface where the bullet is seen to touch the sides, leaving the bore without any sharp edges."

It does not seem possible that so slow a twist as that advocated by Mr. Boucher could have given his bullet sufficient gyroscopic stability for a range of 1,800 yards, but the bullet was short. In any case, it is a system of grooving to which attention is to be drawn.

It was in 1865 that Mr. Metford first came into the field with his system of rifling. He had then been experimenting with rifles for a good many years, and had arrived at the conclusion that the bore of half an inch or over which had become almost a fetish with both military and sporting experts was not a necessity, and that in fact, with elongated bullets, which, of course, had greater sectional density than round bullets, a smaller bore had great advantages. Sir Joseph Whitworth had come to the same conclusion. Metford's first rifle, like that of Whitworth, had a bore of .450 in.; and these two were the beginning of the "small bore" rifles for military purposes, though a bore of such size would in modern practice be considered very large.

Mr. Metford's first rifle had five grooves, .004 in. deep. The lands and grooves were of equal width, and the grooves were sharp at the edges. He found, as Mr. Boucher had done before him, that, with shallow grooves, the ramming of the bullet down the barrel cleaned the bore, so that shooting could be continued for a very large number of shots without the fouling causing any difficulty in loading, or causing any inaccuracy in the flight of the projectile.

Mr. Metford's essential discovery was, of course, that his hardened lead bullets were sufficiently expanded by the force of the explosion to take and hold his shallow rifling, and that the soft lead bullets previously thought necessary were not necessary after all. Mr. Boucher had really made the same discovery if he had not allowed his vision to be obscured. He chronicles the fact that his bullets took the rifling perfectly; but he apparently attributed this to a disc of iron which was affixed to the end of the bullet. Like so many other experimenters, he allowed himself to be led from the truth by a

THE NEEDLE-GUN

chimera; and so it was left for Mr. Metford to make the announcement that tolled the death-knell of deep grooving and mechanically fitting bullets, and opened the gates for the breech-loading rifle and the vast possibilities it contained.

In following the development of rifling systems we have gone on rather fast, and must now return to consider the other important developments which took place in the breech-loading system.

The first breech-loading rifle to be adopted for military purposes was the well-known "Needle-gun," invented in 1839 by Dreyse as a sporting gun action. Despite the fact that it suffered badly from the same defects as its predecessors, and that the escape of gas and flame at the breech made it impossible to fire it from the shoulder after the first few shots, it was adopted by the Prussians in 1848, after many experiments and improvements had been made since the Prussian authorities became interested in it in 1842. The "Needle-gun" can justly lay claim to be the parent of modern breech-loading rifles, inasmuch as it was a bolt action. In the earlier pattern the cocking of the action was performed by pulling back on a milled cocking-piece that was connected with the "needle," or striker, and situated at the rear of the bolt. In later models this was performed by the action of drawing back the bolt, as is done in all modern bolt actions (see Plate XIII.).

The success of the Dreyse weapon was not at first apparent, though it had made a sufficient impression on the British authorities for them to issue to a cavalry regiment, in 1857, some American "Sharp's" carbines for experimental purposes. A few years later the French converted their Minié rifles into breech-loaders, adopting the Tabatière system, which has many points similar to the Snider (see Plate XVII.).

In 1864 the British Government, thoroughly awakened by the success of the Prussian breech-loader in the war with Denmark, appointed a committee to consider the best form of breech-loading action of our Army rifles. It decided in 1866 on the Snider action, and the Enfield rifle was promptly converted into a breech-loader on this system.

The Snider system was rightly considered as merely a

stopgap until a rifle designed and built as a breech-loader could be found worthy of adoption for the British troops. In 1866 the Chassepot rifle was adopted by the French army, and in that year a new Commission was called to consider the best rifle for our own Army. The Chassepot was an improvement on the Prussian "needle-gun" rifle. The "door-bolt" principle, which is now found in some form or another in all military rifles, was still somewhat in advance of its time; but the French certainly made the best they could of it, realising that it was the quickest action to operate that had yet been invented. Gas-escape being still, after twenty years, the great drawback of the "needle-gun," a rubber washer, or obdurating pad, was fitted to the bolt-head of the Chassepot, though it did not have altogether the effect that was hoped. The bore was .433 in. There were four grooves with a depth of .0118 in., and having a twist of one turn in 21.2 in. to the left, or counter-clockwise. The length of the barrel was 32¼ in. The tremendous advantage given by the breech-loading system over muzzle-loading had been demonstrated both at home and abroad, and the victory of the Prussians over the Austrians, the latter being armed with a muzzle-loader, drove the lesson home with telling force. It was rightly considered that the British Army should wait no longer for a weapon that would place it on terms of advantage with the foremost Powers. The time was marked by considerable military activity, and there was a sincere wish that the troops of this country should not be behindhand in the matter of arms. A Commission to consider the matter was formed in 1866.

Knowledge of breech-loading systems was small, and the Commission had really little good material to go upon, despite the fact that 120 different rifles were submitted to them. Paul Mauser was quietly but steadfastly at work in Germany, and John Rider, in America, was experimenting with what was soon to become known the world over as the Remington action; but neither of these actions was yet ready, though one or more Remington-action rifles actually arrived in this country whilst the Commission was sitting, and were shot at the Wimbledon meeting in that year. The Henry action, which was one of the

PLATE XIII

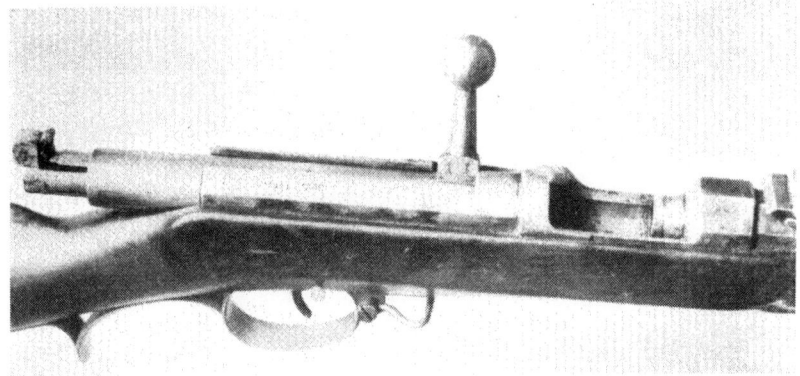

PRUSSIAN "NEEDLE GUN"
The first bolt action rifle. Picked up after the battle of Würth

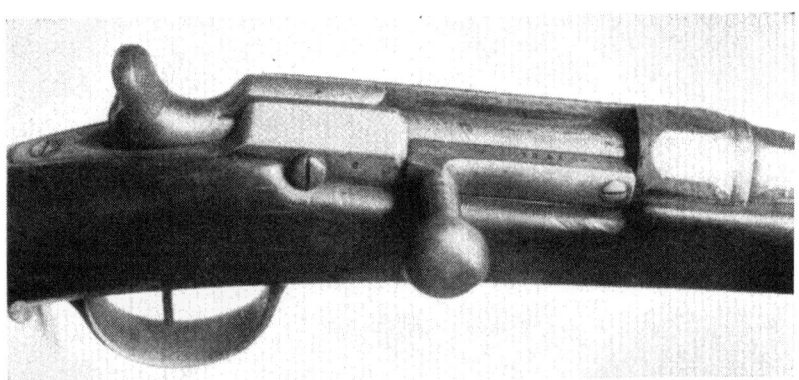

FRENCH CHASSEPOT (ZOUAVE)
This specimen was picked up after Würth

SINGLE SHOT MAUSER RIFLE
This rifle, except for a few small improvements, is similar to the first Mauser accepted by the Prussian Army. Taken from the Chinese at Taku

THE 1866 COMMISSION

best known in England at that time, was a development of the action of Sharp's carbine, which had been used with success in the American Civil War, and was issued to some British cavalry regiments nearly ten years before. The breech-block dropped when the trigger-guard lever was depressed, and enabled the cartridge to be inserted. Sharp's rifle had suffered from the fact that it was used with a linen cartridge, and as a consequence there was the usual bad escape of gas and flame from the breech. It was, of course, a percussion-cap rifle, and there was a sharp edge to the breech-block which cut

Fig. 14.—Remington Improved Breech-loading Action for Military Service (see also Plate XVII)

the base of the cartridge and exposed the powder to the flame of the cap. With the metal-based cartridge, containing its own cap, that was now available, Henry's action answered very well. The Peabody action, an American invention which was the forerunner of the well-known Martini principle, was submitted; but its reputation was not so good on this side of the Atlantic as its merits warranted.

The breech action was still in a very undeveloped state, and the work of many independent men, striving in different directions, and along diverging paths, had produced a chaotic state of affairs which did not render the Commission's work easy. When it became evident that the breech-loading system must be adapted to the rifle, there were several courses open to

RIFLES AND AMMUNITION

experimenters. It was possible to take one of the systems already being used for shot-guns—one of these systems could be altered and adapted to fit it for rifle work; or an entirely new system of breech action could be thought out. The inventor of the Dreyse needle-gun adopted the second of these courses. He had, in 1838, put on the market a sporting gun fired by a long needle. The loading of this gun was performed by pulling back a lever, when the barrels slid forward a little way and dropped down slightly, when the paper cartridge could be placed in the chambers. It was evident to Dreyse that this system was of no use for military purposes, and, striking out with the original needle and his cartridge as a base, he produced the first bolt-action rifle, which, like his sporting gun, was hammerless.

It is difficult now to realise how very largely military authorities and the gun trade were bound to conventions, though a little reflection will convince one that there is still in this direction a great liking for established precedent. In the early days of the breech-loading rifle the ramrod was still fitted and carried on the under-side of the fore-end. It was not sufficiently long to be used as a cleaning-rod, and, of course, a ramrod is an anomaly in a breech-loading rifle, so it came to be called a "clearing-rod," and was undoubtedly occasionally useful in cases where the extractor failed to act properly, when it could be dropped down the barrel to start the spent case.

The clearing-rod, therefore, was of some occasional use, but there were other additions to the rifles of that time, which as examples of the result of the slavish following of accepted models are hard to beat. A German inventor perfected a quite reasonable hammerless breech action. The gunsmith to whom he took it informed him that his customers must have a hammer, and so the inventor took his action back and fitted to it a perfectly useless hammer, which is cocked when the striking-pin is cocked, and falls on a blank anvil on pressing the trigger. The hammerless rifle now having been turned into a hammer rifle, was put on the market, and sold in considerable quantities. But this example of conservatism is badly beaten by another

CONVENTION V. PROGRESS

one. Another German manufacturer put on the market in all good faith, as something which would appeal to his customers, a two-groove air-rifle firing a flanged ball. The rifle was good enough in itself, though it was fitted not only with a purely ornamental hammer, but with a ramrod also. Both these appendages were about as useful as the buttons on the back of a man's tail coat.

Despite the lead taken by Dreyse and others, there was a very slow appreciation of the fact that a breech-loading rifle almost of necessity demanded a self-contained cartridge. Inventors clung to the idea that the only effective form of ignition was that provided by a nipple and percussion cap, and much ingenuity was displayed in combining the nipple ignition with a breech-loading mechanism. The action invented by the American, Gilbert Smith, for instance, had to be provided with a rubber cartridge case, the base of which had to be perforated to admit the flash; whilst in actions such as those of Prince and Terry (see Figs. 16 and 18) the cap flame had to pierce the case of the cartridge to fire the powder. Both Prince's and Terry's actions are interesting as being early attempts to improve Dreyse's bolt-action idea.

The victory of the breech-loading principle was not won without a hard fight and many bitter words. It is interesting, as illustrating the struggle which any new principle has to make for recognition, to note that the very virtues of the breech-loader were turned against it by its enemies. It was alleged that with it a soldier would be able to fire so fast that his ammunition would soon be expended and he would be left without a defence against his

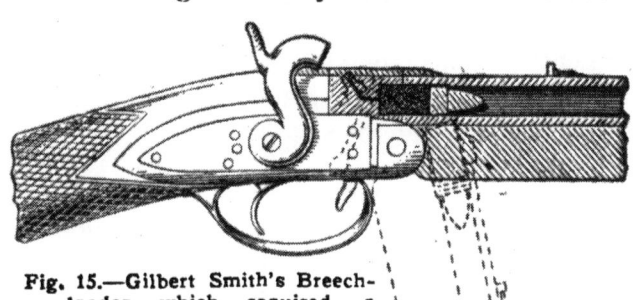

Fig. 15.—Gilbert Smith's Breech-loader which required a rubber cartridge case with a cardboard base perforated to admit the flash from the cap

slower-shooting enemy armed with a muzzle-loader. Champions of the breech-loading principle were told that the breeches would blow open and kill the firer or his friends rather than the enemy.

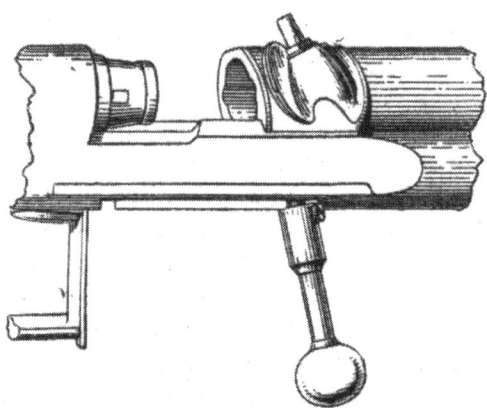

Fig. 16.—Prince's Sporting Rifle Action. The whole barrel was slid forward by the bolt handle

No doubt breeches did blow open. They blow open to-day in certain circumstances, but this danger could not outweigh the many advantages of the breech-loader for both sporting and military purposes. Again, it was contended that after a few rounds the back fire from a breech-loader was positively dangerous, and in the case of the early Continental breech-loading rifles this was so. But when the French adopted the Chassepot, they had thought out a nearly successful method of sealing the breech, and it only wanted the coming of the metal cartridge case for that drawback to completely disappear.

The result of the 1866 Commission was a negative one. It reported that though the rifles and the cartridges submitted to it had many good points, not one of them was of sufficient excellence to make possible a recommendation that it should be adopted in place of the Snider. In 1867 the Commission was formed again, and was bidden to arrive at some definite conclusion.

Acting upon their experience gained the year before, the members of the Commission decided to divide the question before them into two parts, or rather into three. The type of rifling and size of calibre was one head of their investigations, the type of breech action was the second, and the cartridge was the third. The names of the experimenters whose barrels were selected for testing, on the ground that they were known to

Plate XIV

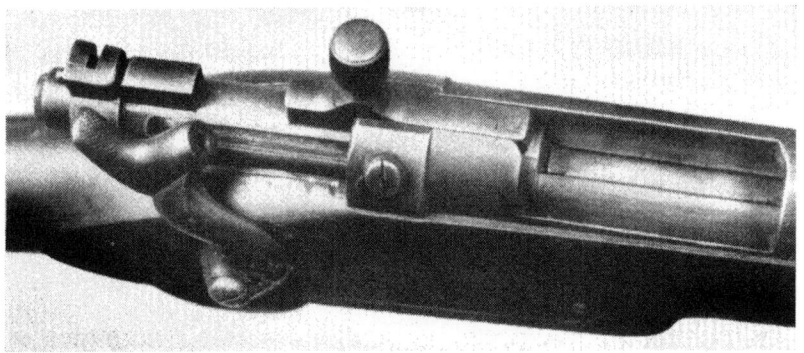

KERR'S BOLT ACTION RIFLE
An early attempt to produce a British bolt action rifle. Another view of this action appears in **Plate XIX**

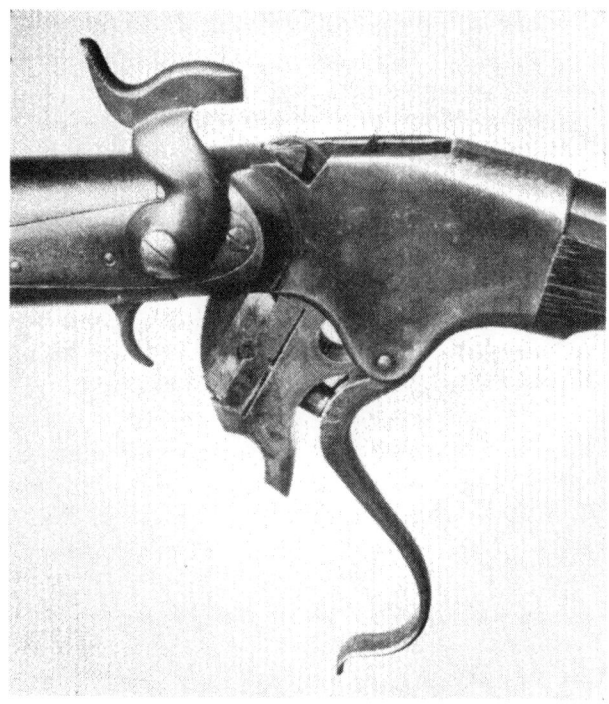

THE SPENCER REPEATING RIFLE
The Spencer was an early American "repeater" with a butt magazine. It was patented in 1860

THE 1867 COMMISSION

give good shooting, having been shot at the N.R.A. meetings at Wimbledon, were Messrs. Henry, Lancaster, Rigby, Westley Richards, and Whitworth. Mr. Metford did not accept the invitation. The Small Arms factories at Enfield and Woolwich also sent barrels for competition. All the actions which had any pretension to military efficiency were under review.

With a view to keeping the dimensions of the cartridge within reasonable limits, certain standards were laid down, and to ensure that all the barrels started under the same conditions, they were to be fitted to the Henry breech action, which commended itself as one likely to give little trouble, though it had not been decided upon as the action for the new service rifle. The result of the deliberations and the trials of the Commission was the Martini-Henry rifle, the Henry barrel being fitted to the Martini hinged-block action, which before adoption was modified by the Enfield factory.

In making their selection from the material supplied by the best brains of the day who had given any consideration to the production of a military rifle, the Commission did not make an altogether happy selection. The Martini action is a good one, but the extraction it gave was weak, and the defect continued to give trouble as long as the Martini-Henry rifle was in use. The bolt-action had been suggested by the needle-gun and the Chassepot, and at least one bolt-action, the simple and well-made piece of mechanism turned out by Kerr, was submitted.

As regards the form of rifling selected, the Commission perhaps was not to blame in that the very best form of rifling then available, which was the invention of Mr. Metford, was not submitted to them; for Metford, wearied with work and ill, and having a keen recollection of the bitter disappointment caused to him by other Government inquiries, did not submit his barrels to the Commission for examination.

Representing, as they did, the highest point to which ballistic engineering had been taken in those days, it is interesting to examine the barrels that were submitted to this Commission. Sir Joseph Whitworth, fresh from his classical series of experiments, sent his hexagonal bore, which has already been described. The Lancaster rifle had an oval bore, giving the effect of a two-groove rifle, which, like the Metford segmental grooving, wears well and does not foul badly. Rifles with this system of oval grooving have always been a speciality of the Lancaster firm, and are still manufactured and sold for sporting purposes. The Henry rifling, which was adopted by the Commission, was remarkable for the number of angles it contained, all capable of holding fouling. It had seven grooves, separated from one another by sharp edged lands, the consequence being that there were fourteen sharp corners into which fouling could get and remain despite cleaning efforts. The Westley Richards barrel was very similar to the Whitworth one (see Plate XV.).

The Martini-Henry rifle was officially adopted as the British service arm early in the year 1871. In that year two or three Continental nations, who had also been inquiring as to the best available small arm, came out with bolt-action weapons which were a great improvement on anything yet seen as a military arm, and had the advantage that when, but a few years later, the repeating or magazine system had to be adopted, they wanted only small changes to fit them for their new rôle. In 1871 Holland armed herself with the Beaumont, Italy with the Vetterli, and Germany with the Mauser. The really go-ahead nation, however, was little Switzerland, who about 1870 adopted the Vetterli repeating rifle, which, with its tube in the fore-end, was the first magazine arm to be used by any army.

The entrance of Paul Mauser into the field of rifle invention marks a point of distinct interest in the history of the weapon. Mauser was the son of a soldier, an artificer of the German army, and subsequently the head of the gunmaking department of the Oberndorf works, to which position he had risen by his own industry and intelligence. Young Paul, who was employed under his father at the works, early showed that mechanical genius which was to make his name famous throughout the world. His early endeavours were in the direction of tool making and the improving of methods of manufacture in the works. Whilst performing his military service the youngster had many practical demonstrations of the disadvantages of the needle-gun, and returned to the works with the idea for an improved breech-loading weapon simmering in his fertile brain. He told these plans to his brother Wilhelm, and together they made the first Mauser rifle, the principle of the action being Paul's idea.

Nothing more was done in the matter for several years, but in 1863 the two brothers again turned to their rifle and considerably improved it. Oddly enough they got no encouragment from their own Government, and took their invention to Austria, where they were lucky enough to make the acquaintance of Mr. Norris, of the Remington Company, who was quick to see the merits of the bolt-action weapon presented for his examination by these two earnest young men. He entered into an agreement with them, and they went to Liége to commence the manufacture of their rifle. Paul had by this time become the leading spirit, and it was his pluck which kept the two from despair during their long wait for recognition. A measure of success came at last in 1872: in February they were definitely told that their rifle had been adopted for the German and Prussian Army (see Plate XIII.).

The Prussian Government, having recognised the merits of the Mauser rifle, were not mean in expressing their appreciation in a material form. They gave the brothers Mauser a bounty in order to enable them to perfect their invention on a larger scale, and in 1873 they gave them an order for 100,000 rifles of the Model '71, on condition that they purchased the Royal Rifle Manufactory at Oberndorf. The brothers were not long in finding the necessary financial backing, and so the foundations of the great and highly successful Mauser firm were laid. Paul was all along the mechanical genius, his brother Wilhelm devoting himself chiefly to the commercial side of their business and negotiations.

Meanwhile other Powers were hard at work looking for the best that could be found in the way of small arms for their troops. In 1872 a board of officers met to consider the best form of breech action for the small arms of the United States army. In this connection it is interesting to notice that the

74 RIFLES AND AMMUNITION

British authorities were not the only ones who failed to grasp the significance of Continental developments along the line indicated by the bolt action invented by Dreyse. It is curious that Great Britain and the United States of America, in both of which countries the sport of rifle shooting was well developed and had a considerable following, should have been content with actions which were by no means the best that could be found even at that time. Though the inquiries of the United States Board were limited to the selection of a breech action, and though it had before it for examination some of the best actions then extant—including the Terry bolt and the Remington action, which had been adopted by the United States Navy Board in 1867—they chose the distinctly inferior "Springfield" action, in which the breech block was hinged at the forward end and turned back over the backsight to extract the spent shell and allow a new cartridge to be inserted. This action was not much better than the Snider, considered either from a mechanical or a military point of view. The breech block hinged at the forward end had already been adopted by Belgium for their Brendlin-Albini model of '67, the only essential difference being that the Belgian action had an extremely simple method of locking the block to prevent it being blown open at the moment of discharge, whilst that of the Springfield action was by comparison complicated and not nearly so efficient. The calibre of this rifle was .45 inch, and the rifling consisted of three plain concentric grooves .005 inch deep, equal in width to the lands. The pitch was one turn in 22 in. The forward hinged block was also a feature of the Russian Berdan action, the hammer of which was arranged to act on the bolt principle, working through the back of the action body and impinging on a striker in the block.

The Springfield action, which was really a modified form of the Roberts action, had been issued for trial on the "Springfield musket" in 1870. This was approved by the Board in 1873, and, with minor alterations, remained the service rifle of the United States army until the adoption of the Krag in 1896. An interesting development of the Springfield rifle was the Officers' Model, which was issued in 1875. This rifle,

PLATE XV

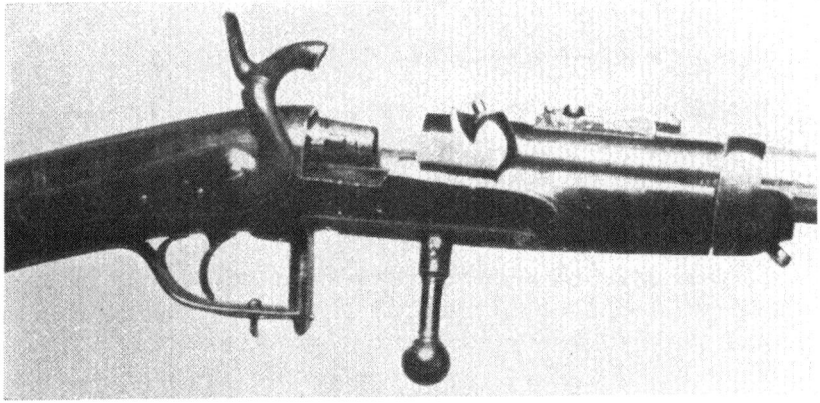

PRINCE'S BREECH-LOADING CARBINE
Made by the well-known gunmaker, Mr. Prince, about 1859. The whole barrel slid forward to open the breech

THE MONT STORM CAVALRY CARBINE
This breech-loader is marked "Tower 1860"

THE WESTLEY RICHARDS MILITARY RIFLE
The barrel has Henry's rifling. The action resembles the Martini

THE SPRINGFIELD RIFLE 75

which was chequered and engraved and fitted with a detachable pistol grip, was nothing more nor less than a well-made sporting and target rifle. It was fitted with "globe and pinhead" foresight, and in addition to the "buckhorn" backsight on the barrel, had a well-made peep backsight fitted on the small of the stock, and graduated for ranges of from 50 to 1,100 yards. The rifle had also a trigger which could be used at will as a hair trigger. It is interesting to note that in the official description of the rifle the clearing-rod, which was carried under the barrel, is still referred to as a "ramrod."

At the time when the Springfield action was adopted by the Army Board of Officers, the United States was already becoming known as the producer of fine breech-loading rifles. In 1864 the Stevens firm had established their first plant for the manufacture of weapons with the well-known Stevens dropping-block action, whilst in 1866 the equally well-known Winchester Repeating Arms Company laid down its first plant. The first of the great American trio of small arms manufacturers, the Remington Arms Company, had been in the field for an even longer period. Somewhere about 1816 the founder of the firm, the son of a smith, made his first rifle, and by 1828 he had bought a large farm at Harper's Ferry, where he built his works. The Remington Factory is still situated on that site, now no longer given over to peaceful agricultural pursuits. The history of the Remington business is an interesting one.

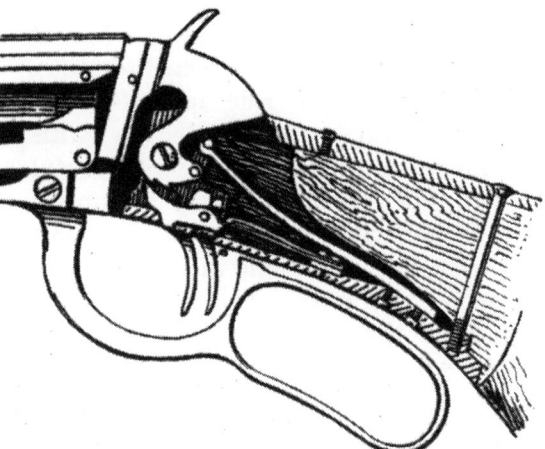

Fig. 17.—Double-set Trigger (Winchester). The scear is taken nearly out of the bent by pushing forward the rear trigger. The slightest touch on the front trigger will then fire the rifle. The front trigger can be used also in the ordinary way

From almost the very first it was associated with the production of war weapons. It produced many thousands of the rifles used in the Civil War which the North waged against the South, and even earlier; in 1845 it had turned out several thousand Jencks carbines for the war with Mexico.

This American factory—which owes its origin to the incident of a boy whose father refused to buy him a much-coveted rifle, and who therefore determined with characteristic pluck to make one for himself—armed many of the European Powers at one time or another. France, Sweden, and Spain had many thousands of their rifles in the '60's and '70's, whilst the Egyptian and Chinese armies were also armed by them. It is not generally known that about the time when Paul Mauser was making his early experiments, the Prussian army was on the point of ordering Remington rifles, and would indeed have done so but for one of those tiny incidents which sometimes suddenly become big in importance.

The story runs that Samuel Remington had practically closed with Prussia for an order of two hundred thousand rifles. The Prussian Army Board, after severe tests, was enthusiastic in favour of the arm, when the King came to the place of demonstration and asked to see it. Samuel Remington handed him a loaded rifle and stood back, confident that the monarch's verdict must be in line with that of his experts. Wilhelm raised the weapon, took careful aim, and pulled the trigger. The hammer merely snapped on the cap. A bad cartridge had chosen this of all moments to play its disheartening trick, and had come in the way of a deal involving many thousands of pounds. The impatient and hasty King merely threw down the rifle in disgust, and the deal was off. One wonders what effect that bad cartridge had on the subsequent development of Paul Mauser and his rifle. It is only when one views such events down the perspective of years that speculation as to their possible bearing on one another can be indulged in. At any rate, it was not long after that that Paul Mauser got his first official order, and made the Mauser rifle the weapon of the Prussian, and of the German, army.

THE LEE ACTION

It is one of the proud claims of the Remington factory that the experiments which resulted in the Lee action, which has been for years the bolt action of the British arms, were carried out in their works. The Remington-Lee rifle was used by the Chinese in their war against the French in the '80's with some considerable success.

In telling the story of those interesting years which witnessed the adoption of the breech-loading system by all the military Powers, we have somewhat neglected the sporting arm. We have, however, already pointed out that, once the rifle became the recognised military small arm, the history of the military weapon was, save for small details, the history of the sporting weapon also. The most important developments in connection with sporting rifles were in the direction of improvements in the ammunition used, and a description of these would be out of place in this chapter.

The military weapons of the transition period were all of large bore, and none of them developed a velocity of over 1,500 feet per second at the muzzle. With the single exception of the French Chassepot, the rifling of all of them was twisted in a right-handed direction. Though many of these arms were sighted for ranges up to and exceeding 2,000 yards, there were few of them that were of much use for accurate shooting at ranges over 500 yards—at any rate, during the early years of the transition. As knowledge grew real effective range was increased, but anybody who has fired a Chassepot, for instance, will realise the futility of sighting it for 1,200 metres; whilst even the Snider, modestly sighted for an extreme working range of 1,000 yards, found itself considerably taxed at that distance.

CHAPTER IV

The History of the Cartridge up to the Adoption of the Solid-drawn Case for Military Arms

THERE is, unfortunately, no record of the name of the genius who first thought of making up gunpowder, patch and ball into one unit for each charge. Probably the idea originated with no one man, and, in any case, the practice is of considerable antiquity. The earliest recorded use of the cartridge for military arms is in the Swedish army in the early eighteen hundreds. The "Text Book of Small Arms" attributes this innovation to King Gustavus Adolphus; but there is good ground for believing that cartridges were used generally on the Continent by sportsmen at the end of the sixteenth century. In any case, the germ of the cartridge idea can be seen in the beautiful breech-loader of Henry VIII., preserved in the Tower of London. This weapon had provided for it metal cases which were loaded with powder and ball, and had a touch-hole and flash-pan. The date is 1537 (see Plate IV.).

By the time the breech-loading system was adopted for military purposes, the cartridge had been considerably developed. For the muzzle-loader it consisted, as we have already seen in the case of the Minié, of a paper tube attached to the bullet. The portion of the tube above the bullet contained the powder, which could be poured down the barrel when the top of the tube was torn or broken. The tube was then torn off at the base of the bullet, and the portion of paper round the bullet, which was lubricated, acted as a patch. The Minié was the first cartridge used in the British Army.

The Enfield rifle cartridge resembled the Minié very closely, and is only mentioned here because it is of some historical importance. It was said that the use of a particular kind of

THE MUTINY CARTRIDGE 79

tallow as a lubricant on the Enfield cartridge was the cause or the excuse for the disturbance which began the Indian Mutiny. It is certain that in 1857 a native worker at the ordnance works at Dum Dum, some six miles north-west of Calcutta, spread a rumour that the new lubricating tallow was a mixture of hog's fat and cow's fat. If the rumour was designed to produce unrest, it could not have been designed with more devilish ingenuity, for such a mixture offended the religious feelings of both Hindus and Moslems. A deputation of native soldiers waited on the head of the Dum Dum works, and suggested that the bullets should be lubricated with beeswax. No notice was taken of them at the time, but it is significant that two years later the lubricant of the Enfield cartridge was changed to pure beeswax (see Plate IX.).

The Government bullets of the period were made by compression, and presented several advantages over the bullets made in the ordinary way by casting in a mould. They were uniform in size and weight, had a smooth, true surface, and were free from internal air holes. The machine which formed these bullets was the invention of a Mr. Anderson, chief engineer of Woolwich Arsenal; and so good were the bullets he turned out, judged by contemporary standards, that a writer in the *Field* laments (in 1859) that Volunteers could not obtain them "unless the Government should permit them to purchase from their stores."

Though, through military use, cartridges for the muzzle-loader were well known, the sportsmen of the years round about 1860 did not often use them, preferring to load from a powder flask, in the manner that had the sanction of some hundreds of years of practice to justify it. By this time it was possible to get a rifle powder that was reasonably sure, and Messrs. Curtis and Harvey were already building up a reputation for a good article. In sporting and target shooting so much was left to the individual taste of the user himself, that a vast deal of private experiment was continually going on in the direction of finding out the best shape of bullet, the best charge and the best caps. This general interest in the vital problems of rifle shooting necessarily resulted in a keen under-

80 RIFLES AND AMMUNITION

standing of the essentials, and prepared the ground for a quick recognition of the merit of the great improvements which were soon to come.

As regards the ammunition used in breech-loaders, the self-contained cartridge—that is to say, the cartridge having in it bullet, powder and cap—was not in general use in the middle years of the nineteenth century, though one or two types had been available for a good many years. The most general form of breech-loading cartridge consisted of a thin shell of paper or other material containing bullet and powder. The flame from the percussion cap passed down the nipple, and had to pierce the thin covering of the powder to fire it.

An early breech-loading cartridge of considerable interest was that employed in the Sharp rifle, which was one of those experimented with by the British War Office when it began to be apparent that the breech-loading action might perhaps have some advantages over the muzzle-loader. The cartridge consisted of thin linen or paper, and the simple falling-block of the action had a sharp edge which cut off the base of the cartridge as it returned into place, exposing the powder to the flame of the cap. The cap was not of the ordinary cupped type, but was a disc of copper which was most ingeniously fed on to the nipple from a magazine when the trigger was pulled and the hammer started to descend. A contemporary critic tells the tale of the defects of the system in these words: "This plan acts very well when free from the action of the wind, but if it is at all submitted to the action of this agent, the disc is blown away, and the consequence is a miss-fire. Independently of this defect, however, the amount of recoil and the noise in the ears caused by the escape are so great as to ensure its rejection by the sportsman." The escape at the breech, always a great trouble in the first breech-loaders, was subsequently done away with in Sharp's rifle by the adoption of the solid-drawn cartridge case. This solid-drawn case, of a curious shape, was one of the earliest of the kind to be used. In its base was a small hole to allow the flame to reach the powder. Though we have handled the cartridge, a specimen of which is in the museum of the National

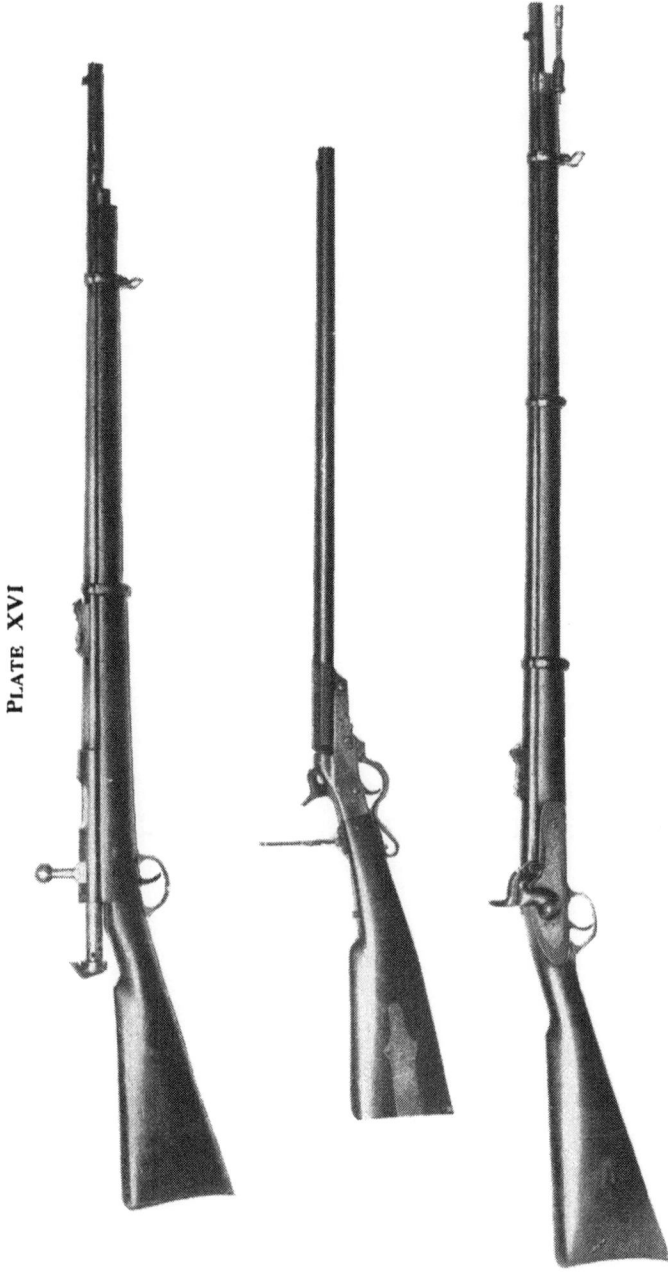

PLATE XVI

THREE SPECIMENS FROM THE N.R.A. MUSEUM

At the top is a finely preserved Chassepot (1870), presented by Major P. W. Richardson. In the middle an American Maynard, dated 1857, and fitted with an orthoptic backsight. This type of rifle was used with deadly effect during the American War between North and South. At the bottom is Gibbs' military muzzle-loader, dated 1861 (presented by the executors of the late Mr. Metford)

TERRY'S CARTRIDGE

Rifle Association at Bisley, we have not seen the improved Sharp rifle in which it was used, and it is somewhat difficult to imagine how the action was arranged to take the cartridge, the widest part of which was where the bullet entered the case (see Plate XVIII.).

A device which was in use in rifles where the flame of the cap had to pierce the paper was to prepare the paper with nitre, so that it burned very rapidly and was consumed entirely with the powder. Such a cartridge was used in Prince's rifle, which had a big vogue amongst sportsmen in the middle of the nineteenth century. Mr. Prince used this form of cartridge in the military rifle which he prepared for the consideration of the War Office. Like Sharp's rifle, Prince's military pattern had a capping apparatus, by which he claimed to be able to fire it sixteen times in a minute!

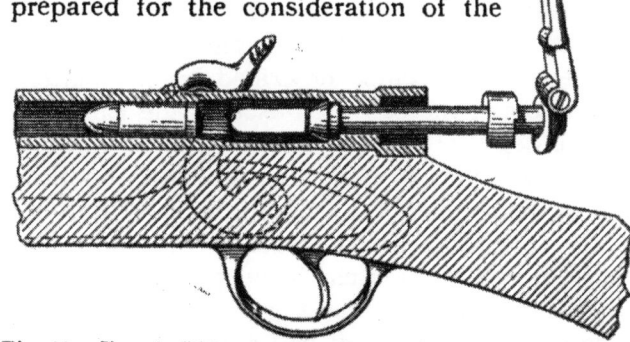

Fig. 18.—Terry's Rifle showing the cartridge with its base wad in position. No wad is shown in front of the bullet

The cartridge used in Terry's rifle, which was another of those experimented with by the British Army, is of very considerable interest, because it is the first one made with a bullet bigger than the diameter of the bore from land to land, thus introducing a principle which has been retained to the present day.

"The cartridge is made of strong brown paper, and is secured to the end of the ball by some adhesive substance," says Mr. Terry, in his own description of his invention; "it has glued to the back of it a wad, well saturated with tallow for preventing the gun from fouling after repeated use, the action of which will be hereafter explained. By referring to the illustration, it will be seen that the cartridge is placed directly under the channel or bore which leads from the nipple in such a position that when the cap is discharged by the fall of the hammer, the explosion of the powder takes place from the centre of the cartridge, and not from the end, as is usually the case. The object of this arrangement is for the purpose of detaining the tallowed wad in the barrel at the time the ball is ejected from it by the force of the exploded powder; it there remains ready to be forced forward by the next ball and cartridge inserted, and leaves the barrel when the discharge again takes place. It will therefore be understood that there is always a wad left behind every discharge, ready to be pushed forward by the following charge."

Of the size of the ball a contemporary description is as follows: "The chamber in which the cartridge lies is of the diameter of the circle described by the bottom of the rifling grooves, and the ball used exceeds the Enfield ball in diameter by the depth of those grooves. The barrel has a gradual bore from the larger to the lesser diameter, so that when the discharge takes place the ball is gradually driven into the rifling grooves, and presents precisely the same appearance as an Enfield ball does after it is discharged. In this way the patentee states he obtains greater range, force and accuracy, with the same weight of ball and powder, than can be obtained by any other rifle."

It is interesting to record that, despite the inventor's faith in his method of using a ball bigger than the bore, his rifle could not compete with the muzzle-loader of the time. A Terry rifle was entered in the 1862 contest at Hythe to determine the rifle to be used in the final stage of the Queen's Prize. Sad to relate, it retired ingloriously from the contest.

Notwithstanding the ingenuities displayed in designing, for the breech-loader, cartridges which contained only the powder and ball, events were combining to sweep them into the limbo of past and discarded achievements. The cartridge containing its own ignition was no new thing. Pauly's idea of combining a paper fulminate cap in the cartridge itself, and firing the charge by piercing the cap with a needle, was probably the first effort in this direction. Other inventors

PLATE XVII

AN EARLY PATTERN REMINGTON
The rifle here pictured was taken from Arabi Pasha at Abu Klea

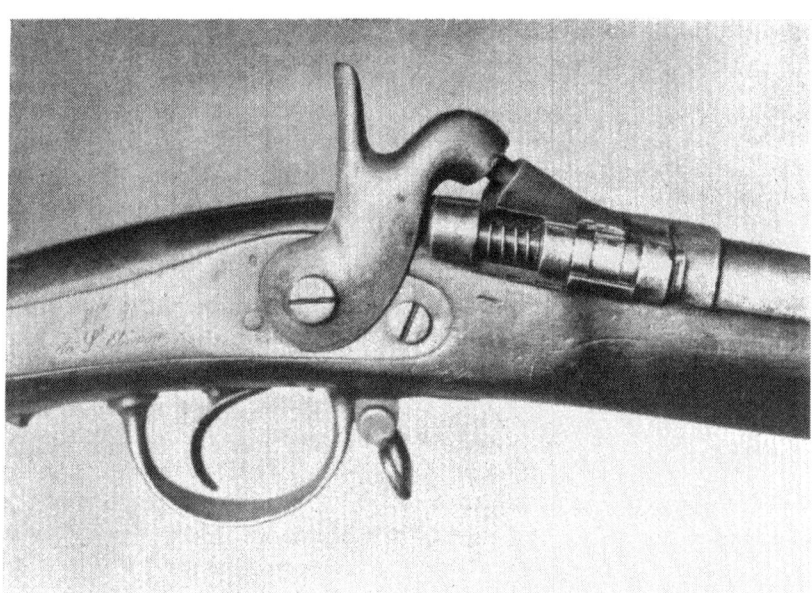

THE FRENCH TABATIÈRE RIFLE
This conversion from the muzzle-loading Minié was very similar to our Snider. The specimen figured was picked up after the bombardment of Alexandria

MOSER'S CARTRIDGE

were slow to take up the idea, for it was not until 1831, over twenty years after Pauly had put his cartridge on the market, that a certain August Demondion patented, in connection with his breech-loading gun, a cartridge which had attached to it a percussion tube, which doubtless suggested itself to him as a convenient development of Joe Manton's tube ignition for muzzle-loaders.

It is curious that, though military experts were supposed to be anxious to make the rifle an efficient weapon, development in cartridges should have been almost entirely the work of those who were seeking to improve the shot-gun. The explanation is, of course, to be found in the fact that military officers of those days in all countries were considerably hampered by tradition.

The first hint of the needle-gun cartridge, which in the Dreyse rifle was to cause a great sensation amongst military men, was found in the Moser cartridge introduced into this country in 1831—as a means of quickly loading a special muzzle-loader fired with a needle. The fulminate was on a card wad placed against the base of the bullet, and the needle had to pass right through the powder to reach it. Dreyse in 1838 adopted this cartridge, with trifling modifications that did not do away with its many disadvantages. The needle, being constantly subjected to the heat of the explosion, very quickly became so corroded that it broke. The case was, besides, of paper or linen, and did not in any way obturate the breech, so that the escape of flame was often positively dangerous.

It was not until 1847, nearly forty years after Pauly had shown that a self-contained cartridge was possible, that we find any definite and real improvement. In that year a gun-maker named Houiller, also working in Paris, made and patented the pinfire cartridge in a form very similar to that in which it existed for very many years, and in which it can still be obtained under the name of the "Lefaucheux" cartridge. Houiller also made a rimfire cartridge, and experimented with a central fire case. Exact details of his work are now impossible to obtain; but he used a metal base to all his cartridges. Paper cases, linen cases, cases of skin, and even of rubber, had all been tried and found wanting, in that they did not seal the breech. The ingenious Houiller must be recorded as the originator of those methods of cartridge manufacture which we know to-day. The advantages of his pinfire cartridge with its metal base were quickly recognised by users of the sporting gun. The metal expanded and filled the breech, so that there was no, or very little, escape of flame—the great trial and bugbear of all users of breech-loaders at that time. The popularity of the Lefaucheux gun was due in a great measure to Houiller's cartridge.

We must still, in continuing our history of the cartridge, look to Paris and to gun-makers, as opposed to rifle-makers, for improvements. Somewhere between 1856 and 1860 a M. Pottet began to experiment with the idea of improving on the now very popular pinfire cartridge. He may or may not have known of the work Houiller had done on the central fire cartridge; probably, living in Paris, he did. At any rate, he concentrated his endeavours on the central fire principle, and produced a shot-gun cartridge with a metal base and having the cap in the centre of the base. A modification of this case was introduced into this country in 1861, and was subsequently the basis of much law-court bickering. The Pottet case was very similar in appearance and construction to those now used in shot-guns, and it may be said that, as regards principle, the shot-gun cartridge difficulties had been successfully solved; improvements in detail were all that had to follow.

Rifle cartridges still lagged behind in their development along lines which had proved themselves to be correct. The Prussian Zundnädelgewehr, or needle-gun, was the only breech-loading military weapon, and its reputation as a fighting weapon obscured in popular and perhaps in military estimation some of the worst of its faults. At any rate, when the French adopted in 1866 the Chassepot, they neglected to avail themselves of the metal-based cartridge; and whilst using the central-fire system, still handicapped their weapon with a supposed-to-be "consumable" case, which naturally presented no deterrent to the escape of flame at the breech.

When the British Small Arms Committee met in 1864, it

METFORD'S HOLLOW-NOSED BULLET 85

was lucky to have in its constitution some officers who had knowledge of the recent developments of the cartridge, and they gave some considerable attention to the ammunition which was to be used. The cartridge which was adopted for use in the Snider was of stiff paper and had a metal base. The shooting of the rifle with this cartridge did not, however, satisfy the authorities, and they directed further investigations.

It now became the turn of Great Britain to show the way in regard to the military rifle cartridge, and that we were able to take the lead we owe chiefly to the inventive genius of two men—Colonel Boxer and Mr. Metford.

We have already mentioned Mr. Metford's explosive bullet and his connection with the Pritchett bullet. With these successes he was not satisfied, but continued his investigations, with the result that he discovered that his explosive bullet gave much more accurate results on the target than did the ordinary solid Enfield projectile. Mr. Metford's engineering and scientific knowledge, together with his practical acquaintance with the rifle, led him to seek in the right place for the reason for this added accuracy, which was that in making a hole in the nose of his bullet to take the bursting charge, without deducting from the normal weight of an Enfield bullet, he had taken the weight from the centre of the projectile and placed it on the circumference, where it materially aided in the maintaining of a steady rotation. Having put his discovery to a practical test in 1862 and 1863, by using a hollow-nosed bullet, without a bursting charge, in competition, which competition he won, he made his discovery public in 1864. The announcement was made in a letter to the Committee of the Rifle Conference which met in London in January. The Conference was not in any way official, but was the direct outcome of the interest in rifle shooting aroused by the Volunteer Forces and the National Rifle Association.

Colonel Boxer was not a private investigator, and the business of finding a better cartridge for the Snider had been referred to him by the Committee of Small Arms of 1864. Luckily he was a man well fitted to hold his important position at the Royal Laboratory, and tackled the problem with energy and understanding. The result, obtained after considerable labour, was a cartridge in which the paper was replaced by thin coiled brass. The "Boxer" cartridge, as it came to be called, finally settled the problem of completely obturating the breech, and showed the way for many further improvements.

Colonel Boxer's epoch-marking invention, and Mr. Metford's equally important discovery in bullet making, combined in the Snider cartridge served to place the British small-arm well in advance of that of any other country. The advantage was not to last long, but it was a fitting outcome of the tremendous interest in rifle shooting which had swept over the country with the Volunteer movement.

It will be interesting here to compare the capabilities of the cartridges of the three breech-loading military rifles which were in use in 1866. The Prussian needle-gun cartridge has already been described, as has that of the Chassepot. It had a lead bullet of 478 grains, 1.12 in. long, with a diameter of just over .53 in. The powder charge weighed 74 grains. It was supposed to be capable of use up to nearly 700 yards, but at half that distance its performance was very bad. The Chassepot had a 386-grain bullet, only .98 in. long, with a diameter of .46 in., and a powder charge of 86.5 grains. The bullet was larger than the bore, on the principle already discussed with regard to the cartridge for the Terry rifle. The Chassepot was supposed to be available to about 1,300 yards (it was sighted for 1,200 metres), but about half that range was the limit of its military efficiency. The Snider cartridge held a charge of 70 grains. The bullet was .002 in. smaller than the bore, being .573 in., and was made to expand by means of a wooden plug in the base. Its length was 1.042 in., and its weight 480 grains. The rifle was sighted to 1,000 yards, and could be used with sufficient accuracy for military requirements to nearly that range.

The work of Mr. Metford in further developing the military small arm cartridge cannot properly be considered apart from his investigations with regard to the rifle itself, and it has, therefore, already been dealt with in the previous chapter; but in considering the history of the cartridge we must not forget

PLATE XVIII

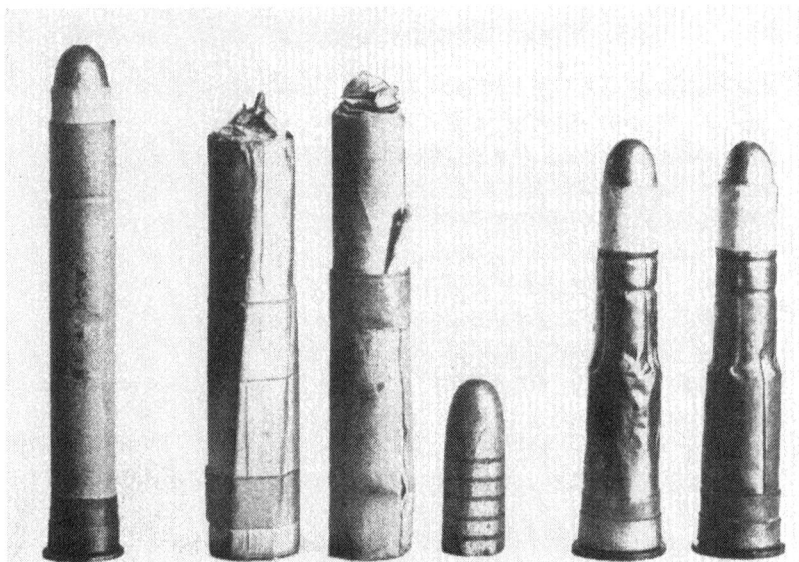

The Henry cartridge | Cartridges and bullet for Whitworth muzzle-loader | The original coiled brass cartridge for Martini-Henry rifle

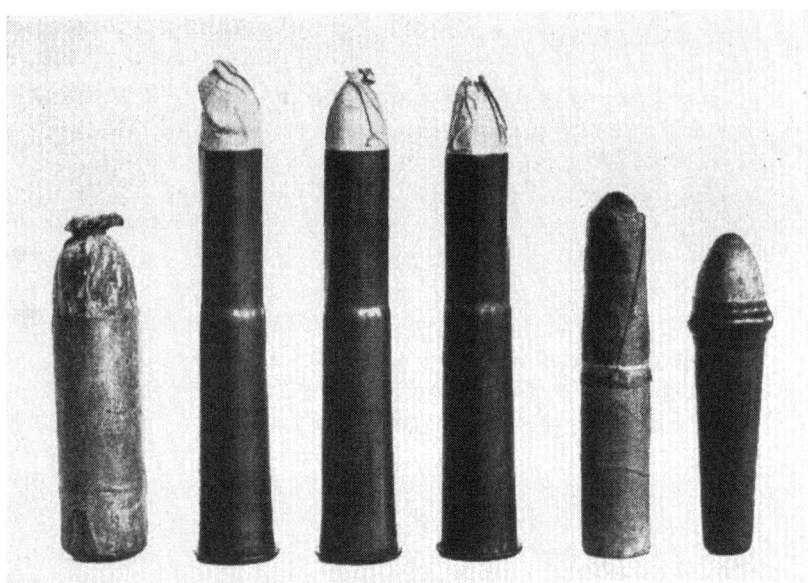

Needle-gun cartridge | Early solid-drawn cartridge used by Mr. Metford | Chassepot cartridge | Brass cartridge for Sharp's rifle

TYPES OF EARLY CARTRIDGES
Photographed from specimens now in the Museum of the National Rifle Association

THE SOLID-DRAWN CASE

that he was at this period hard at work on a succession of experiments in conjunction with his good friend, Sir Henry Halford, and that those experiments lasted for very many years, with results of the utmost importance, both as regards the bullet, the cartridge case and the rifle itself. As we have seen, he definitely laid it down that a bullet of sufficient length with regard to its weight did not need a cup in its base to make it expand to fit the grooves, and that soft lead was not needed to make this expansion possible.

The success of the Snider cartridge soon set other nations experimenting with the idea of bettering it, and an almost immediate result was the cartridge case made out of solid-drawn copper or brass. It is not possible to determine the origin of solid drawing as applied to cartridges, but Paul Mauser had evidently been experimenting with it for some time previously to 1870, for it was used in his rifle adopted by Germany in 1871. Mauser's first rifle, which had been produced about 1864, was fitted to fire a cartridge with a paper case and a gas-tight head. The bullet was probably the steel projectile with soft metal "driving bands" in which he did not lose faith for many years.

It is charitable to suppose that the 1869 Committee which recommended the Martini-Henry rifle did not know of the development of the Boxer cartridge into a solid-drawn article, for they recommended that the Boxer should be adopted for use in the new arm, though it was already proved that the thin coiled brass of the case was very likely to be damaged if at all roughly used, and that this disability must be considerably extended in the longer cartridge which would now be necessary. In adopting a cartridge, however, important changes were made. The diameter of the bullet was reduced from .577 in. to .45 in., whilst it was kept at the same weight, 480 grains, as the Snider bullet. This meant an increase in length, and consequently an increased ballistic efficiency. The velocity at the muzzle was only 110 f.s. higher than that of the Snider, being 1,350 f.s., but the better shape of the bullet told its tale in the trajectory. Another important change that was made was the adoption of a hard lead bullet. This change was no doubt

88 RIFLES AND AMMUNITION

directly inspired by Mr. Metford's experiments, though the Committee did not, unfortunately, have the benefit of his direct help.

Meanwhile the solid-drawn brass case was proving its superiority over any other kind with a conclusiveness that left no room for question. Mr. Metford, always quick to realise anything making for accuracy, adopted the solid-drawn case for his military breech-loader, with one of which Sir Henry Halford won the Duke of Cambridge's Prize for such rifles in 1871. Mr. Metford's case had several advantages over the Boxer-Martini cartridge in addition to being of solid construction. The paper patch of the bullet was almost completely covered by the case, and not exposed to tearing and abrasion for the greater part of its length, as it was in the Martini cartridge. The lubrication in Mr. Metford's design consisted of two wax impregnated wads, which served their purpose admirably without being open to the objection that at anything over normal temperature they were liable to melt and run into the powder, as was the case with the wad of solid beeswax which lay between powder and bullet in the Martini cartridge (see Plate XVIII.).

Austria adopted the solid-drawn case for the Werndl rifle about 1873, and other nations followed suit as opportunity served. Opportunity might have served Great Britain at any time, for solid-drawn cartridges were used by us for machine-gun work very soon after the invention of the metallic case. However, the comparative cheapness of the coiled case appealed to the representatives of "a nation of shopkeepers," and it was not until the Egyptian War of 1888 had proved how unfit the coiled case was for a hard campaign that solid-drawn cases were made. Even then they were provided for foreign service only.

When this important change was made, a new Small Arms Committee had been sitting about two years. They evidently saw that the solid case could no longer be ignored, for in 1886 they recommended for the new Martini-Enfield rifle a 380-grain hard-lead bullet of .402 in. diameter, with a charge of 85 grains, all contained in a solid-drawn brass case, the

THE MARTINI-ENFIELD CARTRIDGE

cap chamber of which, in accordance with the practice now followed by other nations, was raised out of the solid metal of the base.

The solid-drawn cartridge case had now established itself beyond doubt or question. It had all the qualities which were needed to allow the breech-loader to be developed to its full capabilities. The solid case expands perfectly to seal the breech, it is light compared with its strength, and will stand any amount of ordinary rough usage without hurt. With this we may leave for the time being the history of the cartridge. Subsequent developments were mostly in the direction of improving the bullet and the charge, though the case itself gave a good deal of trouble to the manufacturers.

CHAPTER V

The Development of the Bolt-action and Magazine

OF the single-loading rifles adopted up to 1886 by the various military powers, only Germany, France, Holland, Italy, Portugal, Russia, and Servia had taken the bolt-action pattern. All the other countries had some kind or other of block action. In 1871 Germany had adopted the Mauser action to a .433-in. calibre barrel. The same year saw the Beaumont rifle with the same calibre adopted by Holland, and the .41 Vetterli taken into use by Italy, and the Berdan II. by Russia. In 1874 France replaced the Chassepot with the Gras, which was a large-calibre weapon firing a hardened lead bullet and using a metallic cartridge case. Of its kind it was a very efficient weapon, and remained in service for a good many years until, in common with all the other large-calibre rifles, it had to give way to the demand for flat trajectories.

The essentials of a bolt-action are, the bolt itself, which is like a door bolt in shape and is provided with just such a handle for operating it as the door bolt has, a "bolt race," or "bolt way," in which the bolt can slide, and means of locking the bolt when in the closed position so that it shall not be blown open by the force of the discharge. As a matter of convenience, the body of the bolt is made to contain the striker and mainspring, but there were some early forms in which the blow to ignite the charge was given by a hammer.

The locking of the bolt is provided for by having at some place on the bolt itself one or more lugs or outstanding pieces which, on the bolt being turned over into the locked position, engage against a resistance shoulder or shoulders in the action body. The force of the explosion is taken up by the bolt, which because of the engagement of the lugs upon the

THE BOLT-ACTION

shoulders cannot escape backwards. The force is transferred through the lugs and shoulders to the action body.

Even when Dreyse manufactured his first needle-gun rifle the bolt-action was no new thing, for somewhere about 1830-35 a gunsmith named Durst Egg, of 1 Pall Mall, London, was selling a percussion breech-loader with a bolt-action which locked home on the interrupted screw system. Attention was at first directed to the bolt-action because it seemed to present possibilities of a better sealing of the breech than had been possible with any of the block-actions extant before the era of the metal base cartridge; but subsequently inventors and mechanical experts addressed themselves to the task of introducing improvements which would allow of a greater rapidity of fire and would make for safety and ease in working.

The compression of the mainspring is usually so arranged that a portion of the work is done on opening the bolt and the rest on closing it; this is to prevent the whole task falling on the hand during the last action of pushing the bolt home. In Mauser actions the initial compression is about half, the rest of the compressing is done on turning the bolt down. This crowding of the heavy work into a small space does not make for rapidity of fire.

The persistence of the bolt-action until it had replaced all other types for military purposes is not an accident. When the demand arose for an increase in the rapidity with which the rifle could be fired, those nations which had adopted the bolt-action found themselves very favourably placed for converting their existing weapons into magazine arms. It is true that some forms of block-action, notably those of the Remington and Winchester type, have been very successfully developed into magazine or repeating actions, but, generally speaking, for military purposes it has been found that the bolt-action is the only one which works with maximum efficiency in conjunction with a magazine. We find, therefore, that those nations which had already a bolt-action rifle were first in the field with magazine weapons. As a matter of fact, Italy started experimenting with the magazine principle almost as soon as the Vetterli rifle was taken into use, and the Vetterli-Vitali rifle can

RIFLES AND AMMUNITION

claim to have been the first magazine arm issued to any army, though the officers of the little army of Switzerland had been experimenting with their adaptation of the Vetterli rifle as early as 1869. This Swiss experimental rifle had a magazine tube in the fore-end, the idea of which was no doubt borrowed from the American repeating rifles which were already on the market. It was with this form of magazine that the rifle was subsequently issued.

Systems of supplying cartridges rapidly to the chamber for quick firing had existed for very many years before there was any possibility of using them successfully. Some very early forms of these have been discussed in previous chapters, and we can take up the story at, or about, 1840, the year before Prussia adopted the epoch-marking needle gun. In 1840 Colonel Colt, whose name is still a household word, took the already

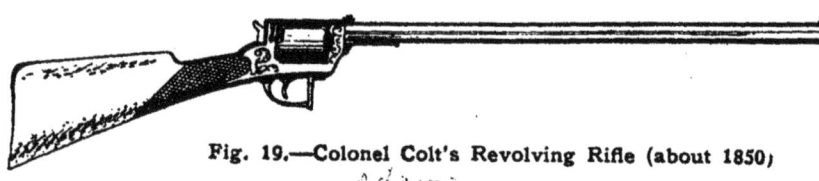

Fig. 19.—Colonel Colt's Revolving Rifle (about 1850)

existing idea of a series of revolving chambers, and from it evolved a fairly successful repeating rifle on the revolver system. It is often stated that Colonel Colt invented the revolver. As a matter of fact, what he did was to make the revolver possible by using for it a metallic cartridge case. The revolver principle had been known since the sixteenth century.

As a rifle Colonel Colt's idea proved to be a failure. As a means of adapting the rapid fire principle to pistols it has made history.

Appropriately enough, America, which has long been looked upon as the home of quick action, was for some time foremost in the development of rapid-fire rifles; the need for such an improvement being doubtless very apparent to hunters and backwoodsmen in their daily intercourse with wild life. The means of obtaining rapidity were not at first, however, so easy to see as the need for it. After Colonel Colt's revolv-

PLATE XIX

KERR'S RIFLE

An early British attempt to evolve a bolt action. This rifle was submitted to the Committee which decided on the Martini-Henry. In Kerr's action the bolt and hammer act separately

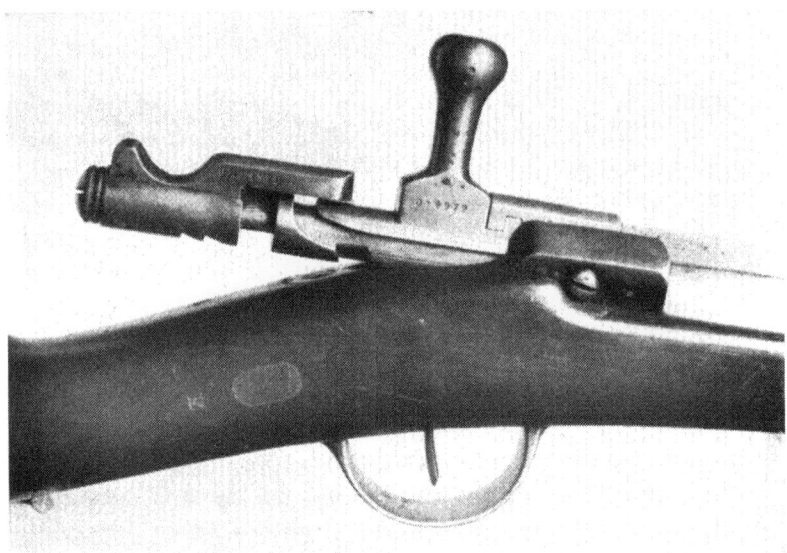

THE FRENCH GRAS RIFLE

This rifle replaced the Chassepot as the arm of the French infantry

THE WINCHESTER REPEATER 93

ing rifle had proved to be of little value there was a lull in the development of the magazine arm. Then in 1860 came the adaptation of another old idea, and that was to have a succession of cartridges in a tube in the stock. In its original form, with loose powder, the butt magazine had been a source of the gravest danger. With metallic cartridge cases its possibilities were considerably extended. The Spencer rifle, in which this principle was first successful, was patented in 1860. The mechanism for feeding the cartridges into the chamber one at a time was ingenious and effective. A hinged block-action opening backwards was used, and the block itself was made to carry the cartridge from the tube magazine into the chamber. Henry's rifle, patented the same year, had the cartridges in the fore-end, and the block slid backwards and forwards. From the Henry the famous Winchester repeater was developed. The use of the Winchester repeater by the Turks at the siege of Plevna proved to be of such great value to them, that the Powers who had been hesitating as to the advisability of fitting themselves out with the magazine rifles immediately began to give a great deal of attention to the matter.

The tube form of magazine having been first in the field it is somewhat surprising that it did not attain a greater success. After the Winchester people had supplied their rifle to Turkey the French adopted the fore-end tube for the Kropatschek rifle, which was served out to the Marines in 1879 or 1880. In 1881 Switzerland brought out the Vetterli with its fore-end tube magazine, the result of twelve years of experiment. In 1884 the Mauser rifle of Germany was turned into a magazine arm by the addition of a fore-end tube, and three years later Norway came out with the Jarman rifle, and Mauser supplied Turkey with a similar weapon to that which had been ordered for the German Army. This last, with the addition of the French Lebel, which was adopted in 1886, and the Japanese Murata, completes the list of military arms fitted with tube magazines, and of them all have passed away but the Lebel.

Rifles with tube magazines are usually now known as "repeating rifles," whilst those with the box type of cartridge receptacle are generically termed "magazine rifles." In the early days of the magazine weapon it was suggested that the word "magazine" should be used to describe only such rifles as were provided with a cut-off, whilst repeating rifles would be all those magazine rifles without a cut-off. Fortunately, this classification did not meet with much favour. The classification usually now accepted is to place all tube magazine rifles under the heading "repeating," and to call all fitted with a box cartridge container "magazine rifles." It might perhaps be possible to take the division further and say that repeating rifles are those which have the tube magazine and the block action, whilst all rifles with the bolt action and a magazine, no matter what the type of magazine, are known as magazine rifles.

The types of rapid-fire weapons which were experimented with when the need for magazine fire became apparent may be divided into seven distinct classes. There were two types of tube magazine, both of them originating in America. As we have already seen, they are that in which the magazine is under the barrel and that in which it is in the butt. The tube magazine under the barrel has already been mentioned with reference to the early American repeating rifles and the French Kropatschek. It should be mentioned that Portugal adopted this latter rifle in 1893, and that the Japanese rifle known as the Murata was not taken into use until 1894.

Of magazines in the butt there is not much to say. They found even less favour from a military point of view than did the magazine-under-the-barrel type.

Of both these tube magazines it may be said that the cartridges lie in the magazine with the bullet of one pressing against the base of the other, and it is likely that an accidental explosion may take place in the magazine owing to the bullet striking the cap with sufficient force to fire it. In the Murata rifle an endeavour was made to overcome this difficulty by making the cap with a distinctly cup-shaped surface, so that the bullet could press against the outer edge of the cup without being able to strike the sensitive part. To aid in this the point of the bullet was made very blunt. There is, as well, the danger of the bullets being driven down upon the charge by the pressure of the spring or by the sudden jar of grounding arms.

TUBE MAGAZINES

Extreme pressures are likely to be developed by a cartridge which has its smokeless powder compressed or the space between charge and bullet reduced. For all that users of the French Lebel rifle do not seem much troubled by either of the two faults which have been mentioned. It has, however, a

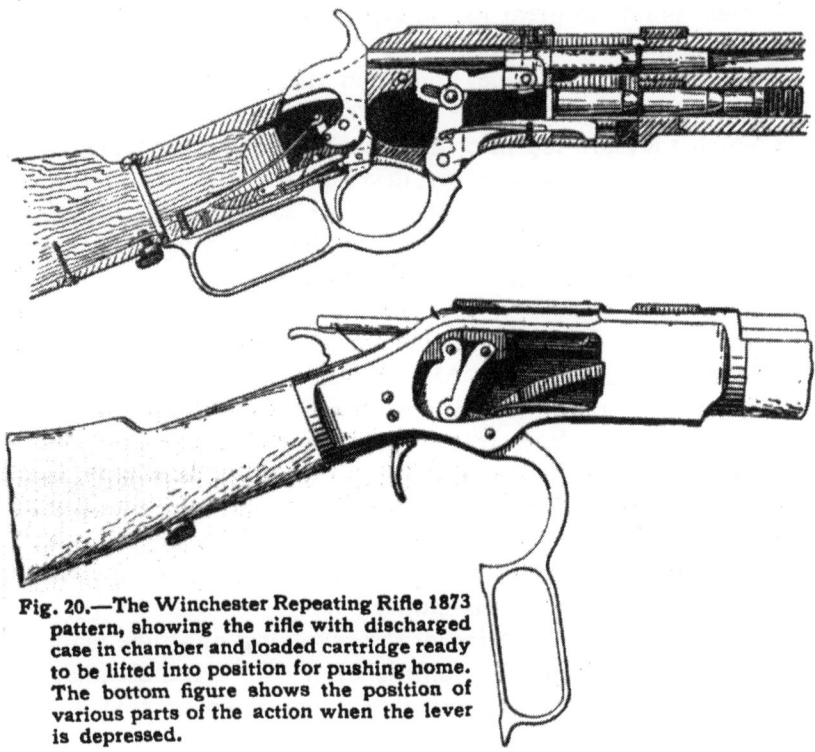

Fig. 20.—The Winchester Repeating Rifle 1873 pattern, showing the rifle with discharged case in chamber and loaded cartridge ready to be lifted into position for pushing home. The bottom figure shows the position of various parts of the action when the lever is depressed.

fault inherent in all tubular magazines, and that is that the charging of the magazine is of necessity slow. It is necessary to push the cartridges one by one into the tube, and, of course, as the spiral spring becomes more and more compressed the pressure that is used to push the cartridge home beyond the holding-stop increases. It has also been found that in high-power rifles, in which the tube-under-the-barrel system is used, the heat developed by rapid fire is sufficient to melt any lubricant which has been placed on the bullet, and also in some cases to heat the cartridges to such an extent that their ballistics are very considerably altered. It may be said that another disability attaching to the tubular magazine under the barrel is that the balance of the weapon is altered from shot to shot when the magazine is being used. This defect is not so great in the type of weapon which has the tubular magazine in the stock.

The revolving magazine, in which the cartridges are held in a series of water-wheel-like buckets, or in a series of tubes, from which they are fed into the chamber when they reach the right position, was considerably developed in the two or three years preceding and following 1890. The Savage magazine rifle of that date was perhaps the best, but the revolving magazine could not hold its own against the simpler patterns which had even then been designed. A development of the revolving magazine which has met with considerable success is the Schoenauer, used with the Mannlicher rifle of Greece, and a favourite pattern for use in sporting Mannlicher rifles. In this pattern, which dates from 1903, there is only one rotary platform. The cartridges are fed in from the bolt-body, and the rotary platform revolves on its axis against the pressure of a spring. When the magazine is full and it is desired to feed from it the spring pushes the cartridges round and upwards in succession until the box is empty.

An interesting combination of the revolving and tube magazines was brought out by Mannlicher in his original model. We have not been able to examine a specimen of this arm, but as far as can be ascertained from contemporary descriptions there were three or four tubes, each with its feeding spring contained within the main magazine tube, which were placed in the butt. The rifle was of the bolt-action type, but the bolt was not developed to anything like the perfection of the modern Mannlicher. The tubes were apparently revolved with each shot, so that cartridges from each in turn were presented to be driven forward into the chamber by the bolt-head. A magazine of such a type would contain about eighteen or twenty cartridges, but would have disadvantages which would greatly out-

PLATE XX

THE HOTCHKISS MAGAZINE RIFLE

This rifle, dated 1877, has the straight bolt handle characteristic of modern Continental small arms. The magazine is not satisfactory, judged by modern standards, but the bolt compares favourably with others of its period

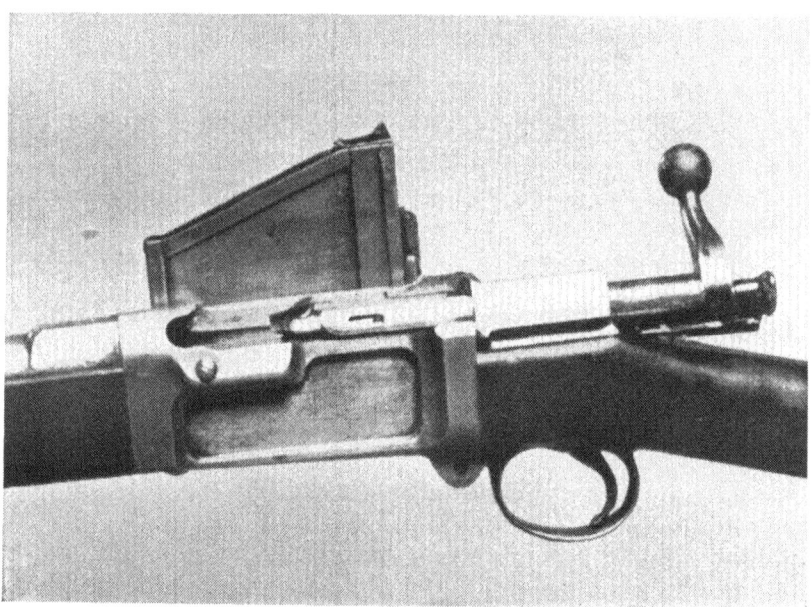

THE LEE-BURTON MAGAZINE RIFLE

The peculiarity of this action is the gravity feed magazine. The bolt, which was manufactured before the adoption of the Lee system for the British service, shows the characteristic cocking piece and bolt handle. This rifle was one of those experimented with by the Committee which chose the Lee-Metford rifle

MANNLICHER'S FIRST MAGAZINE

weigh the advantage given by such a reserve of fire. For one thing the charging of this magazine was bound to be even more slow and laborious than the charging of the ordinary single-tube pattern, and the containing of a big tube in the butt must have been a source of great weakness.

Mannlicher's next development was in the direction of placing the magazine over the chamber. The magazine, which would contain eight cartridges, was attached over the bolt-way, so that the cartridges could be fed in by the bolt-head as they dropped from the magazine. A magazine projecting up over the bolt is, of course, extremely liable to injury and seriously interferes with aiming operations, which is quite sufficient to condemn it at once. Several rifles with this type of magazine were made experimentally, but none of them ever achieved any distinction as a military arm until the magazine had been altered to a more reasonable form (see Plate XX.).

It was soon found as a result of these various experiments that the only possible place for the magazine, if maximum efficiency is to be developed, is beneath the centre of the bolt body, the cartridge being fed upwards by a spring and taken forward by the return of the bolt, one at a time. These magazines are quickly charged or emptied, can be easily examined by the soldier to see whether they are full or empty, and have none of the disadvantages of the types of magazine previously described. Such magazines developed for some years along two main lines. In the first place, there were those rifles the magazines of which were so arranged that when they were charged the rifle could not be used as a single loader. Another class of rifle, of which the British Service rifle before the introduction of charger loading is a good example, was so made that the charged magazine could be held in reserve for any length of time, the rifle meanwhile being used with cartridges singly fitted in. Yet another class might be said to possess some of the properties of both these types, and any rifles which fall into these three classes can be used as single loaders so long as the magazine is empty.

Any estimation of the advantages or disadvantages of these systems must take into consideration the fire effect which it is desired to obtain. When the British Lee-Metford was designed it was thought that the very best results could be obtained by a rifle which would admit of comparatively slow aimed fire for a certain time and would then allow of a sudden burst of extremely rapid fire. To such an end the magazine was admirably designed. The box, which originally held seven and afterwards ten cartridges, could be completely closed by the cut-off, when the rifle could be used as a single loader, with the magazine full of cartridges in reserve.

But as speed of fire became of more and more tactical importance, it was seen that the time occupied in loading such a magazine as that of the Lee-Metford, where the cartridges had to be put in one by one, must give place to something allowing of greater rapidity. Attempts were made, as in the Lee straight-pull rifle, to allow for quicker loading by providing a means of lowering the magazine platform when it was to be charged. By this means the time taken in overcoming the pressure of the spring is eliminated. Such a system is to be found in the Canadian Ross rifle. A thumb piece, conveniently placed for the thumb of the left hand, may be depressed to lower the magazine platform. The cartridges can then be poured in off the right hand, and with practice considerable dexterity in performing this can be obtained. It is, however, still too slow for modern requirements.

The obvious way of speeding up the loading of the magazine was to provide some method of putting several cartridges into the box with one operation. The original method of doing this was to make up the cartridges into a kind of metal skeleton box which, on being placed in the magazine, really became part of the magazine and remained in it until the last shot was fired, when the skeleton box fell out at the bottom of the magazine and left room for the insertion of a fresh packet of cartridges. This method was open to many disadvantages. In the first place, the light metal framework which kept the cartridges together was extremely liable to bend or become deformed in some way or another, either by blows, pressure, or the rusting action of the atmosphere. Unless the frameworks were in first-class condition jamming in the magazine was extremely likely to

CLIP AND CHARGER LOADING 99

happen. In order to get over these difficulties packet loading developed in two directions. One was by holding the packet of cartridges together by means of a narrow strip of metal clipping them together at the base, and from which they could be swept into the magazine by the action of the thumb. This system is now known as the charger-loading system, and is a feature of the Mauser rifle and of those based on the Mauser model, and was that adopted when the British Service rifle was converted for packet loading. The other development of this system of loading is associated with the Mannlicher arms. The clip which holds the cartridges together has been reduced to very small dimensions, so that it is like the clip of the charger-loading system, little more than a strip of metal bent to hold the cartridges together at the rim. In this system clip and cartridges are placed in the magazine all together, and the clip falls out from the bottom of the magazine when the last shot has been discharged.

It is interesting to trace the gradual conversion of military authorities from the ideas which obtained when magazine fire first came into use to those which now hold sway in most armies. We have already touched on the idea which provided for a reserve of fire for emergencies. This was, in the early days of the magazine, thought to be its primary use. With the development of packet loading military authorities could not be easily divorced from this idea, and so we have the interesting spectacle of a complicated system of ammunition supply which provided for a certain portion of the ammunition to be in clips, so that the magazines could be loaded rapidly, and a certain proportion to be put up as boxes of single cartridges, so that the soldier could use his magazine as a single loader until the necessary moment for rapid fire arrived. Musketry officers of countries which had no cut-off provided for their magazines taught their men to load from the clip and then use their rifles as single loaders by firing the top cartridge and then replacing it from a supply of single cartridges as long as slow fire was ordered. The soldier was required to keep five cartridges always in his magazine, but it would be interesting to know what happened if this system was ever actually used in warfare. The probability is that the soldier would do what is now regarded as correct practice, and that is, load in his clip, fire it either slowly or rapidly as considered necessary, and then load in another clip. The British practice is now to regard the cut-off solely as a means of isolating the magazine when the arm is to be carried for some distance with a charged magazine.

Modern tendency is in the direction of having as little as possible of the magazine box exposed below the surface of the woodwork, but it becomes a question whether a large magazine, with the enhanced possibilities given by increased capacity, is not of more value than the complete protection of the magazine box. The modern compressed steel magazine will stand quite an extraordinary amount of knocking about, and there can be little doubt that a magazine capable of holding ten rounds has a moral if not an actual superiority over one holding only five or six rounds.

To the late Mr. James Paris Lee is usually attributed the honour of being the pioneer of the box-shaped magazine. This interesting personality, who was for many years employed by the Remington Arms Company in the United States, was a Scotsman by birth. In 1835, when James P. Lee was but four years old, his father, a jeweller and watchmaker by trade, emigrated to Canada and settled in Ontario, where young James was naturally drawn towards guns and gunning by the very nature of the country surrounding his home. When he grew to manhood James P. Lee became a watch and clock maker, and became noted for his skill and dexterity in the use of tools. His first known invention in guns was a rifle which he built with a hollow steel butt containing a series of box magazines into which the cartridges were loaded against a spring in a similar manner to that which is used in all box magazines of the present time. These magazines contain now forty shots, and the mechanism was so arranged that with the firing and ejection of each cartridge a rod drove a fresh cartridge into the chamber and transferred cartridges from each of the magazines forward into the magazine nearer the breech. Unfortunately for Mr. Lee's invention, there was at the time at which he patented it, 1856, no metallic cartridge case, and therefore his rifle shared the

PLATE XXI

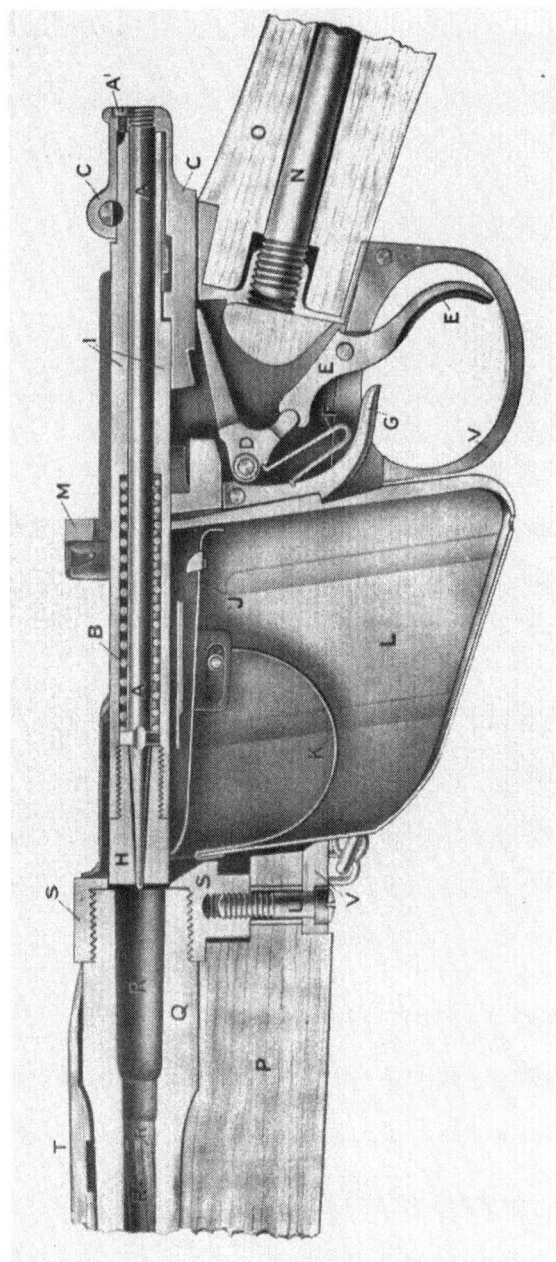

By courtesy of the Birmingham Small Arms Co., Ltd.

THE ACTION OF THE LEE-ENFIELD

A. Striker
A¹. Striker-keeper screw
B. Main spring
C. Cocking piece
D. Scear
E. Trigger
F. Scear spring
G. Magazine catch
H. Bolt head
I. Bolt body
J. Magazine platform
K. Magazine spring (much improved in subsequent models)
L. Magazine
M. Charger guide
N. Butt screw
O. Butt
P. Fore-end
Q. Barrel reinforce
R. Chamber
R¹. Lead
R². Rifling
S. Action body
T. Handguard
U. Trigger-guard screw
V. Trigger guard

fate of all breech-loaders of that period. Mr. Lee was responsible for a system of converting the muzzle-loading Springfield of the United States into a breech-loader, and also for inventing a small breech-loading rifle which had some vogue amongst American and Canadian hunters. An ingenious invention of Mr. Lee's was an adaptation of the Martini block, which he submitted to the British Government in 1875. This block was operated by a hammer instead of by the under-lever, and with this action Mr. Lee supplied a magazine which he attached to the left shoulder of the shooter. The magazine held thirty rounds, and fed the cartridges into the rifle by gravity. It is said that twenty-eight shots per minute could be fired with the Lee-Martini action and the Lee magazine.

In 1877 Mr. Lee patented a box magazine and a bolt-action rifle, which subsequently became the British Service rifle. In an early form, and known as the Remington-Lee, this rifle was used by China, and in a slightly improved form by the United States navy.

The development of the bolt action is still proceeding and can by no means be thought to have reached its final form. Whether or not the lines of its development will be altered by the necessities of providing for automatic fire is a question for a future answer, but it seems probable that the magazine rifle will remain the standard military small arm for many years.

CHAPTER VI

The Demand for Higher Velocities and how it was met by Reduction in Bullet Diameter and the Invention of Smokeless Rifle Powder

THE general adoption of the brass cartridge, drawn solid from a blank, opened the way for a large number of improvements in the ammunition as well as in the rifle. As regards the ammunition, it quickly became obvious, now that there was no possibility of back-fire in the breech, that it would be possible to get higher velocities by using heavier charges, and experiments in this direction were soon begun.

In this instance the lead was taken by Switzerland, owing to the almost inspired deductions of Major Rubin, head of the Swiss army laboratory at Thun. Whilst all other nations were more or less content to believe that, with a diameter of something over .4 in., the bullet had been reduced as far as was expedient if good results were to be obtained, Major Rubin saw that the efficient military bullet would have to be very much smaller than this. By reducing the bore of the rifle, and consequently of the bullet, he would be able to get a high velocity and a flatter trajectory without the expenditure of a charge of powder that would produce an excessive recoil.

Rubin was faced with several difficulties, not the least of which was that, with a long bullet, he would have to give it so severe a spin that even hard lead would not stand the great torsional stresses, nor would that metal be adaptable to the severe friction of a high velocity. Being a man of originality and boldness, Rubin made a great departure from accepted practice, and by so doing originated the compound high-velocity projectile as we know it to-day. He still retained lead, with its high density, its ductility and non-elasticity, as the main item of the bullet; but he cased his lead in an outer envelope of copper, with the result that he at once had a projectile that answered his requirements.

Another difficulty which had to be faced was the large charge which was necessary to give the bullet a high muzzle velocity. With loose black powder, such as was generally used, it would have been necessary to have a very clumsy bottle-necked cartridge, or else a very long one, to allow sufficient room for the charge. To a soldier of Major Rubin's experience neither of these expedients could commend itself. He therefore compressed his charge into a cylinder which had a hole running through the middle of it, along which the flame from the cap could pass. This form of charge also delayed the complete burning of the powder, and prevented the developing of excessive initial stresses.

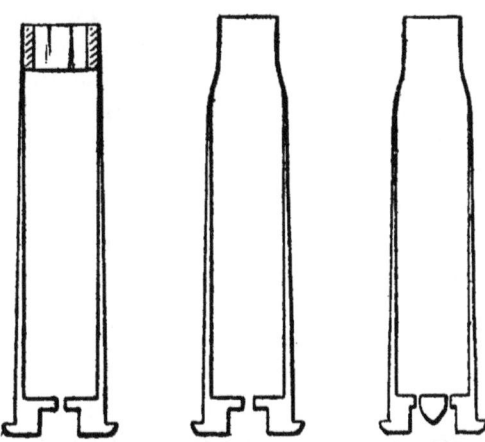

Fig. 21.—The development of the .303 Case. The left-hand section shows the original case with the brass ring at the neck adopted from Rubin's model. The middle section is the first necked case. The base has a single flash hole and was fitted with a loose anvil. The third is the modern case with the anvil pressed out of the solid brass of the base.

The original Rubin cartridge was something of a compromise in the manner it was made up. Having designed his bullet and got over his powder difficulty, Rubin was faced with a problem for which he did not at once see the solution. To take his cylinder of compressed powder, the case had to be somewhat bigger in diameter than his bullet, which only measured .295 in. (7.5 mm.) across its base. The powder cylinder was therefore placed in the case, and the difference between the outside diameter of the bullet and the inside diameter of the case was made up by the provision of a brass ring. The ring gave considerable trouble, and was soon discarded in favour of necking down the end of the case to the size of the bullet.

Rubin's cartridge and rifle were offered to his army authorities in 1883. Apparently they were not satisfied that it offered sufficient advantages over the magazine rifle they had adopted but two years previously, and it was left to Portugal to be the first to use the compound bullet. The bullet they took into use for their Guedes single loader of .315 calibre had a copper envelope and a hard lead core which was exposed at the point.

Meanwhile, a British committee had been appointed in 1883 to go into the whole question of the small arm for the services. We have already told of the adoption of the solid-drawn case by this committee, but the next useful step it made in regard to ammunition was not until 1887, when it made practical acquaintance with Rubin's cartridge, which by this time was considerably improved. The bullet had been enlarged to .30 in. As a result of their experiments, a compound bullet of copper-nickel alloy, with a lead core, was adopted for the .303 rifle. The charge, like that of Rubin's cartridge, was a compressed cylinder of black powder, in this instance weighing 70 grains. The velocity given by this cartridge was just over 1,800 f.s.

The rifle and cartridge had now developed beyond the capabilities of black powder to use to advantage the improvements that had been effected. But a remedy was at hand, and did not wait long before it was taken into use.

Smokeless powder, which is an organic substance, usually cotton, nitrated by treatment with nitric acid, had been known for many years, and long before its use in guns or rifles was possible experimenters had dreamed of manufacturing it in such a way that it could be so used.

That well-known chemist, Oscar Guttmann, in a treatise on "The Manufacture of Explosives" (1909), quotes a very early mention of a nitrated substance being suggested as a

PLATE XXII

THREE MODERN MILITARY RIFLES

These three rifles were used in the Olympic Games Competition at Bisley in 1908 and presented to the N.R.A. At the top is the Danish Krag, in the middle the Swedish rifle presented by the King of Sweden, and at the bottom the French Lebel

SCHÖNBEIN'S COTTON POWDER

substitute for gunpowder. Having talked of the "Feuerwerksbuch," which was compiled about 1410, Mr. Guttmann continues as follows:

"This book was lent to other master-gunners, who severally copied and enlarged it, until in 1534 it was printed in Frankfort-on-the-Main under the title 'Büchsenmeysterie.' In this printed edition we find a prescription, 'How to shoot out of a gun as far with water as with gunpowder. Take 6 parts of nitric acid, 2 parts of sulphuric acid, 3 parts of liquid ammonia, and 2 parts of oleum benedictum (crude tar oil), and charge the gun to a tenth part of its bore.' It further advises quaintly: 'Light it quickly, so as to get away in time. See that the gun is very strong. With an ordinary gun you can shoot 3,000 paces with this water; but it is splendid.' This is the first evidence of a nitrated organic substance having been used as a propellant."

It is not on record that anyone tried this fearsome mixture, and certainly it did not replace black powder, despite the joyful promise of a range of 3,000 paces for the bullet fired by anybody with sufficient pluck to make use of the invention.

Serious experiment with smokeless powders dates from 1846, when Schönbein reported that he had discovered a "cotton powder" which he thought might be used for guns, pointing out that his powder burnt without smoke and left behind it in the barrel very little residue. This announcement was of considerable importance to those who were working with black powder, and almost immediately—in the same year, in fact—guncotton was tried in rifles.

In its crude state this nitrated cotton was, of course, much too violent to be used as a propellant, and guncotton was subsequently developed into a disruptive explosive, though it forms the basis of our own cordite powder.

So important was Schönbein's discovery deemed that next year a "Commission de Pyroxyle" was appointed in France, and soon afterwards the army experts of all the chief European Powers were experimenting. Accidents, many of them serious, followed as a matter of course, for but little was known of the highly complex nature of the substances under examination,

106 RIFLES AND AMMUNITION

and so dangerous were guncottons held to be that work on these were almost entirely abandoned, save in Austria, where General Von Lenk still held to his belief that in "rauchschwaches pulver" (smoke-feeble powder) lay the solution of many military difficulties. His experiments lay mostly in the direction of so modifying the guncotton that it would lose its excessively brisant qualities and become, as it were, "amenable to discipline." The means by which it was sought to control the rate of combustion were mechanical. Von Lenk had his guncotton made in long yarns and woven into compact masses; but with little success, though he himself was so far convinced that he was on the right lines that in 1862 he had a number of field batteries adapted to use his cartridges.

About this time Sir Frederick Abel began to experiment in England, and made many important discoveries as to the correct conditions to be observed in the manufacture of guncotton.

About this time Sir Frederick Abel began to experiment in England, and made many important discoveries as to the correct conditions to be observed in the manufacture of fact that nitrated organic substances could be given a colloid, or jelly-like form which made their use as propellents a possibility.

In 1847, but one year after Schönbein had published his data with respect to guncotton, Dr. Hartig, a Brunswick Councillor of Forestry, made a discovery of first-class importance. He showed that it was possible to dissolve guncotton in acetic ether, and it would then, without altering its chemical state, become a clear, stiff jelly when the excess of ether had evaporated. If the ether was allowed to evaporate entirely, a white residue remained behind which had the same property as the original guncotton, but exploded much more slowly than guncotton. Here, then, we have the first indication that the rate of combustion of guncotton could be controlled.

The powder invented by Captain Schultz, in Berlin, about the year 1864, was made originally from small discs of wood, which after being boiled in soda and steamed for many hours, were nitrated. It was a very excellent sporting powder, but no good for rifle purposes. So excellent did the Schultz powder become when it was made of pulped nitro-cellulose that it became one of the best known of sporting powders, and is still sold in Great Britain by the British company that was formed to work it.

The first man to make a nitro powder suitable for rifles was a certain Frederick Volkmann, who in 1870 and 1871 patented a powder which he called "collodin," which was made from finely chopped alder wood. After that had been subjected to a severe washing and bleaching process, the minute pieces of wood were nitrated with a mixture of nitric and sulphuric acids, and after a further treatment with potassium nitrate, or barium nitrate, the nitrated wood particles were dissolved in ether alcohol. After a certain amount of drying, the material so obtained became a dough-like mass, which could be moulded or pressed into any shape desired. Volkmann was evidently quite well aware of the exact result of the processes he went through. He was aware, for instance, that he had produced a substance not in the least degree porous, for he states that his solid form of powder will stand immersion in running water for any length of time without change. He knew as well that he had arrived at a means of controlling the speed with which the powder consumes, for he distinctly states that the rate at which the powder burns can be governed by the degree to which the solution of the grains in ether alcohol is allowed to proceed, and to the amount of pressure to which the dough is subjected. He states definitely that experience enables the manufacturer to regulate the rate of combustion exactly. Volkmann had evidently gone a very long way towards producing a high-class propellant when, in 1875, the Austrian Government closed his works because, forsooth, his explosive was regarded by them as an infringement of their gunpowder monopoly. It is probable that collodin would have disappeared from history as completely as it did in fact but for the lucky chance which enabled Mr. Oscar Guttmann to procure a copy of Volkmann's patents, a translation of which in English is appended to his "Manufacture of Explosives." In 1870 patent specifications filed in Austria were not published, and as a consequence practically nothing whatever was known of Volkmann's work when his progressive efforts came to an untimely end.

Nothing much more was done with regard to the production of a smokeless rifle powder till about 1884, when a young French chemist named Vielle was working on problems connected with the governing of the rate of combustion of nitrate powders. A few years previously Mr. Walter Reid had patented a mixture of soluble and insoluble nitro-cellulose, which was subsequently known, and achieved a wide popularity which it still retains, as E.C. powder. Vielle's discovery consisted in the fact that he reduced nitro-cellulose to a true jelly, and from this jelly he made thin sheets which were cut up into small squares for loading into the cartridge. The original Vielle powder contained a certain quantity of picric acid, but this was abandoned for the poudre B, which became the French military powder, and was the first smokeless powder to be adopted by any Power. It is often stated that this poudre B was so called in honour of the famous General Boulanger; but in the absence of any direct evidence that this is so, it seems far more likely that poudre B was simply a second effort of Vielle, his first effort, the powder containing picric acid, being probably known as poudre A.

So far our history has concerned itself with the development of the nitro-cellulose powder, but we now come to an important development which was brought about by the introduction of nitro-glycerine into the components of rifle powders. Nitro-glycerine was the discovery of an Italian chemist, who first made it somewhere about the year 1850, perhaps a year or two before. At any rate, the date is not of very great importance, for nothing was done with this extremely violent explosive until about ten years later, when Alfred Nobel recognised its utility for blasting, and began to manufacture it commercially. The extremely violent properties of nitro-glycerine necessitated some steadying agent, which was found in the extremely porous earth known as Kieselguhr, and by the mixture of nitro-glycerine with this inert substance the famous dynamite was produced. In the course of further experiments Mr. Nobel found that it was possible to dissolve a soluble nitro-cellulose in the nitro-glycerine; and in this way he manufactured blasting gelatine. Experiments to determine the correct amount of these two ingredients which were to be used led to the discovery that it was possible to so mix and treat nitro-cellulose dissolved in nitro-glycerine that a hard colloid substance could be produced, and that this substance had all the properties which would make it desirable as a rifle propellent. Mr. Nobel's discovery led to further inquiries, and to the production, in 1888, of ballistite.

We are now in a position to consider the exact relations between the development of the propellant and the development of the bullet and rifle. We have seen that, about the year 1888, the British Small Arms Committee had adopted the bolt-action magazine rifle of small bore, and that there had previously been very considerable activity in the direction of the provision of magazine rifles among Continental nations. Now, directly the magazine rifle had been adopted it became evident that a smaller cartridge than that generally available was necessary if the rifle was not to be too unwieldy for comfortable use, and that such a reduction in the size of the cartridge was also of considerable importance if the soldier was to be able to carry a sufficient number of rounds to enable him to continue firing his magazine rifle for a considerable time.

If the cartridge were to be reduced in size, the amount of space available for the charge must of necessity be curtailed. The compression of black powder had failed to produce the effect expected of it, and it was seen that the only alternative was the development of a nitro-cellulose powder, or some other explosive based on the nitration of an organic substance, into an efficient rifle propellant. What was wanted was great energy in a small space, the said energy to be sufficiently under control for rifle purposes. At the same time, the reduction in the size of the cartridge would not of necessity reduce it sufficiently in weight unless the bullet itself was considerably reduced. Here the military expert found himself up against what at first sight seemed to be a dead wall. To reduce the bullet, as Rubin had done, to a little over 7 mm. seemed suicidal to the soldier used to the heavy shock-producing and man-stopping capabilities of the large lead bullet of the times. Some military men were known to be in favour of placing stopping power before even ranging capabilities, though the development of a long-range, quick-firing artillery must have made it evident to the thoughtful that ranging power was perhaps the most important of all the attributes of a military bullet. As there seemed no other way out of the difficulty, the bullet was considerably reduced in diameter; but its weight was kept up by giving it a length of several times its diameter. This, of course, resulted in a high sectional density. Sectional density is a figure arrived at by dividing the weight of the projectile by the square of its diameter, and is of extreme importance in ballistic calculations. A study of the figure derived from the formulæ given enables the expert to arrive at very definite ideas with regard to ranging power and other attributes of the bullet under examination, while it is, in conjunction with another figure, known as the co-efficient of reduction, used to arrive at the ballistic co-efficient which is essential to nearly all ballistic calculations dealing with the progress of a bullet through any medium. The mathematical excursions of Guilamôt and Hebler, together with the practical experience of Lorentz and Rubin, had already showed that velocity over considerable ranges could be obtained even better with a bullet of no greater diameter than an ordinary lead pencil than could be obtained with the heavier bullet of much less length but considerably more diameter. It is obvious to us now that the smaller surface a bullet presents to the resistance of the air the less resistance will it have to overcome; but it should be remembered that the knowledge of atmospheric resistance is of comparatively recent acquirement, and that, indeed, it was not until bullets were projected with an initial velocity above that of sound (1,100 f.s.) that the extent of air resistance became of really vital importance to the ballistician.

The essential features of a bullet and cartridge on these new principles had been quite well understood by Rubin and

PLATE XXIII

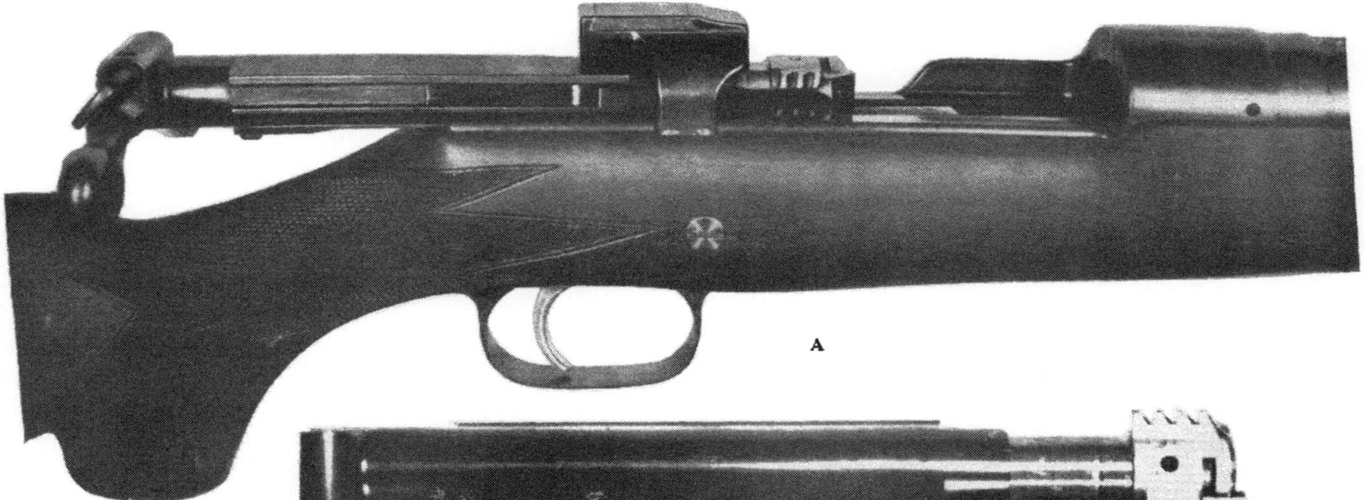

THE CANADIAN ROSS RIFLE ACTION

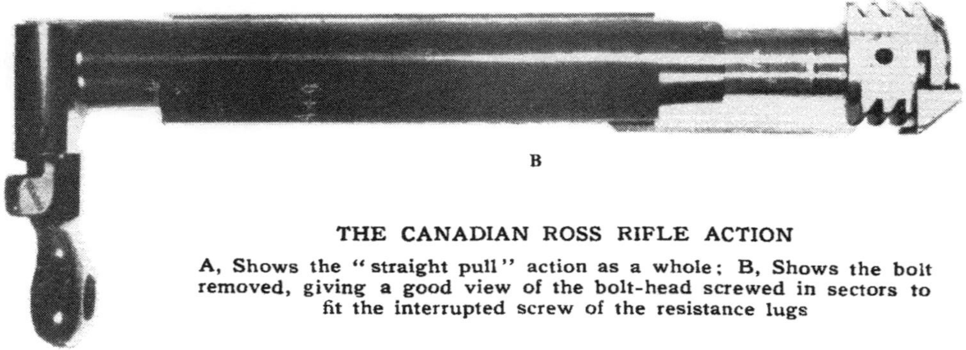

A, Shows the "straight pull" action as a whole; B, Shows the bolt removed, giving a good view of the bolt-head screwed in sectors to fit the interrupted screw of the resistance lugs

BLACK POWDER SMOKE

his imitators in this country, as we have shown; but the new type could not be successfully adopted, because black powder failed to give a sufficiently high velocity and produced too much smoke to be used in rapid fire. In the old days of the muzzle-loader the great cloud of smoke which was emitted from the rifle on discharge was not of vast importance, for in those days there was no attempt at concealment in battle, and the loading was so slow that the powder-cloud had plenty of time to roll away before the next volley was discharged. But, with the breech-loader and the speed-up of the rate of discharge to five, eight, and then over ten shots a minute, when such rapidity of fire was desirable, the smoke of black powder became, to say the least of it, a highly dangerous nuisance. In calm weather one man firing rapidly was speedily enveloped in a cloud of his own making, so that it was impossible for him to see to take proper aim, whilst a company or regiment could so fill the atmosphere that the smoke of their rifles made it difficult for them to breathe.

Now we have the cartridge ready for smokeless powder, and smokeless powder almost, if not quite, ready for the cartridge. It was necessary to combine the two. The British experts were not satisfied that they could yet see their way to do this, but some of the Continental nations were not so shy of the new powder. As we have seen, France had led the way in 1886, Germany followed in 1888, whilst others progressed quickly in their wake. At last it was seen that in a smokeless powder lay the only hope of developing the capabilities which were known to exist in the Lee-Metford magazine rifle and the new small-diametered bullet. It must not be thought that at this period the British Government was unacquainted with or negligent of the advantages of the smokeless powder. There were many difficulties in the way of the adoption of a powder for British use, for, in the advance of our world-wide Empire, British arms were subject to extremes of heat and cold, and had to stand an amount of carriage and general knocking about far in excess to which the cartridges of any Continental nation would be subjected. The expert view of the situation is briefly summed up by Lieut.-Colonel Fosbery in a speech made by him in 1891, whilst the Explosives Committee, with Sir Frederick Abel as president, was nearing the end of that long series of experiments which were to result in the production of the explosive known as cordite for British arms.

"At present," said Lieut.-Colonel Fosbery, "so far as is known to me, we are still in search of the ideal explosive; one, in fact, which shall pack into the smallest possible space, develop the utmost energy, and keep indefinitely under all possible circumstances; and until we have found this, or, at all events, some reasonable approach to it, we cannot with a light heart adopt, as our Continental friends have done, a smokeless powder for the use of our troops. Gunpowder we know all about; it is a good, honest mixture, and, severely tried as it frequently is ashore and afloat, it may be reckoned upon to do its duty as long as we keep it dry. But when we come to high explosives—especially when these are chemical compounds, and from their very nature more or less unstable compounds at that—we, more than any other people, must exercise the utmost precaution in their general adoption, and be sure that neither the damps and heats of India, the salt air in our naval magazines, nor the cold of Canadian winters, will set these treacherous substances fermenting, decomposing, or exploding."

Nitro-cellulose powders in their earlier forms were open to several objections, the most important being that they were far from stable. Though knowledge of the properties of guncotton had, owing to the work of Abel, been considerably enhanced, it was still not possible to make guncotton powders capable of withstanding a succession of big changes in climate. The British Explosives Committee followed the lead of Nobel in using nitro-glycerine as a solvent for guncotton, with the aid of another solvent, in this case acetone, which is subsequently dried out. Camphor had been used by Nobel in the making of ballistite in order to make the surface of his ballistite grains, or blocks, harder. The use of camphor was open to two important objections. One was that in the process of manufacture of ballistite heat has to be used to get the camphor into the surface of the grains, and that subsequently the

AN IDEAL SMOKELESS POWDER

camphor evaporated, changing the ballistic qualities of the powder. It should be mentioned that a small proportion of vaseline was used in the manufacture of the original cordite. The properties of an ideal smokeless powder are : (1) A high velocity with a moderate pressure, (2) smokelessness, (3) harmlessness of the vapour given off, (4) stability, (5) safety in manufacture and handling. The high velocities and moderate pressures given by smokeless powders are due in the main to the fact that, as they are impervious, they can only burn on their outside surface, with the consequence that combustion proceeds comparatively slowly. The amount of time which the explosive takes to burn can be very accurately governed by the amount of surface which is presented for combustion. Of course, the time expended in this way is but a minute fraction of a second, and yet the explosive chemist has to gauge this time so accurately that he can regulate the burning of the powder so that combustion is finished just as the bullet leaves the muzzle. With smokeless powder the force available for propulsion is much greater than with black powder, because there is far more energy stored in the smokeless powder when the two propellants are prepared bulk for bulk. Pressures are far more evenly distributed along the length of the barrel than they were with black powder.

With regard to smokelessness, it may be said that the simplest knowledge of chemistry enables one to realise that smoke is only non-consumed matter in a very fine state of division. Black powder produced a large quantity of this soot, which, besides being projected into the air, was deposited along the bore. Smokeless powders, in which almost the entire material is converted into gases, leave practically no deposit in the barrel, and but a light whiff of smoke to indicate that the rifle has been fired. Much of the visible material which comes from a barrel firing smokeless powder is water vapour.

It is desirable that the gases given off by the combustion of the powder should be non-injurious to the firer. This is of importance because, though in calm weather and with the wind blowing from the firer, the gases are carried away by their own velocity as well as by the wind, if the wind is blowing toward the firer, even the velocity of the gases as they leave the muzzle will not prevent them being blown back.

It is probable that carbon-monoxide and some more or less complicated oxides of nitrogen are produced at the moment of explosion of a nitro powder; but the high temperature changes some into less harmful gases, whilst the sudden change in pressure and volume which instantly follows the emission of the gases from the barrel accounts for the translation of others to harmless combinations. At any rate, the gases from the combustion of propellants have not yet been known to harm anyone, though during the present war there is reason to believe that many deaths have resulted from asphyxiation caused by confining within a small area large quantities of gases, evolved by the explosion of a shell containing a disruptive.

As has already been indicated, stability is of the highest importance in a military cartridge. The charge should not react in any way with the metal of the case, nor should it be liable to undergo within itself any chemical or other change. The stability of cordite, as it is now manufactured, is remarkable, and for this reason it is still preferred in our Service to the nitro-cellulose powders, which offer other advantages. Safety in manufacture is brought about by the exercise of tremendous care. It is probably correct to say that powders containing nitro-glycerine are not so safe to manufacture as those made of nitro-cellulose; but the great care exercised in the making of cordite has resulted in a very high degree of safety being attained. As regards the safety in handling, once the explosive is manufactured, all the military powders have this to a high degree. They are incapable of being ignited when made up into cartridges save by the definite explosion of the primer.

The stability gained by a nitro-glycerine powder was purchased at a very high cost in other directions. The hot flame of the cordite explosion is very wearing on the barrel, and rifles in which cordite is used suffer from gas cutting and erosion to an extent far in advance of the same trouble

PLATE XXIV

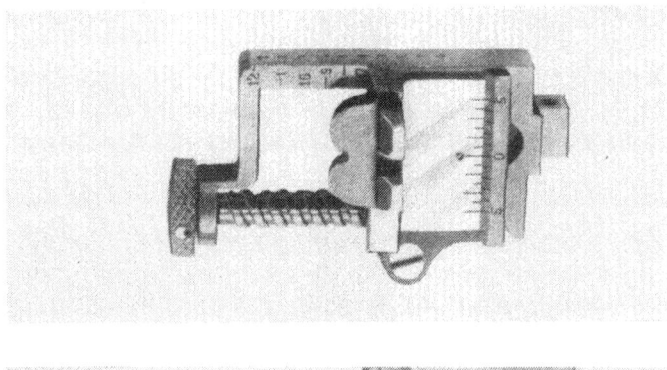

THE ROSS RIFLE MILITARY BACKSIGHT

The left-hand picture shows the leaf down, the middle picture the leaf up, and the right-hand the leaf detached from the mounting. The sight is excellently placed for using the orthoptic hole but badly placed if the V is to be used

CORDITE AT BISLEY

in rifles in which nitro-cellulose powders are used. Service rifle users in Britain very quickly became aware of this disability. The following paragraph from "Arms and Explosives" of August, 1894, tells its own tale:

"The War Office authorities are always informing us that cordite is making rapid strides in popularity in the Services, both for small-arm and ordnance purposes. Such a statement is practically impossible to controvert so far as the Regular branches of the Services are concerned. These have but little opportunity of preferring one powder to another, inasmuch as they are, in a vast majority of cases, bound to use Service explosives. Even here it is well known that those officers who go in at all largely for rifle-shooting very often employ their own private fancy in powders, without, however, giving such publicity to the fact as to lead the authorities to believe that they dislike cordite. It is very different with the case of the Volunteers, and the Bisley meeting affords a far better criterion of the popularity of cordite than any of the naturally prejudiced statements of War Office officials. It is, therefore, interesting to learn that where cordite had to meet with full, fair and free competition with other powders it came out very badly. Particulars have appeared in the public Press, which tally pretty accurately with our own information, as to the powder used in one of the leading M.B.L. competitions at Bisley—the Duke of Cambridge prize. Although cordite was served out gratis to the competitors, only two out of twenty-two used it. All the others seem to have preferred one or other of the various guncotton or nitro-cellulose powders now on the market. Indeed, it is claimed by the representatives of one of these that it won all the M.B.L. long-range competitions. When men of the experience of Sir Henry Halford, not to mention many others, publicly show their preference, and justify it by their success, for other powders than that officially adopted for the Services, something more is required to convince us of its growing popularity than the asseverations of the War Office. So far as we could gather at Bisley, the feeling was that the man who respected the bore of his rifle should be very chary of subjecting it to the heat developed by cordite, and that as a shooting powder the latter was not to be relied upon."

It is certainly true that in the early stages of the development of cordite it was not as accurate as it might have been; but this unfortunate feature of cordite has now been removed to so great an extent that it can compete on equal terms with the most highly developed nitro-cellulose powders. As regards the destructive effects of cordite, recent modifications in the specification have done little or nothing to remedy the complaint. The shooting in the 1914 match rifle competition at Bisley demonstrated to admiration that, though M.D. cordite can be made to shoot with wonderful regularity, its destructive effects increase rapidly when charge and velocity are put up. Five hundred rounds of .280 cordite ammunition leave the barrel very worn and badly gas cut at the breech end.

The history of the British cartridge-case and bullet in the first few years after its adoption is interesting and instructive in that, when considered together, they indicate the growth of knowledge and the adaptation of design to cope with difficulties which presented themselves in practice.

It has often been said that the correct method of procedure is to evolve a cartridge which will give the desired results, and then produce a rifle to fire it. We believe that Major Rubin did follow this course, but he is apparently the only man who has ever done so. Certainly in 1888 the Lee-Enfield rifle was chosen first, and the cartridge evolved with much trouble and expense subsequently. In this case, there was the excuse that the main point of the Committee's deliberation was the adopting of a magazine rifle, and that it could not be expected to think of the cartridge first. Neither could it know that black powder was so soon to be tumbled from the position it had occupied for centuries, and its place taken by a more complete and less easily understood propellant—one which, whilst solving some of the Committee's difficulties, would upset a great number of their carefully worked out calculations.

The original cartridge-case was almost an exact copy of that of Colonel Rubin. It had a rimless base, and the bullet was held into the top of the case by means of a split ring,

THE FIRST .303 CASE

just as in the original Rubin model. The reason for this straight form of case was that which has already been indicated in dealing with Rubin's experiments. A large pellet of compressed black powder had to be got into the case. Though there was provided at the end of the chamber a definite shoulder which should have been capable of preventing the case from travelling too far up the barrel, the case in its rimless form was turned down almost at once, and a rimmed base substituted for the more practical rimless form. Probably extraction difficulties with the experimental .303 rifle were the cause of this change.

The ringed bullet seating having proved inefficient, the case was then necked down to take the bullet. Here was fresh trouble, and lots of it. First of all, the necking had to be done so that the largest possible black powder pellet

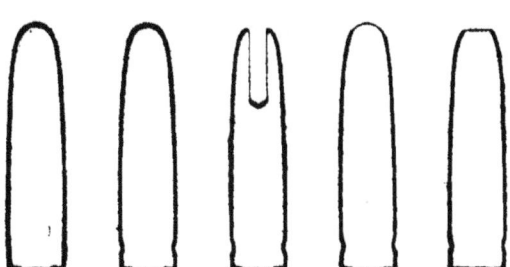

Fig. 22.—The development of the .303 bullet. On the left is the original .303 bullet in section, next to which is the Mark II. bullet with a flat base and thickened up shoulder and head. The centre bullet is the notorious Mark IV. The remaining two are respectively the Dum-Dum and a flat-headed solid base bullet which was tried before The Hague Convention put it out of court for military purposes

could be got into the case, and the shoulder was arrived at solely with the black powder pellet considerations in view. The pressure on the neck produced unequal annealing, and this trouble was very apparent in the early days of the solid-drawn cartridge-case. Because a case looked right did not of necessity mean that it was right. The first shot would often crack the case, or blow its neck off, and then started another round of painstaking inquiry and of experiment to find what had gone wrong in this instance. The cap chambers in these early forms were simply circular holes formed in the base and having a smaller hole communicating with the interior of the case. A cap containing its own anvil was placed in the cap chamber.

When the black powder pellet was abandoned in favour

of the cordite charge, those manufacturers and experimentalists who were dealing with the case found that their work had to be done all over again. The case had to be made a little stronger; but the principal difficulty was found to be with the cap. Caps which fired black powder perfectly gave extremely poor ignition with the new smokeless powder. Eventually these troubles were got over by providing a bigger and stronger cap, and by forming the anvil of the brass of the cartridge-case itself. Instead of the one centrally placed flash-hole two were now provided, one on either side of the anvil.

The .303 bullet in the first ten years of its life went through even more changes than the case. The first service bullet, which had a slightly concave base, was found to be provided with too thin an envelope, and to have too little turnover at the base. With the coming of cordite, a Mark II. bullet was introduced, with improvements in the direction of gradual thickening up of the cupro-nickel of the envelope towards the nose, and of giving more covering to the exposed lead of the base. The hollow base of the early form of the bullet was given up for a curious reason. It was found that wads were occasionally so closely held to the base of the bullet by air suction that even the high initial velocity of the bullet's flight failed to detach them from the base, with the consequence that the bullet proceeded upon a most erratic course.

Next came reports from officers and soldiers that savage tribes, with whom we were always conducting wars, refused to be sufficiently impressed by the Mark II. bullet; in fact, they often ignored it altogether, and, having been hit in four or five places, came on to unpleasantly close quarters. Major-General Tweedie had, as early as 1889, foreseen this difficulty, and had taken out a patent for a bullet which had the envelope at its nose weakened by cuts, or by thinning the case so that it would expand on impact. The Government, having experimented on their own account, decided that what is now known as a hollow-nosed form would serve their purposes better, and produced the Mark III. bullet, which was similar to Mark II., except that there was a hole through the cupro-nickel nose extending for the fraction of an inch into the lead core. This

PLATE XXV

Photo: Clarke & Hyde

ROLLING THE BARREL "MOULD" OR BLANK

Ten pairs of rollers are arranged close together alternately vertical and horizontal. The short bar of steel is put in one end and comes out a rod of the right length for the barrel at the other. The rollers are shaped so as to reduce gradually the diameter of the rod or blank

bullet failed to do what it was required—that is to say, expand on impact—and was discarded as soon as it had been invented. The Mark IV. bullet, which had the hole in the nose, and had the envelope thinned also at the nose, proved itself capable of mushrooming quite respectably on impact. An advantage that this bullet showed, which was quite an unexpected one, was that its shooting was distinctly better than that of the ordinary Mark II. form. Many theories were promulgated to account for this, one being that the cavity in the nose made a kind of peg on which the bullet could spin, and that as a consequence the bullet would not gyrate in its flight. As a matter of fact, the reason for this increased steadiness was probably exactly the same as had given the increased steadiness to Mr. Metford's explosive bullet; the balance of the bullet was improved by the placing of the centre of gravity a little farther back. With all its advantages, the Mark IV. bullet came quickly to an end of its useful life, for in 1899, when the Mark IV. cartridge was issued to the competitors at Bisley, it was found that the lead core showed a decided tendency to part company with the envelope, an accident which was exasperating enough when the divorce took place in the air, but which was positively dangerous when the core flew out of the muzzle, leaving the envelope tightly fixed to the rifling, and making an obstruction which, with the next shot, would cause a very serious rise in pressure when the next bullet tried to pass the obstruction. The Hague Convention also came into force forbidding the use of expanding or exploding bullets, and so in the Boer War return was made to the Mark II. bullet. There was, a little previously to 1900, a tremendous controversy about the respective merits, etc. of the Dum-Dum and the Tweedie bullets. Major Tweedie's bullet has already been mentioned. The Dum-Dum bullet, the patent for which was granted in 1897, was invented by Captain Bertie-Clay, of the Indian ammunition works at Dum-Dum. This bullet had, like the Mark IV., an opening at both ends; but the Dum-Dum bullet was simply a bullet exactly the same shape as the Mark II. but with the lead at its nose exposed. There was no cavity at all in the nose of Captain Bertie-Clay's bullet. Another variant introduced about this time was a bullet with a solid base and having the lead at the nose exposed. The idea of this, of course, was to prevent the core blowing out of the envelope. We have heard a great deal within recent months of the use of the Dum-Dum bullets by the belligerents in the Great War, and this is a curious fulfilment of a prophecy which was made in 1900. In an article on expanding bullets in "Arms and Explosives" a writer, signing himself "Cyclops," says:

"The term 'Dum-Dum' has taken the public fancy, and sooner or later it will be catalogued up as classifying all bullets which mushroom upon impact."

We have now traced the development of military rifle ammunition almost to the point where it is to-day. Subsequent improvements have been of a revolutionary character, and are of such great interest that they demand a chapter to themselves.

CHAPTER VII

Modern Military Rifles Critically Examined

ACTUAL war experience seems to point to the conclusion that, given a good, serviceable rifle—and all the rifles of the Great Powers and many of those of smaller Powers come into this category—the fighting value of the weapon depends more on the practical skill of the user than on any mechanical refinements which engineering or ballistic knowledge may have suggested.

As a matter of fact, the differences in effectiveness of all the best rifles are so small that they can easily be mastered by the human element. Good points can be nullified by lack of skill, whilst the handicap that should be introduced by a bad feature in a rifle may easily be more than made up for by highly developed aptitude on the part of the users. In one type of rifle, also, a weak or unscientific feature may be counterbalanced by another extremely good one. An instance of this may be seen in our own latest pattern short rifle. This still has the very unscientific bolt, with the lugs at the rear end of the bolt instead of close up to the base of the cartridge-case; but the slight inaccuracies brought about by this might easily be made up for on active service by the ease and rapidity with which the backsight can be adjusted with the thumb only of the left hand. The bolt is the worst to be found on any modern military rifle; the backsight is the best.

For the purpose of a critical survey of the modern military rifles of the Powers it will be convenient to divide them into three groups:

        1. Mauser and Mauser types.
        2. Mannlicher and Mannlicher types.
        3. Other rifles.

122   RIFLES AND AMMUNITION

This grouping is not altogether an ideal one, but it is perhaps the best that can be devised. All modern rifles have breech actions of the bolt type, and all are under .316 in calibre; so that it is not possible to divide them into "bolt rifles and others," or "large bores and small bores." A division according to bores might be made, making the separation at .30 in. Of rifles with calibres of .30 in. and over there are eleven important examples. Of smaller bores there are ten examples worth considering. It is notable that of the smaller bores seven are 6.5 mm. = .256 in.

Before considering the various rifles now in use for military purposes, it is important to arrive at a clear understanding of the ideals which the designer of a military rifle must keep before him. In this we cannot do better than be guided by the general rules laid down by the "Text-Book of Small Arms" (1909). They are as follows:

"1. *Durability.*—The rifle should be simple, compact, and strong; free from risk of derangement due to accident, long wear and tear, rough usage on active service, exposure to wet or sand, or fouling from long-continued firing. It should be capable of being easily cleaned and inspected, and if, after long use, any part does break down it should be easily and cheaply repairable. The mechanism should be capable of being stripped without the use of tools.

"2. *Rapidity of Fire.*—Filling the magazine and loading the cartridges into the chamber should be quick, easy and certain operations. The sights should be simple, and not liable to shift during firing; they should be capable of being quickly set, easily seen, and accurately aligned.

"3. *Accuracy.*—The graduations should give the correct elevation for the distances marked; the foresight should be placed so as to give the true direction; and the points of impact on the target of a group of shots fired at the same mark should be close together.

"4. *Lightness and Handiness.*—A light rifle can be easily carried by the soldier, and, in rapid firing, raising it frequently to the shoulder does not cause so much fatigue as it would in the case of a heavy rifle; consequently, in prolonged firing,

PLATE XXVI

Photo: Clarke & Hyde

A DROP FORGING HAMMER

The correct shape and Knox form of the breech end of the barrel are obtained by reheating and pressing between a pair of dies, one of which is held on the anvil and the other on the hammer

or in snap shooting, better results should be obtained with a light rifle. For deliberate shooting a fairly heavy rifle is easier to hold steady. Lightness is governed by the strength of the barrel and breech-closing mechanism necessary to resist the explosion of the charge and the tendency to vibrate excessively; by the solidity required to stand rough usage; by the length of the rifle; and by the weight necessary to check the recoil. With regard to the length of a rifle, a long barrel gives increased velocity; it enables the sights to be farther apart, which increases the accuracy with which aim can be taken, and it gives a longer reach in bayonet fighting. A short barrel is handier, and vibrates less than a long one of equal thickness; this latter point tends to improve the consistency of the shooting. The body is kept as short as possible for the sake of compactness, and the length of a rifle is altered by varying the length of the barrel. The length of the butt cannot be varied much, as the distance from the butt-plate to the trigger depends on the length of the soldier's arm. In the British service butts of three lengths are now issued, so that the soldier may be properly fitted, with a view to improving his snap shooting, in which the balance of the rifle is very important. The centre of gravity should be a little behind the point where the fore-end is gripped by the left hand, so that when the soldier throws his rifle up to his shoulder it may point at the required object. If the centre of gravity is too far back, the rifle, when quickly brought to the shoulder, tends to point above the object, and vice versa.

"5. *Good Ballistics.*—The initial velocity should be high, the proportion between weight and area of cross section of the bullet should lie between proper limits, and the shape of the bullet should be well adapted for overcoming the resistance of the air, so that the trajectory may be flat."

These ideals in the design and manufacture of military rifles will be the criterion in our consideration of the various types of war rifle now in use. To have a thorough understanding of the difficulties in the way of designing a perfect rifle a few more points should be considered.

To give perfect shooting, the barrel of a rifle should be

free to vibrate along its whole length, and the action should be symmetrical—that is to say, its weight should be evenly disposed within its mass. To the first of these conditions no military rifle can possibly conform; to the second of these conditions no rifle can be made to conform—that is, to be operated conveniently by hand and fired from the shoulder.

A perfectly symmetrical action is an impossibility for practical use because, in the first place, considerable power must be employed to pull back the body of the bolt, pressing at the same time the spring into the cocked position and extracting the spent cartridge-case. This is most conveniently performed by the aid of a knob, or handle, projecting to the right of the bolt. The attaching of this necessary bolt to the action at once distributes the weights unevenly. The bolt could be operated by the aid of a ring or projection immediately in the rear of the bolt; but the power that can be exerted by one finger through a ring, or by the finger and thumb on a milled projection, is so much less than that which can be exercised by the whole hand on the bolt as now fitted that such a device, though theoretically correct, is practically quite unsound. The body of the action, too, is the result of compromise, even when, as is the case with the Mauser, Mannlicher, and all modern actions, the resistance lugs of the action-body are placed symmetrically and in an up and down direction, it is necessary that half the action-body behind the chamber should be cut away on the right to give a clearance for the ejection of a spent cartridge.

As regards the barrel being free to vibrate from chamber to muzzle, experimental rifles such as are used in the match rifle class at Bisley are so made, but the exigencies of active service necessitate there should be a long wooden fore-end to protect the rifle from being bent and injured, and to support the bayonet. This wooden fore-end, together with the long upper wooden covering with which many modern rifles are fitted to protect the hand of the soldier after rapid fire, are bound to the barrel by means of steel bands, to the under-side of which the Ds and swivels to take the sling are usually attached. Even when these bands are carefully arranged and packed with some elastic material, as in the highest class military target rifles, there is bound to be a very extensive interference with the natural vibration of the barrel, a secondary result of which is often the deposit of excessive metallic fouling at the points where the bands grip.

The weight of the modern military magazine rifle is between 8 and 9¾ lb., without the bayonet, the lightest at present in use being the Belgian Mauser, which is 8 lb. ½ oz., unloaded and without bayonet; whilst the heaviest is the Krag-Jorgensen, of Denmark, which weighs 9 lb. 11¾ oz. The length varies between the 3 ft. 7½ in. of the Swiss Schmidt-Rubin to the 4 ft. 4¾ in. of the Danish rifle. These lengths are, of course, without bayonet.

The first class of rifles to be considered are those of the Mauser type. The real Mausers, manufactured by the Mauser Company, or under licence from them, are in use by Belgium, Turkey, Spain, Germany, and Brazil. The earliest pattern is the official arm of Belgium, and the latest that of Brazil. The Portuguese rifle is the Mauser-Verguiero, and those of the United States and Japan are similar to the Mauser in so many particulars that they must be classed amongst them.

The Mauser action, from which rifles of this class take their name, is simple. The essentials of the action are a bolt of solid construction, with the locking lugs opposite one another at the forward end, close to the cartridge-case. The end of the bolt, through which the striker impinges, is not a separate component. The Mauser Company claim that this is an advantage, as the rifle cannot be rendered useless by the loss of the bolt-head; and that the shock of the explosion being taken direct on to the bolt-head, and transferred straight through the lugs to the resisting shoulders, there is less likelihood of any inequality in the taking of the pressure by the lugs developing. Against this may be put the fact that a separate bolt-head can be replaced by a longer one should the constant hammering of the lugs allow so much play that the bolt-head does not come sufficiently hard up against the base of the cartridge, or should it become damaged in some other way. The length of the bolt-head can also be adjusted when fitting a new barrel if it is removable.

A difficulty which is always apparent in bolts having no separate bolt-head is in the disposal of the extractor so that it will not revolve with the bolt. If it does so revolve, as in the old 1888 type of Mauser, a portion of the end of the barrel has to be recessed to allow a clearance for the end of the extractor hook; besides which there is the unnecessary friction of the hook against the cartridge rim. Mauser got over this difficulty in his later pattern at the expense of the simplicity of the bolt. He recessed a groove right round the bolt, and fitted an extractor with a long spring, the spring being held to the bolt by a ring which fits the groove. When the bolt is revolved a quarter turn to extract the fired case the extractor does not revolve. With this type of extractor dust and grit are likely to be carried by the oily surface of the bolt under the extractor spring on closing the bolt. They are caught and retained by the undercut grooves of the spring, eventually clogging it and preventing extraction.

The forward end of the body against the breech is deep to allow of the slots to take the locking lugs being cut in it. These slots are difficult to get at, and therefore not easy to keep clean and free from obstructions.

The Mauser rifle is extremely durable, and conforms well to the ideal as regards simplicity, compactness and strength. The bolt can be taken to pieces without the use of tools. The magazine being of the true box type, with no opening at the bottom, is not liable to have dirt and dust forced into it when firing in trenches or over loose earth cover; loading is by charge, grooves to take it being cut in the body. The empty charge is flicked away in driving the bolt forward. The stock and fore-end is in one piece. The barrel is screwed into the action body in the usual manner, and when the bands, nosecap, hand-guards, and magazine have been removed the body and barrel can be taken from the stock by unscrewing two screws. These two screws also hold the trigger-guard and magazine-frame, which are made as one component, in place. The **Belgian Mauser** has an extra outer tube fitted over the barrel,

THE MAUSER BOLT 127

but quite free from it except at the breech and muzzle. This tube, which holds the barrel and prevents it touching the woodwork of the stock, would seem to give certain very decided advantages.

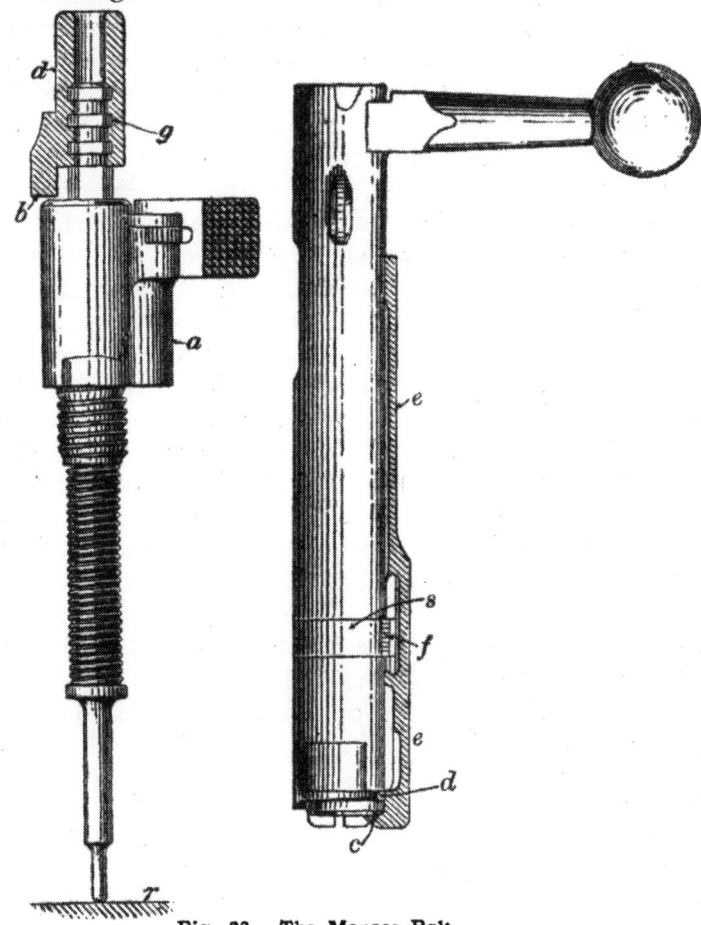

Fig. 23.—The Mauser Bolt.

The diagram shows the striker, safety catch (*a*) and cocking piece free from the bolt body. The spring is being depressed to free the cocking piece (*d*) which in the position shown has its stud (*b*) free, and can be turned a quarter right or left when the interruption screw (*g*) is free, and the cocking piece can be lifted off the striker, setting free the safety catch and spring. *c* Extractor hook. *d* Guide groove. *e* Extractor spring. *f* Dovetail projection. *s* Spring band.

RIFLES AND AMMUNITION

Target shots and rifle experimentalists have long been aware that the wooden fore-end exercises considerable influence on the shooting of the barrel, and the most successful match rifle shots at Bisley in recent years have gone to considerable trouble to make sure that the wooden fore-ends of their experimental rifles touched the barrel nowhere, thus assuring themselves that there was no possibility of varying temperature causing the barrel to bear with different pressure on the wood, and so causing a shifting of the zero of the sighting, and altering also the vibration of the barrel. The worst effects of the wooden fore-end in contact with the barrel are felt when the wood warps owing to wet or heat, or both combined. In such a case the warping is more than likely to bend the barrel and render it unfit for accurate, or, in bad cases, for any shooting. A tube prevents, or reduces to a minimum, these effects of the wooden stock, and at the same time acts as a hand-guard and as a guard to protect the barrel from external injury in the rough usages of active service. An additional advantage is claimed because the sights are affixed to the casing-tube, and the barrel itself is not liable to be affected by the unequal heating to which it has to be subjected when the sight-beds and blocks are brazed directly to the barrel.

That the casing-tube has some grave disadvantage to outweigh these advantages is evident from the fact that Paul Mauser, whose idea it was, discarded it for the rifle he started making for the German army in 1898, and has not used it in any model subsequent to that of 1888, which is the one Belgium has stuck to since 1889. It was found out in practice that to make a rifle sufficiently light to fall in line with military ideas the barrel has to be much thinned, and the casing also cannot be of sufficient strength to make it an efficient guard against damage. Rust is liable to set up under the casing, thereby still further weakening the already weak barrel. The sights on the casing are very liable to be displaced by blows which even slightly deform the thin casing, so rendering the weapon useless for accurate shooting until a fresh zero has been taken, or the sights have been restored to their original positions. The casing also introduces unnecessary complications in the

Plate XXVII

Photo: Clarke & Hyde

TESTING FOR STRAIGHTNESS

The straightness of the bore is tested by looking at the multiple reflections of the muzzle in the bore. The slightest curvature can be detected

Photo: Clarke & Hyde

BARREL SETTING

If a barrel is not straight it is set by being tapped with a copper-shod hammer. Barrel setters are marvellously expert at giving just the right strength of tap to the barrel

manufacture of the rifle, adding to the cost and the time expended both in making and repairing. It should be noted that the Belgian Mauser has a barrel so light that it vibrates unduly.

With regard to rapidity of fire, the capabilities of the Mauser rifle vary. The loading of the magazine in all types can be performed easily. In 1893 Mauser fitted to the Turkish rifle a platform which projected up into the bolt-way in such a manner that if there are no cartridges in the magazine the bolt catches on the platform end and cannot be closed until the platform has been pushed down by the fingers. This was

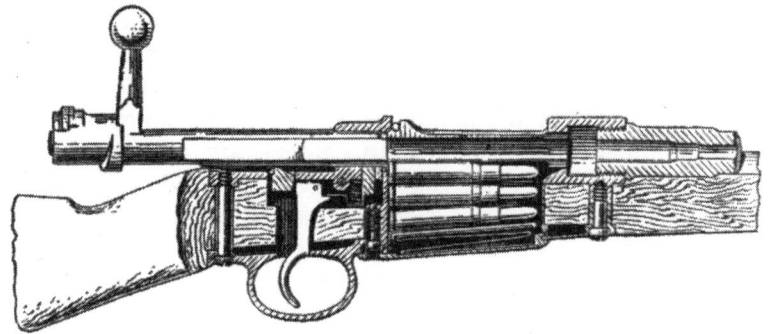

Fig. 24.—The Mauser Action in Section

adopted to warn the soldier that his magazine is empty. It was repeated in the Spanish model 1896, but has not been utilised in later models.

The heavy German and Spanish patterns come up clumsily to the shoulder, their rather straight stocks not aiding a rapid alignment of the sights. Even after considerable practice they do not commend themselves as being efficient snap-shooting weapons to those used to the handier and shorter rifles of Great Britain and the United States. All the Mauser military arms seem to lack that perfection of balance which is so marked a feature of the short Lee-Enfield. The Mauser rifles of all patterns have a tendency to favour a high shot, particularly at short ranges and with rapid fire. The straight butts are so made to make aiming comfortable at long range, where

J

the downward bend of the British and most other rifles necessitate the cheek and chin being well away from the butt, with a consequent loss of steadiness. Mauser rifles are not fitted with long-range sights.

The foresight of all Mauser models are dovetailed into the foresight-block, and are of the ordinary barleycorn pattern. The Belgian sights are fitted to the casing. In all other patterns the block is in one piece, with a ring or collar which is fitted over the barrel, and is pinned and soldered into position. This plan does away with brazing, and has much to recommend it. The backsights of the Mauser rifles have nothing particular to recommend them when compared with the latest British sight. They are fitted with notches corresponding with the lines representing hundreds of metres, and as they are not fitted with fine adjustments, the sights can only be used with sureness when the teeth of the clamping catches are in the notches. The clamping catches are released from the right side, necessitating the hand being placed right over the sight to move it. In the German model the notches allow of the sight being used at intervals of 50 metres, but though the graduations are placed on the top and side of the backsight-bed they are not very easy to see.

Mauser adhered to four grooves for all his rifles, the twist being in every case to the right. The figure of the rifling is concentric (similar to that known in Enfield), but Turkish and Spanish models have slightly rounded edges.

A very high degree of accuracy over a long barrel life has always been claimed for the Mauser rifle, and the claim has been fairly well sustained in practice, though, of course, barrel life is more or less dependent on the type of ammunition used. The following report of a test made at Oberndorf may be of interest:

"On one occasion 15,005 rounds were fired at the rate of 720 a day, a portion of the shots being rapid fire. It was stated that after 9,000 rounds only a slight diminution of accuracy was observable; but even after this prolonged trial the rifle was considered to be absolutely fitted for actual war service."

THE BRAZILIAN MODEL 131

Actual tests carried out with the new 7 mm. rifle made for Brazil gave the following results:

900 yards	25-in. angle
1,000 ,, ...	27-in. ,,
1,100 ,, ...	36-in. ,,

These tests were made at Bisley, April 4 and 18, 1914; ammunition D.W.M., 154 grain bullet, pointed. The velocity was given as 2,920 fs., but no means were available for checking this. The accuracy of this rifle and ammunition at very short ranges was somewhat remarkable. At 25 yards four shots were through the same hole, and the fifth touching the hole; at 50 yards all five shots were in 1 in.; and at 100 yards the five shots made a group of a shade over $1\frac{1}{2}$ in.

The retaining of the bolt in the action-body is a problem which has been well overcome in the Mauser models. A small lever is hinged on the left side of the body toward the rear, and is kept pressed flat against the side by an interior spring. From the small lever a tooth projects through a slot in the body and stops the travel of the left locking-lug of the bolt. If it is desired to withdraw the bolt, the lug may be allowed to pass by pulling out the lever, and so removing the tooth from the groove in which the lug travels. The ejector, which reaches the base of the cartridge through a slot in the left locking-lug, works on the same pivot as the bolt-retaining lever. The only objection to the Mauser bolt-retaining system is that if the wood about the body swells, or grit and dirt get between the underside of the lever and the woodwork, it is liable to jam.

The United States service rifle, known officially as the "Short Magazine Rifle," and unofficially as the "Springfield," is, as has already been stated, a copy, so far as the action is concerned, of the Mauser. It has the characteristic Mauser bolt with no separate bolt-head, and an extractor which does not revolve with the bolt. The striker differs from Mauser models, and is made in three pieces; a long rear portion on which is the cocking-piece and the tongue of metal on which the single bent is formed. The rifle can be cocked by hand by means of a milled head. The idea of making the striker in three pieces is so that, should the pin break at the point, which is the usual place for this accident to happen, a new striking-pin can be adjusted without it being necessary to replace the whole striker. Another difference between the United States rifle action and that of the ordinary Mauser action is in the retaining-bolt. This is on the left-hand side of the rear of the bolt-body, as usual, but it is so arranged that it will give three positions. In one, when the thumb-piece is right up, showing the word "on" engraved on it, the bolt can be drawn back but insufficiently to clear the cartridges in the magazine. If the thumb-piece is put down to show the word "off" engraved on the other side of it, the bolt can be withdrawn sufficiently far back to enable the cartridges to rise from the magazine; and thus the retaining-bolt has been ingeniously adapted to act as a cut-off. The third position given by the retaining-bolt enables the bolt to be withdrawn completely for cleaning and inspection purposes. The magazine is similar to the ordinary Mauser pattern. The trigger is similar to that of the Mannlicher pattern, which is shown in detail on page 135. The double pull-off is common to all the Mauser rifles, as well as those of the Mannlicher pattern. The Mauser is the more simple, the Mannlicher the smoother working.

The backsight of the American rifle is peculiar in that it has a peepsight. To enable this to be used the sight has had to be placed a good deal farther back than is usual with rifles fitted with "V" or "U" sights only. The American backsight is also fitted with two "U's" which, because of the nearness of the backsight to the eye, are rather difficult to use. The sight is made slightly askew to the left to give an automatic compensation for drift to the right. The length of the rifle without bayonet is a shade over 3 ft. 7 in. There are four grooves .004 in. deep, of a concentric figure, turning to the right once in 10 in. The bore is .3 in.

The Japanese rifle introduced in 1907 is a remarkably close copy of the Mauser. This weapon is of particular interest owing to the large numbers which were taken into use by Territorial and Service Battalions early in 1915 for instructional

PLATE XXVIII

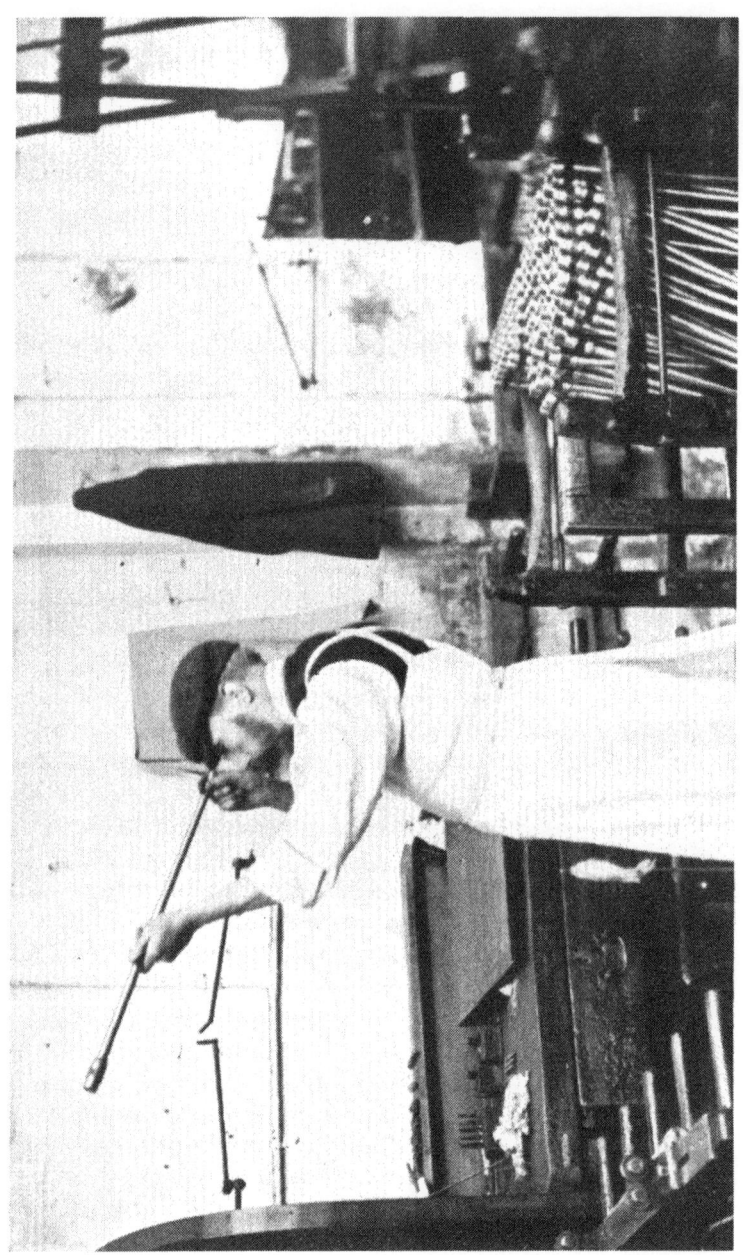

Photo: Clarke & Hyde

INSPECTING THE BARREL IN THE RIFLED STATE

When the rifling in the bore has been cut, the barrel is examined to see that it is free from flaws. It is also tested to see that the depth and pitch of rifling are correct

THE JAPANESE RIFLE 133

purposes, thus setting free for actual warfare rifles firing our own ammunition. The bore is .256 in. or 6.5 mm., and ranks with others of this calibre as the smallest now in use for military purposes. The magazine is entirely protected by the woodwork of the stock, and will take five cartridges, which are loaded in from a clip. When the magazine is empty, the end of the magazine platform rises against the face of the bolt-head and prevents the bolt from being closed unless the magazine is recharged or the platform depressed with the finger. The whole weapon is well balanced and accurate, but the sights are not strongly constructed and, being entirely unprotected, are extremely liable to injury. The backsight leaf is graduated from 500 to 2,000 metres, and at right angles to the rear end of the leaf there is a separate backsight for 400 metres. The barrel is encased in wood from the backsight to the lower band. According to British notions, the Japanese rifle is somewhat light in construction; though it is an inch and a half longer than the Territorial pattern, it weighs 10 oz. less. The rifling is of the Metford type, four grooves taking one turn in 7.875 in.

Rifles of the Mannlicher type fall naturally into two groups: those having straight-pull actions and those with actions of the more usual turning-bolt type. All Mannlicher rifles have separate bolt-heads, though only those of Holland and Roumania (turning-bolt actions) are capable of being rotated without the bolt. The bolt-head of the straight-pull rifle is not a bolt-head in the usually accepted meaning of the word; it is really a bolt with a solid head, turning in one piece, the motion being imparted by an outer sliding sleeve.

The only straight-pull Mannlicher is that of Austria, and the same pattern which is used by Bulgaria. The bolt can be opened and closed by drawing the bolt-knob straight backwards and pushing it straight forwards. It is, of course, necessary that the locking-lugs should be so revolved that they come clear of the resistance lugs; and this action is performed in a most ingenious manner. The bolt is, as usual, a hollow cylinder containing the striker and the mainspring. On the outside of it are two ribs, horizontally placed, which work to and fro in grooves in the action body, preventing the bolt being turned in the body. The bolt-head, which has on its end the resistance lugs, fits with a long tail into the cylinder of the bolt proper. It has two spiral slots or grooves cut in it in which work the small "feathers" in the inside of the bolt proper. When the bolt proper is moved in either direction, these feathers, by working in the grooves of the bolt-head tail, cause the bolt-head to twist, and thus lock or unlock the lugs.

The trifling gain in rapidity of action brought about by the straight pull of the bolt is most distinctly negatived by the very much more complicated bolt and bolt-head which is necessary to do away with the ordinary turning motion. It is said that a straight-pull action is less likely to get jammed in dusty or sandy country; but if sand does get into a straight-pull action the jam is usually far more complicated in its effects than the jam which occurs in a turning-bolt rifle. The wear on the grooves and feathers of the Austrian straight-pull very soon causes a good deal of play.

The extractor is fitted with a long tail, which lies between the bolt-head and the bolt-sleeve, where it is held so that it cannot revolve with the bolt-head. The hook projects down over the top lug of the bolt when the action is closed, and is supported by the other lug when the action is open. The extractor is complicated by the necessity of fitting it to a straight-pull action. Primary extraction, which is given in the straight-pull Mannlicher by the cam shape of the end of the grooves in which the locking-lugs work, is distinctly weaker than the primary extraction which can be got by an ordinary turning-bolt action. In the Mannlicher rifles the scear and ejector are made up together in three components. The bent fits into the body of the scear, and is pivoted on the scear-pin, which passes through the action-body. The ejector is pivoted on to the front of the scear, and is kept in a forward position by a small spiral spring. The trigger does not work on a pivot, but is supported in the groove, so that at a certain point the leverage is changed and the double-pull effect is produced.

The rifle without the bayonet is of medium weight, being just over 8 lb. 5 oz., the exact weight depending, as in

THE MANNLICHER

every other rifle, on the density of the wood used in stocking. The whole weapon is well balanced, and comes up to the shoulder nicely. For snap-shooting purposes the straight-pull action gives, as has already been said, some slight advantage in speed, and the clip-loading, by which a clip of five cartridges is placed in the magazine in one action, is also of slight advantage. With the clip form of loading, unloading is also facilitated. In the Mannlicher type it is possible, by pressing a stud, to remove a full or partially full clip without actuating the bolt mechanism. When a clip is empty it falls out of the bottom of the magazine through a hole left for that purpose. This hole is a disadvantage, as dust and mud, which are always

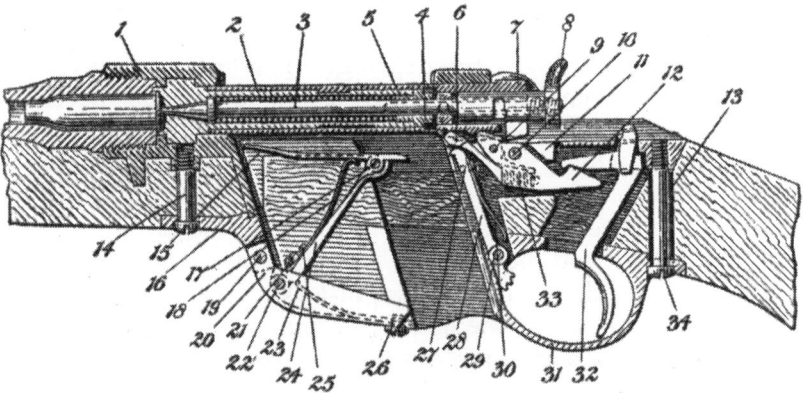

Fig. 25.—The Austrian Straight-Pull Mannlicher

1. Action-body
2. Mainspring
3. Striking pin
4. Collar
5. Bolt-head tail
6. Ejector
7. Bolt body
8. Cocking piece
9. Ejector pivot pin
10. Scear and bent pivot pin
11. Scear bent
12. Scear body
13. Rear securing screw housing
14. Front securing screw
15. Cartridge elevator platform
16. Front magazine and guard tang
17. Platform pivot
18. Elevator platform spring
19. Magazine trough screw
20. Magazine trough
21. Platform spring screw
22. Elevator pivot
23. Cartridge elevator spring
24. Cartridge elevator
25. Platform spring stud
26. Elevator spring screw
27. Clip catch spring screw
28. Clip catch
29. Clip catch pivot
30. Clip catch spring
31. Trigger guard
32. Trigger arm
33. Scear-spring
34. Rear securing screw

the accompaniment of active service, can easily get into the magazine, causing jams and other troubles. Clip-loading necessitates a downward extension of the magazine, as the cartridges remain in a single column, whereas in the charger-loading types they can be made to arrange themselves in two columns when they are swept out of the charger. There is also an element of delay with the straight-pull Mannlicher in the occasional resistance of the cartridge-case to the first pull of the bolt. This fault, which is at present common to all rifles of the straight-pull principle, is due to the lack of really efficient primary extraction.

The sights are of the ordinary pattern, and call for no special comment. The backsight is attached to the rear end of the backsight bed, and when raised in the upright position is held up in the usual way by a spring. The leaf is engraved with elevations from 600 to 2,600 paces, even 100 paces being the smallest graduation. The spring stud on the slide releases a catch which fits into notches on the outside of the right-hand side of the back of the leaf. These notches correspond with 200-pace graduations. The locking-stud of the slide being on the left-hand side can be freed by the thumb of the left hand. As with all notched sight-leafs, it is difficult to get the slide fixed in intermediate positions.

The rifle is 4 ft. 2 in. long without the bayonet, the barrel being 30.12 in. The calibre of the barrel is 8 mm., or .315 in. It is rifled with four grooves of concentric figure, with bevelled edges. The twist is one turn in 9.8 in., to the right.

Regarded as a whole, the straight-pull Mannlicher, though it is an excellently made weapon, is rather too complicated to be a first-class military rifle. In military efficiency it is considerably behind the turning-bolt Mannlicher rifles and the Mauser rifle.

The Mannlicher turning-bolt action is nearly as simple as the Mauser action. The two principal examples in use are the Roumanian pattern of 1893 and the Dutch pattern of 1895. No tools are necessary to strip or assemble the bolt, and it is without complicated parts. There is a separate bolt-head, which admits of a speedy repair being made, should the bolt-head

THE DUTCH PATTERN EJECTOR 137

become damaged, without replacing the whole bolt. The locking-lugs are disposed like those of the Mauser type, so that when the bolt is locked home the lugs lie vertically over and under the bolt.

The bolt-head, when attached to the bolt, appears as a disc of steel projecting beyond the lugs and carrying the extractor, and in the Dutch pattern an ejector, and the Roumanian a stud of metal. The bolt-head is capable of revolving, and when the bolt is turned either the ejector or the metal stud, before-mentioned, engages in a slot in the action-body and prevents the bolt-head from revolving with it. By this arrangement the advantages of a rotating bolt-head, and the consequent simplification of the extracting mechanism is obtained without putting the lugs much farther back on the bolt than they are in the Mauser type. Both extraction and ejection in the Mannlicher turning-bolt action is good. Cam-shaped grooves lead from the locking-lug seatings in the head of the action-body, and when the bolt is turned over in the first action of unlocking a very powerful primary extraction is given by the backward travel of the lugs in these grooves. Friction is reduced by the fact that the bolt-head does not grind against the base of the cartridge, as it does in the Mauser type of bolt. In the Dutch pattern the ejector is on the bolt-head, and can slide backwards and forwards on it for a limited travel. The ejector is fitted with a tail which bears on the bolt. When the bolt is drawn fully back the tail strikes against the retaining-bolt and the ejector is driven forward. It pushes against the left edge of the cartridge-base and pitches the case out to the right. This ejection is very efficient, and works sweetly and without undue violence even when the bolt is driven back very hard. The Roumanian ejector is towards the rear of the action-body, acting on the underside of the bolt. A tooth projects upwards into a slot in the underside of the bolt-head when the bolt is drawn fully back, and, catching the base of the cartridge, flings it out upwards and, owing to the pressure of the ejector, to the right.

The rifle can be fully cocked by raising the bolt-knob and depressing it again. If this is done quickly after a bad hangfire an accident might easily happen, as the lugs are cleared from the resistance-pieces by the action of turning the bolt. There is no means provided for drawing back the cocking-piece without raising the bolt-knob.

The turning-bolt Mannlicher action is a favourite with match rifle shots, partly because of its separate bolt-head, and also because the pull-off can be nicely adjusted to give a clean, even disengagement of scear and bent. The action is capable of standing up to pressures considerably higher than the danger-point of the British Service action, which may be fixed at 20 tons on the square inch. In regard to resistance of pressure, the turning-bolt Mannlicher is perhaps not quite equal to the Mauser; but the pressure which would put either of them to a severe test would be quite extraordinary in rifle work. Both Mauser and Mannlicher actions have given every satisfaction in the way they have stood the strain of the constant shooting of the heavy charge of the .280 match rifle cartridge.

Of rifles which can be classed as neither Mauser nor Mannlicher there are only six in use by military powers. They are the Lebel, the Nagant, the Schmidt-Rubin, the Krag-Jorgensen, the Ross, and the Lee-Enfield. Of these the Ross and the Schmidt-Rubin have straight-pull actions and the rest have the ordinary turning-bolt action.

We will examine the two straight-pull rifles first, considering them, as we have those falling in the two main groups, in relation to their efficiency from a military standpoint.

The Schmidt-Rubin rifle of Switzerland is interesting because it was the first short pattern small-bore, high-velocity rifle definitely designed to agree with the military ideal of handiness. The Swiss rifle of 1893 was short, but in the 1900 pattern, which is here under consideration, the length between muzzle and butt was reduced to 3 ft. 7.12 in. The barrel is covered with wood for almost its entire length, and the weapon presents a very workmanlike appearance. It is, however, somewhat deficient in balance, being rather heavy in the action; the butt is also very short, making it difficult to use in the prone position. The bolt is more complicated than that of the Austrian Mannlicher. Briefly it consists of a cylinder which

PLATE XXIX

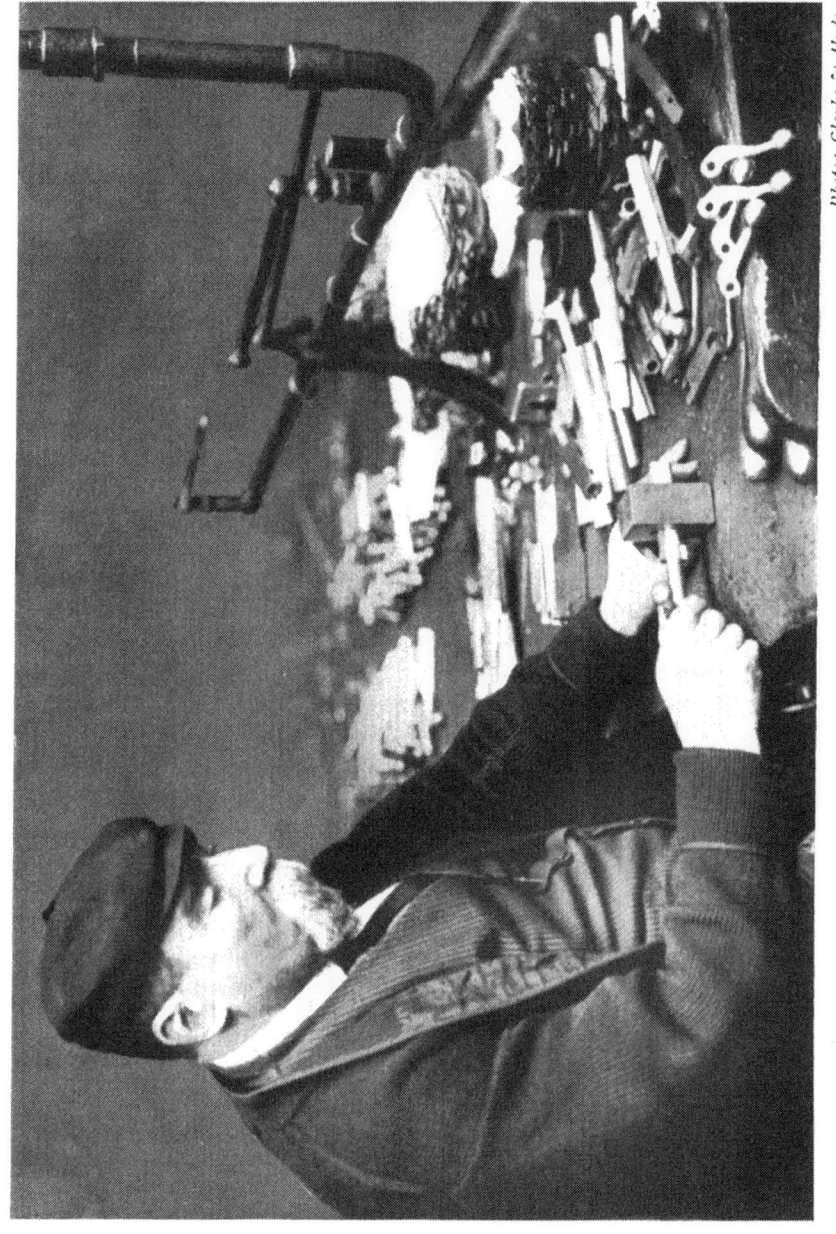

GAUGING BOLT BODIES

In the manufacture of the modern rifle gauging plays a very important part. The limits of toleration are always small and sometimes none is allowed. A few parts are gauged at stated intervals in the machine room, but all machined parts are gauged and inspected by a qualified man before they are passed

Photo: Clarke & Hyde

contains the striker and mainspring, a sleeve bearing the locking-lugs, and a rod bearing the handle which, by a reciprocal motion, revolves the locking sleeve. The action-body and bolt are very long, and the locking-lugs are placed a long way back from the bolt-head. When the bolt is closed the lugs are behind the magazine opening. Such a length of metal between bolt-head and lugs allows of an amount of play under firing stress which is not conducive to straight shooting. The evil of this length of free bolt is minimised to some extent by the fact that the lugs are locked in a vertical position, so that errors due to unequal taking up of pressure by the lugs will increase the depth rather than the breadth of the group.

The extractor is of the long-tailed pattern, and is secured to the bolt by a stud which locks into a hole in the bolt cylinder. Primary extraction is fair and the ejection is good. The trigger mechanism, of the double-pull variety, is simple and efficient. The magazine takes six cartridges and is charger-loading.

The rifling is of concentric figure, with slightly rounded edges. There are only three grooves, and these are very shallow, being but .0039 in. deep. The twist is to the right.

The sights are a barleycorn foresight and "V" backsight. The barleycorn is dovetailed into a foresight block at right angles to the axis of the barrel, and is capable of being laterally adjusted with a hammer. The foresight-block is made in one piece, with a ring which is soldered on to a swell on the barrel. The backsight is placed close to the breech, lying over the chamber. It is pivoted at its forward end, and has only one aiming "V," which is cut in the rear end of the leaf, which is turned up at an angle of about 45 degrees. A slide works on the end side of the leaf, engaging in a series of ratchets which are cut to give sighting for every 100 metres from 1,200 to 300. The sight is well made and capable of standing rough usage.

The Ross rifle is the arm of the Canadian forces; and as it is a Canadian production is looked on with considerable affection by the sons of the Maple-leaf. It is regarded by them as being very considerably superior to the Service rifle of the Mother Country, and the consistently good shooting of the Canadian teams which have visited this country has fostered the idea. In thus praising the rifle at their own expense, the members of the team probably belittle themselves unduly, for they have to use the same cartridge as their British fellow subjects when firing at Bisley, and there is nothing in the design of the Ross rifle that could make a great deal of difference in the usually good shooting of the Mark VI. ammunition. The difference would come into play if a heavy cartridge had to be used—one which the British action would not stand up to—then the stronger bolt of the Ross rifle would give it a tremendous advantage (see Plate XXIII.).

The Ross action is described in the "Text Book of Small Arms" as being a modification of the Mauser, but it is difficult to understand the grounds for the assertion. The action, which is the invention of Sir Charles Ross, may be said to resemble the Mannlicher straight-pull action in that the necessary turning of the bolt itself to free the locking-lugs is done by the straight backwards pull of an outer bolt sleeve, the straight pull being transformed into a turning motion by the aid of spirals. Here the resemblance ends. The Ross spirals are cut on both bolt and sleeve, and engage one with the other, giving a very strong and positive action. Cocking is effected on the withdrawal of the bolt. The trigger is of the double-pull variety, and is so arranged that it gives a very sweet, clean release. There is no charger guide or other means of loading the magazine with clips. The magazine platform can be depressed by means of a finger-piece on the right-hand side of the stock, and cartridges can then be poured in.

We will now examine the four turning-bolt action rifles in the last section.

The French Lebel rifle of the 1886 pattern has a bore of 8 mm., or .315 in., enjoys the distinction of being the first small-bore rifle adopted for military purposes by any nation and the first rifle in which smokeless powder was used. Its chief peculiarity is that the magazine is tube shaped and lies along the fore-end, and the balance of the rifle is therefore disturbed a fraction as each shot is loaded into the chamber from the magazine. The cartridges, eight in number when the magazine is full, are pushed base first towards a lifting

THE FRENCH LEBEL RIFLE 141

carrier by a strong spiral spring. The carrier is pivoted towards the rear of the action, and on withdrawing the bolt a cartridge is lifted by it into such a position that the returning bolt catches the upper edge of the rim and drives it into the chamber. A turn-down projection on the forward end of the carrier acts as a stop to prevent the next cartridge from being driven under the carrier. The magazine is loaded through the action-body, and there is another stop provided on the lever which elevates the carrier to further assist in retaining the cartridge in the

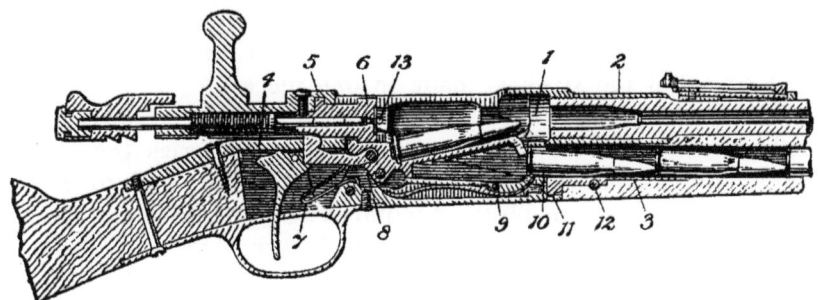

Fig. 26.—The Lebel Rifle
1. Locking recesses and lug groove. 2. Body reinforce. 3. Magazine reinforce. 4. Body tang. 5. Connecting rib. 6. Bolt-head. 7. Scear spring. 8. Carrier axis pin. 9. Retaining spring pivot. 10. Cartridge in magazine. 11. Fore end position hook. 12. Magazine tube pin. 13. Ejector screw

magazine until the bolt is drawn back for the purpose of loading another cartridge into the chamber.

The stock of the Lebel rifle, like that of the British Service rifle, is in two pieces, and is therefore open to familiar criticisms that it is weak and more expensive to produce than stocks and fore-ends in one piece. The stock is only attached to the action by two screws, one passing right through the butt from the metal of the trigger-guard to the metal of the tang of the body, and another passing through the tang into the butt.

The foresight is a low U-shaped blade, and is worked with the foresight-block, which is dovetailed into the barrel at right angles to its axis. The backsight-bed is attached by solder in front of the chamber. It is pivoted at the front end, and is used in two positions from 400 to 800 metres. The sight is down, the slide engaging in steps cut on the top side of the sight-bed for elevations from 900 to 1,900 metres. The leaf is raised to a forward position, and the slide adjusted by marks on the leaf. There is a "U" cut in the foot of the leaf which gives the elevation of 250 metres when the leaf is turned right forward so that the cap rests on the barrel. The aiming "U's" are semicircular notches cut in the bottom of shallow grooves. This type of backsight is familiar to sportsmen, and is undoubtedly capable of being used with quickness in snap-shooting. The French have also a carbine for shooting the Lebel cartridge from a box-magazine which will contain three cartridges. The bolt and action are similar to that of the Lebel rifle, but the stock is made in one piece.

The bolt is strong and simple. There is a separate bolt-head which moves with the bolt in turning. This carries the extractor, and therefore the rear of the chamber has to be recessed for a quarter of its circumference to allow for the movement of the extractor-head. The locking-lugs are close up against the base of the cartridge. The trigger mechanism is simply arranged to give a double pull.

The rifling of the Lebel twists to the left, like that of the British Service rifle; it makes one turn in 9.45 in. It has four grooves of a concentric figure. The grooves are .0059 deep.

Judged by modern standards, the Lebel is not a first-class military weapon. It is heavy, and does not admit of being handled smartly enough for the quickest snap-shooting purposes (see Plate XXII.).

The Russian rifle, known as the "3 line" or Nagant, is a clumsy weapon, though without the bayonet it weighs under nine pounds; it is always carried and fired with the bayonet fixed, and then weighs about 9 lb. 12 oz. The butt is not of good shape, and the "small" is thick and clumsy to hold. The bolt is complicated, beyond the necessities of a turning-bolt, by the provision of a "connecting-bar" which holds the bolt proper and the bolt-head together. The bolt-head is separate from the bolt, and is not actually fitted to it, but on to a hollow cylinder which is attached to the connecting-bar. The rear part of this cylinder, through which the striker passes,

PLATE XXX

Photo: Clarke & Hyde

THE MECHANICAL REST USED IN TESTING SERVICE RIFLES

A full regulation sight is obtained by means of a special telescope, which rests on the blade of the foresight and the shoulders of the backsight. The rifle is laid by hand wheels

THE RUSSIAN RIFLE

fits into the front of the bolt proper. The bolt-head turns with the bolt and carries the extractor. The cocking-piece is provided with a shaped head for cocking without opening the breech, and turns with the bolt, which is not in accordance with usual practice. In all other rifles the cocking-piece is prevented from revolving by the use of grooves and studs in suitable positions. The locking-lugs are close to the base of the cartridge when the bolt is locked home, when the lugs are placed horizontally instead of vertically, as is usual. Primary extraction is obtained in the usual manner by means of cam-shaped grooves to lead the bolt backwards when the bolt is first turned upwards.

The magazine is a fixed box beneath the bolt-race, and can be loaded with five cartridges by means of a charger. A feature of the Russian rifle is the "interrupter," which is intended to prevent the delay caused by "double loading," or the moving of two cartridges forward towards the chamber at the same time. In bolt-heads so designed that the extractor rides over the rim or into the groove on the cartridge-base immediately the cartridge is fed upwards by the magazine platform double loading is practically impossible. If the extractor-claw does not engage with the base of the cartridge until the bolt has been pushed home, double loading is very likely to happen when excitement causes the soldier to forget to work the bolt smoothly. The Russian "interrupter" is a flat metal plate working in a slot in the action-body, and so arranged that a tooth on the inside edge of the plate holds down the next cartridge whilst the one above it is being fed forward into the chamber. It is impossible to feed in another until the previous one has been completely extracted and ejected. This simple piece of mechanism works very well.

The barrel is covered with a handguard as far as the upper band, which is separate from the nose-cap. The handguard is lined with thin brass sheeting, which is riveted to the wood. The handguard is held in place by tongues of the brass lining, which fit into grooves in the bands.

The sights of the Russian rifle are of the old style "V" and barleycorn, the backsight being of the leaf pattern, pivoted to the bed at its forward end. When the leaf is down it gives elevations from 400 to 1,200 paces by means of saw-tooth steps on the ramps at the side of the bed. In an upright position the slide can be moved upward to give further elevation to 2,700 paces, or 2,200 yards, approximately. The slide retains its position on the leaf by friction, aided by a small spring, and is not capable of being very quickly adjusted.

The bore is of .3-in. calibre, or 7.62 mm. The grooves are four in number, making one turn in 9.5 in. The figure of the rifling is concentric, with edges slightly rounded. The grooves are .007 in. deep.

The Danish Krag-Jorgensen has a unique feature in its horizontal fixed box magazine. This magazine is so arranged that the cartridges are fed in at a door on the right-hand side, and are pressed round to the left of the bolt-race. The benefit of this particular form of magazine is that it is not necessary to open the bolt to charge the magazine; but, on the other hand, it is ill-adapted for charger-loading, and though a charger has been designed for use with the Krag-Jorgensen 1889 pattern, it is heavy and also clumsy to use.

Another peculiarity of the Krag-Jorgensen rifle is that there is only one locking-lug in the usually accepted sense. This is on the end of the bolt, close to the head, and when the bolt is locked home the lug is downwards. A resistance-piece, or rib, on the right side of the bolt bears against a shoulder on the end of the body, and helps to take up the recoil from the bolt and transfer it to the body. The demerits of this unsymmetrical disposal of the resistance does not need labouring, but they are probably not greater than in the British service rifle bolt.

The barrel is made rather thin, and is cased in a tube of metal which protects the barrel and acts as a handguard. The merits and demerits of this practice have already been discussed in connection with the Belgian Mauser. The striker has a separate head of sound and solid construction, and is very unlikely to be broken or deformed. None of the other parts of this rifle call for special comment (see Plate XXII.).

THE BRITISH RIFLE

The first British magazine rifle—the Lee-Metford Mark I.—was approved in December, 1888. This rifle was the result of the work of a Committee which sat for the first time in February, 1883. Two years and six months later the Committee recommended the Lee action, the invention of the American, James P. Lee, particulars of whose work have been given in Chapter V. This action was associated in the Committee's report with the Bethel-Burton magazine, the whole rifle being known as the Lee-Burton (see Plate XX.). The Committee also recommended the Owen-Jones rifle. As a result of a trial carried out with these rifles, the Lee-Burton and an improved form of the Lee action with a more serviceable magazine were tried again with Mr. Metford's .402-in. barrels. Lee's own magazine, which was placed under the bolt-race, proved its superiority, and the Burton form was discarded. Meanwhile the Committee had been conducting their experiments in connection with reduced calibres for military rifles, details of which have already been given, and early in 1888, the .303-in. Lee-Metford rifle was actually in existence. Later in the year some three hundred odd of them were prepared for experimental purposes. The summer having been taken up with these experiments, the manufacture of the Lee-Metford Magazine Rifle, Mark I., was started at the beginning of 1889. The adoption of smokeless powder for the charge necessitated several alterations, and the Mark I. was converted to the Mark I*, the manufacture of which was started about February, 1892. In the meantime another Committee had been appointed to consider the Mark I. pattern, and as a result of various reports submitted to them they suggested some improvements in the direction of simplifying the bolt, and recommended a magazine which would hold ten cartridges. This rifle, known as Mark II., began to pass out of the manufacturer's hands in January, 1892. In 1895 a safety catch was added to the cocking-piece, and the rifle so fitted was known as Mark II*. The change from Lee-Metford to the Lee-Enfield rifle was due to the fact that the shallow Metford grooves were very susceptible to erosion. The next change was the taking away of the clearing-rod and the groove made to hold it, the rifle with this

K

alteration being known as Lee-Enfield Mark I.* There have also been various makes of Lee-Enfield and Lee-Metford carbines, but the biggest change that was made after 1895 was the conversion (in 1907) of the Lee-Enfield to the charger-loading Lee-Enfield, in which the magazine could be filled by means of chargers containing five cartridges each. During the South African war of 1899-1902 the authorities decided to arm the whole of the Regular Forces—Infantry, Cavalry, Artillery, etc.—with the same kind of weapon, and the short rifle was designed. The first approved pattern of this, known as Short Magazine Lee-Enfield Rifle Mark I., was approved in December, 1902. Some long rifles were converted into a Mark II. pattern of the short rifle early in 1903. The Short Magazine Lee-Enfield Mark III. was approved in January, 1907. Mark IV. is the same pattern, but converted from long rifles.

The Short Rifle Magazine Lee-Enfield is the small-arm of the British Regulars, but there are many other types of rifle in use by the forces of the Empire. Even in times of peace Sniders and Enfield carbines are still to be found in daily military use in outlying stations, whilst the Martini-Metford .303 carbines and the Martini-Enfield .303 carbines are in use in large numbers by native soldiery and police. These carbines were made by converting the Martini-Henry rifle to the smaller bore. The Martini-Henry is also in use by native soldiery of the Empire. Lee-Enfields and Lee-Metfords of early marks, both rifles and carbines, are in use, and there is also the charger-loading pattern Lee-Enfield or Lee-Metford which is popularly known as the "Territorial Pattern," and is a remarkably good shooting rifle. There are some Winchester rifles in use by the Canadian North-West Mounted Police, but otherwise all rifles in use by His Majesty's forces, either military or civil, are made within the Empire.

The British habit of subjecting anything British to a severe course of fault-finding has been responsible for the gradual forming of the opinion that the Empire is the worst provided for as regards small-arms of any of the Powers. In the year or eighteen months before the outbreak of war, the hint that the War Office was experimenting with a new rifle roused

PLATE XXXI

Photo: *Clarke & Hyde*

THE FIRST SHOOTING TEST AT 100 FEET

A couple of shots are first fired to determine if the fore-sight is of the right height and correctly placed. These matters adjusted, five rounds are fired. To be passed the rifle must make a four-shot group 1 in. broad by 1½ in. high

popular interest, and many questions were asked in Parliament and many letters written to newspapers. The burden of most of the Parliamentary answers and most of the letters was that the British Service rifle was bad, the bolt, in any case, was unscientific, and would not stand the high pressures necessary for the high velocities demanded by the most up-to-date practice; the short rifle did not shoot well.

Then came the outbreak of the Great War, and Britain had to go in with the arms she had—only to find out in a very short time that, instead of being the worst small-arm in use, the short Lee-Enfield was the best. Actual war tests proved that a "weak and unscientific" bolt may have advantages not possessed by stronger action designed on lines which meet the approval of engineers. The bolt-action of the British rifle can be worked at very high speed, and this speed is possible without any serious sacrifice of strength or accuracy.

One of the criticisms against the British Service rifle is that the lugs which lock the bolt against the shock of discharge are placed so far back on the bolt that there are several inches of unsupported metal between the bolt-head and the lugs, and that the slightest irregularity in the seating of the lugs on the resistance shoulder and resistance grooves allows this unsupported metal to play sideways, and causes irregularities in the shooting. The body of the action is also complained about on the score that it is weak. From a mechanical point of view, both these condemnations must be supported by the critic; but a careful engineer who bears in mind how successfully the short Lee-Enfield has borne the severest test any rifle has yet been put to, may be allowed to emphasise the fact that both body and bolt of the British Service rifle are difficult and expensive to machine, and that, in the first instance, complaints as to the lack of scientific design in our rifle have come from manufacturers.

Simplicity is the outstanding feature of every detail of the British action (see Plate XXI.). The trigger mechanism is worked on two pivots, and is much less complicated than either the Mauser or the Mannlicher trigger action. In the short rifle a double pull off has been obtained in a most ingenious manner by providing two points of contact between the trigger arm and the lower arm of the scear. The first point provides a long light pressure, and the second, which takes the scear nose from the bent, provides a harder but quicker pull. The transference of the contact from one point to the other is brought about by the change in relative position of the lower scear arm and the trigger arm.

The short Lee-Enfield rifle is admirably balanced, and is suited in every way for the snap-shooting and rapid fire of which the British Army has made itself master. The backsight, which is hinged towards the muzzle of the rifle, and which is elevated by the action of a slide on a curved ramp, is the simplest and best provided on any Service rifle. It can be changed with the utmost ease by the pressure of the thumb of either hand. Considerable nicety of adjustment is provided for. The left side of the top of the leaf has engraved on it each 25 yards of elevation from 200 to 2,000 yards, and these 25-yard marks can be further subdivided into five-yard settings by means of a worm wheel on the right of the slide. On the right of the top of the slide are 100-yard divisions from 200 to 2,000 yards. Both backsight and foresight are well protected. The barrel is protected by a handguard for the whole of its length. The rifling of the barrel of the short rifle is so constructed that the grooves deepen from chamber to muzzle in order to reduce friction. There are five grooves of Enfield figure twisting to the left, as is usual.

Enough has been learned already from the Great War to upset several preconceived notions in rifle design. Speed and accuracy of fire may be of far more importance than an excessively flat trajectory; a simple construction and one that will not easily seize up even in most adverse circumstances may be of greater value than great strength; whilst the sacrifice of loss of reach in a short rifle may be more than compensated for by general handiness.

CHAPTER VIII

Military Rifle Ammunition of To-day

THE modern rifle cartridge is to the eye a fairly simple construction; a more or less bottle-shaped brass case has in its open end a bullet made of lead covered with cupro-nickel, or other suitable metal or alloy. At the closed end of the cartridge-case is a percussion-cap, and in the interior of the brass case is a smokeless powder charge. Simple as the cartridge appears, it is, however, an exceedingly highly developed product, each feature of which has been designed for a special end and fulfils a special purpose.

An ideal cartridge must be light, so that as large a number of rounds as possible may be carried by the soldier; but the strength of the complete cartridge, and its capability of resisting hard usage, must not in the slightest be sacrificed for considerations of weight. The cartridge-case must be of adequate size to enable sufficient powder to be loaded into it to give a high velocity to the bullet. The bullet must be of great density and as non-elastic as possible. Most of the dense metals belong to the group which may be called rare metals, but in the common metal lead we have one which is quite sufficiently dense for our purpose, and is at the same time almost ideal with regard to its inelasticity. We therefore find that, with one exception, the modern military bullet is made of a lead core. The exception is the solid bronze bullet used by the French. We have already seen in Chapter VI. that the increasing velocities brought about by the use of smokeless powders and smaller bores made the use of an unprotected lead bullet impossible. The modern envelope mostly in use is that made of cupro-nickel; but this metal, though from its hardness and capability of resisting rust it is certainly in many respects excellent, is by no means the best material for its purpose.

With cupro-nickel envelopes, particularly in association with nitro-glycerine explosives, metallic fouling of a particularly objectionable sort is one of the greatest troubles with which the user is beset. As velocity is increased, and "time up the barrel" is reduced, the residue left by the passage of the cupro-nickel envelope is very considerably increased, so that there can be no doubt at all that before any change in the design of the present British Service rifle can be made, with the object of getting increased velocities and a flatter trajectory, it will be necessary, particularly if we are to retain cordite as our propellant, that some more satisfactory envelope than the present one of cupro-nickel will have to be devised.

Steel or iron would suggest itself as being an almost ideal substance for envelope purposes. It is cheap, it can easily be worked, it is sufficiently non-elastic for the purpose, and quite sufficiently malleable to take the grooves of the rifling. Iron or steel are, however, open to many objections, the principle, from a Service point of view, being their extreme liability to rust, which liability is only slightly reduced by coating them with wax, an expedient which is not possible in the British Service. The carefully made iron envelope bullets which Sir Charles Ross used for his famous .280 match rifle cartridge, though the dipping of the bullet in wax was undoubtedly given the same care which was expended on all other details of its manufacture, would develop rust spots at the point during one winter, even when stored most carefully in as dry a position as possible. Another objection to the steel or iron envelope bullet is that by using it we have in the bore, whilst the bullet is moving up it, similar metals in close contact under conditions which must develop excessive friction.

There can be little doubt that up to the present the very best combination of metals for envelope purposes is that obtained by coating steel with a very thin layer of nickel. The nickel acts, in effect, as a lubricant, both in protecting the steel from rust and also in preventing the contact of two like

PLATE XXXII

THE RANGE TEST AT 600 YARDS

Ten per cent. of the Service rifles which pass the 100 feet test are shot at 600 yards. Nine out of ten shots must lie within a twenty-four inch circle, or the rifle is rejected

Photo: Clarke & Hyde

METALS FOR BULLET ENVELOPES 151

metals in the barrel. Bullets made on this principle have already been adopted by Germany, whilst Greece, Holland, and Turkey use steel envelopes coated with cupro-nickel. With regard to relative fouling set up by nickel-coated steel and cupro-nickel, match rifle shots had at Bisley last year an admirable chance to experiment. Messrs. Eley's .280 match rifle cartridge had a nickel-coated steel bullet. That provided by the King's Norton Metal Company had a cupro-nickel bullet. Without taking into consideration any other qualities of the cartridge, it may be said that very little practical experience sufficed to prove the great advantage which nickel-plated steel had over cupro-nickel in this respect.

Before leaving the question of the material from which bullets are made, it should be noted that they tend to become more complex with advancing ideas. The adoption of the pointed bullet has led to the frequent inclusion of yet another metal in the bullet, in the shape of a plug of aluminium immediately behind the nose of the envelope, and even extending back almost a third of the length of the bullet.

The charge of the modern military cartridge has had devoted to it an enormous amount of thought during the last few years. Chemists of high technical ability are devoting their whole lives to the elucidation of certain problems which arise both in the course of manufacture and during the use of the propellant. It is necessary that whatever propellant is used it should conform as nearly as possible to an ideal which demands a low maximum pressure, which can be kept up until the moment when the projectile leaves the muzzle, this moment of time coinciding with the consumption of the last atom of the charge. The attainment of such an ideal is, of course, impossible, for no explosive can be so governed in its action as to apply a certain pressure to start the bullet up the bore and then keep that pressure maintained without variation until the bullet leaves the bore. Immediately the bullet starts to move pressure begins to fall, but for a short space the tremendous rush of gases from the burning explosive more than makes up for the increasing space at the disposal of the gases, so that the pressure reaches its maximum within about 1½ in. and 2½ in. from the chamber. This distance varies, of course, with different rifles, but it is usually somewhere about that stated. After the maximum, the pressure falls off very rapidly for 4 or 5 in., and then begins to settle down to a more or less steady push, only decreasing slightly until the bullet is expelled from the muzzle.

There are two or three factors which have to be taken into consideration in loading a cartridge so as to utilise the maximum of its efficiency as regards the pressure of the gases evolved by the burning explosive. The most important is, undoubtedly, the nature and form of the propellant, because by these are very largely governed the speed with which it can be ignited and the speed with which it burns. The strength of the cap affects the rate of ignition; the density of loading, or, in other words, the space occupied by the charge in the cartridge-case, affects the rate of burning. Pressure is also governed to a considerable extent by the resistance offered by the bullet to the propulsive effort of the gases. With regard to the first consideration it may be said that the colloid structure of smokeless powders is a very favourable characteristic. A colloid is a substance which is not permeable by gases, and a colloid substance is directly opposed to the porous one. Colloids burn only on the surface, and therefore their rate of burning can be directly influenced by the surface which is exposed. Two or three fair-sized sticks of cordite, for instance, do not expose nearly so much surface as a bundle of smaller sticks containing exactly the same weight as the two or three bigger ones. The smaller sticks of cordite will thus burn with greater rapidity than the bigger sticks. Again, tubular cordite, such as is now used as the charge for the Mark VII. cartridge, burns both on the outside and on the inside of the stick, the hole down the centre of the stick exposing that much more surface to the action of the flame.

The military cartridge, since it reached the form in which we now know it, has been developed along very definite lines. The ideal military cartridge should be so designed that the bullet flies with a very flat trajectory over a long range, so

THE IDEAL MILITARY CARTRIDGE 153

that the soldier will be able to hit any standing figure up to between 800 and 1,000 yards without altering his sight, aim being taken, of course, in the usual military manner, at the foot of the figure. This ideal is not yet realised, though it is now well within the bounds of possibility. Most military rifles have an extreme range, or "random," of something over 3,000 yards, and all of them, with the exception of the Swiss short rifle, are sighted to well over 2,000 yards. The British rifle is sighted to 2,800 yards, and during the Boer War good practice was made at 2,700 yards on one or two occasions by the defenders of Ladysmith. The United States rifle is sighted up to 2,850 yards.

The length of the complete military cartridge has also to be very carefully considered. If the cartridge is long, it is inconvenient to handle and necessitates a long and weighty magazine. The explosion chamber has also to be lengthened unduly, and the cartridge itself is unhandy both to pack and to use. Modern practice limits the cartridge length to something closely approximating to 3 in. The longest serviceable cartridge in use is the pointed bullet, 1903 Springfield, of the United States, which is 3.329 in. The shortest is the Lebel copper-zinc bullet cartridge of France, which is 2.95 in. long. The British cartridge for the Lee-Enfield, both pointed and round-nosed, is 3.05 in.

The weight of the complete loaded cartridge is in the neighbourhood of 400 grains, the heaviest being the 455-grain cartridge for the Austrian Mannlicher and the lightest, Italy's Carcano-Mannlicher cartridge, which weighs close on 332 grains. It will be seen that the weight of the heaviest cartridge is less than the weight of the bullet used in the Martini-Henry rifle.

Stopping power in a military bullet is, of course, of considerable importance, but it is liable to be sacrificed to a considerable extent to considerations of weight, ranging capabilities and flatness of trajectory.

The capability of a bullet to develop stopping power on impact depends in the main on its velocity and its weight. Of two bullets made of the same material in the same shape, and striking with the same velocity, the weightier would cause the more severe shock, having more energy stored at the moment of impact. But this striking force, as it is called, is not of the first importance in considering the wounding effect of the projectile. In discussing wounding effect in contradistinction to striking energy, one has to have regard principally to the velocity and the shape of the bullet, and the material of which it is made. The size and severity of a wound made by a modern small-bore bullet is, of course, governed considerably by the part of the body which is hit. A round-nosed bullet meeting with little resistance usually penetrates cleanly, the exit orifice always being larger than the point of initial penetration, this being due to the driving forward of tissue, etc., with the bullet.

If the bullet meets with any considerable amount of resistance, such as would result from hitting a bone, what is termed an explosive effect is the result. The bullet itself tends to set up and become deformed, the base moving forward whilst the point is checked. The moving bullet thus becomes larger, the bone or resisting tissue is driven forward in short, splintered masses and the wound of exit is very considerably larger than the wound of entrance.

In the later months of 1914 considerable outcry was made in the Press of the belligerent countries as to the use of "explosive" bullets by the combatants. There can be little doubt that these reports were the result of ignorance of the effect of high-velocity bullets striking living tissue and bone. Big game hunters have long been aware that high-velocity bullets fired into a living body at close range have a tendency to fly to pieces, or "explode" within the body, making wounds of a ghastly character. It is very difficult to get any exact data with regard to the range at which this description ceases with military bullets, but since it presumably depends on velocity, as well as resistance, it would vary for each type of bullet used.

Given equal velocities, there is no reason to reject Sir Victor Horsley's dictum that "the destructive effects vary directly as the viscosity of the body," or, in simpler words,

PLATE XXXIII

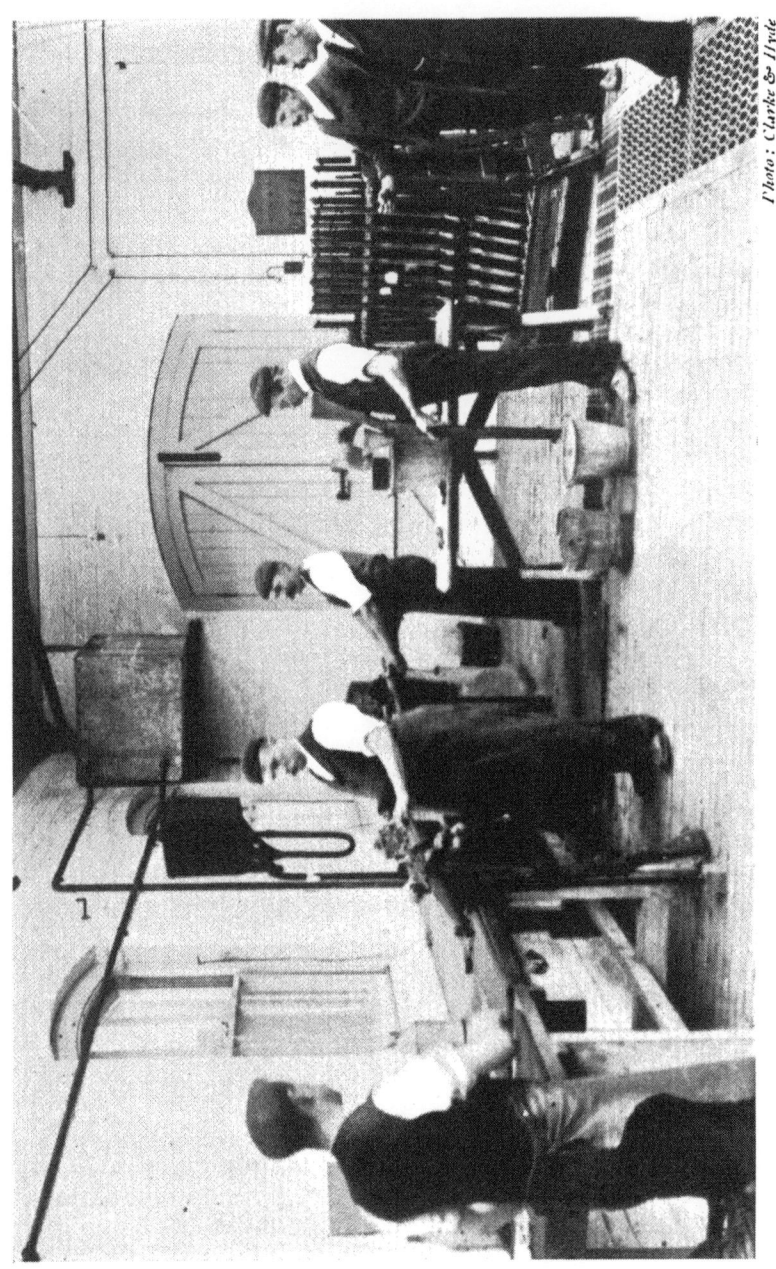

Photo: Clarke & Hyde

WASHING AND CLEANING AFTER TESTING

Once a rifle has had a charge of nitro-powder through it, it is never safe from its great enemy, rust. After testing at the works the barrels are subjected to a very thorough cleansing and oiling

WOUNDING EFFECTS OF BULLETS

the more water-filled the tissues struck, the more will be the destruction wrought. But wounds in warfare are not given and received in circumstances that make for cool, scientific analysis, and when the wounded man comes under the care of the surgeon, all chance of determining the probable velocity of the bullet which made the wound has been lost. It is, of course, likely that in the trench warfare which is going on at the time of writing, a definite idea as to the range at which the wounding projectile struck can be formed. If any attempt has been made to associate such information with definite cases, we shall have some very definite and interesting particulars to work on when the surgeons can stay their work of repairing the wreckage of war, and collate the information they have derived from their experiences. It should be remembered, however, that the work of the surgeon does not interest him so much in how the wound was delivered, but in the best way to repair the damage done. Descriptions of wounds and details as to their treatment are of no use to the ballistician, unless to knowledge of the resisting powers or viscosity of the part struck he can add definite details as to the shape of the bullet and the velocity at which it was travelling.

There is now little reason to doubt that at certain velocities the pointed bullet behaves on striking tissue in a way that tends to the formation of more severe wounds than those given by the blunt-nosed variety. A bullet is spun, as we know, to keep it travelling point first in the air, and the spin is arranged with regard to the fact that air is the medium through which it is travelling. If the medium were water the bullet would have to be given a much accelerated spin, and if the medium is tissue the acceleration must be proportionately greater, varying as the density of the medium through which it has to travel. Now the pointed bullet has its centre of gravity well back towards the base, so that when anything happens to reduce its gyroscopic stability, such as translation into a much more dense medium, the base of the bullet tends to overtake the point, and the bullet travels sideways. This "keyholing," as the target-shot calls it, is bound to result in a much more severe wound than when the bullet travels point first. It is probable that the path of a pointed bullet can be divided into three distinct zones. First, that in which disruptive or explosive effect is to be expected; second, that in which it is travelling at such a speed that, though it does not "explode," it goes through the tissues with little or only slight "keyholing"; and, third, when its velocity is so diminished that it cannot overcome the resistance of the tissues before they have so checked the spin as to cause the bullet to completely lose its gyroscopic stability. Of course, as in all other considerations of the wounding effect of bullets, the resistance which the bullet meets would have a great effect in determining the precise point in its flight at which these distinct performances will take place.

The most remarkable improvement which has taken place during recent years has been brought about by the adoption of the pointed bullet. Just as most other improvements in rifle-shooting were discovered years before they were adopted, and were dropped from some cause or another whilst experimenters tried to find a solution for their difficulties in other directions, so the pointed bullet, in very much the same form as we know it now, was used many years before its virtues became apparent.

In the recently published "History of the National Rifle Association" (Humphry and Fremantle, 1914), the following interesting paragraph occurs, which shows not only how early the pointed bullet came on the scene, but also the origin of the shape of head which was adopted by nearly all nations for their military bullet, and which came to be known as the "Metford" shape. The paragraph occurs in the account of the 1907 meeting at Bisley, and reads as follows:

"It is only by chance that the merits of the pointed bullet were not developed thirty years before. In 1877 some of the American team were using pointed bullets of nearly the same shape" (as those which were used at Bisley in 1907) "in the match for the Palma Trophy at Creedmoor, and one Remington rifle with American pointed bullets was obtained by one of the British team of that year, and successfully used by him

EARLY POINTED BULLETS

in 1878 in England. He induced Mr. Metford, with whom he was on a visit to Sir Henry Halford at Wistow, to consider whether there might not be some advantage in the American shape of the fore part of the bullet; and Mr. Metford took the view that the advantage lay in the general slope of the shoulder, rather than in the actual sharpness of the point of the bullet, having in mind the effect of a gradual wedging action in pushing through and thrusting aside the resisting volume of air. He therefore made experimental bullets by taking a set which were of rather greater weight, putting them on a lathe, and reducing the shape of the fore part of the bullet, then always of a very blunt pattern, so as to bring the weight down to that of his ordinary bullets, and the shape to that of the American bullet, except that the nose of the bullet was not brought to a fine point, but was moderately flat—a point which Mr. Metford regarded as of little importance as regards loss of velocity, and of some importance for convenience of manufacture. With this altered bullet he got at 1,000 yards an advantage of about six minutes in the angle of elevation over the pattern hitherto in use, and the new pattern thus obtained became the accepted pattern for match rifle bullets, and subsequently for military bullets. The sharp point was not tried by him; but though it would no doubt have shown some further advantage, it was easily liable to deformation, military bullets being still made of alloyed lead. Nor could even a proportionate advantage from such an alteration in shape be gained by projectiles moving at 1,300 to 1,500 feet per second (as was then the case), as against this modern military bullet, with its velocity of 2,500 to 3,000 ft. per second."

Of course, pointed bullets had been made and used before 1877 (General Jacob's, for instance), but as they were associated with a length little greater than their calibre, and with low velocities, they cannot be regarded as direct parents of the modern shape.

The virtues of the pointed bullet might have been discovered, again in this country, at a date when they could have been put to some practical use. About 1895 experiments with reduced charge or "gallery ammunition" were being carried out at Woolwich, and one of the cartridges experimented with was given a bullet with a very pointed nose. It showed no advantage, as was to be expected, with the low velocity used for short-range work and was abandoned. But what might have happened had any one connected with those experiments taken the trouble to load such a shaped bullet into a service case, and taken it to a longer range with the service charge?

To understand the advantages of a pointed shape in bullet construction we must consider very briefly the conditions which govern the passage of a projectile through the air. If the projectile could proceed on its path uninfluenced by terrestrial gravitation, and if it were, at the same time, travelling in a vacuum, it would continue on its path with its axis coincident with the axis of the rifle to infinity. Its trajectory would be a straight line, and the sighting of the rifle would be "point blank" for any range. The rifle and projectile manufacturers combine their efforts to approximate as closely as possible to this ideal of a straight-line trajectory. The best they can do, however, only results in flattening the trajectory curve. In practice the flight of the bullet is always influenced by the action of gravity and the resistance of the air, and no portion of the path of the bullet can be a straight line.

Terrestrial gravitation begins to pull the bullet towards the earth immediately it is unsupported—that is to say, immediately it leaves the muzzle of the rifle. The effect of the gravity pull on the path of the bullet can be readily appreciated by studying the two diagrams on page 159 (Figs. 27 and 28). In Fig. 27 the right line M B represents the path of an unimpeded bullet, the time taken to pass from M to B being n seconds. But gravity acts with a constant force, the effect of which can be calculated by means of the formula

$$h = \frac{1}{2} gt^2$$

where h represents the vertical drop of the bullet; $g = 32$ (the value of acceleration of drop due to gravity—i.e. 32 f.s. per second), and t is the time of flight in seconds over the range M R. If we suppose that in $n - x$ seconds the projectile would

PLATE XXXIV

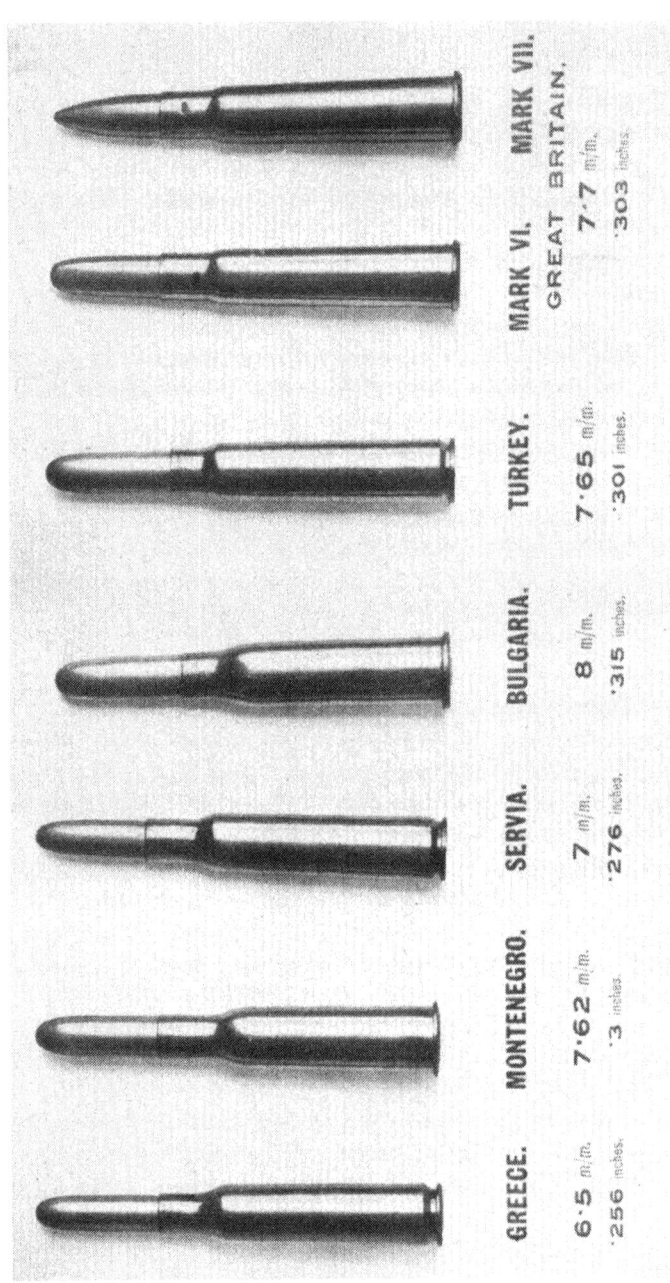

TYPES OF CARTRIDGES USED IN THE BALKAN WAR COMPARED WITH BRITISH CARTRIDGES

TERRESTRIAL GRAVITATION 159

have travelled to A, then we can place its actual position at H, because in $n - x$ seconds it would have fallen to H. Similarly in n seconds the bullet would have fallen from B to R.

Now we will consider Fig. 28. Suppose a bullet will travel to A_1 in x seconds if it is unimpeded in its flight. In the same

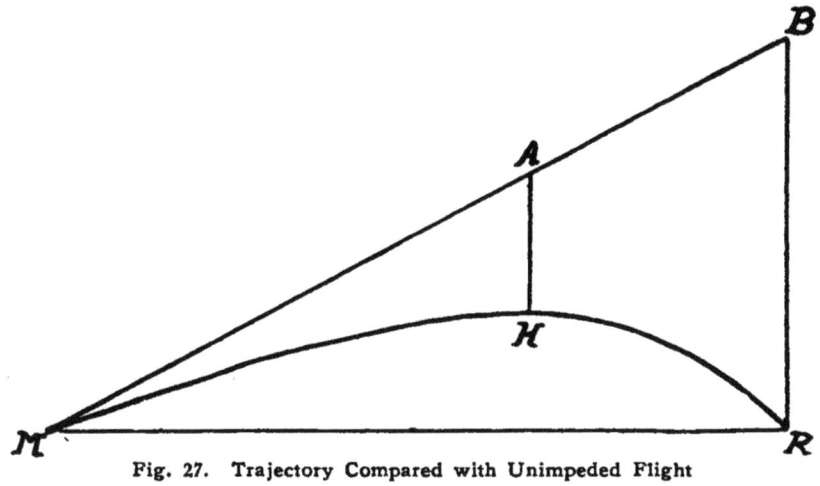

Fig. 27. Trajectory Compared with Unimpeded Flight

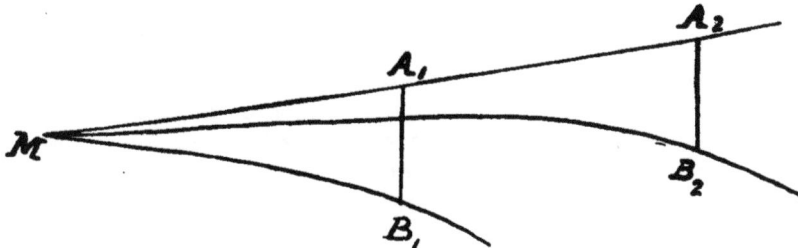

Fig. 28.—Flatness of Trajectory due to Speed

time it will drop to B_1. Another bullet which can overcome air resistance better will travel to A_2 in x seconds, and since the pulling force gravity is constant, the drop of the two bullets in the same time will be through the same space

$$(A_1 - B_1 = A_2 - B_2).$$

From this it is clear that since in a given time a bullet will fall through a measure of space which bears an exact and fixed relation to the time of flight, the problem before the ballistician is to project his bullet to the greatest possible distance in the least possible time.

It is demonstrable that a bullet projected to infinity in zero time would follow a path coincident with its axis of projection, and the path would coincide with the path the same bullet would follow if it were unimpeded by gravitation and air resistance.

Now let us consider the effect of the resistance of the air on the flight of the bullet. It is well known that if there were no air resistance to be overcome, and the bullet was influenced once it left the muzzle solely by terrestrial gravitation, its flight would be a parabola, the vertex or maximum ordinate of which would be at a point equidistant from the beginning and end of the flight. It would also follow that the ascending and descending branches of the trajectory would be equal, the angle of projection and the angle of descent would be equal, and the initial and final velocity would be equal.

Once the resistance of the air is taken into account, all the mathematical balance of the parabolic curve is destroyed. In the first place, the bullet loses velocity during the whole of its flight. For instance, the .280 Match cartridge gives the 186-grain bullet an initial velocity of 2,760 f.s. The remaining velocity at 1,200 yards is only 1,250 f.s. Over 1,200 yards with that cartridge there is a loss of 1,510 f.s. of velocity in a time of flight of 1.97 seconds. An angle of elevation that would give the bullet a range of 1,500 yards *in vacuo* would only result in a range of 875 yards in air (see the nomograph of rifle elevation facing page 168.). The difference is just over 40 per cent., and the percentage difference increases with an increase of range.

The resistance of the air is then a factor of the utmost importance in determining the space through which a bullet can be projected in a given time. Air resistance operates to continually take from the bullet its stored-up energy, which, if there were no air resistance to be overcome, might be employed in covering space. Owing to air resistance the velocity constantly decreases, whilst the distance fallen is always increasing; it follows that the curve of the trajectory constantly

THE FLIGHT OF A BULLET

increases. The angle of descent is greater than the angle of projection, and the vertex is not in the centre of the trajectory, but nearer the first graze.

It will be observed that the way to get a flatter trajectory is to reduce the time of flight over a given range. The initial velocity cannot be increased very much with the old-shaped bullet, because the effect of recoil on the shoulder has to be considered. What has to be done is to provide a bullet which will not have to waste so much of its stored energy in overcoming air resistance.

The recent photographs of bullets in flight which are published in this volume (Plates XXXIX. and XL.) were obtained by the method devised by Dr. Ernst Mach, of Prague, and subsequently used and improved by Boys, Doyle, and others. In its flight the bullet is made to touch certain wires, and discharge an electric spark which illuminates the projectile. At the same time the lines of different air tension caused by the passage of the bullet are photographed. A reference to Plate XXXIX. (Fig. 1) will enable the characteristic phenomena recorded by such photographs to be recognised. The bullet photographed is of the ordinary blunt-nosed type. The heavy bow wave and the lighter stern wave are beautifully shown, as is the rarefied air area and the trail of eddies in the wake of the bullet. Between the bow and stern waves can be seen the lesser waves caused by the shoulder of the bullet. On the same plate (Fig. 2) will be seen a photograph of a pointed bullet in flight. It will be noticed that the point of the bullet is well through the bow wave, the angle of the wave is much more acute, because of the extra velocity of the pointed bullet. Professor Boys' photographs (Plates XXXVII. and XXXVIII.) should be compared with those on Plate XL. showing a pointed bullet in flight.

A bullet with a very blunt nose pushes some of the air in front of it, just as do the bullets fired base first and shown on Plate XL. Such a blunt-ended bow wave indicates high air resistance on the bullet.

It is impossible to write a history of the pointed bullet without referring to Captain J. H. Hardcastle, the inventor of the "Swift" bullet, who was very largely instrumental in getting the pointed bullet experimented with and adopted in this country. Captain Hardcastle's monograph on "Pointed Bullets," printed in No. 9 of Vol. XXXIV. of the *Journal of the Royal Artillery*, is a most fascinating explanation of the virtues of the pointed shape, and an illuminating history of the bullet after its sensational appearance in match rifle shooting in 1907.

"The advantages of the new shape, in practice, are two, although both arise from the same cause," says Captain Hardcastle. "The lengthening of the point is the cause, and its efficiency is derived from the reduction of the resistance of the air. At 2,400 f.s. the resistance of the air to a projectile of 1-in. calibre with an ogival head of $1\frac{1}{2}$ diameters radius is $25\frac{1}{2}$ lb. If the head is of Metford shape the resistance falls to 20 lb., but with the new point the resistance is about 14 lb., or barely half of the old standard shape used by Bashforth, which is still very common in the projectiles of modern heavy ordnance. In consequence of this reduction, the two benefits appear in practice. (1) The ballistic co-efficient is increased, with all attendant advantages; and (2) the wind loses its resisting effect in proportion as the ballistic co-efficient is raised. It is the latter benefit which commends itself so strongly to target shots, whereas the former is most useful for military purposes."

If lengthening the point is the cause of so much added efficiency, it is reasonable to ask why the point should not be lengthened still more than it is. The answer is that the limit of the taper of the point is set by mechanical considerations. The bullet must not be liable to deformation, nor must it have its centre of gravity so far back that the twist of the rifling necessary to give it gyroscopic stability is excessively severe. The danger with a bullet which is so designed that its point is very long is that the bullet will turn in its flight so as to travel base foremost, and thus have its centre of gravity in a more favourable position. The French Balle D. presents an interesting study in this regard. The point is long, and one would naturally expect trouble in keeping the bullet point foremost. As a matter of fact, the slight taper of the base,

PLATE XXXV

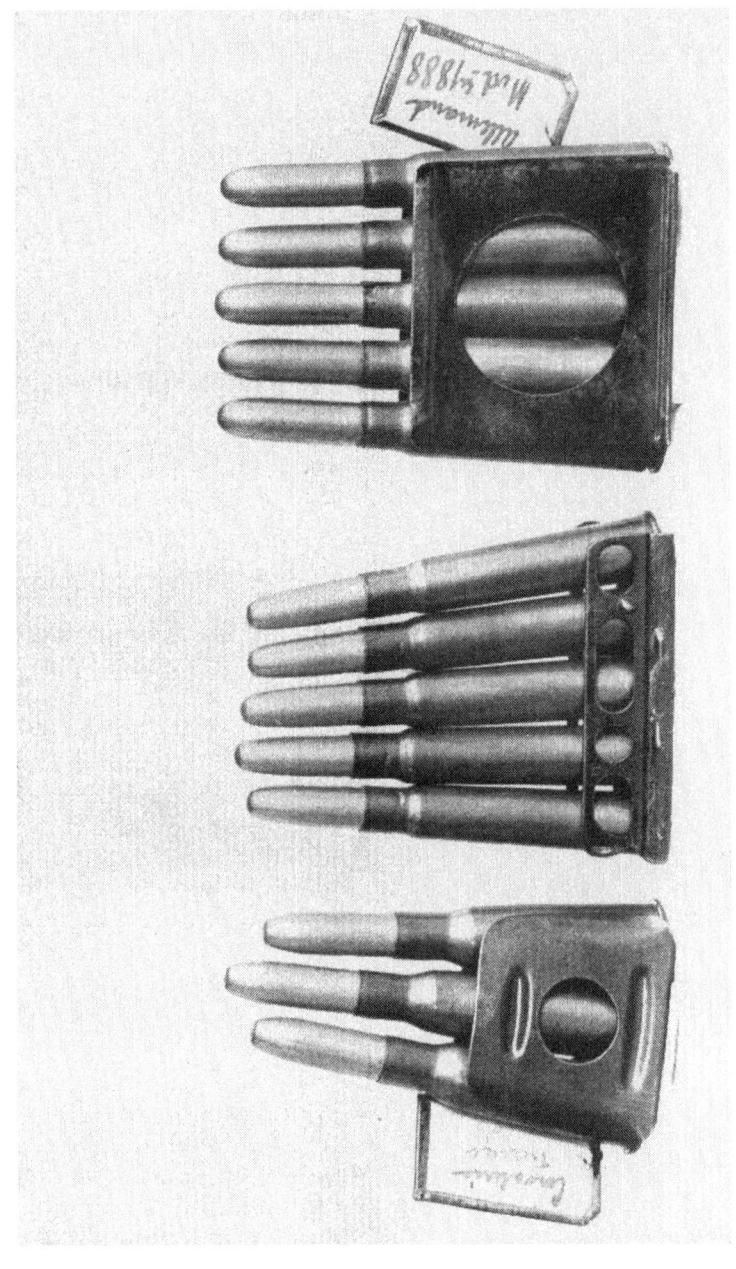

THREE TYPES OF CHARGERS

On the left is the Lebel carbine charger, with the old cartridge. In the centre is the British charger with Mark VI. cartridge. On the right is the first type of charger used in the German army

POINTED BULLETS

though it is not sufficient to affect the rarefied air area when in flight, is yet sufficient to throw the centre of gravity further forward and materially assist the balance of the bullet.

Modern projectiles can be divided in rough and ready manner into two main classes: (1) light bullets designed for a high velocity; (2) heavier bullets designed for a medium velocity. In an article in *Streffleur's Militarische Zeitschrift* for April, 1914, it is suggested that the first of these classes should consist of light projectiles weighing about 150 grains, and characterised by a high muzzle velocity of over 2,600 f.s. Such bullets have a very flat trajectory at the beginning, but because of their small mass lose their velocity, and consequently their flatness of trajectory, comparatively quickly. The second class of projectile weighs in the region of 180 grains, has a velocity of less than 2,600 f.s., and as a consequence the trajectory is not so flat at the beginning. Such bullets, however, lose their velocity far less rapidly than the lighter bullets of the first class, and their trajectories at the longer ranges are considerably flatter. The German Spitzer bullet is a typical example of the first class, and the French Balle D. a typical example of the second class. Match rifle cartridges such as the .280, with 186-grain bullet and 2,700 f.s. velocity, and the .30 Remington U.M.C. match cartridge, with 180-grain bullet and 2,700 f.s. initial velocity, obviously come into a separate class which may be catalogued as experimental target bullets. In order to give a high initial velocity to a heavy bullet, a big charge, with its attendant military disadvantages, must be used.

Bashforth knew and maintained that the shape of the head of a projectile played an important part in determining the air resistance, but despite this many authorities disagreed, and it was not until about 1890 that there was a general acceptance of the fact that the form of the bullet can influence air resistance. The honour of having first adopted a pointed bullet is undoubtedly due to the French, for they were experimenting with the forerunner of the Balle D. as early as 1889, and Captain Hardcastle has in his possession a Balle D. which apparently bears the date 1902. Between 1900 and 1902 the German experiments began, and resulted in 1904 in the production of the "S." or Spitzer bullet for the 7.9 mm. Mauser rifle. It was this bullet with its 154-grain weight and 2,800 f.s. initial velocity which first drew the attention of a very large number of experimenters to the virtues of the pointed shape. Captain Hardcastle says of the account of the bullet which appeared in *Kreigstechnische Zeitschrift* in the autumn of 1905: "When I read this article and examined the figures I perceived that either a deliberate hoax had been perpetrated, or else that something new and of the utmost importance had been discovered, and I reported accordingly, mentally deciding to get direct experimental evidence before taking action."

Other keen ballisticians had also decided to get direct experimental evidence of the figures published in Germany, and in 1906 there were several firms in England who were working with the pointed shape with a view of submitting them at the competitive trials which the War Office were carrying out. The Deutsche Waffen und Munition Fabrik, of Berlin, patented their pointed bullets in Germany in 1904, and in February, 1905, in England.

As has already been pointed out, a very important improvement which the high velocity of the pointed bullet gave it was the decreased liability to deflection by the wind. Captain Hardcastle, who had been studying ballistics under Professor Greenhill, was in a very favourable position to realise accurately the great advantage which the new shape gave in this direction, and when he designed the Swift bullet, which was manufactured by Messrs. Kynoch, it was the resistance to wind deflection which the new shape gave which he had particularly in his mind. His own extremely modest description of what he did is as follows:

"I took the heaviest bullet used in the .303 and put on to it the best point that I could hear of, and used the heaviest pressure that was safe. By so doing I got the shortest 'time up the barrel' and the greatest ballistic co-efficient, and so obtained the greatest vertical accuracy by considering the vibrations, and the greatest horizontal accuracy by eliminating the wind deviation as much as possible. That my reasoning was correct is proved by the result."

Plate XXXVI

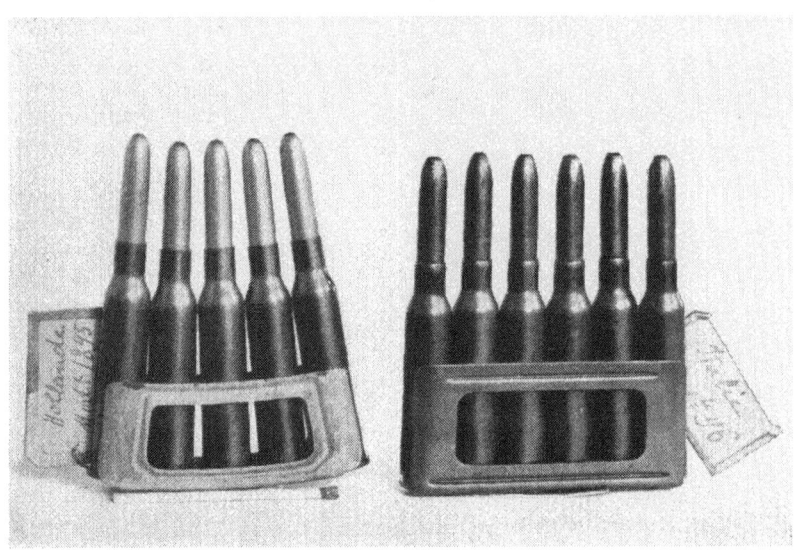

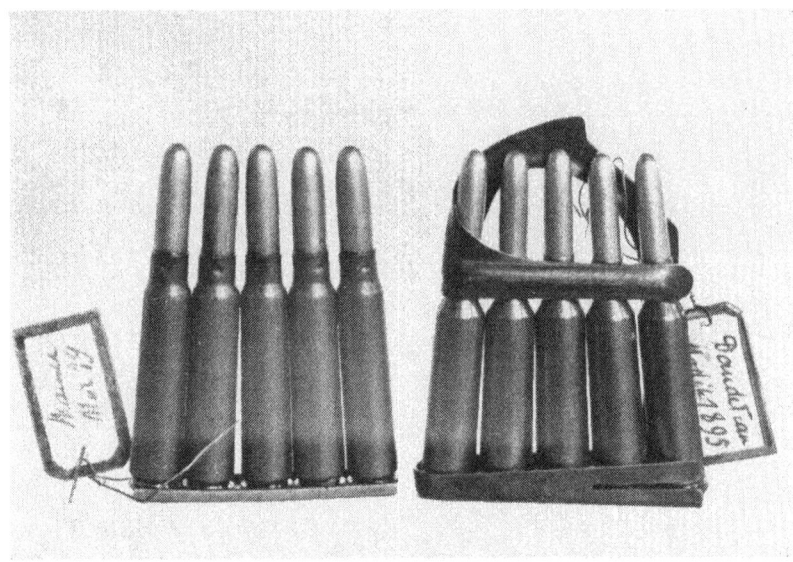

TYPES OF CLIPS AND CHARGERS

In the top picture on the left is the clip of the Dutch Mannlicher, and on the right is the six-cartridge Italian clip. The bottom picture shows the German blunt-nosed bullet cartridge in charger, and on the right the Portuguese Mauser

THE MARK VII

The results which Captain Hardcastle speaks of were truly remarkable. The Swift bullet made its first public appearance on May 29th, 1907, when it was shot on the first day of the English VIII. Club meeting, and took the first prize with a score of 135 out of 150 at 800, 900, and 1,000 yards. A very strong right wind was blowing. The next best score was 129, and the result is all the more remarkable when it is considered that a tyro was the first prize winner, and of course, it being the English VIII. Club meeting, he was shooting against many of the best men in the country. Naturally, after so sensational a win, the bullet was much talked about, and in the Scottish meeting a little later in the year a world's record at 800, 900, and 1,000 yards was made by Mr. Caldwell with 223 out of 225, using the Swift bullet. Another triumph for Captain Hardcastle's projectile was the Irish VIII. meeting, where the shooting took place in a very fierce wind, and his bullet won easily. By the time the Cambridge Cup Competitions were shot towards the end of June in 1907, more than half the competitors were using the Swift bullet, and the result of the Cambridge Cup, which was another triumph for the bullet, together with what had gone before, effectually finished off the career of the Metford nose as far as match rifle shooting was concerned.

The Bisley Meeting which started on July 8th saw practically every match rifle-shot using the new shape bullet, which in a couple of months had superseded the design which had been used with success for more than twenty years.

As regards military bullets, the pointed shape cannot be said to have come yet into general use. France and Germany, the first two to adopt it, have been using it with considerable success for some years. Great Britain has also used it during the last year or two and found it most effective. The British Mark VII. bullet is of cupro-nickel with a hard lead core and an aluminium plug under the nose. It weighs 174 grains, and is given an initial velocity of 2,440 f.s. by a charge of tubular modified cordite. The only other pointed bullets in use are those of the U.S.A., Japan, and Brazil. The U.S.A. .30 bullet, like the bullet of Germany, belongs to the light type of pro-

RIFLES AND AMMUNITION

jectile with a comparatively high initial velocity. The weight is 150 grains, and the initial velocity 2,700 f.s. The Japanese bullet is 140 grains in weight, and is given an initial velocity of 2,500 f.s. The new Brazilian bullet is undoubtedly the most effective of all the light weight, high velocity bullets yet turned out. The sample bullet sent over to this country in the beginning of 1914 by the Deutsche Waffen und Munition Fabrik Aktiengesellschaft had a bullet of nominally 154 grains, and the result of weighing a dozen samples showed an average of almost exactly that weight. The initial velocity claimed by the manufacturers was 2,920 f.s., and the ballistic co-efficient .54. From these it was estimated that the

Time of Flight over

25 yds.	900 yds.	1000 yds.	1100 yds.	1200 yds.
= .003090 secs.	1.268 secs.	1.467 secs.	1.680 secs.	1.912 secs.

Elevation (in minutes of angle) for

	200 yds.	900 yds.	1000 yds.	1100 yds.	1200 yds.
Minutes of angle	4.5'	27'	32'	37'	48'

As a matter of fact, after a true zero had been taken at 25 yards and all necessary allowances had been made, the backsight elevation found necessary at 1,000 yards was 38 minutes of angle, which premises an n value of about .6 and a C of .47. The average wind force during the tests was between twelve miles per hour and sixteen miles per hour, with occasional stronger puffs. The angle was between 75 degrees and 50 degrees. According to a wind chart estimated from the figures supplied by the manufacturers, necessary corrections would be between 6 and 9 minutes of angle. Allowing for the drift of 2 minutes to the right, the corrections were found to be between 6 and 10 minutes of angle. The manufacturers claimed a 27-inch group at 1,000 metres (1,094 yards), but the shooting at Bisley failed to give a better group than 36 inches at 1,100 yards, and 27 inches at 1,000 yards. In any case these groups are excellent for a military cartridge, and the time of flight undoubtedly compares most favourably with that of match rifle cartridges, the resulting trajectory being better—i.e. flatter—than that of any other military cartridge in

THE CARTRIDGE OF THE FUTURE 167

existence. We have described this bullet and its performances at some length because it is the latest effort of the premier German ammunition manufacturing company.

With regard to the bullet of the future, it can be said without fear of contradiction that finality has not yet been reached. One direction of improvement which is obvious to anyone who considers the various types of military bullet now in use is a further reduction in calibre, the aim being to increase velocity and so flatten trajectory without the attendant disadvantage of excessive recoil. The advantages offered by a reduction in rifle calibre are so many and the disadvantages so few, it would seem certain that a very few years will bring many changes. A small calibre rifle can be made lighter than a large calibre arm, an advantage of importance to the soldier. His cartridge supply can be increased without adding to his burden. The nervous shock attending the firing of a number of shots rapidly would be materially decreased by the use of a small calibre light-recoil rifle. Add to these the increased steadiness in shooting due to the small disturbance of aim in a rifle of light recoil, the increase in the "point-blank" range due to the flatter trajectory, the great saving of raw materials in manufacture, and other minor advantages, and we have put forth a strong case for the small calibre military rifle. Many experiments have been carried out in America with small-bore rifles for sporting purposes, notably of .22 calibre, and although developments have not got beyond the sporting stage, enough has been seen to indicate considerable possibility from the military standpoint. At present a bullet of 150 grains weight represents the most advanced military thought. The trend of present-day experiment seems to indicate that at no distant date bullet weights will drop to 100 grains or even less. Without some radical change in propellants there would seem to be no other method of obtaining increased velocities, keeping in mind the military necessity for limitation of recoil.

It is, of course, possible that future developments in warfare may be in such a direction that the rifle is ousted by the machine gun and automatic rifle. In that case it is probable that the actual weight of the cartridge and severity of recoil may not be of such importance as they are at present, for the man who carries the automatic rifle or who is No. 1 of the machine gun section would not have to carry his own cartridges, but would have them supplied to him by bearers or wagons; also, the automatic rifle absorbs some of its recoil. This, however, is mere speculation, and as long as the arm of the individual soldier is the rifle, both weight of cartridge and recoil must be the primary consideration in cartridge design.

The accompanying nomograph for rifle elevations is a most ingenious contrivance, for which we are again under obligation to Captain Hardcastle. It is included here because it is likely to be of interest to the reader who is comparing the potentialities of various bullets.

As will be seen from the directions printed upon it, its primary use is to give the angle of elevation necessary for any rifle projectile of which the muzzle velocity is known.

The angle of elevation, as has been explained elsewhere in this work, is simply the angle at which it is necessary to point the barrel above the object to allow for the action of gravity. The amount which the bullet will drop is governed by the time of its flight, and this in turn depends on (a) the initial velocity and (b) the ability of the bullet to maintain this velocity, or, in other words, to overcome the resistance of the air. The reader will at once see that this last quality has a most vital bearing on the time of flight, and therefore on elevation; and it was, in fact, to obtain this property in a bullet technically known as the ballistic co-efficient that the spherical ball was abandoned in favour of an elongated projectile.

The air-resisting qualities of a projectile depend upon (a) its weight in proportion to the area exposed to the direct resistance of the air, and (b) the shape of its nose and shoulder.

With a given charge of propellant, the heavier the projectile the lower will be its initial velocity. Hence a gain in air-resisting quality is either greatly modified, or is completely negatived by loss in velocity unless the powder charge is increased, and this is distinctly limited owing to considerations of rifle weight and recoil.

PLATE XXXVII

Photo: "Navy and Army Illustrated"

A BRITISH SERVICE BULLET IN FLIGHT

This is one of the famous photographs of bullets in flight taken by Professor C. V. Boyes, F.R.S. The double stern wave should be noted—one proceeds from the cannelure, and the other from the end of the rarefied air area

RIFLE ELEVATIONS

All cartridge improvements, therefore, aim at providing a high velocity with a high ballistic co-efficient, or at providing one of these features without sacrificing too much of the other. The method of calculating the ballistic co-efficient of a projectile is stated elsewhere in this book.

A first consideration of the problem to provide a scale or device for calculating the elevations of all rifles, with their hundred and one different sized bullets and different velocities, made it seem impossible of accomplishment. A close study of Captain Hardcastle's nomograph will show the ingenious manner in which he has solved it.

First of all, there is a perpendicular line running down the middle of the page called the Reference line, which is introduced to establish the particular relation of muzzle velocity and ballistic co-efficient applicable to the projectile for which the elevation is required. The scales for muzzle velocity and "C" or ballistic co-efficient are set on either side of the reference line, and a straight edge joining the appropriate figures will indicate the reference point on the reference line.

Having marked the reference point of the particular bullet, turn now to the range scale on the right. Five perpendicular lines are given, the outside one being applicable only to bullets having a ballistic co-efficient of .35, the inside one to bullets having a ballistic co-efficient of .75, and the intermediate lines to bullets having respectively the figures of merit shown at the foot of the range scale.

The five perpendicular lines are divided off into range scales by a series of radiating lines, marked with their respective distances, the intersections of the radiating lines with the perpendicular lines forming the range scale of each line respectively. So that when dealing with a bullet which has a ballistic co-efficient of, say, .5, the range line marked 0.5 is the only one to be referred to.

A straight line drawn from any point on the appropriate range line through the reference point to the elevation scale on the left will show the angle of elevation necessary for the range.

It need hardly be stated that where the elevation for one

170 RIFLES AND AMMUNITION

distance is known, a reversal of the process mentioned will show the muzzle velocity.

There is a method of finding out the ballistic co-efficient from the nomograph, given the elevation for one range and the muzzle velocity, as follows:

Insert a pin through the elevation line at the known elevation, and another pin through the velocity line at the known velocity. Take two lengths of black thread, each a foot long, looped at one end. Pass one loop round each pin, and pull the threads taut across the face of the sheet. The elevation thread is now stretched across to the appropriate radiating range line and it intersects the reference line at some point. Now stretch the velocity thread across the reference line at the same point—to the "C" line—and read the ballistic co-efficient. Compare this figure with the intersection of the other thread on the radiating range line, and see if they agree. If not, move the threads until the figures for "C" agree, bearing in mind that both threads must intersect the reference line at the same point.

The MV and the sectional density $\left(\frac{w}{d^2}\right)$ of most military bullets can be found in "The Text-book of Small Arms." For convenience in reference a few are given in the table below. To use the nomograph $\frac{w}{d^2}$ must be converted into C by the formula $\frac{w}{nd^2}$. The value of n can be conveniently taken as stated in the sheet on which the nomograph is printed.

TABLE OF MV AND $\frac{w}{d^2}$

	Shape of nose	MV	$\frac{w}{d^2}$
British	round	2060	.3205
"	pointed	2440	.251
German	round	2093	.322
"	pointed	2882	.2115
French	pointed	2380	.276
Belgian	round	1968	.325
Russian	round	1985	.324
Japanese	pointed	2500	.289
United States	pointed	2600	.238
Austrian	round	2034	.334

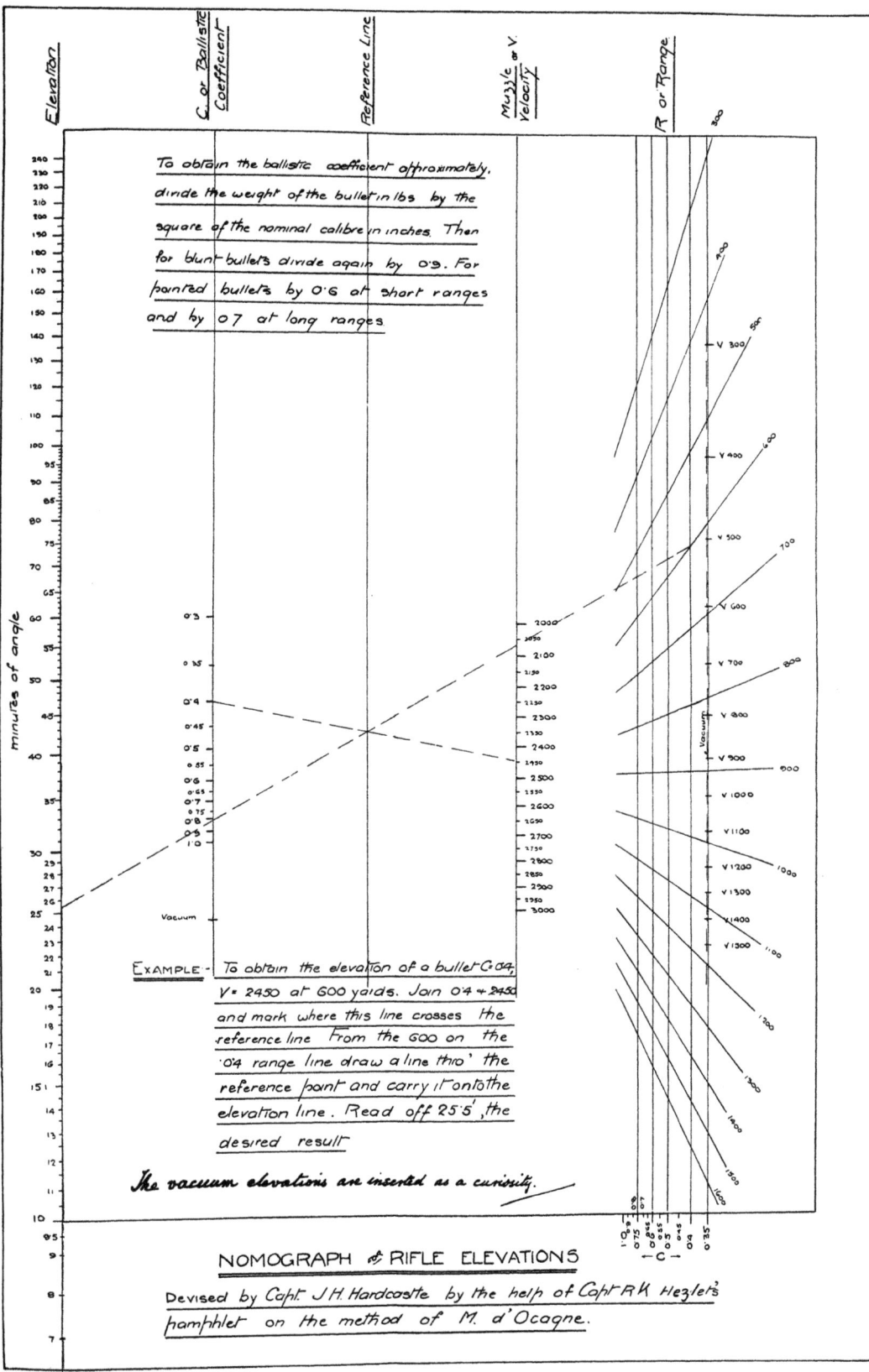

CHAPTER IX

The Sporting Rifle—Its History and Development

THE divergence of military ideals in small arms from those of the sportsman, and the concentration of effort on perfecting the rifle for war purposes, have led to the evolution of a class of rifle particularly adapted to the killing of game, and differing in many respects from the military weapon.

In the early days of rifle development, as has already been pointed out, the sporting rifle led the way. Most of the improvements were made on behalf of game-hunting users. The extra time and trouble taken in loading a muzzle-loader were of little moment to the sportsman, but the accuracy of the rifle was a great consideration. He used a double-barrelled weapon, finished to perfection by workmen who were artists. His rifle represented the utmost skill of the gunmaker of his day. On the Continent of Europe there was an early disposition to specialise rifles for target shooting as distinct from game and military shooting, which specialisation grew more distinct with the advance of knowledge and skill on the part of rifle users.

In the years between 1820 and 1850 British gunmakers were beginning to acquire that reputation for turning out high-grade sporting rifles which has never since left them. The British love of sport, particularly sport with some danger in it, together with the unique opportunities afforded by our world-wide Empire, led to a growing taste for big-game shooting. The American backwoodsman, who had usually to deal with smaller game, and always had to be economical of his lead, developed the "Kentucky" small-bore rifle. The British gunmaker, knowing that as a rule his customers did not have to carry their own rifles and ammunition all day, and that they frequently had to deal with beasts which would kill if they were not killed, made large-bore weapons to fire a heavy ball. The "Kentucky" or "pea" rifles have developed into "rook and rabbit rifles" and the "miniature" .220 target rifle, whilst the large-bore rifles have developed along lines appropriate to their purpose. Between the two are many varieties and calibres for special kinds of sport.

The great fault with sporting rifles in the early part of the nineteenth century was that the trajectory was very curved even over such a short distance as 150 yards. The energy of the bullet when it struck was not great, so that it suffered both in penetration and in stopping power. The need was felt for a rifle that was capable of firing a bullet with a higher velocity and a flatter trajectory, so that within a reasonable range aim could be taken at game without altering the sight elevation.

About the time when Delvigne was coming to the conclusion that in the conical bullet lay the only hope for the military rifle, Sir Samuel Baker, the well-known game-shot, began to experiment with the idea of firing a heavy charge behind a fairly heavy load, and so getting a high velocity and good striking force and penetration, with as flat a trajectory as possible over sporting ranges.

The rifle he designed was no weapon for the lone hunter, for it weighed over 20 lb. The ball, which was round and flanged like the Brunswick ball, weighed 3 oz., and the charge was 16 drams of black powder. The Bristol gunmaker, Mr. Gibbs, a name still known and honoured, made the rifle, and Sir Samuel Baker shot elephants with it in 1841. This rifle was the muzzle-loading prototype of the black powder "Express."

The Brunswick rifle was adopted by the British army in 1836, and as has been told it was far from being a success; but the flanged ball and deep grooves provided, as Sir Samuel Baker had seen, a ready means of getting over the stripping of the bullet which took place with distressing frequency when a heavy charge was used and sufficient twist was given to the rifling to rotate the bullet with enough rapidity to give it gyroscopic stability.

Baker's sporting rifle attained some considerable notoriety, and when, in 1853 or 1854, a demand arose for a rifle which could be used with success for big-game shooting in South Africa, several makers—Purdey, Gibbs, and Greener among them—reverted to Sir Samuel Baker's adaptation of the Brunswick, but used a conical bullet with two flanges on it. It should be remarked that about this very time General Jacob was perfecting his four-flanged bullet and rifle in India; his rifle, though primarily designed for military purposes, was at that time an almost ideal big-game weapon. In 1856, Purdey built to the order of two well-known big-game shots rifles on the two-groove pattern, constructing them to fire a big charge of powder. He called the type the "Express Train" because of the large initial velocity, and because the express train at that time had taken the popular imagination. That was the origin of the word "express" used to denote a rifle with a high initial velocity and flat trajectory over sporting ranges.

Once the express type had been developed there came further divergencies. The ideal of the manufacturer was to get a rifle that would shoot "point blank" up to, say, 150 yards. Conveniently ignoring the known effects of terrestrial gravitation, some makers of express rifles claimed that their weapons fulfilled the ideal they had set up. As a matter of fact, the ideal had to be adjusted to fit in with natural laws, and "point blank" came to mean that range at which the object could be hit without adjusting the sights from their lowest point. If, for instance, the vulnerable part of a beast measured 6 in. in diameter, the extreme range at which the trajectory of the bullet did not rise more than 6 in. above the zero line made by the line of sight would be the point-blank range of that rifle used at such a target. It will be realised that used in this sense the "point blank" of a rifle varies with the size of the target it is desired to hit.

In order to get this "point-blank" range the bullet was considerably reduced in weight, and at the same time in calibre, whilst the charge was left at somewhere near its old size. Immediately this was done, there came a complaint from men who went after the bigger game that the lighter bullets, though doubtless very excellent, lacked stopping and shocking power, and so there were developed two classes of rifle: the large bore which was used for elephants, tigers, lions and similar beasts, and the express rifles which were used for less dangerous "big game." In the process of improvement the two classes rapidly became more or less merged as the large-bore rifles were given a bigger charge to speed up the bullet, and the power and weight of the bullet of express rifles were extended up into the realm of those of the large-bore rifles.

When the trials of sporting rifles were organised by the *Field* newspaper, and held at Putney in October, 1883, six classes were thought necessary in order to cover the whole ground. They were those for double, four, eight, and twelve bore heavy rifles; those for the .577, .500, .450, and .400 double-express rifles; and a class for rook rifles. Mr. W. W. Greener, whose firm did not compete, is of opinion that these trials were not fully satisfactory as far as the gun trade and sportsmen in general were concerned. As a matter of fact, there were only six competitors, and though these were some of the best-known gun and rifle makers of the time, the trials were at short notice, and a number of firms which might have come in felt that they would not be doing themselves justice if they did not have a chance to manufacture special weapons. A complete account of these trials is to be found in "The Modern Sportsman's Gun and Rifle," where Mr. Walsh ("Stonehenge") has given a complete résumé of the happenings. It is not necessary to repeat the details here because sporting rifle manufacture has, since those trials, been completely revolutionised. Some general particulars will doubtless be of historical value, however, and therefore it may be said that the amount of accuracy obtained was thought at that time remarkably good, and some of the diagrams compare more than favourably with those obtained at the present time. In the trials, recoil, trajectory, and target group were all taken into consideration.

The express rifles all gave trajectories with a maximum ordinate of between $4\frac{1}{2}$ in. and 5 in. over 150 yards. Major Fremantle, in the course of a critical study of the results of the trials which he gives in "The Book of the Rifle," points out that the tendency of makers of express rifles in those days was to lighten the bullet to such an extent in order to get high

PLATE XXXVIII

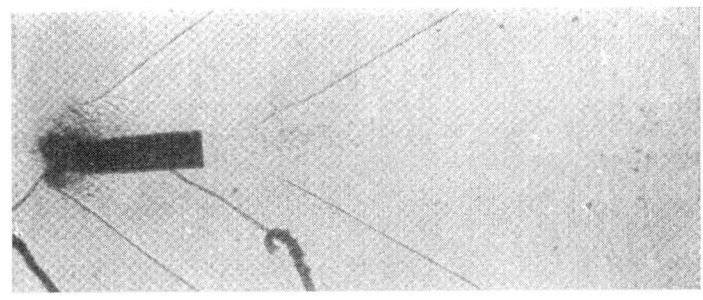

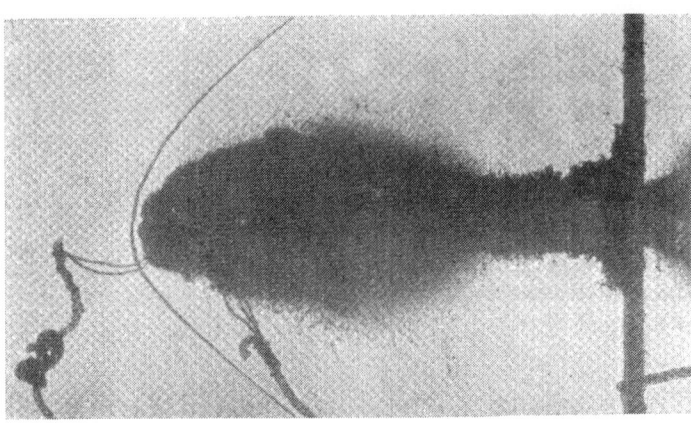

PROFESSOR BOYES' PHOTOGRAPHS

The top photo shows a Lee-Enfield bullet in flight. The bow wave, stern wave and rarefied air area are clearly marked. The bottom pictures show, first, a Lee-Enfield bullet entering a sheet of glass, and, second, the bullet leaving the sheet surrounded by splinters. Note the much enlarged bow wave

velocity that stopping power and penetrative capabilities were sacrificed to a degree which tended to bring this class of rifle into disrepute with sportsmen. He also points out that the Holland express rifles, which won in the trials, all fired heavier bullets than the rifles submitted by Messrs. Holland's competitors in their particular classes.

The approximation of one class of rifle to another, which has already been mentioned, was distinctly visible in the rifles submitted for these trials. Some of the rook rifles distinctly came within the express rifle category, while the .577 express, which to differentiate from the large bores was restricted to rifles under 12 lb. in weight, was nevertheless quite capable of being used for the same purposes for which the smaller of the large bores was designed. A very interesting rifle submitted in the rook rifle class was that sent by Bland. It was of the .295 bore and was a distinct forecast of the kind of rifle which was, a quarter of a century later, to become very familiar to frequenters of miniature rifle ranges. This rifle was fitted with an orthoptic backsight with vernier scale and with a fine foresight capable of being adjusted for wind. It is interesting to note that in 1883 the .400-calibre rifle was known as a "small-bore" express.

Some months before the *Field* held its sporting rifle trials, a committee was constituted to consider the advisability of adopting an improved military rifle for British service in place of the Martini-Henry. The work of this committee extended over five years, and resulted in the adoption of the Lee-Metford magazine rifle. When the high velocity military rifle became an accomplished fact, it was in effect a rifle built to shoot express cartridges, and in addition to attain accuracy at a very long range. Gunmakers quickly recognised that they were face to face with a very severe problem. It was not long before the problem was really acute. Sportsmen, tempted by the new weapon, neglected the old double-barrel express, and more often than not averred that the magazine was quite sufficient to guarantee a second shot, if a second shot were needed, and in addition a third or fourth or fifth was also available. Gradually, however, the old ideas on the subject of the second barrel began to prevail again. It was found that, no matter how swiftly and with what precision and ease a bolt mechanism was operated, it was impossible to get off the second shot as quickly as with the aid of a second barrel. It must be sufficiently obvious that the movement necessary to shift the finger from the first to the second trigger is not nearly so much as is required to withdraw the hand from the trigger-guard, draw back the bolt, return the bolt, and place the finger back on the trigger again.

The small-bore, high-velocity cartridge had come to stay. It remained therefore for the gunmaker to adapt his methods to suit the new conditions, and very soon a number of makers were experimenting with the construction of double-barrelled rifles to shoot the .303 cartridge. The problems which had to be faced were many and not easy of solution. For instance, the laying of the barrels required to be arranged to suit altogether new conditions; for the sportsman knowing the ranging capabilities of the new cartridge demanded that 300 yards should be the least distance up to which he could rely on getting accurate shooting, and this, of course, necessitated a very long parallel flight. Then there were difficulties which arose because of the extra pressure and shock given by the cordite cartridge, and it was only by the utmost patience and determination that the efficient small-bore double rifle was evolved. These double rifles were almost exclusively built upon the shot-gun principle, that is to say, the breech was exposed by "breaking" the rifle, the barrels being hinged to the stock and action. It will be understood that here again were difficulties which, in common with others, had to be overcome, with the knowledge that over all lay the sportsman's desire for a perfectly balanced arm, finished in that manner which is associated with the work of the British gunsmiths. At last, however, the problems were solved, and the principles began to be extended to bigger bores. Meanwhile, the magazine rifle still continued to hold its own with a certain section of the sporting public, so that we have the modern express rifle developing along two lines, the magazine rifle of .280, .303, .375, and occasionally big bores like Gibbs's .500, and the true double expresses which are built in all calibres.

BALL AND SHOT GUNS

A further development has been in the direction of adapting the automatic, or auto-loading principle, to sporting rifles, under which category we place such weapons as the Browning automatic and the Winchester auto-loading, the latter being in all calibres up to .500.

For sporting purposes automatic rifles do not suffer from the grave disabilities which prevent their present adoption for war work. In the hands of a sportsman the automatic mechanism is likely to receive that care which is necessary if it is to be kept in proper working order, and since two or three shots are all that are likely to be fired in quick succession, the problem of ammunition supply need not enter into the discussion. What really does matter is that, the more complicated a piece of mechanism, the more moving and bearing surfaces there are in it, the more springs and holes and rods are necessary to work it, the more likely is it to suddenly develop some minor defect which temporarily puts it out of action. Rifle actions, which have to resist a series of violent shocks, and which may not be weighted with metal much beyond the mere safety margin, are in the nature of things liable to annoying break-downs when they are of complicated design. The perfection to which the automatic action has now been brought, and the fact that break-downs are the exception, not the rule, in severe range tests, does not do away with the fact that the automatic is more likely to fail than the double-barrel or the magazine rifle. It is also more expensive than the magazine rifle. There do not seem, for sportsmen, sufficient advantages at present in the automatic rifle to outweigh its disadvantages.

An interesting development is presented by the rifles which are designed to project both shot and ball as they are needed. Generally these weapons are smooth bore for the greater part of their barrel length, and have an inch or two of the muzzle of the barrel rifled to give the bullet the necessary rotation to enable it to maintain sufficient gyroscopic stability for the distance it has to travel. Messrs. Westley Richards have put on the market a number of these rifles from 28 to 12 bore. The guns do not require any special mention as they are, except for the special boring to take the rifle cartridge, essentially shot-

M

guns. Such composite weapons are extremely useful in countries where mixed shooting is the rule. The most interesting part of the problem presented by such rifles is concerned with the ammunition, and this will be dealt with in the next chapter.

The following list of calibres will be useful in that it gives some idea of the wide range of bores which have been developed for sporting purposes.

TABLE OF SPORTING RIFLE CALIBRES	
H.V. Express Rifles for Big Game Shooting	Small Game Rifles
.600	.50
.577	.45
.577/.500	.44
.505	.405
.500	.38
.475	.32
.500/.465	.303/.301
.500/.450	.33/.30
.450	.30/.30
.404	.25
.400	.22
.375	
.360	
.354	
.375/.303	
.303	
.280	

CHAPTER X

Sporting Rifle Ammunition

THE problems before the makers of cartridges for the modern sporting rifle are not altogether easy of elucidation, and though a very large amount of progress has been made in the direction of adapting the nitro-powder-loaded cartridge to the needs of the killer of game, there still remains a good deal to be done, particularly in the direction of getting high and well-maintained velocities with heavy bullets without developing excessive pressure and recoil. To a certain extent the problems are those which present themselves when military cartridges are under consideration, but the large range of size of sporting cartridges, both above and below that of the military variety, gives, of necessity, a chance for the overcoming of difficulties which are only rarely met with in manufacturing procedure as regards the military article.

As has been suggested in a previous chapter, the sporting rifle for use with black powder had been very considerably developed, and was in a state of comparative finality when the development of propellent nitro-powders brought higher velocity, and, consequently, longer ranges and greater striking energies, within the range of possibility. The first hint of trouble for the cartridge maker came, of course, when the result of Colonel Rubin's experiments began to be known, and when the Rubin cartridges were experimented with in this country. About 1895 a very considerable number of military rifles, both of the British and Continental makes, were being used by sportsmen. The nitro-powder cartridges available for use with these military weapons were found to give so flat a trajectory that, within an extended sporting range, errors of distance estimation which, with the old black powder expresses, would have meant a missed or maimed beast, with the new rifles did not prevent an effective kill.

The new cartridges were not, of course, without their detractors. We have already alluded to the controversy which arose with regard to the efficacy of magazine loading as against a second barrel, but a far more serious argument had to do with the lack of stopping power which was very early apparent in the hard-cased bullets demanded by the new method of cartridge making. The rifle manufacturer's answer to the charge of lack of shock effect was to develop a series of bullets which would expand, or mushroom, on impact. The idea was, of course, to utilise as much as possible of the bullet's energy in the work of stopping and killing the animal struck. The man in the street is immensely impressed if he is told that a modern military bullet will go through five men one after the other, and wound the lot of them, but this factor does not interest the sportsman in the least. What he wants is a bullet which will stop his quarry, and bring it down dead within the fewest possible yards of the place where he originally hit it.

Mushrooming depends entirely on the resistance offered by the substance struck, and so although the military calibre bullets were turned out with thin noses and hollow noses and split sides, and with exposed lead at the nose, the sportsman still felt that there was a chance of his game getting away even when hit. While recognising the many advantages of the nitro-powder cartridges, he began to think longingly of the old black-powder expresses with their larger calibres and very much heavier bullets.

It was not long before enterprising gunmakers, with years of experience behind them, saw the necessity for turning out a nitro-express cartridge to meet the demands for a larger calibre bullet. Men, such as Purdey and Rigby, who knew all there was to know on the subject of black-powder expresses, found themselves with very little knowledge on the subject of the behaviour of cordite, which was the only nitro-powder then available for rifle use. A cartridge with a larger bullet was wanted, and the only means they had of supplying it was by enlarging the military cartridge and, as they did so, keeping

PLATE XXXIX

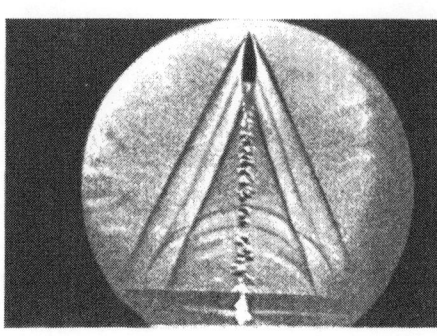

2. A POINTED BULLET IN FLIGHT

In this photograph the sharper angle of the lines from the nose and tail indicate a higher velocity. It will be noticed that the point of the bullet projects through the head wave. In other respects the phenomena to be observed in the two photographs are similar. There are the head and tail waves, the rarefied air area, the track of whirls, and the compression lines caused by rotation. This bullet is the German "S".

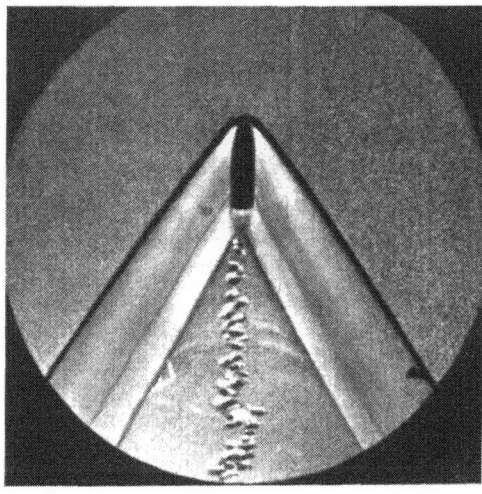

1. AN OGIVAL-HEADED PROJECTILE IN FLIGHT

The lines flowing from the bullet at an angle are lines of different air density. From the nose of the bullet comes the "head wave," or wave of compression. From the base there is the tail wave. Immediately behind the base of the bullet is a rarefied air space, and in the rear of it a track of air whirls. Between the head and tail waves are the compression waves caused by the rotation of the projectile. This projectile is the Italian service bullet

TROUBLE AND DISAPPOINTMENT 181

all the proportions the same. The early cordite expresses were based entirely on the sizes which had been developed for black powder use, and trouble occasionally arose from people trying to use these new cartridges in rifles built only for use with black powder. It is possible to load sporting cartridges with nitro-powder for use in rifles designed for black-powder cartridges, and this in the early days was occasionally done, the cartridge being loaded so as to give the same trajectory as the black-powder cartridge had done. This, of course, gave the shooter the benefit of a considerably reduced recoil.

Just as the manufacturers of cartridges for the military rifle had at first experienced a very great deal of trouble with the brass, so the makers of these new express cartridges had trouble with their cases. Old rules were quite useless in the new conditions. Before the problems were correctly solved, many rifles were ruined because of split cases and blown-out caps. Many and bitter were the evidences placed before the cartridge manufacturers that the intensely hot gases evolved by the ignition, under pressure, of cordite, were capable of cutting and eroding highly finished steel faces in a truly wonderful manner.

Another trouble which manufacturers of early cordite cartridges had was that cordite, and particularly the early forms of cordite, is capable of developing unexpected tricks when subjected to high temperatures. Black powder, dirty and evil smelling though it was, behaved in the same way on the Equator as it did when shot in the Highlands of Scotland. Stable as the British constitution, it could be depended upon absolutely to do what was expected of it. Not so the new cordite, the skittish and flighty behaviour of which caused much weeping and gnashing of teeth in Birmingham and other places where gunmakers "most do congregate." It was found that rifles sighted and adjusted in Great Britain in the usual way by respectable and methodical gunmakers who had been at the same thing all their lives, would, in the hands of experienced rifle-shots in India, refuse utterly to bring the game to ground. Again, rifles manufactured by reputable firms, and which had passed the proof-house in the proper and correct manner, bulged in the barrel and gave way at the breech in a way which was always annoying and often dangerous.

It was a considerable time before it was discovered that an increase of temperature will cause cordite to give an increase in pressure and velocity. When this fact was discovered, the obvious remedy was to turn out special makes of cartridges for use in tropical countries. Cordite is much more stable now than it was in the early days of its manufacture, but the increase of pressure due to heating up has not been done away with altogether. How the difficulties were overcome in the early days may be judged from the following two paragraphs taken from one of the famous series of "Lectures to Young Gun Makers," published in "Arms and Explosives." The particular lecture from which the quotation was taken appeared in June, 1904, and is one of a series of lectures on the cordite express rifle and ammunition, which is, as far as we know, the only technical and authoritative information on the subject which has appeared:

"It followed from the nature of these rifles that their use was almost exclusively confined to tropical countries where the game for which they were intended abounds, and although black powder behaves alike in countries with widely different ranges of temperature, with cordite this is not so. The high average temperature which obtains in tropical country affects the behaviour of cordite in a manner that was not at first appreciated. It soon, however, became apparent that rifles which had been manufactured and adjusted in this country gave trouble abroad, not only because of the increased strain that the higher pressure put upon the mechanism, but also because the resulting increase of velocity altered the elevations for which the sights had been adjusted. It was, in fact, found that rifles which were sighted and adjusted for certain charges in this country would only produce the required level of result if the amount of powder charge was reduced in proportion to the increased activity of the explosive when used abroad.

"It was long before this seemingly obvious proposition was practically applied in regard to cordite rifles. Now that the

MODERN CARTRIDGES 183

theory of the subject is fully understood, the ammunition manufacturers are loading cordite ammunition with two sets of charges, viz. full charges for the sighting and adjustment of the rifles in this country, and reduced charges for reproducing the required standard of result abroad. The amount of reduction in powder charge necessary is arrived at by firing the ammunition in a heated condition, the charge being selected which gives the combination of pressure and velocity which is accepted as standard in this country for full charged fired at the normal temperature of the English climate. A temperature of 120° F. is accepted as representing foreign conditions of service. In this way the gunmaker is fully assured that the sighting and adjustment arrived at in this country will be applicable to the same rifle when fired abroad with reduced charges. He is similarly easy in his mind that the rifle which works well in England will not give trouble abroad by reason of an increase above the level of pressure with which it has been tried and adjusted at home."

The reason that cordite was so largely used for sporting purposes in the early days of the use of smokeless powder was because that particular propellant was being largely manufactured for Government purposes, and whilst it was the subject of continuous experiment, it was at the same time sufficiently standardised for the purposes of the cartridge loader. Cordite is now far from enjoying the monopoly which once belonged to it, but it is still for many purposes the most dependable powder that can be used. Many of the objections which attached to cordite when regarded as a military powder need not be taken into consideration when it is looked at from a sporting point of view, and, on the other hand, its great virtue of stability and good keeping powers are of the utmost value to the sportsman as they are to the ordnance man.

In the case of sporting-rifle cartridges the purchaser does not, as a rule, have so free a choice in regard to powder as does the buyer of shot-gun cartridges. The rifle manufacturer has usually had the cartridge worked out exactly to his requirements, and the charge is, in almost every case, one of the standard makes of smokeless powder.

In regard to the bullet, there is far more latitude for the exercise of individual peculiarities, likes and dislikes. Besides the more or less standardised forms of soft-nosed or hollow-nosed bullets, there are numbers with special forms of weakened envelopes, such as the special split-case bullets sold by Messrs. Jeffreys, or the special bullets manufactured for Messrs. Holland and Holland.

A recent development in sporting cartridges is the magnum cartridge, in which a case of bottle-shaped outline, having a big loading capacity, is used in order to further flatten the trajectory of the bullet. The use of such cartridges, which develop fairly high pressures, necessitates an exceedingly strong breech action, but the cartridges themselves are favourites with those who desire a flat trajectory over a long range. The magnum cartridge resembles an exaggerated military cartridge.

The most interesting sporting cartridge of recent years is the .220 high-power, which, in the B.S.A. rifle designed to shoot it, develops the remarkably high velocity of 3,000 f.s. The bullet is of hard lead, with a cupro-nickel base extending a little more than half-way up the sides of the bullet. The lead nose is pointed, and the whole cartridge presents an exceedingly workmanlike appearance. For a range of 150 yards the maximum ordinate is only one and one-third inches, and at 300 yards it is 6 in. high. This means that up to 300 yards the rifle can be used against deer and other soft-skinned game without alterations of the sight. Starting with such a high velocity the bullet is naturally extremely explosive in its action on striking, and is said to break up immediately it enters the skin of deer or bear. Rabbits shot with it are killed whenever struck, provided the hit is in the body, but the bullet is hardly suitable for such small game as it mutilates the body unduly, and has too big a ranging power for use on an average British rough shoot.

Users of high-power or magnum cartridges occasionally encounter annoying extraction difficulties owing to the force with which the case is expanded against the walls of the chamber, and the weak extraction provided in some sporting rifles. For really high-power cartridges the bolt-action is

STANDARD SIZES NECESSARY

usually most effective. Certainly Messrs. Gibbs's .505 cartridge gives no trouble in the special rifle designed for it.

The tendency of sporting-rifle ammunition makers is towards the excessive amplification of types. It would be a good thing for shooters, and doubtless also a good thing for the trade, if it were possible to standardise certain types and sizes of cartridge for certain shooting, just as the .22 long-rifle cartridge has become the standard for miniature-rifle shooting throughout the world. The trouble is that many big-game shots have very decided ideas as to what a cartridge should be like, and are willing to go to a deal of trouble and expense to have some small alteration in design made. Other men follow their lead, and the demand for yet another type of cartridge is created.

CHAPTER XI

The .220-in. Calibre Rifle

WE have preferred in the title of this chapter to use the strictly technical definition of a class of rifle the development of which has been one of the outstanding features of rifle manufacture during the last fifteen years. The adjective "miniature" as applied to this rifle was distinctly unfortunate, though through association the word has ceased to have its original meaning of littleness, for those who understand, when applied to a rifle. The word, however, still retains its original meaning for the man in the street, who, until he gets used to handling one, thinks of the miniature rifle as a toy. The word "small-bore" reintroduced by the National Rifle Association a year or so ago to do duty in place of the word "miniature" is equally unfortunate. The change from the Martini-Henry to the .303 rifle is still sufficiently fresh in the memory to make the word "small-bore" still apply to the modern military rifle, as opposed to the older, large-calibre weapon firing a lead bullet.

Call it "miniature" or "small-bore," or what you will, there can be no doubt that the .220 calibre rifle has been instrumental in re-creating in the Briton that love of marksmanship which in years gone by was one of his proudest boasts. It should be realised that the rifle did not arise from the demand caused by the Miniature Rifle Clubs, but existed previously in various forms. The clubs themselves were the direct result of, in the first instance, some pointed remarks on the British lack of skill in marksmanship made by Lord Salisbury at a Primrose League meeting, and afterwards to the energy and perseverance of that great soldier, the late Lord Roberts, who became president of the Society of Miniature Rifle Clubs, and did all in his power to impress on the people of this nation the great

LORD ROBERTS'S BATTLE CRY 187

necessity for acquiring skill in arms. His ambition was to see a rifle club in every village, and the men and boys of the nation practising shooting in their leisure time as do the citizens of Holland and Switzerland. Lord Roberts's ambition was not wholly satisfied, but there were in the country some 400,000 members of rifle clubs when, shortly after the outbreak of war, he addressed a letter to what he was proud to call "his rifle clubs," asking the members to do more even than they were doing. Before he died he read the proof of the first Roll of Honour issued by the Society of Miniature Rifle Clubs, a Roll of Honour which was to swell until it contained the names of many thousands of members of miniature rifle clubs serving their King and Country, either in the Navy, the Army, or the Territorial Forces.

When Lord Roberts first insisted on the necessity for rifle-shooting practice, and patriotic men and women all over the country started the movement he had inaugurated, it at once became obvious that the ordinary Service rifle, with high-power, long-range ammunition, was quite inadequate to the situation. For one thing, it was impossible to get ranges to serve the needs of the inhabitants, and for another thing the expense of firing the Service ammunition was absolutely prohibitive to many men, and those the class of men to whom it was most wished to appeal.

The promoters of rifle clubs, therefore, turned to low-power rifles which would throw a projectile with reasonable accuracy over a short range. When the National Rifle Association issued their first pamphlet concerning the formation of Miniature Rifle Clubs, which they did in February, 1902, they laid down that the rifles must comply with the following regulations: The calibre was not to exceed .303 in., nor were they to be more than 8 lb. in weight, except it be the Service rifle with Morris tubes. The trigger-pull was not to be less than 4 lb., the butt to be plain, without projections at toe or heel. Any sights, except telescopic, might be used. Repeating and magazine rifles were strictly prohibited.

It will be seen at once that these regulations allowed a very great latitude in the choice of rifle, but they barred weapons of military weight. At least twenty different sizes and designs of cartridge between the .22 short and the .32 Winchester were available, and as a consequence the rifles taken into use were as varied in design as were their capabilities.

It was not long, however, before it was seen that, to quote the words of Mr. E. J. D. Newitt, an early and enthusiastic worker in the miniature rifle movement, "the most suitable rifle and ammunition should combine the minimum of energy and cost with the maximum of accuracy." The cost of shooting is affected more by the cost of ammunition than by the cost of the rifle, and it was the fact that the .22 rim-fire cartridge was the cheapest on the market which assisted in determining the size of rifle which was to become standardised as a miniature or small-bore rifle. At the same time, the .22 cartridge was remarkably accurate, and could compete quite favourably with the bigger and more expensive cartridges over the short ranges used for rifle-club shooting. By 1905 the Society of Miniature Rifle Clubs had standardised the size of bore permissible in competitions for their prizes and trophies. According to their first set of regulations, "the miniature rifle may be of any pattern, single-loading or repeating, of any calibre not exceeding .23 of one inch, or 6 mm., or a rifle of larger calibre fitted with any device for firing miniature ammunition." The latter part of this rule was designed to allow the use of Morris tube rifles, that is to say, the Service rifles fitted with a rifle tube to reduce calibre, and also to permit the use of what were known as adaptors. These were, in most cases, false chambers with the exterior contour of the cartridge of the arm for which they were designed. A cartridge containing a bullet of the right calibre for the rifle, but with a very much reduced powder charge, was fitted into this false breech or adaptor, and by this means the Service rifle could be used for shooting at short ranges, and so shot at less cost than with the full-power ammunition. These adaptors were far from satisfactory, one of the principal reasons being that the sharp twist of the Service rifle is adapted for the nickel-cased bullet, with a velocity of over 2,000 ft. per second, and is quite unsuitable for use with lead bullets having a velocity of only about 1,000 ft. per second.

PLATE XL.

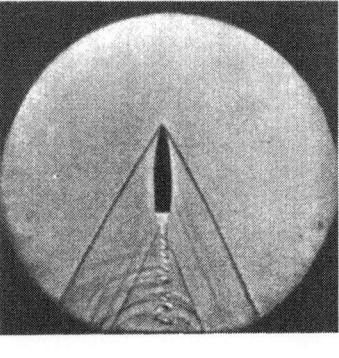

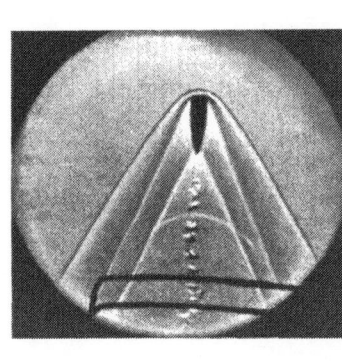

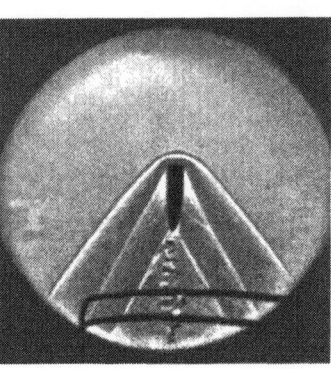

BULLETS FIRED BASE FIRST

In the case of bullets fired base first there is a very strong pushing out of the head wave of compression, and only a small rarefied air space and formation of whirls behind. It is not to be supposed from this that bullets with pointed bases would be an advantage. As a matter of fact, they are very unstable. The rarefied air space and whirls would seem to indicate steadying as well as retarding influences

FRENCH "BALLE D" IN FLIGHT

The French "Balle D" has a slightly tapered base which they claim has helped in the production of a projectile of high ballistic qualities

Note.—These photographs should be examined in conjunction with those printed in Plates XXXVII, XXXVIII and XXXIX

THE MORRIS TUBE

The Morris tube, which before the coming of the .220 rifle had a great vogue in the Army and Volunteer Forces for the teaching of musketry on short ranges, had, like the adaptor, a good many disadvantages. It required a considerable amount of care to keep it in perfect order, and as usually found on rifle ranges was capable of nothing but heart-breaking inaccuracy. Properly looked after, the Morris tube could undoubtedly do very good work, and modern samples made to shoot the .22 cartridge are almost as accurate as .22 rifles bored from the solid tube. It is only fair to the old Morris tube to say that it was the cheapness of the .220 ammunition as compared with the .295/230 cartridge of the Morris tube which led to its being superseded. A lot of men who developed into first-class Volunteer shots had their initial training with the aiming tube.

The .220 rim-fire cartridge was an American invention, and in the years 1901 and 1902 practically the only rifles chambered to use it were those of American manufacture, though there were both Belgian and French rifles available as soon as the demand became known. Among the American rifles were many with well-known names. There was, for instance, the Winchester musket and the Stevens "Ideal." In an improved form both models are still being used by rifle club members at the present time. The Remington was another well-known model which early came into extended use. These American rifles were all of them fitted with a form of sliding-block action whereby on the depression of an under lever the block either slid vertically downwards, or downwards and backwards. They were at first fitted with extractors, but not with ejectors, the ejectors being a refinement that was introduced to meet the demand of those who wished to fire rapid practices. The well-known Francotte firm of Liège were early on the scene with their adaptation of the Martini action fitted to a .220 barrel, and the Martini action also made itself apparent in the miniature rifle made by Messrs. Greener.

In 1902 there were already many criticisms from military men that the shooting experience gained on rifle ranges was not of the kind likely to be of value from a military point of view. Though many of the civilian rifle clubs were at that date of a semi-military character, that is to say, they indulged in drill and were taught by ex-military men, the rifles they used were extremely unlike the ordinary military pattern. Towards this, the N.R.A. rule limiting the weight to below 8 lb. had some considerable influence, and it was only when the majority of shooters, through the Society of Miniature Rifle Clubs, brought pressure to bear on the parent association that the weight of the miniature rifle was extended so as to include any reasonable design.

But to return to the criticisms of 1901 and 1902. We have heard these criticisms many a time, and it is interesting to see how little they have varied during the passage of years. In 1901 an Army officer wrote to a morning paper saying that if the men were to be taught to handle the rifle so as to use it efficiently in time of need, they must be taught with the kind of weapon they were likely to have to use in war. Efficient use came only with familiarity, and there was no possible excuse for making each man familiar with a light and childish weapon when he would have to use one very considerably heavier when he came to fight.

The answer to such criticism was obviously to adapt the Service rifle to fire the reduced bore cartridge, and in February, 1902, Messrs. Buck & Co. put on the market the now familiar Service rifle bored for the .22 rim-fire cartridge. In 1904 the Birmingham Small Arms Company were manufacturing a similar weapon, and since that date it has been possible to get the successive types of Service rifle constructed to shoot the low-power cartridge.

During the present war very many thousands of recruits have had their first introduction to a Service rifle through the medium of these .22 Service weapons, and there is no doubt at all that as a quick introduction to the full-charge weapon nothing can equal the same pattern barrelled and bored to take the miniature cartridge. A man can be taught to shoot with any rifle, and if he only goes far enough it will not subsequently matter what class of rifle he takes up he will be quite at home with it within a few minutes. But when a man has to be taught

THE FIRST "MINIATURE" MEETING

quickly to shoot, there is nothing like letting him stick to the type of weapon he is to use.

The first Miniature Rifle Prize meeting held in Great Britain took place at the Crystal Palace from March 23 to April 1, 1903. The meeting was opened by General Sir Ian Hamilton, supported by Earl Grey. The programme included twenty-five competitions, thirteen for individuals and eleven for teams. For the prizes over one thousand nine hundred and seventy-one competitors entered, representing forty-eight rifle clubs. The shooting was conducted at two ranges, the shortest being 20 yards and the longest 50 yards. The targets were adaptations of the N.R.A. dimensions. The bull's-eye at 20 yards was a black of $\frac{7}{8}$ in. diameter scoring five marks, with a central ring scoring six marks. The inner was 2 in. in diameter, and the rest of the 6-in. square target counted as the outer. At 50 yards the black scoring five was $1\frac{3}{4}$ in. in diameter. At this range there was also the central, counting six. The 50 yards target was 12 in. square. The standing position was adopted for the 20 yards range, the prone position for the 50 yards range. This rule applied to all competitions except the Championship, where shots were fired both standing, kneeling, and prone at both ranges.

One of the chief results of this meeting was the prominence which it gave to the unreliable character of shooting from the Morris tube. So unsatisfactory were the results obtained that it was determined at future meetings held by the Society of Working Men's Rifle Clubs a separate class would have to be made for it as it was quite unfit, except in specially lucky circumstances, to compete against the much cheaper and less complicated Belgian and American rifles made to fire the .22 cartridges.

The shooting at this meeting was nothing like the class which we have now learned to expect of the miniature rifle, but it must be remembered that aperture sights and orthoptic spectacles were not permitted, and both rifles and ammunition were in an undeveloped state. The championship was won by the well-known Service rifle-shot, A. J. Comber.

The results obtained by the Miniature Rifle Competition at

Bisley in 1903 were of very little importance as regards the development of the rifle. This competition was so arranged as to allow .25 ammunition to be used, and it was, in fact, with a Stevens's .25 rifle the competition was won.

In 1904 the National Rifle Association and the Society of Miniature Rifle Clubs held a meeting in conjunction at Olympia from April 25 to April 30. The ranges were still 20 yards and 50 yards, but the targets had been altered to conform more nearly to N.R.A. usage, the central being done away with and the bull's-eye, scoring five marks, being reduced to four-fifths of an inch at 20 yards. The prone position was adopted for both ranges at all competitions, with the result that there was considerable improvement as regards the scores. A. J. Comber, the N.R.A. Gold Medallist, was again a prominent competitor, as was also Mr. Fulton, sen. An interesting feature of this particular meeting was the inclusion of a special competition for ladies, the first of a long series of ladies' competitions which have been a feature of the S.M.R.C. competitions for years past. In 1904 the Stevens and Winchester rifles were still pre-eminent, with the Francotte cadet model a good third. British-made weapons were, however, beginning to acquire a reputation, and among these the models manufactured by Greener had the biggest following. There was also on the market the "Cestus" rifle made by Messrs. Cogswell & Harrison, a model which has a considerable interest because it foreshadowed in general design the cadet rifle which was soon to be fathered by the War Office.

By the end of 1905 the civilian rifle movement had got such a hold on the country that the War Office became actively interested, and decided to seal a design to be known as a cadet rifle, to be used by Cadet Corps, Rifle Clubs, and similar organisations. The War Office called to their assistance experts from the N.R.A. and the Society of Miniature Rifle Clubs, and apparently they started out with the very best intentions in the world. The rifle was to shoot the .22 cartridge, and was to cost about 30s. When it was known that the War Office was going to help by the turning out of a cheap and really efficient rifle, the rifle club members were in high glee. But bitterly were

THE WAR OFFICE MINIATURE

they disappointed when the completed article came out. The War Office miniature rifle was doomed to failure from the start. It shot quite decently, because it was manufactured by the Birmingham Small Arms Company and the London Small Arms Company, who know how to manufacture rifles to shoot well, but the design passed by the War Office will not permit of the rifle being sold at less than 45s. or 55s. fitted with magazine to hold five cartridges, whereas there were already several excellent rifles on the market at about the same price. The War Office miniature rifle was too light for ordinary use, as $5\frac{1}{2}$ lb. will not give sufficient steadiness for the best shooting. The hollow form of the rifle was expensive, with many unnecessary refinements. A little later the Birmingham Small Arms Company showed what could be done by turning out a bolt-action rifle, the bolt of which was very similar to the War Office miniature bolt, at a price of 30s.

Despite the activities of the War Office and some of the big firms, the real boom of the civilian rifle movement did not come until a genius in the gun trade had discovered that it was possible to convert old Martini-Henry rifles to fire the .22 bullet. Who this genius was it is difficult at this date to say. To that well-known gunsmith, Mr. W. W. Greener, is usually given the credit for first showing that these old rifles could be fitted with new barrels, bored eccentrically so that the old striking-pin could be utilised for detonating the primer of the rim-fire cartridge. Once the idea had taken on, the conversion of Martini-Henry rifles went on apace. The Society of Miniature Rifle Clubs and the National Rifle Association secured from the War Office the right to convert these weapons and to sell them at 25s. to members of clubs affiliated to them. The converted Martini, as it was called, is the most excellent cheap rifle it is possible to obtain. It is of correct military weight in nine hundred and ninety-nine cases out of a thousand, and it shoots well enough to put ten shots in succession into a half-inch carton at twenty-five yards. It is not easily damaged, and, in fact, it fulfils all the ideals of a rifle club weapon.

If in its very early days the Society of Miniature Rifle Clubs discouraged at its meetings the use of any but military sights, it was not long before it saw the unwisdom of its ways and ruled that sights for miniature rifles should be of any pattern, fixed or adjustable, both vertically and laterally, with a proviso that this rule did not allow the fitting of magnifying glasses, telescopes, or spirit levels. These rules were promulgated in 1905, and so wise and broad-minded were the whole of the regulations that there can be no doubt that they had a very marked effect on the popularising of rifle shooting and the spreading of the rifle club movement. To get the private citizen to take an interest in rifle shooting it must be made reasonably easy. The orthoptic sight provides just the aid which is wanted to make target shooting a fascinating sport. As a matter of history the whole of these early regulations will be quoted here, as they are of considerable interest, and the only volume we know of in which they were published has been out of print for some years.

"REGULATIONS

"(1) *Miniature Rifle Clubs.*—A miniature rifle club is a club which, being affiliated to the Society of Miniature Rifle Clubs, carries on rifle shooting wholly or partly with miniature rifles on miniature ranges with miniature ammunition, as defined in paragraphs (3) and (4).

"(2) *Miniature Ranges.*—A miniature range is a range not exceeding 100 yards in length, upon which miniature rifles and ammunition, as defined in paragraphs (3) and (4), are used.

"(3) *Rifles.*—A miniature rifle may be of any pattern, single-loading or repeating, of any calibre not exceeding .23 of one inch, or 6 mm.; or a rifle of larger calibre fitted with any device for firing miniature ammunition, as defined in paragraph (4). Sights may be of any pattern, fixed or adjustable, both vertically and laterally, but in competitions promoted by the Society rifles may not be fitted with magnifying glasses, telescopes, or spirit levels.

"A miniature pistol may be single-loading or repeating, with any sights as described for miniature rifles, and taking any miniature ammunition as defined in paragraph (4).

"(4) *Ammunition.*—A miniature cartridge may be rim fire or central fire, with projectile of any calibre not exceeding .23 of one inch, or 6 mm., and, in case of bottle-shaped cartridges, the shell may not exceed .297 of one inch.

THE SOUTHFIELDS RIFLE CLUB

"The powder charge may not exceed 7 grains of black gunpowder, or its equivalent in any other explosive. The projectile must be of lead, not cased with other metal, and not exceeding 50 grains avoirdupois in weight.

"(5) *Targets*.—Targets shall be of the following dimensions:

"For shooting up to and including 25 yards, a card of 6 in. square having ten rings, the central being ½ in. in diameter, and increasing by half-inches to 5 in.

"For 50 yards, a card 12 in. square having ten rings, the central being 1 in. in diameter, and increasing by one inch up to 10 in.

"For 100 yards, a card 21 in. square having ten rings, the central being 2 in. in diameter, and increasing by two inches up to 20 in.

"(6) *Scoring*.—The score value of the central ring shall be 10, and of the other rings in a descending scale: 9-8-7-6-5-4-3-2-1."

The immediate result of these regulations was in the direction of standardising the .220 calibre rifle as the weapon to be used by the citizen rifleman. At one blow the Society cut itself off from all traffic with adaptors and with any of the powerful ammunitions which were then beginning to masquerade as miniature cartridges.

This progressive policy on the part of the Society of Miniature Rifle Clubs was the outcome of a similar enlightened policy on the part of the famous Southfields Rifle Club, in its day one of the most progressive and far-seeing clubs in the country. The Southfields club was fortunate in having among its original members and on its committee two or three men who were unconventionally minded. Among these men were E. J. D. Newitt, W. E. Pimm, George Barnes, and W. Kenset Styles. These men fought for, and succeeded in getting passed, a policy of freedom in regard to choice of rifle and sights, limiting the cartridge to the .22. Now, Mr. Newitt, and, if we remember rightly, Mr. Pimm also, were on the original committee of the Society of Miniature Rifle Clubs, and they worked so hard in the interests of freedom of choice that they were very largely instrumental in getting the regulations we have quoted passed by the Council. That, at the same time, Mr. Newitt succeeded in getting the Council to adopt the so-called "decimal" target is perhaps a matter for regret.

The Southfields Rifle Club then became missionaries whose lessons were not the less convincing because in many instances they involved the winning of many competitions. In October, 1905, the Midland Railway Rifle Club, which was then, as it is now, an extremely strong institution, had a S.M.R.C. open meeting on their range by permission of the chairman and directors of the Midland Railway Company. A Southfields team of ten men went to Derby, with the result that Southfields won the team shoot and between them took almost every prize there was. In one competition a Midland Railway man scraped in at the bottom place, and only two other clubs were represented in the prize list at all, out of some twenty-three prizes given for individual competition. This result, which the Southfields men credited, and rightly credited, to the fact that they were all using, and had been using for some time, orthoptic sights, was such an eye-opener to the rest of the miniature rifle world that among the progressive clubs practically nothing else was talked about, and no one could rest until he had procured an orthoptic backsight to see whether his shooting would be similarly improved.

The miniature rifle at this period being practically freed from all shackles, except those which confined its bore and chambering to the firing of the .22 rim-fire cartridge, was free to develop along lines which would give it the maximum efficiency at the minimum cost. The rifle manufacturers very wisely refrained from endeavouring to compete with the cheap converted Martini rifle, and confined themselves to the developing of a high-class rifle which should, without doubt, give better results than could possibly be obtained with a rifle designed for one purpose and converted, however ingeniously, to another. As we have said, Messrs. W. W. Greener had been in the field with miniature rifles almost from the very start of the movement, and they continued to turn out sound and workmanlike weapons which were a pride and pleasure to shoot with and to own. For all that, and despite the efforts of one or two other British firms, the cream of the rapidly

THE BRITISH MINIATURE RIFLE 197

growing market was still going abroad at this date, say about 1907, almost entirely to the American Stevens firm, who, encouraged by the demand for .22 rifles in their own country, were making models to suit every purpose and every purse. It was then that the Birmingham Small Arms Company took a hand in the game, and brought all their great resources and enormous experience in repetition machinery to bear on the problem of turning out an article which would beat the American producers on their own ground. Of course this great corporation was "grinding its own axe," but that does not do away with the fact that the men in the employ of the B.S.A. who had to do with this particular branch proved themselves remarkably gifted with insight into the needs of the rifle club member, and also public-spirited in that they have not hesitated to spend money in experimental work and in educating the public to a proper appreciation of the rifle and rifle shooting. It may be said that in fighting the American rifle-maker the Birmingham Small Arms Company adopted American methods, and used them in a truly and thoroughly British way. Their reward is that to-day they are probably the best-known arms manufacturers in the world, not excepting even the Mauser and Mannlicher firms. The miniature rifle is an article which goes into the home of the many. The B.S.A. miniature rifle has found its way all over the British Empire, into France, Norway, Sweden, Denmark, and even, before the war started, into Germany. In America it has begun to more than nibble at the stronghold of the cheap American arm, and that despite the high tariff against it.

This by the way and in contravention of the oft-quoted statement that the British rifle-maker is non-progressive and is being beaten all over the world.

The British miniature rifle of the present day most in use in clubs and competitions weighs between $7\frac{1}{2}$ and 9 lb., and is a thoroughly sound and well-made article. The action is generally a Martini, or an adaptation of the Martini such as that first introduced by the Francotte Company, and now adopted by the B.S.A. The fore-end of the best models is usually thickened and shaped to the hand, and the grip is thinned down so that the thumb and fingers of the trigger-hand can grip it comfortably. The barrel should be fairly heavy, and, as a matter of fact, is so in those rifles manufactured with an understanding of the requirements of a really first-class miniature rifle. There has been a tendency during the last year or two to make the barrels unduly long, probably because in the search for extreme range certain ammunition manufacturers began to increase the load of the cartridge and put up the velocity very considerably. Now that particular phase has gone, there is no reason why the barrel should be more than 27 in. or 28 in. As a matter of fact, one of the finest miniature rifles we have ever seen was a Stevens with a 26-in. barrel, bored by the famous American gunsmith and experimenter, H. Pope. The rifling of this particular barrel was shallow and extremely well finished. Any arguments that the short barrel did not enable the best to be got out of the ammunition was positively negatived by the fact that the rifle hardly ever shot outside a 2-in. group at 100 yards, and very frequently pulled the group down to 1¾ in., and even on one or two occasions to 1¼ in.

The novice buying a miniature rifle should, if his purse will allow him to go to £3 or £4, purchase a model by a well-known maker. The secretary of his rifle club will usually be able to advise him; but if he has not such an advantage it may be as well to say that a converted Martini, if he can get it, is good enough to start with; but if he takes up this rifle at first he is bound to have a better model sooner or later, and he may just as well have it sooner, as it will considerably add to his pleasure and the profit he gets from his instruction. The fore-end should be well fashioned to the hand, and the balance should be about 4 in. in front of the trigger-guard. He should see that the trigger-pull is smooth and gives the impression of a clean snap. Anything of the nature of a dragging pull is to be avoided. This feature is well looked after in the higher-price models. If the novice has to content himself with a cheaper rifle, a shilling or two spent on having the action properly attended to by a qualified gunsmith will be money well spent.

PLATE XLI

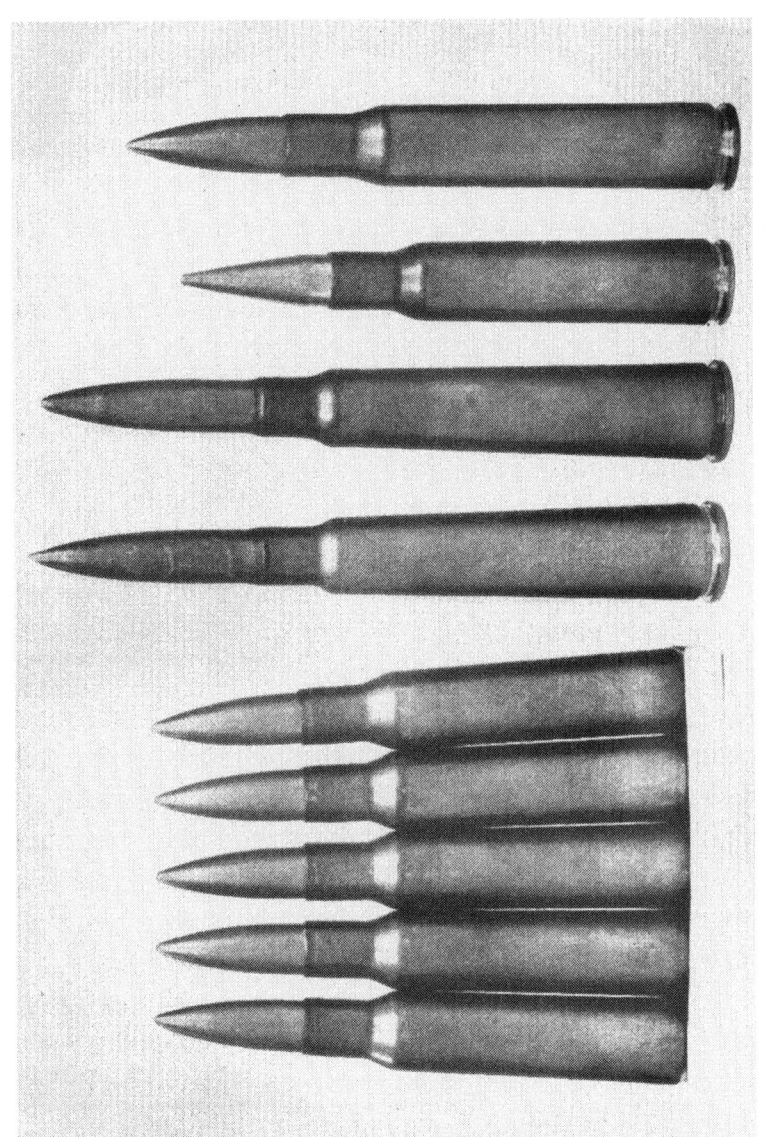

TYPES OF HIGH-VELOCITY AMMUNITION FOR TARGET SHOOTING

On the left in the clip is the 7 m/m D.W.M. cartridge which the Mauser Rifle Co., Ltd. introduced at the beginning of the 1914 season. In the centre is the King's Norton .280 match cartridge, which had the greatest list of wins in 1914. Next to it on the right is the Eley .280. The pencil-shaped head of the K.N. 7 m/m target cartridge is somewhat remarkable. Only a little more than half the bullet protrudes from the case. The last cartridge on the right is the very successful .30 U.M.C. cartridge with 180 grains bullet

THE "MINIATURE" RIFLE DEFINED

The following are the latest regulations of the Society of Miniature Rifle Clubs as regards rifles and sights:

RIFLES

63. A miniature rifle may be of any single-loading pattern, of any calibre not exceeding .23 of 1 in. or 6 mm.; or a rifle of larger calibre fitted with any device for firing miniature ammunition, as defined in paragraph 70.

64. No repeating or magazine rifle allowed.

65. The trigger-pull must not be less than 4 lb., and must be tested with a dead weight. Competitors must submit their rifles for testing to any officer appointed for that duty, at any time during the continuance of a meeting, and any competitor whose rifle fails to pass the test will have his score disallowed and may at the discretion of the Committee have all previous scores also disallowed. If a rifle fails to pass the test, the Range Officer will, if the competitor so desires, retain it in his possession and retest it after a period of not less than five or more than ten minutes, and if it then passes the test the score will be allowed. In the event of an appeal to the Committee from the decision of the Range Officer, the rifle must be at once handed to the Range Officer and will be retained by the Committee until the appeal has been considered.

66. Slings may be used.

SIGHTS

68. The Society recognises two varieties of sights:
    (a) "Any." Sights of any pattern, fixed or adjustable, both vertically and laterally, but not fitted with glasses, telescopes or levels.
    (b) "Military." Sights of a pattern identical to those in use on any rifle in any branch of H.M. Service in the British Isles.

69. Orthoptic spectacles are not permitted in Military sight competitions.

The "paragraph 70" referred to in rule 63 defines miniature ammunition in such a way as to exclude any cartridge not of a strictly "miniature" description. A reference to page 194 will show that the definition of a "miniature" rifle has changed very little between 1905 and 1915. The rules of the National Rifle Association with regard to "small-bore" rifles and sights are substantially the same as those quoted above.

CHAPTER XII

The .220 Cartridge

AS regards numbers, there is no doubt that in times of peace the .220 cartridge is the most extensively manufactured of any particular size of ammunition. The tremendous development of the rifle club movement in the British Empire and in America, as well as among the Continental nations, has resulted in a demand of many hundreds of millions of rounds every year of the various sizes of this cartridge.

The .220 cartridge is a development from the percussion cap fitted with a bullet, which is known as the "Flobert" cap. The first .220 cartridges were made in America, and the idea was slowly developed for small game shooting and for gallery practice.

In the early days of civilian shooting at short ranges the .220 cartridge had not sufficiently made its mark to indicate it as essentially the best for this purpose, though by 1902 there were already many exponents of gallery shooting who held that up to 50 yards there was nothing to beat the .220 calibre short ammunition. At that time the long-rifle cartridge, which is now the standard size for all club rifles, was practically unobtainable in this country, and therefore a large number of other cartridges, which do not come within the scope of this chapter, were used by men who wished to shoot at ranges over 20 yards. These included such powerful ammunition as the .310 Greener, with 1,320 f.s. initial velocity, and the .32/40 Winchester, with 1,450 f.s. velocity. Such cartridges are, of course, not miniature cartridges in any sense of the word, and it only needed an adequate supply of the long-rifle cartridge, coupled with firm legislation by the governing societies, to put them out of court. The .220 cartridge as originally used in

THE THREE "MINIATURE" SIZES

this country was loaded with black powder, and the bullet was usually lightly seated in the case without any crimping. These uncrimped cartridges were naturally somewhat difficult to handle, as the bullet could easily be twisted out of the case by awkward loading, and if it were necessary to unload the rifle without firing the cartridge, it was quite usual to leave the bullet behind when the case was extracted. The black powder, though extremely reliable, fouled the barrels a good deal, so that it became usual to clean the rifle after every ten shots.

The miniature cartridge is made in three standard sizes. The short has a 30-grain bullet, as has also the long cartridge, whilst the long-rifle cartridge has a 40-grain bullet. For practical purposes the long cartridge may be excluded. It is seldom used, and rifles are hardly ever chambered for it in this country. There is no reason at all why, for shooting at 25 yards, the short-rifle cartridge should not be used; but almost all open competitions in this country include shooting at 100 yards, and for that purpose the long-rifle cartridge is necessary. Though rifle manufacturers frequently state that short and long cartridges can be used in weapons chambered for the long-rifle variety, it should be distinctly understood that by doing so the user seriously endangers the accuracy of his rifle. The use of a short cartridge in a chamber which is longer than it sets up corrosion behind the lead, with the result that there is an escape of gas immediately the short cartridge is fired, and when it is attempted to use a long cartridge in the same rifle the metal of the case is expanded by the explosion of the charge into the corroded place, and extraction is rendered difficult, if not impossible.

The problems before the manufacturer of a .220 cartridge are complicated by the fact that in so small an article there is practically no room for any toleration. With a smokeless powder charge weighing about three grains, a fraction more or less will make a considerable difference to velocity, and the least difference in the thickness of the copper of the case may lead, on one hand, to tight and difficult loading into the chamber, or, on the other, to the frequent piercing of the cases when the striker hits the rim.

Cases are now crimped on to the bullet, and as a consequence the bullet is always more or less deformed where the crimping has been. It is necessary that the crimping machines should work with considerable accuracy, or the bullets will be badly unbalanced when they leave the muzzle of the rifle.

The miniature bullet is made of lead alloy, the hardness of which is carefully calculated for the velocity which the bullet is to be given up the barrel. It is cast with two or three cannelures, which serve to reduce the friction of the bearing surface and to hold a lubricant. It has been frequently stated that these cannelures have the effect of greatly improving the steadiness of the bullet's flight, but it is difficult to see how the cannelures can affect in any way the flight of the bullet, to which is imparted sufficient rotation to give it proper gyroscopic stability. The same statement was made very many years ago about the very deeply indented bullet invented by Captain Tamisier.

The lubrication of the bullet is provided for in most makes of cartridge by dipping the bullet in specially prepared fat which will solidify on cooling. This, of course, makes the cartridge very dirty to handle, and some manufacturers have sought to confine the lubricant to the interior of the case by mixing a lubricating powder with the propellant. The civilian rifleman, however, is more concerned with the accuracy of the ammunition supplied to him than with the cleanness of his fingers, and, be a cartridge ever so bright to look at, he will have none of it if it is incapable of placing ten consecutive shots inside a 2-in. ring at 100 yards.

The accuracy of modern miniature ammunition is indeed remarkable. Five or six consecutive shots through the same hole in the target at 25 yards is an experience which has come to almost every really good holder of the miniature weapon, whilst there is now never an open miniature meeting without several scores of 100 at 100 yards, and very many of 99 and 98. Two or three years ago a well-known London miniature club started a competition which was known as the Century. In those days possibles at 100 yards were comparatively rare, and the idea of the competition was that a

MINIATURE CARTRIDGE FAULTS

ticket, at the price of 1d., could be taken out and a "century" could be shot concurrently with any other competition at 100 yards or by itself. The competition was to run on until some member of the club made his 100 yards "possible," when he would take as a prize a gold medal and the whole of the proceeds of the entries, less 10 per cent. which went to the club. The competition was won soon after it was started, and then ran a matter of thirteen or fourteen months before it was won again, though the club counted among its members many of the best-known metropolitan shots. When it was won for the second time the prize-money was worth between £4 and £5. After that, small improvements in the ammunition and in the rifles, but principally in the ammunition, made the hundred yards "possible" more and more frequent until the "century" at 100 yards became of little more importance than one at 50 yards.

The man who shoots with a miniature rifle and cartridge is often curiously hard to please, particularly if he has attained to that degree of excellence in holding it which will permit him to be reasonably sure of making 98 or 99 at 25 yards on the standard decimal target. He buys his ammunition usually at 2½d. for ten rounds, or at 2s. a hundred by the box, the difference between the price charged by the factor and the price charged by the club being sufficient with a reasonable number of shooting members to keep the club in a sound financial state without resorting to demands on the public for donations.

Though the ammunition is so cheap, the shooter usually criticises it adversely at the slightest provocation. Men who ought to know better have upon occasion used their influence, as officers or committee men of a club, to get a brand of ammunition banned by their members just because, in some competition, the particular man in question only succeeded in making 96 or 97 where he expected a 99 or a "possible." To these selfish individuals it does not seem possible that they themselves should be in error. Every shot which is not in the "carton" is "due to faulty ammunition," and they do not hesitate to write and tell the ammunition manufacturer all about it.

Now, in manufacturing small cartridges by millions it is not to be expected that every shot will be projected truly centred and with the exact velocity of those shots which have preceded and will follow it. Such a standard of perfection is not humanly possible. For all that, the careful rifleman who knows his business and is capable of differentiating between his own errors, those caused by the ammunition, and those caused by the rifle, will tell you that the number of faulty cartridges in any 100,000 lot sent out by one of the big firms is surprisingly small. It is possible to fire many thousands of rounds without having a deviation which can be attributed to ammunition trouble.

The ammunition faults which do exist are those which are not apparent to the casual club member until they are demonstrated to him by someone in the know. A year or so ago there was a demand for extreme accuracy in the miniature cartridge up to 200 yards, and a well-known German firm, in endeavouring to provide this, produced a more powerful .220 cartridge which was still within the definition of the word "miniature." The high velocity resulting in a good deal of lead fouling in the bore of rifles in which it was used, the manufacturers reduced the velocity slightly, but still kept it in the neighbourhood of 1,200 f.s. They also made some alterations in the priming composition, and though they produced a cartridge which was hardly to be beaten for its high level of accuracy, was yet most deleterious in its action on the barrels. Of course, the firm in question altered the composition of their cartridge when they found out what was happening, but the information was given them by a firm of rifle manufacturers, and not by a member of the shooting public.

With regard to shooting at 200 yards, it may be said that, though this range is within the capabilities of the cartridge, it seems unnecessary to force the little .220 bullet over such a distance. The only thing to be said in favour of 200 yards shooting with the miniature rifle is that it gives its devotees some very useful lessons in wind judgment.

CHAPTER XIII

Simple Ballistics

THERE are many men who shoot from year's end to year's end without concerning themselves in the least with the why and the wherefore of the phenomena they are constantly witnessing. Such men may develop into good marksmen—many of them do—but they are missing much of the most interesting part of rifle work and are preventing any possibility of their becoming really high-class shots. Others may be interested in ballistic matters, but, having little liking for mathematics, are scared off the field of inquiry by a formidable-seeming algebraical barrier bristling with apparently abstruse formulæ. As a matter of fact, the whole of Part II. of the "Text Book of Small Arms," which deals with the ballistics of small arms, can be comprehended by anyone who has a working knowledge of the simplest mathematics. Logarithms are necessary to reduce the otherwise unwieldy and uninteresting arithmetic to reasonable proportions, and an acquaintance with the method of working with a calculating rule is worth cultivating.

The science of ballistics may be classed as a physico-mathematical one. It has to do with the motion of projectiles, and also takes account of the means of imparting motion, the movements of the rifle, and the stresses and pressures developed in the act of imparting motion to the projectile. It is concerned with the observation and recording of phenomena and the measurement of such effects as are capable of being stated in terms of time, space or matter. The modern ballistician does as much investigation with the slide rule as he does with the delicate measuring instruments which science has placed to his hand; but the amateur will probably find his chances are small of working with crusher gauge or chronograph, and he will have to content himself with squared paper and other folk's figures as a basis for his calculations. He will be able, nevertheless, to pursue many fascinating problems to a logical conclusion, and will quickly find his shooting benefiting by the clear conception of the actual facts of a bullet's flight which he will gain in his excursions. We can conceive of no more interesting way of spending a winter evening than with slide rule and notebook, working out angles of elevation, wind tables and trajectories for bullets one hopes to use during the following season.

It is premised that the ordinary rifle shooting enthusiast will concern himself with only that portion of rifle shooting mathematics which deals with the branch of the science which comes under the heading of "exterior ballistics"; that is to say, that portion which deals with the motion of the bullet after it has left the muzzle of the rifle. "Interior ballistics" has to do with the motion of the bullet within the bore of the rifle. It is far more obscure, and is perhaps of more interest to the ballistic engineer than to the rifle-shot himself.

Before one can conveniently tackle any ballistic problem it is necessary that the ordinary terms used in the science should be thoroughly understood. The text-books on the subject content themselves with a series of definitions, but it will be convenient to explain matters in a more conversational, if less brief, manner than is possible in a definition table.

We will suppose, therefore, that we have a rifle to our shoulder, and are taking aim at a mark, using the sight in a proper manner in doing so. An imaginary line passing through the sights and joining the centre of the eye and the point aimed at is the *line of sight*. This line of sight makes an angle with the plane of the horizon, and the angle thus made is known as *the angle of sight*. The *line of departure* is the direction in which the projectile is moving immediately it leaves the barrel. The *axis of the rifle* is a straight line passing down the centre of the bore. The line of departure and the axis of the bore may be coincident, but in practice they usually form an angle one with the other, and the angle so formed is called the

PLATE XLII

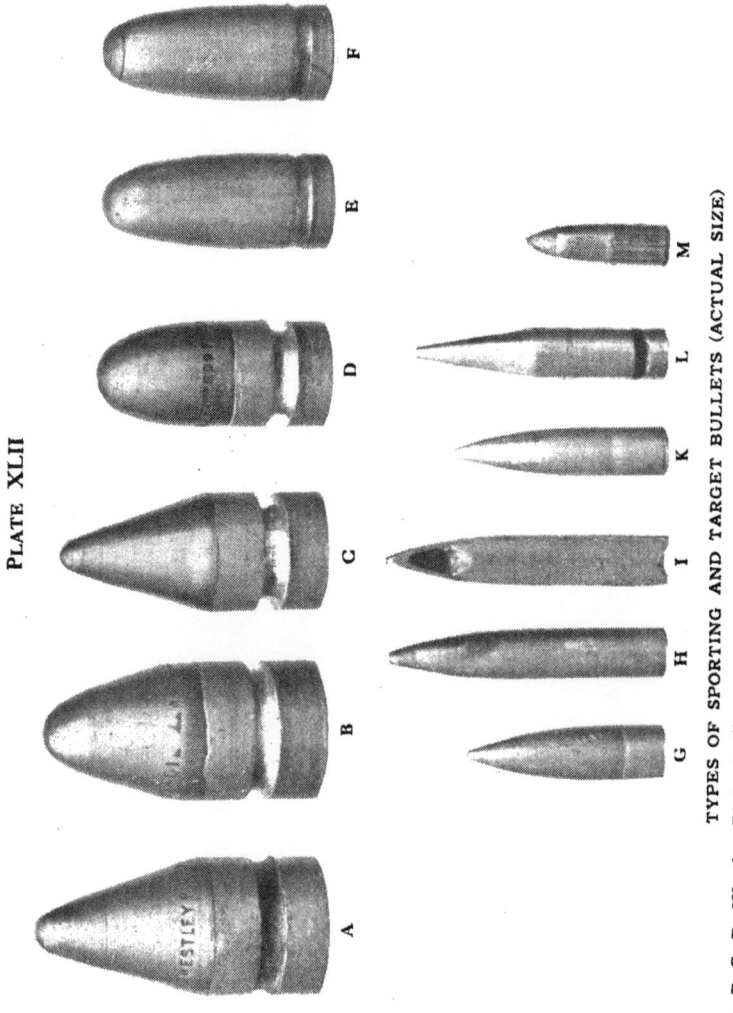

TYPES OF SPORTING AND TARGET BULLETS (ACTUAL SIZE)

A, B, C, D. Westley Richards "Explora" ball and shot-gun bullets
E. Gibbs .505-in., 525 grains, bullet
F. Gibbs .505-in., 525 grains, bullet, soft nosed
G. The "reduced charge" pointed bullet experimented with in 1895
H. K.N. .280 match rifle bullet
I. Section of the Ross .280 iron envelope bullet showing the hollow nose which led to its being disqualified for shooting at Bisley
K. The 7 m/m Mauser bullet for Brazilian service rifle
L. The 7 m/m K.N. target bullet
M. High velocity .220 sporting bullet—"The Imp"

DEFINITIONS

angle of jump. If the line of departure is below the axis of the bore, the angle of jump is said to be a "negative" one. If the line of departure is above the axis of the bore the jump is "positive." The *trajectory* is defined as a curve described by the centre of gravity of the bullet during its flight. The greatest height, or *maximum ordinate*, of the trajectory curve is not in its centre, but towards the point of impact. The *range* of a bullet is the distance between the muzzle of the rifle and the place where the trajectory cuts or intersects the line of sight.

These are by no means all the definitions which are given in the text-books, but they are quite sufficient to be getting along with, and are only stated in full in order that the reader who is not familiar with the exact definition of these terms so commonly used in rifle shooting shall be able to clearly visualise the facts which the definitions refer to. It should also be understood that no attempt is made here to go beyond the Government text-books. We feel that many men will like a clear explanation of the simpler ballistic problems stated in a way that does not take so much for granted as do the "Text Book of Gunnery" and the "Text Book of Small Arms."

A projectile is propelled from the muzzle of a rifle with a certain amount of energy stored in it. This energy is used in the work of overcoming the resistance offered by the air to the bullet's flight. The bullet has only a definite amount of stored energy, and the more it expends in pushing its way through the air, the more quickly is the energy exhausted and the bullet's flight finished.

The amount of resistance which the air offers to the flight of a projectile has been the subject of many experiments since, in 1687, Sir Isaac Newton dropped spheres of glass from the dome of St. Paul's, filling them with mercury, water and other substances, so that he could observe the behaviour of balls of different weight having the same size and surface. Newton assumed that the resistance was proportional to the square of the velocity. This has since been found to be true for low velocities (below about 900 f.s.) and for high velocities over about 3,000 f.s., but for the most useful range of velocities between these figures no such simple rule will suffice.

The experiments of the Rev. Francis Bashforth, which have already been referred to, gave the world the key to the mathematics of rifle shooting. Bashforth established the law that the resistance of the air was proportional to the square of the diameter (or cross section) of the bullet. This in ballistic work is always written "d^2." The resistance, of course, increases with increase of velocity. But knowing this, we are still a long way off any means of definitely stating in figures the resistance of the air to a projectile. It is necessary to state the resistance of the air to a standard projectile, which in this instance is 1 in. in diameter. To mentally visualise this we must imagine the standard 1-in. diameter bullet travelling at a velocity (which the text-books write as "$v\ f/s$") which results in a certain number of pounds (p) resistance.

The resistances for various velocities from zero to about 4,000 ft. per second were worked out twelve or thirteen years ago by the Ordnance Board, and the resistance to the air at these velocities plotted as a curve, which is figured in Part II. of the "Text Book of Small Arms."

The curve shows that the resistance of the air to a 1-in. projectile travelling at 1,000 f.s. is about 2 lb. With a very little increase of velocity—say to about 1,100, which is the velocity of sound—the resistance is more than doubled. At 1,500 it is nearly 10 lb.; at 2,000 f.s. velocity it is about 16 lb.; at 2,500 f.s. it is nearly 23 lb.; at 3,000 f.s. it is as nearly as possible 30 lb.; at 3,500 it is 39 lb.; and at 4,000 f.s. it is 49 lb.

But this only tells us the resistance to a projectile of a certain diameter. To arrive at the resistance of a projectile of any other diameter, it is necessary to multiply the pounds of resistance of the standard 1-in. projectile at the velocity for which it is desired to know the resistance by the square of the diameter (sectional density) of the bullet which is being investigated. This may be stated as the following formula:

$$R = d^2 p \text{ lb.}$$

For instance, to find the resistance of a bullet .3 in diameter, travelling at 3,000 f.s. velocity, $.3^2$ would be multiplied by 30.

THE CO-EFFICIENT OF REDUCTION

But even now we are a long way off the correct figures for resistance. Bashforth's standard projectile had an ogival head, struck with a radius of two calibres. Modern projectiles have heads which are very favourable to the overcoming of resistance, and in order to take this into consideration we introduce a co-efficient κ which is known as the "co-efficient of shape." It will be understood that the larger the radius of the curve of the bullet's nose, the longer will the nose be, and as the value of κ is regarded as unity for the Bashforth's standard head, then the larger the radii of the ogive the less will be the value of κ.

It is not necessary here to go into particulars of the way the exact value for κ is arrived at, as this co-efficient is mixed up with others which can for practical purposes be taken together and stated as a number which is near enough for rough calculations.

Bashforth's experiments were made with the muzzle-loading weapon, and when the breech-loader came into use it was found that it was possible to use a bullet which flew much more steadily, and to allow for this and for advantages gained by improvements in shape, etc., a co-efficient σ is introduced. There is still another co-efficient which has to be taken into our calculations, and that is the one which allows for differences in density of the air. This is indicated by the letter τ. We now have the formula in this condition:

$$R = \kappa\,\sigma\,\tau\,d^2 p$$

The use of these figures, which would have to be worked out for every separate bullet, and each day they were fired on, is unnecessary, because we do not need for ordinary calculations anything like this amount of accuracy. The co-efficients κ, σ, τ are, therefore, lumped together in one and denoted by the letter n, and is then called the "co-efficient of reduction." In almost all cases it can be taken that the co-efficient of reduction for blunt-nosed military bullets is 0.9, and for sharp-nosed military bullets is 0.6. At long ranges it is advisable to treat the sharp-nosed bullet as having a co-efficient of reduction of 0.7.

We are now in a position to investigate for ourselves one of the most important figures in ballistics, and that is the "ballistic co-efficient"—always indicated by C. This figure is arrived at by dividing the sectional density of the bullet, multiplied by the co-efficient of reduction, into the weight of the bullet in grains (7,000 grains to the pound). The formula is indicated thus:

$$C = \frac{w}{nd^2}.$$

The ballistic co-efficient indicates in figures the bullet's capability of overcoming the resistance of the air and its ability to retain energy. With it and a knowledge of the muzzle velocity of the bullet we can work out, with the aid of the ballistic tables, many interesting little problems.

It is not always necessary, however, to work ballistic problems in the regulation way. Many of the things we want to know can be got at in a rough and ready manner with sufficient accuracy for practical purposes.

For instance, the construction of a trajectory curve according to the books is a long and complicated business not lightly to be undertaken. First of all, one must know Sladen's formula.

The square of double the time of flight in seconds is the height of the vertex in feet, which is written simply:

$$H = (2T)^2$$

To plot your trajectory for any range you must choose a number of intermediate distances and calculate the time of flight, necessitating some fifteen operations for each distance. Thus the height of the trajectory for each point can be calculated and the trajectory plotted on squared paper, with the vertical scale exaggerated as ten is to one or to some other proportion.

There is a much simpler way of plotting a trajectory if you know the elevation necessary for your bullet at various ranges.

To find the ordinate of a trajectory, in inches, at any intermediate range subtract the elevation of the intermediate range from the elevation of the full range, and multiply the remainder

FORMULA FOR WIND DEFLECTION

by 1.047 (the subtention of 1 in. of angle) and by the number of hundreds of yards (for example 255 yards = 2.55).

Let us construct by this means a table of the height of the trajectory of the new Japanese pointed bullet at 300, 400, 500 to a 600-yards range. This bullet has a C = .48 and an MV = 2,500 f.s.; from these, by using Hardcastle's nomograph (page 170), we can arrive at the following elevation in minutes of angle:

Elevation for 300 yards = 9 minutes of angle.
,, ,, 400 ,, = 13 ,,
,, ,, 500 ,, = 17 ,,
,, ,, 600 ,, = 22.5 ,,

All that now remains is simple arithmetic:

22.5 − 9 = 13.5
13.5 × 1.047 × 3 = 42.4 inches.

The other intermediate points worked on the same principle give us the following heights of trajectory:

At 300 yards   42.4 inch.
At 400 yards   39.7 inch.
At 500 yards   28.8 inch.

Another very useful practical formula is that by means of which, knowing the speed of the wind in miles per hour and the C of the bullet, we can work out the necessary adjustment for wind deflection in minutes of angle.

$$\delta = \frac{M \times N}{C} \times \frac{\overline{K}}{1320}$$

where M = miles per hour (wind), N = range in hundreds of yards, $\overline{K}$ = the average value over the trajectory of Bashforth's "K." On the authority of Captain Hardcastle, $\overline{K}$ can usually be written as 90.

We will again work with the new Japanese bullet, and

suppose the range to be 600 yards and the wind twelve miles per hour:

$$\frac{12 \times 6}{.48} \times \frac{90}{1320} = 10 \text{ minutes.}$$

Of course, the result in this working is only correct if the wind is blowing straight across the range. If it is blowing at any other angle with the line of fire, the effect must be reduced by the following formula:

$$W_a = W \sin \theta$$

where W_a is the right angle component of the wind force.

There may come some occasion when, knowing the ballistic co-efficient of a bullet, we want to find one of its components. This may be done quite simply in the following manner:

To find d from $\frac{w}{nd^2} = C$

$$\left(\frac{w}{2} \times \frac{1}{c}\right) = \left(\frac{nd^2}{w} \times \frac{w}{n}\right)$$

$$\therefore \frac{w}{nc} = d^2$$

$$\therefore d = \sqrt{\frac{w}{nc}}$$

On the same principle the value of n can be extracted from $C = \frac{w}{nd^2}$. Thus

$$n = \frac{w}{d^2 c}$$

This is, of course, perfectly simple and easy to the reader who has not let his algebra go rusty, but our excuse for including these elementary figures—"Ballistics for Babies," as they have been called—is that there are many men who wish to know how to tackle simple ballistic problems without having to dig in the mazes of the text-books.

A few more formulæ of practical value may be of use to such men, and are here inserted as being the simplest method of working the various problems.

TRAJECTORY CURVES

To find striking energy of a projectile:

$$E = \frac{V^2 \times W}{2g}$$

Where V is velocity, W is weight in lb., g is gravity.
Example: Find striking energy of .303 Mark VI. bullet at 200 yards.

Striking velocity at 200 yards is 1,700 f.s.
Weight of bullet is 215 grains or $\frac{215}{7000}$ lb.
Gravity = 32

$$\therefore \frac{1700^2 \times \frac{215}{7000}}{64} = \frac{\frac{2{,}890{,}000}{1} \times \frac{215}{7000}}{\frac{64}{1}} = 1386.9 \text{ ft. lb.}$$

To find height or vertex of trajectory, knowing time of flight: Double the time of flight, then square the answer. The result is the height in feet.

Example: Find vertex of trajectory of French Lebel at 1,000 yards range, time of flight being 1.87 seconds ("Text Book of Small Arms").

$$1.87 \times 2 = 3.74$$

```
        3.74
        3.74
       -----
        1496
       2618
       1122
      -------
     13.9876  or about 14 feet.
```

To draw a trajectory curve showing the heights of the trajectory above the line of sight at all points in a range:

On squared paper (ruled preferably to tenths of an inch) draw a straight line representing the range, taking care to mark off each 100 yards. The beginning of the line should be marked 0, and the end of the line with the full range. Horizontal scale 1 in. = 100 yards, or 50 yards as desired. By means shown in preceding examples calculate the ordinates for each 100 yards of the range. Plot the trajectory at these points, making the vertical scale $\frac{1}{10}$ in. = 1 in., 2 in., 6 in., or 1 ft. as desired.

Draw a curved line from the beginning of the straight line marked 0, through the points plotted, to the end of the straight line.

The ordinate of the trajectory for any point in the range can then be read off.

Care should be taken to indicate on the sheet the vertical scale, which for rifle trajectories should never be less than twenty times, and may with advantage in certain cases be made even 200 or 300 times, that of the horizontal scale.

To draw an elevation chart from an elevation table:

On squared paper (ruled preferably to tenths of an inch) near the foot of the sheet coinciding with one of the thick lines of the squared paper. Mark off the ranges from the left, the beginning of the line being marked 0, and the scale being 1 in. = 100 yards.

From 0 draw a vertical line and mark off each vertical inch as 10, 20, 30, etc., each tenth of an inch representing one minute of angle of elevation. Directly above each range, plot the angle of elevation from the elevation table.

With a curved ruler draw a curved line from 0 through the points marked above each range. Carefully drawn an elevation chart will enable the angle of elevation for any range to be read off to one-tenth part of a minute of angle and to one yard of distance.

In drawing elevation charts the various elevations necessary may be plotted by using Captain Hardcastle's nomograph (facing page 170).

A rough and ready method of calculating the drop of a bullet between two distances, knowing the elevations, is to subtract the smaller elevation from the larger in minutes of angle, and multiply the remainder by the number of *hundreds* of yards. The result will be the answer in inches approximately. For example, the angle of elevation for 600 yards being 37 minutes, and for 500 yards 28.5 minutes, the difference 8.5 × 6 = 51 in. drop between 500 and 600 yards.

ZEROING THE SIGHTS

To find the sighting of a rifle by shooting on a 10, 25, or 50 yards range:

The sighting of a rifle coming straight from a factory or gunsmith's shop may be unsuited to the purchaser. The sighting may be tested in the following manner on a short range:

Measure the distance from the tip of the foresight to the axis of the bore. This may be done by measuring the distance from the tip of the foresight to the underside of the barrel, and subtracting half the outside diameter of the barrel.

Prepare a white paper or cardboard target as follows: On the sheet, which should be not less than 8 in. wide by 12 in. high for the shortest range, draw a thick horizontal black line 2 or 3 in. from the bottom. From the centre of this line draw a vertical line to the top of the sheet. Both lines should be of one thickness, depending on the range—e.g. not less than ⅛ in. thick for a range of 10 yards, and ½ in. to 1 in. thick for 50 yards. Beneath the horizontal line and parallel to it at a distance equal to the measurement between the tip of the foresight and axis of the bore, draw a thin line invisible to the firer.

Place this target at any distance from the firing-point not less than 10 yards and not more than 50 yards, taking care that the vertical line is plumb.

Aim at the intersection of the thick horizontal and vertical lines, the tip of the foresight just "touching" the underside of the horizontal line. The rifle should be fired from the prone position, with the left hand rested on some suitable support, such as a bag, cushion, or rolled coat.

Fire with great care a group of not less than three shots. Measure the distance from the centre of the group to the thin line in inches. Multiply this measurement by 100, and divide by the number of yards in the range fired from. The answer will be the number of minutes of angle of elevation. If the shots are below the thin line the sighting of the rifle will be negative.

This is practically the same as the operation known as "zeroing" when the rifle has adjustable sights. The target should be prepared in exactly the same manner as has been described, and the shooting should if possible be done at 12½ yards range. The object of zeroing is to adjust the sights so that they require a perfectly straight aim on a windless day at a particular range. No rifle will shoot truly to the aim at all ranges because the "drift" of the bullet is causing it continually to edge off in the direction of the twist of the rifling. Most Bisley Service rifle-shots who take the trouble to zero properly adjust the rifle to shoot truly at 500 or 600 yards by sighting it to shoot two minutes of angle to the *right* at 25 yards. Match rifle-shots, on the other hand, usually take a true vertical and horizontal zero, and make their drift allowance either plus or minus as the wind is from the right or left. When the sights are truly adjusted the centre of the group fired should have its centre on a spot which is situated exactly below the point of aim at a distance corresponding to the height of the foresight over the axis of the bore, plus the drop of the bullet over the distance of the target from the muzzle. The drop of the bullet can be ignored, as it is seldom more than .005 in. at 25 yards with modern military bullets. In adjusting the sights to bring the group to its desired spot, it should be remembered that one minute of angle is represented by ⅛ in. at 12½ yards and by ¼ in. at 25 yards. When the group has been centralised a few shots should be fired, the sight being raised to correspond with the elevation for say 200, 500, 600, 900, or 1,000 yards. If each strikes the black vertical line of the target, then the sights are fixed to the rifle in an upright position.

It may, of course, be said that no real work can be done without a very thorough knowledge of mathematics, and an aptitude for applying that knowledge to ballistic problems. Our answer is that there are very few men doing "real work" in the science, and that those who are will welcome the modest attempt to introduce the rifle-shooting amateur to a side of his sport about which he is, more often than not, almost completely ignorant.

Part II

RIFLE SHOOTING—THEORY AND PRACTICE

Part II

RIFLE SHOOTING—THEORY AND PRACTICE

CHAPTER I

Shooting in War, in the Field, and on the Range

RIFLE shooting is a complex subject. It is true that all rifles are merely mechanical appliances designed to project missiles accurately, but it must not be forgotten that the uses to which they are put are widely divergent. The big-game rifle-shot, for example, has little in common with the target-shot, and the military marksman bears small resemblance to the stage exponent of trick shooting. In some respects, however, similarity exists between one form of rifle shooting and another, but there are sufficient differences to call for the subdivision of rifle shooting under three heads—namely, Military Shooting, Game Shooting, and Target Shooting.

Taking each in the order of its importance, which is the order given above, a short dissertation may not be out of place.

Military Shooting, besides being the most important, is by far the most difficult branch of rifle shooting. It is carried out, almost invariably, under conditions of great stress, excitement and danger; of fatigue, and frequently of privation. The problems presented to the marksman in war are of greater diversity than in any other form of shooting, the conditions under which they arise are seldom known until the moment calls for action, while the actual shooting has to be carried out under almost every conceivable condition which militates against steadiness and accuracy.

Until comparatively recently, the soldier was merely a mechanical pawn in the game of war. He was not allowed to have any initiative, and even knowledge was not considered an altogether desirable quality. In recent times, however, things have changed. Nowadays the private soldier is encouraged, nay, compelled, not only to learn the technical minutiæ of all that pertains to rifle practice, but also to acquire a fair knowledge of fire tactics, which are based on the assumption of considerable initiative on the part of the private soldier.

Military marksmanship of a high order calls for extensive knowledge on a wide range of subjects pertaining to the science of musketry—for physical fitness, initiative, resource, and intelligence. The marksman on active service must be a good judge of distance; must be strong, and in a high state of physical training; must have good eyesight, and be able to describe accurately the position of any objective; must be able to meet an awkward situation without flurry, and have the grit to "make a good show" under severe climatic conditions. Mere quiescent steadiness is no test of the soldier marksman's shooting ability. In active service he will seldom (except in defence) have time or opportunity to steady down, for most of his shooting will be done after violent physical exertion, aggravated by considerable mental excitement. For this reason he must be in good training. The better his physical condition, the less will exertion affect his steadiness.

All this may prompt an observation that active service shooting is only of the roughest, wildest and most haphazard kind. So it is, *comparatively*. But the reason why it is so, is not because the conditions render accurate shooting impossible, but because of the difficulty of training men to overcome these conditions. The very highest exponents of marksmanship would find active service conditions a shocking handicap to accurate shooting, but even so their shooting would be immeasurably better than the average of the rank and file soldier. By this it is not intended to infer that the British Army is deficient in marksmanship. Far from it. When the difficulties of teaching a large body of men to shoot accurately are considered, the marksmanship of the British Army is remarkable.

GERMAN SCHOOL OF MUSKETRY

But the standard attained is only comparative. Much better results can be obtained by better marksmen, for the difficulties are not all insurmountable. They are certainly great, but their greatness only calls for a higher order of marksmanship than we at present have.

In this connection a recent publication in France gives the statement of a musketry expert, that the French Musketry authorities consider the limit of skill in marksmanship in the French Army to have been reached, the proof of this being that for many years all regiments have shown almost identical results! This is almost, though not quite, as amusing as the arguments of the German School of Musketry, which are sufficiently entertaining to merit recounting. They are also instructive as showing the curious working of the Teutonic mind.

The German "expert" says in effect that active service conditions make accurate shooting impossible; also that in any case the soldier is not likely to aim at all; but if he does, he will aim wrongly. With this as the basis he proceeds to work out his argument as follows: If the rifle be accurate, the soldier aiming wrongly will always miss his mark. His only chance of hitting will therefore depend on some inaccuracy in the rifle or ammunition. Therefore it is necessary to give the soldier a rifle which is not too accurate, and ammunition which will develop errors big enough to correct the soldier's bad aim.

These arguments have for years been solemnly enunciated at the German School of Musketry at Spandau. To-day France and Great Britain have reason to be thankful for them.

Turning now to Game Shooting with the rifle. This branch of rifle shooting, especially when hunting dangerous game, calls for some of the qualities necessary to the military marksman. The problems presented to the marksman here, however, are not of great diversity so far as the actual shooting is concerned, but they are seldom easy, and call for good nerves and steadiness.

When the time comes to shoot, the chief difficulties met with are: Judging distance, sighting or aiming, movement, and time.

The first of these will be dealt with fully in another chapter, but as the principal part of the sport consists of stalking the quarry, and as very few rifles will instantly kill a large animal beyond 300 yards, this distance being therefore generally termed the limit of sporting ranges, the problem of judging distance is not nearly so formidable as in military shooting. Aiming difficulties arise through the similarity between animals and their natural background, through too much or too little light, or through having to "aim off" for intermediate ranges not provided for on the sights of the rifle. The movement of the animal may cause other difficulties, and, in addition, the question of time may become an urgent one if a dangerous animal wants to argue.

Target Shooting may be called the home practice in preparation for Military and Game Shooting. It is possible to closely imitate the real conditions, always excepting the "answering hail of bullets" and the charging lion; but a really close imitation requires such extensive range accommodation and produces such meagre results to the firer under conditions of such great discomfort as to make practice uninteresting to any but those whose livelihood depends on their efficiency. Target Shooting, therefore, is, and must always be, of an elementary nature among those who look upon it as a sport or diversion. That is to say, it must be so arranged that the conditions will be sufficiently easy to enable the shooter to obtain results with certainty and in some degree of comfort. The aspiring marksman will persevere with his practice if the results are regular and show improvement, but if he went to the ranges twice for an hour's practice, under service conditions, and never struck a target at all, his enthusiasm for shooting would quickly evaporate.

However, Target Shooting at unknown distances is almost impossible in this country, owing to want of range accommodation. Modern rifle bullets will ricochet off any ground, from wet bog to dry shingles, and the direction and distance of their subsequent flight are very uncertain. Bullets have been known to travel as much as 2,000 yards from a ricochet, and, although extensive danger areas have to be provided behind present-day stop-butts, all range regulations would have to be

PLATE XLIII

THE OFF-HAND OR STANDING POSITION

These two photographs show the correct "stance" for off-hand shooting. The head should be upright and well back from the cocking-piece; the left wrist and arm well under the rifle. Both hands should grip firmly. The body must be balanced equally on both feet

TARGET SHOOTING

revised if unknown-distance shooting became general, and the ricochet were the rule and not the exception.

The provision of measured ranges and the consequent elimination of the necessity for judging distance in Target Shooting is thus the removal of one of the greatest difficulties encountered in war, and all "Service Conditions" at known distances are thus artificial. Other war conditions, it is true, can be embraced in the practice, such as heavy marching, running, obstacles, firing from loopholes, etc. (and, in actual fact, competitions embracing these conditions for teams and individuals are carried out at Bisley every year); but these conditions are not popular, and require a good deal of "drumming" to bring competitors.

But even if such conditions were general, Target Shooting at known distances can never approach service conditions. To lie down in one's own time and group five or ten shots at a known distance into a ring measuring about six inches per hundred yards of range, even at a rate of fire of ten shots per minute, is child's play compared with the problems presented to the soldier in the field. It is some comfort to the target-shot to know that the difference between the two branches of shooting is reflected in the results respectively achieved.

In Target Shooting, as generally carried out in this country, physical condition or training counts for very little. Competitions are conducted under conditions which place the physically unfit as nearly as possible upon terms of equality with the highly trained men. Indeed, there are many instances on record where women of very moderate physique have successfully competed on equal terms with men. This fact alone would appear to damn present-day conditions of Target Shooting as a preparation for war, for in a test of military marksmanship such as obtains in war no woman is likely to make herself conspicuous by success in competition with trained men. On the other hand, as has already been pointed out, conditions which embrace discomfort and hardship are unpopular with those who pay for their practice, and it would therefore be necessary to have generous Government support in ammunition and rifles if existing conditions were to be changed.

Target practice for Game Shooting, on the other hand, need not include violent physical exercise. The hunter is no doubt unwise who fails to make himself "fit" before he faces an arduous "trek," but at the worst his pace is regulated by his fitness, and when he has had enough he can cry "halt." Again, he probably will never be called upon to do any shooting after an exhaustive race, such as happens in war. He does, however, require specialised knowledge in his rifle to be successful, and this will be dealt with elsewhere.

While the accomplished target-shot may be able to hit a comparatively small bull's-eye nine times out of ten shots at a known range, his performance in the field or against game may appear quite ludicrous when his distances are unknown and wrongly estimated. Indeed, when the rifleman finds himself in open and unknown country a new set of circumstances are encountered which set at naught the highest attainment of shooting skill. On the shooting range one betakes oneself to the firing point, which is correctly labelled with the distance. The sights are adjusted accordingly, and the first shot lands comfortably on the target. There may be some slight error due to atmospheric or other causes, in which case a correction of sighting is made, and the firer pumps his remaining rounds into the bull's-eye with confidence and ease.

Now let us see what happens in the "open." If the shooter is hunting game, his objective may suddenly come into view, or he may be stealthily stalking it in the hope of arriving within effective range. When the time comes to fire, he must estimate the distance at which his quarry is, and adjust his sight accordingly. Now, as everyone knows, the sportsman's bull's-eye in Game Shooting is known as the "heart" region, and is a comparatively small area over the heart. Outside this vital area bullets seldom take immediate effect, except through the head; hence, even when shooting the largest animals, the actual target is a small one, being about a foot in diameter in the case of an elephant, and about four inches in the case of the smaller antelopes. In judging distance, therefore, the margin of permissible error is extremely small beyond 100 yards, if the heart region is to be successfully reached. Beyond 100

MILITARY SHOOTING

yards, the drop of the bullet of the average sporting rifle is rapid; in the case of a rifle giving 2,000 f.s. muzzle velocity being about ten inches between 100 and 200 yards, and about eighteen inches between 200 and 300 yards. Put into practical figures, if the shooter estimated the distance to be 150 yards, whereas it actually was 200, his shot would strike some six inches below the point he desired to hit, even if he aimed and fired correctly. Such an error in "placing" a shot will seldom fail to let the animal escape, although perhaps insufficient to cause a complete miss.

In military shooting, still greater difficulties are met with in this regard. Firstly, the limits of effective range are much greater, requiring more accurate estimation. In the second place, the objective is frequently invisible, offering no gauge of visual size to assist estimation. Then the sights which ought to be adjusted with equally greater accuracy are capable of almost limitless error, unless adjusted with the utmost care. Add to this the possibility of operations being conducted under a well-directed fire from a resolute enemy, and the comparison can be appreciated without further enlargement.

P

CHAPTER II

Physical Condition in Relation to Rifle Shooting in War and Peace

GOOD physical condition is the first attribute in a marksman, and so important and necessary is this condition that, before entering upon a discussion of methods of shooting practice, it is deemed advisable to give a detailed account of how "fitness" can be attained and maintained.

A good digestion is a better asset to the marksman than good eyesight, because on the former rests the whole fabric of physical fitness. Bad digestion may throw the nerves out of order, affect the eyesight and heart, sap the strength, and, in fact, render the sufferer unfit to do himself or his rifle justice. Bad eyesight can be corrected by glasses, but the cure for indigestion is not so easy.

Now the best and indeed the only true and natural method of stimulating digestion is by means of judicious physical exercises. Open-air exercises should consist of walking and running, and should be taken either as exercises pure and simple, or in the form of some game which embraces both or one. It may be that circumstances prevent one indulging in games of the kind indicated, or it may be difficult to take running or walking exercises systematically. In such cases a regular course of what is termed "Swedish drill" can be carried out at home, either at night or in the morning, with most beneficial results. A few simple exercises are all that it is necessary to know, and, if gone through regularly, are sufficient to keep one in a continuous state of "fitness." As a rule, ten or fifteen minutes each day is sufficient to keep one's digestive system in good order, but to be in condition for military shooting—i.e. in hard training—a longer time is necessary, with

PHYSICAL EXERCISE

walking and running in addition, for "wind" is an important essential in the trained military marksman.

The following simple exercises may be found useful, all being carried out stripped to the buff:

(1). Stand erect, with heels close together, arms extended straight above the head, thumbs interlocked. Take a full breath, then bend forward and downward with arms still outstretched, slowly exhaling all the time until the extended fingers touch or nearly touch the toes. Throughout the whole movement the legs must not be bent at the knees. Reverse the movement slowly, inhaling, until the original position has been reached. Repeat the exercise several times.

(2). Stand erect with arms at the side or folded. Contract and relax alternately the abdominal muscles without bending the body. Exhale during contraction; inhale during relaxation. Repeat for two or three minutes.

(3). Assume original position as in Exercise 1. Bend slowly over to the right side as far as possible. Then come up to the original position, and bend over to the left, hands extended above the head all the time. Repeat the exercise a dozen times.

(4). Original position as in Exercise 1, except that the feet are slightly apart, body evenly balanced on both. Bend slowly to the right as far as possible, then, without coming back to the erect position, swing the body slowly forward and round to the left, making a pivoting motion from the hips. Continue the pivot motion, swinging the body backward and round to the right again in a circular movement. Continue the pivoting movement until the body muscles cry "enough." During this exercise, exhale when bending forward; inhale when bending back.

(5). Lie down flat on the floor, face up, arms at the side. Raise the legs, knees straight, until they are at right angles to the body, keeping the head on the ground. Resume original position slowly, and repeat six or a dozen times.

(6). Position as for No. 5, but with arms outstretched behind head. Swing the arms slowly forward over the head until they reach the body, then raise the body slowly into a sitting posture by contracting the abdominal muscles. The knees must be kept straight, and the heels on the ground.

Leg exercises and arm exercises should also be taken, but it is not the immediate purpose of this work to do more than show how that most vital part of the rifleman's physical system —viz. the digestion—may be stimulated and improved.

Coming now to the actual practice with the rifle, a considerable saving of time may be made by a systematised method. To assist a proper appreciation of the method, it is necessary to make a digression, taking the indulgent reader back to some elementary principles.

It may be stated as an axiom that no physical movement is ever performed by man perfectly. Error is always present, the degree of such being usually greatest at the first attempt. Improvements are only made by the reduction of error, and accomplishment with a minimum of error is man's nearest approach to perfection.

All movements of the human body are performed by *contraction* of muscle. The force which contracts the muscles is a nerve force emanating from the brain, which projects it to the muscles by way of the nerves, much in the same way as an electric battery projects power to a motor through wires. Roughly speaking, the brain, on comprehending the nature of the movement required, projects nerve force to one or more certain muscles, which thereupon contract, and, being joined to the frame by tendons, pull the frame in the required direction. By contracting two or more muscles, pulling in different directions, variations of muscular movement may be achieved, while speed and strength depend upon the amount of nerve force expended.

From this rough-and-ready description of muscular movement, the layman will perhaps be able to appreciate that movements of great precision depend entirely upon the exactitude with which the brain dispenses its nerve force and the correctness with which it selects its muscular media. It is merely a step in the process of reasoning to observe that the efficient performance of its functions can only be achieved after painstaking education.

PLATE XLIV

THE KNEELING POSITION
The essentials of a good kneeling position are that the body should be firmly and steadily supported; but that the soldier should be able to rise from it quickly

THE PRONE POSITION
The position here pictured is that recommended for target shooting as the steadiest and least fatiguing. The points to note are the flattening of the whole body from heels to lower ribs against the ground, the head upright and well back from the cocking piece, the elbows drawn a little towards one another

THE MUSCULAR BRAIN

Precision of muscular movement requires the education of the muscular brain. In its first attempts, the muscular brain fails through lack of nerve force, as in the case of the infant trying to walk. Having acquired the requisite amount, it fails in direction and distribution of the nerve force; and the extent to which the education of the brain can be carried in rectifying the two last-named faults is almost limitless.

The method by which the muscular brain should be educated is somewhat similar to that adopted in teaching a child to spell—namely, repeating the letters of simple words. A simple elementary movement is selected, and is performed slowly and repeatedly, until the brain understands the exact proportions of nerve force required. At first, each attempt has some error either in direction or force, or even in time, but succeeding trials familiarise the brain with the movement, and it gradually eliminates, or rather diminishes, the fault.

When a particular movement has been so understood that the brain can operate the muscles with precision, other movements are each taken in turn and thoroughly mastered, all faults being detected and, as far as possible, corrected.

Most movements, however, are compound movements; that is to say, they are composed of several distinct motions running one into the other. At first, there will be error in every motion, and if the whole movement is performed at the beginning of practice, the errors made in the first motions will be forgotten before the time comes to repeat them. It is therefore better to separate each motion, and practise it exclusively until the brain has thoroughly learned it and corrected the faults. When all the individual motions have been mastered, then, and not till then, practise the combined movement.

To draw a rough simile, take the game of golf. The complete game requires proficiency in the use of a number of different clubs. If the beginner buys, say, half a dozen of these clubs, and betakes himself to a golf course to play a round for practice, he starts with a drive which has some error. He next resorts to his iron clubs, and possibly tries each in turn before arriving at the second teeing ground. But, when he comes to repeat his drive, so many shots have intervened to claim his attention since his first essay, that he now has no recollection of what his first error was, and he either repeats it or commits a fresh one which, in turn, is again forgotten at the succeeding teeing ground. And so with almost every shot played. What he ought to do is to practise one particular shot at a time, with one particular club, until the brain thoroughly understands it. Each fault is corrected before it is forgotten, and so not only is progress accelerated, but a much higher state of proficiency is reached.

In practising movements in handling the rifle, a similar course should be followed. As an example, let us take rapid magazine fire with the Service rifle. To be properly performed, this must be done without taking the rifle down from the shoulder, and, in the prone position, it is an exceedingly difficult operation to a beginner, for it calls for the projection of nerve force through unfamiliar channels, causing a feeling of awkwardness, and even weakness, out of all proportion to the complication of the movements or the strength required to perform them.

Having taken up a prone position with an empty rifle held in position for firing, the beginner selects the first motion for practice—namely, lifting the bolt knob. The bolt knob is grasped between the thumb and forefinger of the right hand. With as little movement of the *body* and rifle as possible, the bolt knob is raised as far as it will go. The right elbow may be raised slightly off the ground to perform the movement, which can be assisted by giving the rifle a slight twist to the right with the left hand, but *the whole concentration of mind must be on the upward movement of the bolt knob*. Practice in this upward movement should be continued, slowly at first, until it can be performed without material exertion. The second movement is now taken. With the rifle in position as before and the bolt knob raised, draw back the bolt to its full extent. Additional purchase can be obtained for the right arm if the right elbow is raised just clear of the ground. Return the bolt to the position it started from, but, as before, the concentration must be on the first—i.e. the backward—motion. Repeat this until it can be done easily and without discomfort.

HANDLING THE RIFLE

The third motion is the thrusting of the bolt from the open position right up to the chamber until the striker spring is fully compressed. It is practically the reverse of the second motion, but the cocking of the rifle at the end of the motion requires a different distribution and timing of the nerve force.

The fourth motion is the reversal of the first.

As already stated, the primary difficulty will be found to be lack of nerve force, and the apparent weakness will be accentuated by faulty distribution. For this reason, the empty rifle, being easier to manipulate than a loaded one, is recommended for the first practices; but, as progress is made, dummy cartridges can be used, until eventually the recruit is ready to try his hand on the range. In all practices the movements should be gone through slowly first of all. Speed requires force, which the brain cannot impart economically without a full comprehension of the movement. Gradually, as the movement is more and more understood, the pace may be quickened; but the great tendency which should be curbed is to increase the pace too early in the practice, a habit which leads to irregular and jerky manipulation of the rifle.

Generally speaking, the system of practice above described can be followed in regard to all that branch of shooting which comes under the heading of "Handling the Rifle." In many cases, however, some of the motions are so familiar to the muscular brain as not to require much separate practice; but this will, in any case, be apparent when trying them with the rifle for the first time. In all cases mental concentration on the one particular motion is essential to the best progress, but at the same time it is as well to remember that one cannot always be concentrating, and that there are other variations of handling the rifle which, while not so directly beneficial, relieve monotony without retarding progress. Any exercise with a rifle is better than none, even if it consists only of swinging it round one's head. The proficiency of the Regular soldier's musketry owes quite a debt to the manual exercises, for these engender such a command over the rifle in the handling of it, that aiming and firing instruction starts under much more favourable circumstances than in the case of the awkward civilian.

Constant handling of the rifle produces a feeling that the rifle has become lighter. Actually the brain has become so expert in its distribution of nerve force that less power is expended in handling than formerly. This accurate distribution of force becomes most apparent in what is technically known as "holding"—i.e. the steadying of the rifle when firing.

"Holding" is perhaps the most difficult of all the physical actions of shooting, and it is safe to say that it can only be acquired after long and patient practice. "Holding" demands of the muscular brain a perfectly even flow of nerve force which, in turn, necessitates perfectly accurate distribution. To illustrate what this entails it may be of use to describe what takes place when a human being performs the simple act of standing erect.

Without a rigid frame, the tendency of the erect human is to collapse to the ground. With the frame held rigid, but without a suitable base to stand on, the tendency is to fall flat. Partly by the sense of sight, and partly by other physical means within the head, a "sense of balance" is acquired, and any lapse from a correct poise is communicated to the brain through this medium.

The frame of the body is held rigidly erect by the contraction of certain muscles, and the "sense of balance" tells the brain when the poise is lost and in which direction. Instantly a little stream of nerve force is shot down the proper channels or nerves; muscles operating the pedal frames are contracted, and the point of balance is thereby shifted and the poise restored. This restoring of the poise goes on continuously and perhaps every instant whilst one stands. If one stands on one leg, the actions are very apparent and rapid. The rapid change in the point of balance can be likened to placing a small prop in the direction of the fall.

Now, the more delicate the sense of balance is, the better educated the brain becomes in the distribution of nerve force to maintain the poise. Consequently the flow of nerve force is more constant and even, and the erect position is maintained with greater steadiness.

And so with "holding."

UNSTEADINESS IN HOLDING

Unsteadiness in holding a rifle is caused simply by badly controlled nerve force. Practice alone will remedy this, provided the muscular brain is capable of acquiring the education, for it must not be forgotten that extraneous factors, such as the effects of alcohol, may weaken or disturb the muscular brain in the performance of its function.

Apart from this, an intelligent appreciation of (a) the causes of unsteadiness in "holding," and (b) what the muscular brain has to do to maintain the rifle in a steady position, combined with concentration of the mind on these points when practising, will materially assist the learner to derive the most benefit from his practice.

CHAPTER III

Trigger Pulling or "Let off"

ALL our elaborate care in sighting and steadiness of holding will be thrown away if the rifle is moved from its alignment at the moment of firing; if, to use the rifleman's expression, the shot is badly "let off." Trigger pulling is, in fact, as important a branch of rifle practice as holding or aiming. The use of the term "trigger pulling" has been objected to by many authorities, on the ground that it does not correctly describe the act of moving the trigger so that the scear is drawn from the bent and the striker allowed to fly forward to detonate the cap and fire the powder. "Letting off" the shot, it is stated, is accomplished by a "squeezing" together of the forefinger and thumb.

In actual fact the trigger is pulled; there is no other way of describing the proper action. To combine the movement of forefinger and thumb, or, in fact, to bring the thumb into play at all in letting off the shot, is bad. The function of the thumb of the trigger hand is to assist the second, third and fourth fingers to maintain a firm grip of the rifle, and nothing more. The trigger finger should be so completely under control as to be capable of independent action. Indeed, the trigger finger ought to be able to maintain an even pressure, or no pressure, while the grip of the other fingers and thumb is tightened or eased. When the time comes, the pressure should be applied by the forefinger alone, independently of anything else, and the more completely the action of this finger is detached the better will its work be.

The objection to the term "pulling" arises through the tendency of the beginner to apply the pressure to the trigger by pulling with the arm, which naturally affects the holding of the rifle, the discharge taking place in the middle of a wild swing. But if the pull of the trigger be confined to the forefinger, the objection must cease, for it is the correct description of the correct action. The development of a slow, squeezing, or dragging action in moving the trigger is much to be deplored; it has had something to do with the military criticism that target shots are "slow." The ideal is a quick, sure movement that releases the bent at the proper moment—but does not impart any movement to the rifle itself.

Trigger pulling can best be learned in the firing positions with an empty rifle. "Flinching" at the discharge is a very common failing of the beginner. In most cases "flinching" is a misnomer. It conveys the impression that the firer is afraid of the recoil and has flinched from it. This rarely occurs even in the most pronounced cases of "flinching." What happens is that the firer at the instant of releasing the trigger allows his attention to be taken away from his holding and aiming and concentrated on the trigger release. This can be demonstrated, for the so-called flinching takes place *when the firer is practising with an empty rifle.* He knows the rifle will not recoil nor make a nerve-shattering noise, and yet he apparently flinches. But the case of the practised rifleman affords a more convincing demonstration. Observe what happens when he encounters a miss-fire. His rifle is held steady and his aim is true right up to the instant the trigger is released. Snap goes the trigger, but there is no recoil. Instantly the rifle muzzle performs a wild "bob" and the shooter's eyes blink. He has "flinched"! The beginner usually blinks his eyes when the striker snaps, and this fault should be entirely eradicated before he is allowed to fire with a loaded rifle, because one of the principal methods by which the shooter detects his own errors in shooting is by taking note of the point of aim at the instant of discharge. To do this successfully it is necessary to see right through the recoil, an impossibility unless the eyes are kept open. The declaration of the point of aim at the moment of discharge is insisted on by teachers of military shooting, and should not be lost sight of at any moment during actual practice work in the initial stages of tuition. Seeing through the recoil can be well learned on the miniature range. A good shot with the .22 rifle often holds so well in the prone position, that the alignment of the sights is the same after the discharge of the cartridge has taken place as it was when he pulled the trigger.

In trigger exercises, the education of the trigger finger and brain will be not only in the direction of smoothness of "let off," but also of time. It is desirable to be able to let off exactly when required, for this is the only way by which the natural unsteadiness of human holding can be counteracted. In this connection, some rifles are very deficient in regularity of trigger pull, the variations being so great that "timing" is virtually impossible. Sporting rifles are usually much better in this respect, although the Mauser and Mannlicher types of military rifles leave little to be desired. Many miniature rifles of the "converted" type with the Martini action give some trouble in this respect, and a little time and money spent in adjusting the trigger mechanism to give a certain pull will be well expended.

In practising trigger pulling in the aiming positions, the power or nerve force applied should be gradual, and the mind concentrated on "reading the weight"—that is, knowing how much force to apply to release the trigger. At the earliest practices the time taken to increase the force until the trigger goes should be considerable, say 30 seconds; but it should not be prolonged so much as to cause fatigue, as by doing so a false impression of the "weight" of the trigger will be acquired. Gradually, as the brain appreciates the amount of nerve force required, the time can be shortened, as the brain will be able to at once apply 80 or 90 per cent. of the requisite pressure without fear of releasing the trigger, the remainder being handed out whenever the "hold" has been secured. This is the complete development of the "quick, sure movement" spoken of above. Careful application of this practice daily for two or three weeks will enable the learner to let off his trigger with great certainty of timing, a most desirable accomplishment, and one which is absolutely necessary when shooting in the standing position.

PLATE XLV

WAR SHOOTING IN THE OPEN

The top picture shows the usually adopted prone position as viewed from the front. Compare it with the lower picture, which shows a more crouching and less visible position which has been developed to give the least possible target with the greatest speed in aiming. (See Plate XLVI)

SNAP-SHOOTING

In rapid shooting, where the trigger release would be thought to be of a rough-and-ready description, good touch is invaluable. The secret of rapid shooting is not the accurate snapping-off from an unsteady rifle. Rather is it the high development of fast loading and a quick steadying of the rifle, affording *some* appreciable time for aim and let off. The steadying of the rifle can best be achieved with the firm and accurate manipulation of the rifle by both hands, and the highest education of the right hand and "detached" trigger finger is necessary to realise to the full the possibility of a steady aim during very rapid fire. The aim being the most important thing, the necessity for being able to pull the trigger in the least possible time without disturbing the aim will readily be understood.

These remarks apply with equal force to snap-shooting, where a quick shot has to be taken at an object suddenly appearing for a short space of time. The difference between "rapid" shooting and snap-shooting is that, in the former, the rifle is kept at the shoulder continuously during the delivery of a rapid fire throughout a prolonged exposure of the target, whereas, in the latter, the rifle is brought up to the aiming position from the "ready," and a quick shot delivered at the target. This necessitates the firmest and surest of handling and perfect command over the trigger to prevent snatching at the trigger and disturbance of the aim.

CHAPTER IV

Eye Training and Aiming

IT is as necessary to "train the eye" to see an object as it is to "train the muscles" to hold a rifle. The terms are used in their popular form, and both are wrong; for the eye is merely a lens through which the brain exercises the sense of sight. The perfection of the eye, as an eye, does not necessarily carry with it the strongest or most accurate vision, although it gives the brain the clearest and best impressions to interpret. Strength of vision depends on the strength and activity of that part of the brain which interprets the visual impression. For example, two people with normal eyesight may develop their sense of sight in different spheres far above their original powers, and yet, apart from their own speciality, each may still be normal. Take, for instance, a sailor and a gamekeeper. Each before entering his calling may be possessed of normal sight. After a few years the sailor, through constant visual exercise at sea, can distinguish ships at abnormal distances, while the gamekeeper can detect game which is quite invisible to the layman. Yet the gamekeeper would be entirely unsuited as look-out man on the question of eyesight, and the sailor would in many cases be unable to distinguish a hare twenty yards off in an open field. Why is this? The impressions or images taken by their respective eye lenses are equally good and clear, but being strange the brain through lack of practice cannot interpret them.

Similarly, a target rifle-shot, in favourable circumstances, can distinguish with the unaided eye a five-inch spotting disc on a black-and-white target at an almost incredible distance. Instances are known where this has been done in this country at 1,200 yards. Yet these same men, if placed on a battle train-

RIFLE SIGHTS

ing ground without special practice, would be inferior to the average soldier in observation of obscure battle targets. Their eyes might be just as good, or perhaps a little better, but the want of practice or exercise of the eye brain would result in failure to interpret the image on the retina.

So much for the primary functions of the eyes. Now let us see how they can be trained.

The first or elementary part of the training of the shooter's eye is aiming. Aiming is the act of aligning the sights of an arm with, or in relation to, a mark or objective. That is to say, the sights may be aligned with the actual objective, or with a point adjacent to it. Before pursuing this subject further it may be advisable to interpolate some descriptive remarks on the subject of sights.

Rifle sights may be classified under three heads—viz. Open sights, Aperture sights, and Telescopic sights. The first named have a foresight consisting of a small perpendicular projection near the muzzle end of the barrel, and a backsight consisting of a plate or bar with a notch cut into it, either fixed or adjustable, and seated on the barrel near the breech end. This is the earliest form of rifle backsight, and, despite the immense improvements in rifles during the last century, it is still the almost universal form of sight used, any improvements being merely directed to making the notch adjustable laterally as well as vertically.

The Aperture sight is the name given to a backsight which, in place of a notch, has a small aperture. The shooter, when aiming, looks through the aperture and aligns the foresight only with the object. It is impossible to say when aperture sights were invented, but at least one example of aperture backsight in the Tower of London suggests very early use. Considering the superiority in accuracy of this form of sighting to the open sights, it is difficult to understand how the latter ever came to be placed on a rifle. The explanation probably is that in the early days of rifled arms, accuracy was of such a negligible quantity that the roughest sight was considered good enough, and custom and conservatism account for their retention (see Plate VI.).

RIFLES AND AMMUNITION

A Telescopic sight consists of a telescope mounted on the rifle, and fitted internally with an arrangement of cross wires or other pointer to mark the centre of the field of view. Aim is taken by looking through the telescope and "placing" the pointer or cross wires on the mark. The telescope is mounted rigidly to the rifle, and in such relation to the barrel as to impart the necessary elevation to the latter when aim is taken through the telescope. Telescope sights are made of various designs, and can be had capable of vertical and lateral adjustment (see Plates XII., XLVIII., and XLIX.).

In rifle shooting success depends, among other things, upon accurate aiming, and accurate aiming depends upon the capability of the eye to appreciate small spaces. With the telescopic and, to a smaller but still useful extent, with the orthoptic sight the eye is aided. In open-sight aiming the eye depends wholly on its own powers. In each of the three different kinds of sights above described the method of aiming differs.

Aiming with the open sights is popularly described as the alignment of the backsight and the foresight with the objective. In a sense this is roughly correct, but it is proposed to deal with it somewhat differently here.

In the theory of rifle fire, there are two imaginary lines proceeding from a rifle, namely, the line of sight, which is a straight line passing through the sights and extended indefinitely, and the line of trajectory of the bullet, which is the line indicating the path of the bullet on leaving the muzzle. The line of trajectory is, for all practical purposes, a fixed and invariable line in relation to the rifle barrel, and the line of sight is a fixed and invariable line in relation to the sights. When the sights are fixed, the line of sight and the trajectory are in fixed relation to each other, as shown in the figure on the next page. In all cases the direction of fire is assumed to be approximately horizontal.

In the figure A B is the line of sight; C D E the line of trajectory. The line of sight A B being constant to the sights, and the line of trajectory C D E being constant to the rifle, it follows that if the backsight F be permanently fixed, the above figure

PLATE XLVI

WAR SHOOTING IN THE OPEN: AN IDEAL POSITION

Note the low position, legs together and nearly straight, exposing as little of the body as possible. In the top picture the soldier is watching his front; in the bottom picture, with the least possible movement, he has come up into the firing position. This is a side view of the new position shown in the bottom picture of Plate XLV

THE TRAJECTORY

represents the rifle, the line of sight, and the path of the bullet invariably at the moment of discharge.

If the backsight F be adjustable, the relationship of the line of sight A B and the trajectory line C D E will be altered with each adjustment of the backsight.

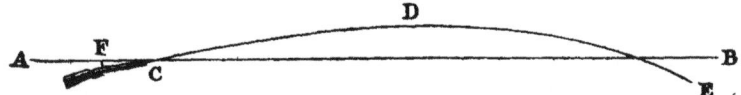

Fig. 29.—The line of sight and line of trajectory. A B is the line of sight; C D E, the trajectory; F is the backsight.

The next figure shows the fixed relation of the trajectory to the rifle irrespective of sight elevation, and how the elevation of the backsight alters the position of the sight line in relation to the trajectory. A B is the sight line when the backsight F is at its lowest setting; $A^1 B^1$ shows the altered position of the

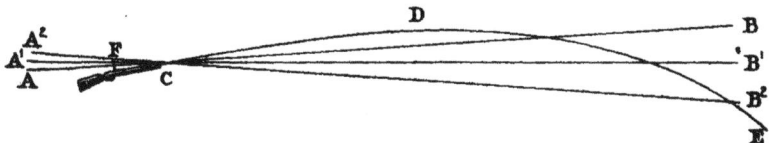

Fig. 30.—The fixed relation of the trajectory to the rifle. C D E is the trajectory; A B is the line of sight with the backsight at its lowest setting. $A^1 B^1$ and $A^2 B^2$ show the altered positions of the line of sight when the backsight has been elevated.

same line when the backsight F has been elevated, and $A^2 B^2$ a further alteration.

The object of the rifleman is to so direct his piece that the path of the bullet or trajectory line will intersect the target or objective, and the medium by which he attains that object is the sight-line. He therefore directs the sight-line in such relation to the objective as he deems will cause the trajectory to intersect the latter. The action is called aiming. To aim, the eye should be brought into the line of sight behind the backsight, and the rifle so held that the eye, the backsight, and the foresight are rigid and in correct alignment. However unsteadily the rifle may be held in relation to the objective, it must be held in rigid relation to the eye, and this is, in fact, comparatively easy. The difficulty lies in *finding* the correct alignment or line of sight, especially in the case of open sights. As the line of sight is an imaginary line passing along the sights of the rifle, correct alignment is obtained by centring, with the eye, the tip of the foresight in the notch. Having found the correct line of sight, all that is required is to "place" the foresight in appropriate relation to the objective. As the trajectory will intersect the line of sight at the distance for which the sights are set, if the objective is at that distance, aim must be taken by placing the foresight on the objective, but if the target is at some greater or lesser distance, the foresight must be placed above or below the objective.

In using aperture sights, the simple operation of looking at the foresight through the centre of the aperture brings the eye into the line of sight, and aim can be taken without any straining after alignment. Moreover, the aperture, if not too large, enables a clear definition of the foresight to be taken and assists rapidity and accuracy of aim.

In telescopic sights, aim is of still greater simplicity, the cross wires or indicator being brought into coincidence with the objective. There is no alignment of sights at all, and there is the additional advantage of having the objective magnified.

To turn back to visual training as applied to aiming. Exactness in aiming can only be acquired by making oneself perfectly familiar with the appearance of the sights in correct alignment, for it is only by this familiarity that the eye can appreciate small errors in alignment. This branch of visual training is quite straightforward, and should be practised at black-and-white bull's-eye targets, first with the aid of an aiming rest, and afterwards in the firing position without extraneous support. Considerable proficiency in aiming is advisable before attempting practice at Service targets.

Visual training requires familiarising the eye brain with the particular objects it is desired to observe. It will suggest itself immediately to the intelligent reader that to train men to visualise British soldiers is not the best training for British

PLATE XLVII

THE BEST GRIP

The right hand must grip the rifle firmly with thumb and three fingers. The first finger should be round the trigger in the position here shown

THE LOADING POSITION

This photograph illustrates the correct military position for loading standing. The butt is in front of the hip. The rifle is firmly grasped and the eyes are on the mark

VISUAL TRAINING EXERCISES

recruits. Neither is it. The best training should provide models or fatigue men dressed in the uniforms of other nations.

In practising visual exercises it is best to take at first objects which are plainly visible. The objects should first of all be fully exposed at short range, so that the learner comprehends exactly what they are. The ranges should then be increased. A second exercise may include these objects in various stages of partial concealment, and this can be varied almost infinitely by using different cover, placing the objects or men against different backgrounds and in varying lights, each exercise being designed to present a task of ever-increasing difficulty.

As with all other practices, a liberal margin of time should be allowed at the beginning, the recruit being impressed with the necessity that seeing is the primary object, time being of secondary consideration. Rapidity will come naturally with practice.

CHAPTER V

Judging Distance

IF it were possible to produce a rifle and ammunition that would shoot with a perfectly flat trajectory to the limit of its practicable range, then the necessity for distance judging would vanish. It is because the path of a bullet through the air is curved that the distance of the object from the firer has to be judged. At short distances, if the target is reasonably large, distance judging is comparatively unimportant, as the trajectory is nearly flat, but at distances over 300 yards troubles are sure to arise. The veriest novice will appreciate that if the rifle is sighted for 300 yards and a shot fired at an object 400 yards off the bullet will strike the ground 100 yards short, and similarly if the rifle is sighted for, say, 600 yards and a shot fired at a prone enemy 500 yards away the bullet will come to earth 100 yards beyond him. Some latitude for error exists according to the height of the target, but the margin is usually small and decreases as distance and curvature increase.

The necessity for judging distance in sport and war being understood, we now come to discuss the means generally adopted to overcome the difficulty, and the methods by which judging distance is practised. In big-game shooting little is known of prevailing methods, writers usually confining themselves to description of the chase, the country, and the bag. Hence it is impossible to find out by the ordinary channels of literature how this necessary accomplishment is attained by the successful hunter, or practised by the aspiring Nimrod. From the vast quantity of military books of instruction, on the other hand, we learn not only how estimation of distance is taught in military schools the world over, but also the appreciation, by all military authorities, of its importance and its difficulty.

JUDGING DISTANCE

Without detailing the various methods of instruction, it may be said that the soldier is put through the most exhaustive exercises and tests to render him individually an efficient judge of distance. Every assistance and encouragement is given him to perfect himself in this branch of musketry, without proficiency in which he cannot be classed as a marksman.

In practising the art of judging distance, one or two main principles can with advantage be kept prominently in mind. In the first place, it is necessary to understand the task we are set out to accomplish. We have to estimate the distance to an objective, (a) by the appearance and extent of the foreground, (b) by the apparent size of the objective, (c) by its visibility—i.e. by the amount of detail which can be seen.

The military method as practised in the British Army is perhaps a fair example of the most approved methods extant. The rifleman is first made familiar with some short unit of distance, say 100 yards, and he is then taught to measure intervening ground with the eye in terms of this unit. Afterwards he is taken through a course of practice in visualising men or objects of known size at known distances, so that he may appreciate the differences in visual angles. A third stage embraces a study of the amount of detail which can be observed in known objects at various ranges. For example, in favourable light, details of the body and dress of a man are distinguishable at 250 yards. Beyond about 400 yards the face cannot be distinguished, although the outline of the figure may be quite distinct. At 600 yards the outline is gone, the body appearing to taper from the shoulders. About 800 yards the tapering is no longer noticeable, the body resembling a stake or post.

These and many other exercises combine to build up a high standard of efficiency in this important branch of musketry.

Now, judging distance is merely an expression in figures of what every human being with sight has learned from birth. That is to say, he has learned to *appreciate* distance, and the proof that he has so learned lies in the fact that objects of known size appear normal at any distance within vision. For example, an average man at ten yards distance appears to the observer to be of average height. At 100 yards distance, although the visual angle is now only one-tenth the magnitude of the visual angle at ten yards, the man still appears normal. The observer's consciousness of distance enables him to interpret the change in magnitude of the visual angle. This appreciation of distance is due, in some degree, to the converging focus of the eyes. An amusing illustration of this is afforded in the parlour trick of placing a cork or other small object on the edge of a table or mantelpiece, and inviting guests to approach it with hand outstretched toward it and one eye closed, and then, having halted at the estimated distance from the object, knock it off with the forefinger by a slow sweeping motion of the outstretched hand. The attempt is seldom successful. The subconscious knowledge of distance is also due to perception of the foreground, and to the effort demanded of the eye to distinguish detail. The latter has a curious illustration in the apparent phenomenon of the appearance of objects in fog. It is common knowledge that a known object—man, horse, tram, etc.—seen through fog appears, at first, to be very much magnified. Now this effect is produced by the fog, but not in the way commonly supposed—namely, by magnification. What happens is that the fog calls for extra effort on the eye to distinguish detail, and this subconsciously suggests a distance greatly in excess of actuality. This false idea of distance produces a wrong interpretation of the visual angles, and, consequently, an exaggerated impression of the size of the object.

Where the size of objects is not known—as, for instance, trees, ships, houses, etc.—the visual angles give little or no assistance in estimating distance, which must be done by reference to foreground and detail. In this, as in all other methods of estimation, numerous factors militate against accuracy, the nature of the foreground and background, the contour of the land, the condition of the atmosphere, and the extent of the light, all combining to make distance-judging the most difficult and unsatisfactory branch of the marksman's art.

A few broad principles, however, may be kept in mind with advantage, but when attempting to put these into practice it

PLATE XLVIII

THE BACK POSITION

The most usual form of the back position is here shown. It is, however, generally recommended that the rifle should not touch the left leg. A good back position gives steadiness and uniformity of hold, with the minimum of fatigue

DISTANCE DIFFICULTIES

must not be forgotten that, while one obvious condition may suggest over-estimation of range, another factor, not quite so obvious, may be at work in the opposite direction.

Generally speaking, ease of vision tends to under-estimation of range; and difficulty in seeing promotes over-estimation. This hardly requires explanation, since near objects are easily seen and distant objects are not, hence the mind has become accustomed to associate distance with difficulty of vision.

Any condition, therefore, of light or atmosphere which assists a clear view of the objective tends to under-estimation of range. Similarly, any marked contrast between the object and the background, tending to throw the former into bold relief, has the same effect.

Another powerful factor in under-estimation is an unrelieved foreground; that is to say, a foreground devoid of feature—as, for instance, a flat plain, a stretch of water, or a mantle of snow. Perhaps the foreground may be entirely absent, as in a wide chasm. Each of these peculiarities lessens or removes those intervening objects which, to the mental eye, give distance to the objective.

Contrariwise, as difficulty of vision tends to over-estimation, all conditions which call for effort from the eyes tend to promote over-estimation of range. Some of these conditions are mist, mirage, haze, dusk, similarity in colours of object and background.

On the subject of foreground, the reader will anticipate that where this is the predominant feature, the eye gives it more than its true value in distance. Looking over a valley, for instance, not only is the actual foreground of greater lineal length than the line of sight, but the impression created in the mind by seeing all of it so prominently displayed gives an entirely flattering idea of the distance.

In the same manner, foreground thickly covered with prominent objects, such as clumps of trees, houses, rocks, or other pronounced features, conveys the same impression. Look along a straight avenue of trees a few hundred yards long, and see what a curious impression of interminable distance it conveys. This is merely caused by the foreground of trees filling the vision to the partial exclusion of the objective—namely, the end of the avenue—which, by contrast, receives a false impression of diminutiveness and consequently of distance.

Now it will be observed that a number of these varying conditions may be present at one time, and that they may act in the same or a contrary direction. For example, the light may favour a clear vision, causing under-estimation of range, while a prominent foreground may correct the tendency, provided both or neither are taken into account. On the other hand, the light may be good, the atmosphere clear, and the foreground flat and featureless. All these conditions would operate towards under-estimation of range, and, if not allowed for, a serious error would be made. In this connection an amusing incident occurs to us as giving an illustration of the bewildering effect of unfamiliar conditions. Two British marksmen of considerable experience in Service rifle shooting were, in the course of a shooting tour, spending a few days at a cattle ranch in Alberta, Canada. One day, returning home after a day's shot-gun shooting, the conversation turned on judging distance for rifle fire. To give point to an argument, one of the two stopped and pointed to a knoll some 200 yards distant. Beyond this knoll appeared to be another of considerable size about 500 yards off, but as the nearer hillock cut out the intervening ground, the distance was distinctly uncertain, especially as there were no apparent objects on the far-away knoll from which to judge. The problem was: "How far off is the second knoll?" The second rifleman, making allowance for the loss of the foreground, gave 600 yards as his estimate, and explained his reason for the figure. His friend pointed out the omission to take into account the clear atmosphere and the rear light, and estimated 800 yards. Number one not being satisfied, they started to pace it out. On arriving at the first knoll, which was 240 yards distant, they made a remarkable discovery. Between the knoll and the second hill was a valley, and in the middle of the valley lay the town of Cochrane, which they knew to be four and a half miles off. The correct distance to the second hill was nine miles!

In war, considerable use is made of range-finders, the best

OBSERVATION OF FIRE

of these being optical instruments of great accuracy, and these are an almost indispensable adjunct to artillery where knowledge of the exact range, especially at long distances, is a *sine quâ non*. It is not, however, the purpose of this work to describe these instruments, as they are hardly a part of the rifleman's outfit.

Another method of ascertaining range in war is by "observation of fire"—in other words, watching where the bullets strike the ground when the rifles have been given a trial elevation, and then making the necessary alteration in succeeding shots until the bullets "get home." This method is quite effective if the ground is suitable for the purpose; but if the ground is such that the strike does not show up, some other method must be tried, the usual expedient being (when range-finding instruments are not available) to direct half the men to use one elevation, and the other half another.

These descriptions of the various methods of ascertaining the range are given to enable the reader to appreciate the difficulties which exist, and are acknowledged by the highest authorities to exist, in the practical use of the rifle. Most of the difficulties will be insurmountable for a long time to come, but some of them can be considerably lessened by a little study and application.

CHAPTER VI

Time Occupied in Aiming

IN deliberate shooting, from five to ten seconds is sufficient time for a marksman to expend on aiming. In target shooting circumstances may arise which preclude the possibility of always getting the shot off in this space of time, as, for instance, when a sudden change in weather conditions necessitates an alteration of the backsight, and consequently a fresh aim, but even this happening does not alter the recommendation that a deliberate aim should not require more than ten seconds.

Prolonged aiming in the endeavour to secure greater accuracy defeats its object through straining the eye, while at the same time the fatigue of holding the rifle in the firing position for a great length of time militates against steadiness. It is therefore very much in the interest of the learner that rapidity of aim should be cultivated, and this ultimate goal should be his aim even while remembering that at first in the early stages of practice the most deliberate methods are advisable.

Even in long-range shooting where objectives require very keen sight and are usually more difficult to pick up, this counsel of rapidity of aim applies in almost greater force, because the strain upon the eye in discerning the object makes it very undesirable to prolong the effort of aiming.

In snap-shooting, the time occupied in aiming should not under favourable circumstances exceed two seconds, counting from the time the butt of the rifle touches the shoulder.

It is perhaps unnecessary to point out that the major portion of this time is expended in "finding" the line of sight or alignment, the time necessary to "place" the foresight on the objective being relatively small. It is for this reason that snap-

TIME OCCUPIED IN AIMING

shooting from the prone position illustrated on Plate XLV. shows such superiority in speed. In that position, while the rifle is resting on the ground the eye of the shooter is in the correct alignment or line of sight, and all he has to do is to raise the muzzle of the rifle till the foresight "touches" the objective. A good rifleman practised in the position can make accurate snap-shooting with half the aiming time of the regular position, and experiment has demonstrated that an exposure of a service target at 200 yards distance for one second has been sufficient to enable a good rifleman to make accurate practice at it.

In rapid firing the actual aim should not take more than one and a half seconds, although many of the best marksmen in the British Army, notably those in the experimental staff of the School of Musketry at Hythe, make good shooting in half that time. Cases are on record of thirty-five aimed shots being fired in one minute, and as this includes the recharging of the magazine five times, the time expended on aiming each shot could not materially have exceeded half a second.

It will be apparent to the intelligent reader that rapid aiming can best be achieved through confident and accurate handling of the rifle, because the quicker the rifle is brought into a steady position, the easier it is for the eye to find the line of sight. Therefore in aiming practice, care should be taken that practice in holding and handling the rifle is not in any way neglected.

CHAPTER VII

Wind Allowance

THE effect of wind upon the course of a bullet in its flight towards the target is a great obstacle to accuracy, and causes considerable disheartening to the beginner. To the latter a bullet seems to have such incredible speed that wind allowance appears quite unnecessary, and when, during a stiff breeze, he fails to find the target with his first shot he is puzzled and discouraged. If, however, the trajectory line is drawn to scale in plan, showing the course a bullet would take in a 500-yards' flight in a strong wind—that is to say, where it is blown say 5 ft. out of the straight course—it will be seen that this deviation of 5 ft. in 1,500 ft. is indistinguishable from a straight line. Allowances of from 1 to 5 ft. at 500 yards are quite common, and, of course, they vary with distance, a "5-ft. wind" at 500 yards requiring an allowance of about 16 ft. at 800 yards and 30 ft. at 1,000 yards.

In war wind allowances are extremely difficult to make, principally because there are few indications observable by which allowance can be made; and, secondly, because in the heat of battle, excitement, hurry, and other exigencies reduce such niceties of rifle-fire to a secondary consideration. In the close phases of battle any attempt to make allowance for wind would merely cause flurry and confusion, and, as a matter of experience, it has been found quite undesirable to have any lateral adjustment upon the backsight at all.

In game shooting with a rifle wind allowance plays a very small and unimportant part, for the reason that sporting distances are short and the bullet velocity is high. Nevertheless, in long shots it cannot be altogether neglected, owing to the extreme smallness of the objective and the necessity for great accuracy. In shooting at extreme sporting ranges of, say, 300 yards with a very light bullet a cross wind will make a considerable difference in the last 100 yards of the flight of the bullet, and therefore a knowledge of wind effects at ranges of, say, 200 and 300 yards is very desirable to the sportsman, and opportunity should be taken to study the effects upon stationary targets.

In target shooting, as generally practised in this country and throughout the Colonies and the U.S.A., every facility is given to enable the shooter to make due allowance for the effect of winds, and as a result of this encouragement wind judgment in those countries has been reduced to a fine art.

The practice is to erect flag poles at various points on the range, and to hoist long streamers to indicate the strength and direction of the wind. A further indication is available in warm weather in the shape of the apparent phenomenon which the rifleman calls "mirage." In warm weather the earth, under the influence of the sun's rays, absorbs considerable heat, and communicates this heat to the air. The heated air immediately begins to rise, and assumes in modified form the appearance of boiling water. If the movement is vertical only, the suggestion of boiling water is complete; but if there is also a lateral movement, the mirage assumes the appearance of a running stream. By using a powerful telescope this air movement is considerably magnified, and the speed at which it travels can be gauged with great accuracy. As it indicates the actual movement of air between the firer and the target, and therefore the air through which the bullet is about to travel, this mirage affords the most accurate means by which wind allowance can be made. Unfortunately, it is only available in hot weather, so that on cold or dull days the only indications are flags, with perhaps additional help from smoke or dust.

It is impossible to lay down any hard and fast rule as to what is sufficient allowance for certain winds. Elaborate tables have been compiled showing that in winds of certain force certain lateral allowances have to be made at certain distances, each variation of the wind being described by a picture representing the appearance of a flag in such winds. It is hardly necessary to point out that a flag made of heavy material will show differently from a flag of light material, and that even if all the flags were made of the same material a shower of rain will convert them into heavier flags and render the description of them quite misleading.

The only reliable teacher in wind allowance is experience. The learner would be well advised to obtain during the early stages of his education the advice of an experienced friend, that he may be saved the discouragement of frequent misses. But he should understand that his sole reliance must eventually be upon his own judgment, and therefore continuous practice is essential to his acquiring good wind judgment.

If the learner have to rely upon his unaided efforts, he had better start at the shortest range, paying particular attention to the exact amount of wind allowance required. The shortest distance at which lateral deviation is appreciable to the beginner is perhaps not less than 200 yards. At this distance a strong breeze will not require more than about three minutes of angle allowance, assuming the rifle is the military .303 and Mark VI. blunt-nose ammunition. Having carefully noted the exact allowance required—and it may be remarked in passing that at this short range great care must be taken that the calculation is exact—the beginner should betake himself to 500 yards, where he will find that three times the 200 yards' wind allowance *in minutes of angle* will bring him near the mark. At 600 yards the allowance will be approximately four times that for 200. Indeed, a reference to the elevation table appropriate to the ammunition he is firing will enable him to make fairly accurate allowances at different ranges by calculating roughly the *proportion* which one range bears to another. Thus, with .303 Mark VI. ammunition, the 500 elevation, twenty-eight minutes, is roughly three times the elevation for 200, which is nine minutes, while the elevation for 1,000 yards, eighty-three minutes, is roughly three times that for 500. Proportionate increase in wind allowance will be found to give sufficiently accurate results to enable the beginner to start practice on wind judgment without material discouragement.

PLATE XLIX

Photo: Gale & Polden, Ltd.

COLONEL J. D. HOPTON

This photograph of the well-known expert on small arms and ammunition is introduced to demonstrate one of the many possible variations of the back position. Colonel Hopton, as can clearly be seen, does not rest his right knee on his left foot, but obtains a steady rest by gripping his left shin with the inside of his right knee

THE "FISH-TAIL" WIND

It must be carefully noted that these proportions are all calculated in minutes of angle, and not in lineal measurement.

The amount of wind allowance is governed by the distance the bullet has to travel and by the force and direction of the air movement. In dealing with direction, it is usual to describe it in terms applicable to the face of a clock, assuming the firer to be in the centre of the clock face and the target at 12 o'clock. A head wind would thus be described as a "12 o'clock wind," a rear wind as a "6 o'clock," a right wind as a "3 o'clock," and a left wind as a "9 o'clock wind."

No wind passing over land is ever perfectly steady. The unevenness of the ground, the trees, and other obstacles break up the general body of the wind and cause it to come in gusts or eddies, with frequent changes of direction. We thus have constant variations in direction and force, all of which have marked effect upon the flight of a projectile.

The most difficult wind to negotiate is commonly known as "a fish-tail wind," which is a wind coming from the direction of 12 o'clock or 6 o'clock. If the wind came in a steady flow from either of these directions, no lateral allowance would be necessary, and the only effect which it would have on the bullet would be an effect upon the elevation, a front wind resisting the progress of the bullet to a greater extent than still air, and therefore requiring more elevation, and the 6 o'clock wind reducing the air resistance to the bullet, and so requiring less elevation.

The unevenness of the air movement, however, causes variation in direction, and in the case of a fish-tail wind these changes take effect first on one side of the bullet and then on the other. At one moment the direction of the wind may be from "1 o'clock," and while the firer is aiming it may have changed round to 11 o'clock, the result being that he finds he has fired with a right wind allowance in a wind coming from the left. The effect is disastrous to accuracy, whether the shot has been fired in sport or in war, the only difference between the two being that, whereas in target shooting the change is apparent from the flags, in war the change is not, and the cause of the inaccuracy is unknown.

The only way to minimise the effect of these rapid-changing fish-tail winds is to shoot quickly, and the man who can, after estimating his wind allowance, get his shot off in half the time his neighbour takes will have just about half the chance of being caught with the change.

In cross winds—that is, winds blowing across the range—variations in direction have not such pronounced effects as in fish-tail winds, though they are likely to come with just as great rapidity. They nevertheless cause considerable variation in allowance, and are, indeed, extremely puzzling for two reasons. Firstly, they are not always observable, and may therefore cause variation in shooting without having been noticed; secondly, a material alteration in the direction of a cross wind may require little or no alteration of allowance, as, for instance, in the case of an 8 o'clock wind suddenly altering to 10 o'clock. Add to this that the alteration in direction may be accompanied by an alteration in force, and it will be readily appreciated that wind judgment provides considerable scope for the exercise of intelligent observation.

When the student has familiarised himself with wind strength and direction, he will be well advised to adopt a method of reading these different from that usually followed by target shots. The method recommended is to judge wind allowance entirely by the appearance and conditions, and not with reference to any preceding shot. In target shooting this is of great importance, but it is equally important in game shooting or in war.

In target shooting the competitor is usually allowed a preliminary shot to ascertain what is technically known as the "error of the day." Having taken this preliminary shot, or "sighting shot," he proceeds with his competition, calculating his wind allowance with reference to the sighting shot, and each subsequent allowance with reference to its predecessor. This method is fairly successful under favourable weather conditions, but in very variable winds its exponent is at a great disadvantage. Especially is this so when the wind changes direction from right to left, where one shot can have no possible relation to another, and the shooter is therefore deprived of the only means he has of reading the wind.

By consistently relying on the appearance of weather conditions as the only guide to estimation of wind allowance for each shot, the learner can build himself up an education which will never leave him helpless, no matter what the weather conditions may be.

In military shooting, however, while this recommendation applies equally, it must not be forgotten that indications as to direction and force are likely to be of an extremely fragmentary nature, and that more often than not a decision has to be come to with extreme rapidity. In such case, if the nature of the ground makes observation of fire possible, obviously the best course is to be guided by the position of the strike.

In target practice, the correction of error from one shot to another is a source of considerable trouble to the beginner, and, indeed, is little understood by many experienced shots who ought to know better.

The beginner, having been told that one minute of angle alteration on his sight will affect the position of the shot on the target to the extent of one inch for each hundred yards of range, proceeds to make corrections based upon these figures whenever such corrections appear necessary. He soon finds, as a result of these corrections, that a minute of angle alteration on the rifle appears to make a difference on the target of at least twice the amount he has been taught, and the idea becomes inseparable from his mind that a half correction is all that ought to be made and that practice does not always bear out theory; but the only time that practice does not bear out theory is when theory has been incompletely or badly constructed. In the above case, the theory assumed that the error demanding correction emanated from one cause, whereas, in fact, it may have been the effect of a number of causes.

To begin with, no rifle has ever been made of such accuracy as to be capable of firing all its shots into one hole at any considerable range. Similarly, no ammunition can be made so accurate as to be capable of this precision. There is, in fact, an unavoidable deviation in rifle and ammunition equal at the present time to not less than one minute of angle. Secondly, no man can hold a rifle with perfect steadiness, the best of marksmen being liable, under the most favourable circumstances, to some slight movement. Thirdly, eyesight is not infallible, and even with the greatest care an appreciable error may creep in. Fourthly, the rifle may not be held perfectly upright, and the resulting error from cant may prove another source of inaccuracy in shooting. Fifthly, an unobserved change in the elements may cause quite considerable errors on the target.

From such a number of sources of error liable to be present in each shot, considerable deviation may be looked for, but where one error may act in one direction, another may act in the opposite direction, and so correct the first, and this, in point of fact, is what most frequently happens. But a time comes when all, or nearly all, errors work in one direction, and it is then that an apparently wild shot, entirely unaccountable, appears on the target. In such a case, the inexperienced learner probably assumes that such error is due entirely to one cause, not necessarily observable, but none the less assumed, and accordingly he makes a full correction. In the succeeding shot, however, the errors are not all present, or perhaps may correct one another, and he finds, to his dismay, that his correction has altered the position of the shot double the distance which "theory" taught him.

In correcting, in target shooting, it is never good to do anything without some definite reason. If a correction in lateral or wind adjustment of several minutes of angle is necessary, the indication ought to be plainly observable in the atmospheric conditions as shown on the flags or mirage. If these indications are not present, then the error must be attributed to some other cause; and here we have an example of the advantage of estimating wind allowance irrespective of any previous shot. If the firer be in the habit of making wind allowance by reference to previous shots, he will be the more apt to be guided by errors on the target, because his teaching will have given him little or no basis upon which to rely for his assumption except the results as they appear on the target;

PLATE L

Photo: Record Press

THE SCHOOL OF MUSKETRY, BISLEY, 1914-15

Members of the National Rifle Association doing part of their course under Hythe instructors to turn themselves from expert target shots into instructors for the New Army

WIND JUDGING WITH TELESCOPE

whereas he who relies entirely upon appearance of conditions will *know* within himself what the correct reading of the existing conditions is, and will be less likely to be influenced by shots on the target.

When atmospheric conditions permit, wind judgment by telescope offers perhaps the most interesting practice of all the various branches pertaining to accurate rifle-fire.

While conditions are only favourable for this work in this country during hot weather, in tropical countries they are almost always present. The heated air arising off the sun-baked ground is usually observable to the naked eye, but it requires the assistance of a powerful telescope, say one of not less power than a magnification of twenty diameters, to enable the observer to read the conditions with sufficient accuracy to make approximately correct allowance. The benefit of wind judgment by telescope is seen at its best in the hands of a team coach in target practice; but in the hands of the expert rifleman, firing individually, it is of almost equal advantage; and it is safe to say that some of the most brilliant wins in Bisley competitions, especially at long range, have been achieved under adverse atmospheric conditions with the aid of a good telescope. One of the reasons why the telescope provides such an advantage is because in most cases when the atmospheric conditions lend themselves to its use the movements of the air are very variable. This applies with particular force in this country, and the reason is probably owing to the frequency with which the sun is obscured by single clouds, thus causing the shaded parts of the ground to cool off, while other adjacent parts are subjected to the full heat of the sun's rays. This causes the atmosphere to be heated in a very irregular fashion, and it is therefore in a constant state of irregular movement. It is not an uncommon sight at Bisley and other ranges in this country to see mirage movement altering from right to left, necessitating a change of wind allowance of 8 or 10 ft. at 1,000 yards, within a space of comparatively few seconds, and this while the indications on the flags showed almost no change at all. In such weather conditions the inexperienced rifle-shot usually retires in hopeless bewilderment, without any idea whether his want of success is due to himself, his rifle, his ammunition, or to the weather.

In order to read air movement, or mirage, it is necessary that the telescope should be very steady. It is almost impossible to gather any idea as to the pace at which the air is travelling unless the telescope is held with the utmost rigidity. For this reason the telescope is usually mounted upon a tripod or other suitable stand.

In many cases, however, individual riflemen have attained considerable success by using the telescope for wind judgment in the following manner: The rifle having been brought into the aiming position in readiness to fire a shot, the right hand, from its position round the small of the butt, is dropped to the ground to grasp the telescope and lift it up to the eye, steadying the body of the telescope along the barrel of the rifle with the fingers of the left hand. This position enables the telescope to be held as rigidly as the rifle, and this is, of course, sufficiently steady to make accurate reading possible. When the firer has satisfied himself as to the correct speed of the air movement, he drops the telescope to the ground and fires as quickly as he can get his aim.

Turn now to the appearance of mirage. Through a telescope it will be found that, when the air movement is such that no lateral allowance is required, the mirage presents an appearance which is well described by the technical expression, "steady boil." It is, in fact, an appearance somewhat akin to the movement of water boiling in a saucepan. A team coach, in such circumstances, would call out "Zero," meaning thereby that the member of his team whose turn it was to fire would aim with the sights set at their lateral zero. The slightest alteration in the atmospheric condition from the steady boil would make itself immediately apparent through a powerful telescope. The "boil" would plainly show that it had started to flow towards right or left, the appearance being akin to clear water running over a bed of shingles. It takes years of experience to teach a man to judge the pace so accurately as to enable him to call the correct lateral allowance. In light, shifting airs, a good wind coach can be trusted to read the mirage with sufficient accuracy to give the wind allowance within half a minute of angle. But beyond an allowance of six minutes accurate judgment becomes very difficult, owing to the similarity in appearance of an air movement of high velocity, until, when the wind reaches a maximum of about fifteen miles per hour, the advantage of a telescope practically ceases. In such a case the air movement is general, and the indications are then observable by other means.

So far we have dealt with simple movement of mirage from right to left; but there are times when the air movement is from other points of the compass, and the experience and knowledge gained of ordinary cross winds is of little help.

When the air movement takes a direction from the target to the firer—that is, a 12 o'clock direction—the "boil" still retains its steadiness, but it has a more animated appearance, much as though it were boiling faster. A 6 o'clock movement, or a movement from the firer to the target, has a similar appearance.

When the movement takes a diagonal direction—as, for example, the direction of a 1 o'clock wind or a 5 o'clock wind—the lateral movement from the right is plainly visible, but is apt to cause a wrong impression of the necessary wind allowance owing to the peculiarity with which it appears to move. In effect, it is the lateral movement of the cross wind combined with the animated appearance of the 12 o'clock mirage above described. This diagonal mirage is very misleading, especially to the beginner, as the animated appearance of the "boil" gives an impression of speed which, in fact, it does not possess. The experienced coach at once detects the nature of the movement by reading the slow lateral travel, as it were, *through* the "boil." The lateral movement is partly disguised by the animation of the boil; but it is this animation which gives the experienced coach his clue as to the true direction of the air movement. He therefore gauges the angle of direction from the extent of the boil disturbance in proportion to the speed of the lateral movement.

It will be seen from this description that wind judgment by telescope opens up a very wide field of study for the ambitious marksman; but we have not by any means exhausted the variety of air movement which comes within the daily purview of the target rifle-shot.

It frequently happens on a day of rapid changes of lateral air movement, particularly at ranges beyond 800 yards, that one movement, say from the left near the targets, may have a counteraction from the right near the firer. It may be that one of these movements may be of greater strength or velocity than the other, or it may be that one movement exactly counteracts the other, necessitating actually no lateral wind allowance at all. In appearance, such a complexity of movement is another source of perplexity to him who relies upon his telescope. If one air movement—say that from the right—is near to the firer, while another is at some considerable distance off, the latter only may be observable through the telescope. This would arise owing to the focus of the telescope being set for infinity, which would prevent the clear definition of anything in close proximity. If the near movement should be too near to be in focus of the telescope, and so not observable, it would probably not be sufficiently strong to have effect upon the flight of the bullet. If, however, both air movements are in proper focus, and one is moving directly against the other, the appearance through the telescope is somewhat similar to that of a 12 o'clock or 6 o'clock air movement. By altering the focus of the telescope, it is possible to discern each movement, particularly the near movement, by pulling out the eye-piece of the telescope, and the distant movement by pushing the eye-piece slightly in. Having by this means ascertained the double movement of the mirage, it is possible by close observation, with the telescope in correct focus for infinity, to determine whether the right or left air movement predominates, and to make a reasonably accurate allowance for it. It will be appreciated that such atmospheric movements are seldom violent, and that at the most a small lateral allowance is called for.

Another phase of telescope work in target shooting calling for experience and care is when the mirage is very faint or intermittent. This occurs when the heat is not great, or during a time when clouds are frequently obscuring the sun. Changes

PLATE LI

A WINTER FIGHTING EXPEDIENT

The steady rainfall that was part of the experience of our troops in France and Flanders for some months of the winter, 1914-15, necessitated special care if rifles were to be kept in working order. One expedient was to cut off the toe of a sock, wring it out in oil, and pull it down over the muzzle to cover the action. When the rifle had to be used the sock was slipped off on to the butt

INTERMITTENT MIRAGE

in air movement in such circumstances are frequent and variable, while the mirage appears and disappears accordingly, as temperature varies. Under such conditions accurate wind judgment by the aid of a telescope is very difficult, and the best effects are only to be obtained by the aid of telescopes of very high power.

When the mirage is almost invisible through the telescope, it is a good plan to slowly open the eye not in use. The apparent effect is to make the mirage "come up" into view. The reason is not clear, but care must be taken that the concentration of sight continues to be directed through the telescope.

On the subject of eyes, a discussion recently arose in the shooting press as to whether it was not advisable to use the left eye for telescope work, leaving the right eye fresh for aiming. Experience is against this suggestion. Riflemen who have tried it have found that the change of sight concentration from right to left, and *vice versa*, has resulted in a slight temporary dullness of sight, which, in some cases, particularly towards the end of a day's shooting, has been sufficiently bad to prevent their aiming for some minutes. In severe cases the aiming eye appears to be unable to focus anything, the sights and target being a hopeless blur. A few minutes rest, or a peep through the telescope with the aiming eye, will, however, completely restore the vision.

CHAPTER VIII

The Trajectory Curve and the Part it Plays in Practical Shooting

WE have already studied the trajectory curve in relation to the line of sight, and have understood that the trajectory for a given rifle, charge, and load is a fixed curve. We are now in a position to consider the part played by the trajectory in practical shooting.

The time of flight of a bullet determines the amount which it will drop before reaching the target, and therefore the amount which it is necessary to direct the bullet above it to counteract the drop. Roughly, a bullet will drop 16 feet in the first second of flight, and there is a constant *acceleration* of 32 feet per second for each second of flight. In the next second the bullet will therefore drop 16 + 32 = 48 feet. In a bullet's flight the drop may be stated thus: 16 feet in one second of flight; 16 + 48 = 64 feet in two seconds of flight; 16 + 48 + 80 = 144 feet in three seconds of flight; 16 + 48 + 80 + 112 = 256 feet in four seconds of flight, and so on.

The time of flight depends upon two things—the velocity with which the bullet is propelled, and the retardation of the bullet due to the resistance of the air. Weight, calibre and shape of a bullet are the three chief factors which determine its air-resisting qualities, the greatest weight being combined with the smallest calibre in a shape which reduces air resistance.

The designer of a cartridge, therefore, strives to impart the highest velocity obtainable to a bullet having the greatest efficiency in overcoming air-resistance, so as to get a minimum time of flight with a minimum drop, and consequently a trajectory which most nearly approaches a straight line.

THE BALLISTIC CO-EFFICIENT

Where the efficiency of a bullet for overcoming air-resistance is known, and the muzzle velocity at which it is projected, it is possible to calculate the time of flight, the drop, and the trajectory for any given range. The air-resisting efficiency of a given bullet is calculated as follows: The weight of the bullet in pounds is divided by the square of the diameter in inches, and by a figure representing the "shape factor." The "shape factor" can only be accurately determined by actual shooting, but for all practical purposes it may be stated at about .85 for a "round-nosed" bullet, and .65 for a pointed bullet, greater or lesser figures being necessary according to the shape or the taper of the nose. The figure of merit arrived at is called the "*Ballistic Co-efficient*" of the bullet.

For military purposes, where a flat trajectory over the comparatively long distance of 800 yards is of great practical value, and for target shooting where lateral air movement has to be overcome, a high figure of merit or ballistic co-efficient is essential in a bullet. The present military bullets of this country, Marks VI. and VII., have a ballistic co-efficient of about .4; the French military bullet is about .46; and the German bullet about .35. This latter represents a low figure of merit or ballistic co-efficient for a military bullet.

The reader will observe that a high ballistic co-efficient depends, primarily, upon a high weight in inverse relation to calibre. As a heavy projectile requires more power to propel it than a light one, it follows that with the same powder charges in equal calibres, the bullet with the highest ballistic co-efficient will have a lower velocity, and vice versa. Consequently if an ultra-high velocity is demanded, some of the efficiency of the bullet as a ranging projectile must be sacrificed. At the same time it should be stated that the powder maker plays a most important part in adjusting velocities to different weights of bullets. Speaking generally, a light bullet requires a faster burning powder than a heavy bullet. A small-grain, quick-burning powder suitable for propelling a 150-grain bullet at, say, 2,700 feet per second muzzle velocity, might only realise 2,300 feet per second velocity with a 200-grain bullet of the same calibre. By altering the size of *grain* of the powder without

RIFLES AND AMMUNITION

increasing the charge, a velocity of 2,600 feet per second may easily be imparted to the latter bullet.

Turning back to the question of the ranging powers of different bullets, it will be seen that a point is reached in the adjustment of velocities, pressures, and weights of bullets when an increase in one can only be had by sacrificing some important quality in another direction. The first essential to a flat trajectory is velocity. The weight of the bullet must therefore be low. The second essential is a high ballistic co-efficient which, with a light bullet, demands a small calibre. The tendency of progress in military rifles must, therefore, be in the direction of small calibres.

In sporting-rifle shooting, where the range is practically limited to 300 yards owing to the very small target offered, ranging qualities in a bullet are of small consideration. Flat trajectory is of vital importance owing to the great difficulty of judging distance, and therefore high velocities are almost the only consideration. The word "almost" is used advisedly, since it must not be forgotten that merely hitting an animal, even in the heart, will not necessarily suffice to bring it down. The aim of every true sportsman is to kill his quarry instantly, and, to do this, great care must be taken to select a suitable projectile. Energy and "shock" must be combined to cause that paralysing effect necessary to prevent a wounded animal getting away, to die, perhaps, a lingering death in some fly-infested swamp. In the endeavour to obtain this nerve-shattering effect in sporting rifle bullets, almost every conceivable shape has been devised. Flat nose, round nose, hollow nose, explosive, collapsible, split points in scores of varying designs and different materials; they form a large and interesting collection.

In making bullets for use against soft-skinned game whose tissues offer comparatively little resistance to a hard substance, difficulty has been met in preventing the bullet from penetrating right through the animal without doing more than inflict a painful wound. The nickel jacket of the bullet has been cut through in various ways to weaken it, and this served the purpose well with an occasional exception, when the bullet either

PLATE LII

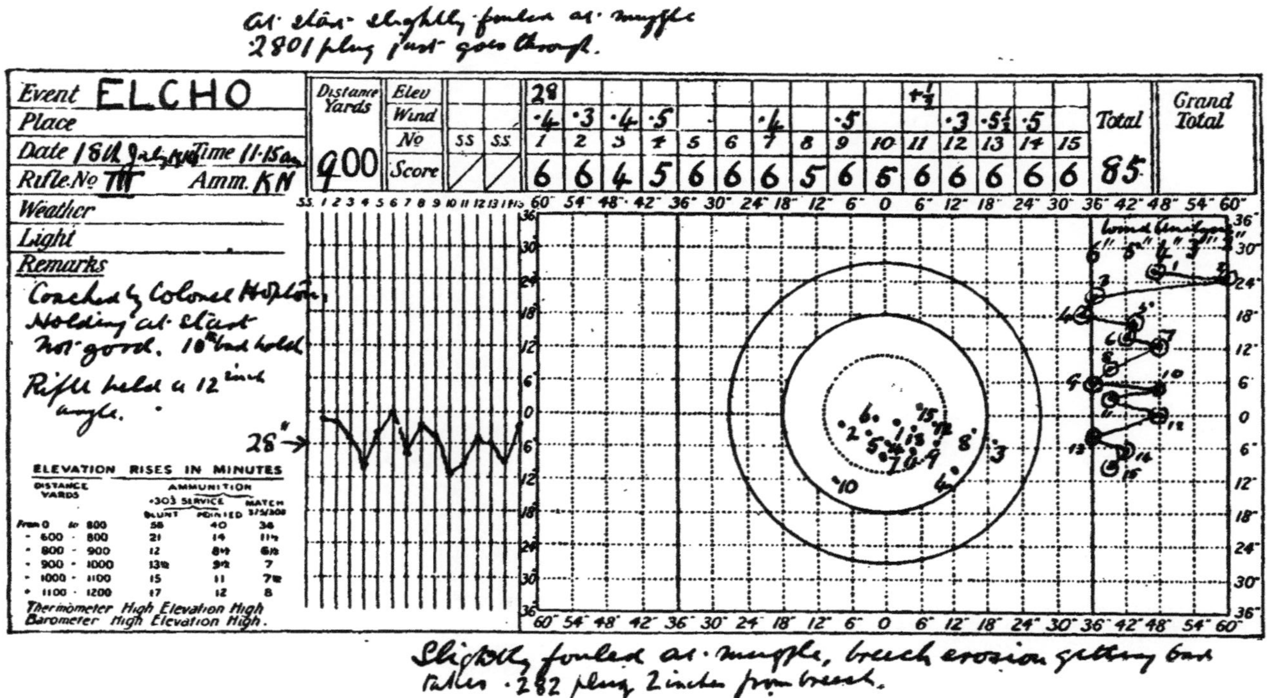

A LONG-RANGE SCORE SHEET

This sheet, taken from a Fraser Score Book used in 1914, shows how score books may be filled in to give all essential particulars. At the top is a statement as to the state of the range. At the bottom a statement as to the state of the barrel at the end of the range. A chart of the angle is made on the left of the diagram to show the position of each shot with relation to the other supposing they had all been fired with the same elevation on the sights. On the right is an analysis of true wind from shot to shot. Big changes between shot and shot often indicate bad holding

SPORTING BULLETS

passed through the animal or broke up before it reached it. Nowadays, it is found that in ultra-high velocities, such as, for instance, 2,800 to 3,000 f.s. muzzle velocity, unweakened *pointed* bullets will break up on impact with soft-skinned game at short range, causing a semi-explosive effect in the animal and making it collapse instantly. This is precisely the effect desired, and it seems reasonable to suppose that when more experience and knowledge have been gained concerning the latest type of sporting bullet, developments will take the direction of a medium calibre rifle projecting a light, pointed bullet at a velocity very much exceeding 3,000 feet per second.

Against the pachyderm, where great penetration is essential, the light high-velocity pointed bullet is of little use. A bullet of considerable weight is required and the nose ought to be round. Pointed bullets are apt to turn on penetration and take devious courses. With a round-nose bullet exceeding 400 grains in weight, 2,000 f.s. velocity is sufficient for all pachyderms, but a little extra in reserve is a comfort. It is impossible to dogmatise on what is necessary and what insufficient for big game, for there is perhaps no subject upon which opinions are more at variance, but if the elephant hunter will be guided by what has been established beyond all controversy and pay no heed to that which provides endless contention, he will arm himself with a rifle which, without excessive velocity, gives a muzzle energy exceeding 3,500 ft. lbs. This entails a bullet preferably of not less than .400 calibre and 400 grains in weight, fired at a muzzle velocity of 2,000 f.s. This constitutes what may be termed a minimum in large calibre big-game rifles, although many sportsmen of experience prefer something much lighter in weight and charge. The heavier rifles, however, in our view, win first claim to true sportsmanship. To attack elephants with a .256 Mannlicher, as many have done with some degree of success, is to be utterly careless of animal suffering. The additional personal danger no doubt adds its charm, but when the first bullet fails to kill, as most frequently happens, there can be little satisfaction in pumping lead into a stricken and suffering body.

One of the best and safest rifles for such big game as

elephant, rhino and African buffalo is the .450 No. 2 Cordite Express. The cartridge for this rifle has a bullet of 480 grains, which, propelled at a velocity of 2,100 f.s. develops a muzzle energy of about 5,000 ft. lb., and a striking energy at 100 yards distance of about 4,000 ft. lb.

No well-delivered shot from this rifle will ever require a second to finish its work, the shock effect being sufficient to bring the largest elephant immediately to the ground.

Although the difficulties of judging distance, as set out in a previous chapter, are very formidable, yet these difficulties may be greatly reduced in military individual shooting and almost entirely eliminated in sporting rifle shooting. All that is required is a thorough knowledge of the trajectory of the particular rifle used. The following explanation of shooting by trajectory instead of by adjusting sights to allow for drop is based upon actual experiment of a very extensive and thorough nature, and carried out by riflemen in almost every stage of efficiency or inefficiency!

As will be seen on reference to the following diagram, the drop of a bullet *after* the trajectory intersects the line of sight is very rapid.

A B is the line of sight, and C D the path of the bullet on leaving the muzzle. The rifle being sighted for 100 yards,

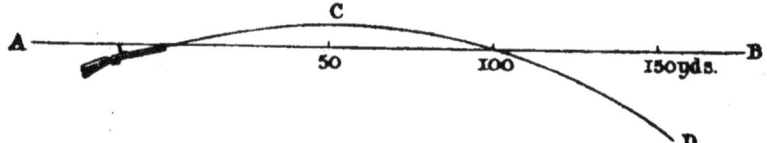

Fig. 31.—Illustrating the rapid fall of the trajectory after crossing the line of sight. A B is the line of sight. C D the trajectory

the bullet crosses the line of sight at that distance, and immediately thereafter it falls very rapidly, until at 150 yards it has fallen a very considerable amount. It follows, therefore, that if an object at 150 yards distance be fired at with the 100 yards sight up in the supposition that it was only 100 yards away, the bullet would fall so low that the object would be missed altogether. At ranges beyond this the drop would be even

TRAJECTORY SHOOTING

more rapid. As distance or range offers great difficulties in estimation, it will be appreciated from this diagram how shots are missed at comparatively close ranges. The next figure shows a trajectory extending over a distance of 350 yards. The maximum height of this trajectory above the line of sight A B is 1 foot, viz. at 200 yards the muzzle velocity being 2,700 f.s. and the ballistic co-efficient .35. Now the shooter knows that

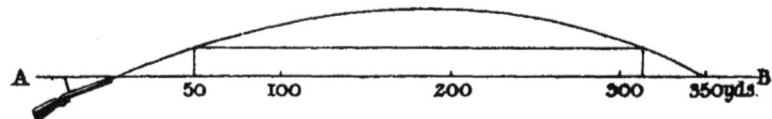

Fig. 32.—A trajectory with a vertex 12 inches high divided into two 6-inch portions. The vertical scale is much exaggerated

wherever he aims the rifle, the bullet cannot rise more than 12 in. above that point of aim, and that at all distances between 50 yards and 300 yards the bullet will strike not less than 6 in. and not more than 12 in. above the point of aim. That is to say, if aim is taken at the belly line of a stag, just behind the foreleg, as shown in the illustration on the next page, and if the stag is *anywhere* between 50 and 300 yards range, the bullet must strike it in the heart region, not less than 6 inches and not more than 12 inches above the point of aim. Indeed, if the stag be missed, the explanation must be one of two: either the rifle was badly held, or the animal was out of range, in which latter case it were better to miss than to hit, since hitting beyond 300 yards usually means a shot placed in an invulnerable part of the animal at a low velocity, causing only a painful wound.

Experiments at stationary stag targets of almost every conceivable variety have demonstrated that within the limits of sporting distances, that is within 300 yards, a good marksman will place 80 per cent. of shots within a 6-inch circle representing the heart of a stag, shooting by trajectory in the manner above described, the remaining 20 per cent. being all on the stag in close proximity to the heart region, while by estimating range and adjusting sights the percentage will be less than half that number, with a large proportion of "clean misses." An objection to the recommended point of aim may be anticipated

RIFLES AND AMMUNITION

by saying that it is at once easier and more definite and accurate than attempting to cover an undefined heart region with a bead, which usually is so large as to hide the whole heart region and a goodly portion of the rest of the deer as well.

Fig. 33.—Stag Target Indicating Position of Heart. In trajectory shooting aim is taken at the junction of the belly and the foreleg, marked **X**. With a 12-inch trajectory every shot fired within certain ranges will strike not less than 6 inches nor more than 12 inches above the point of aim

For running shots, where "aiming off" is necessary, this system of trajectory shooting is equally applicable, there being no great difficulty in aiming ahead of an animal and in line with the breast line. In the case of an animal running directly away, trajectory shooting is particularly useful, as, in the event of an ineffective first shot, by the time the rifle has been steadied for the second, a material increase in the range has occurred. Shooting in the ordinary way, the sights would have to be readjusted or allowance made on the aim for the increase of range, whereas by trajectory shooting the same aim does for any range within sporting distances.

CHAPTER IX

The Effect of Cant

A VERY important side issue of the gravity curve of a bullet is the displacement of the bullet from the objective when the sights of the rifle are canted or leaned over to the side.

The effect of canting or leaning the sights of a rifle is very little understood, even among the general body of practical riflemen. It is part of the general instruction in musketry, that leaning the sights will cause the shot to strike low and to the side on which the sights are canted. It is correct to say that the shot will strike to the side in the direction of the lean, but the loss in elevation is, for all practical purposes, immaterial.

As an illustration, let us assume that we are shooting at a bull's-eye target at 800 yards with the ordinary .303 military rifle and Mark VII. ammunition. As has been previously stated, the effect of elevation on the sights is to cause the barrel, when aim is taken, to point above the target a sufficient amount to allow for the drop of the bullet. The drop of the Mark VII. bullet at 800 yards is approximately 27 feet, consequently at the moment of discharge the barrel is directed towards a point 27 feet above the centre of the bull's-eye.

Now assume that the rifle is canted to the right so that it is now flat on its side with the sights horizontal instead of upright. Aim being taken in the same way, the barrel will now be directed to a point 27 feet to the right of and level with the bull's-eye. Leaving out of account the minor question of jump, if the rifle be fired in this position, the bullet will be projected towards a point 27 feet to the right of the bull's-eye and will fall 27 feet below that point. Reference to the figure on the next page will facilitate understanding.

A is the target at 800 yards range. Aim being taken at the point C in the bull's-eye, with an angle of elevation on the sights of, say, 39 minutes, the barrel is directed at the point B 27 feet above C, and the bullet falls to C in its 800 yards flight. The rifle now being canted to a right angle and aim taken at the point C, the barrel will *point* to D. But the bullet will fall 27 feet to E. If the rifle is canted 45 degrees right, the barrel will point to G, and the bullet will strike at H. Intermediate angles of cant will cause the barrel to point somewhere on the dotted line B G D, and the bullets will fall on their corresponding positions on the dotted line C H E. The continuous line C F represents the path of hits on the target for various angles of cant up to 18 degrees.

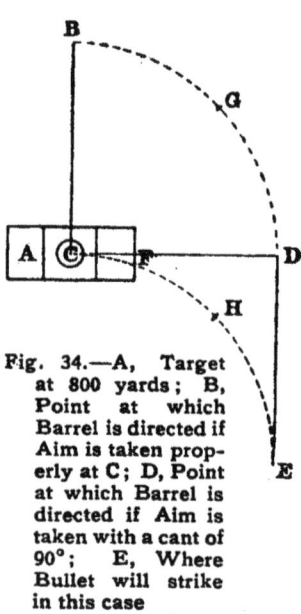

Fig. 34.—A, Target at 800 yards; B, Point at which Barrel is directed if Aim is taken properly at C; D, Point at which Barrel is directed if Aim is taken with a cant of 90°; E, Where Bullet will strike in this case

From this line C F it will be seen that while the lateral deflection is 5 feet at F, the loss in elevation is only a few inches. The loss is, of course, greatly accentuated as the cant is increased, but we are chiefly concerned with the accidental cant which can hardly exceed 12 to 15 degrees.

The above illustration deals with shooting when no allowance is made for wind on the backsight. But when the backsight is adjusted laterally to make allowance for deflection due to wind, a very different set of circumstances operate to produce different results, and we are indebted to that well-known ballistic expert, Captain J. H. Hardcastle, for throwing light upon a phase of the effect of cant which, we believe, has never before been disclosed.

Stated shortly, when the backsight is adjusted to make allowance for wind, canting the sight will still cause lateral deflection in the direction of the cant, but the effect otherwise will be to throw the shot *high* if the cant is with the wind, and low if against the wind.

PLATE LIII

Photo: Record Press

THE PULL-THROUGH IN USE

Men of "Kitchener's Army" clearing their rifles with the pull-through after instruction practices at Bisley

Photo: Record Press

THE BOILING WATER METHOD OF CLEANING

Boiling water is undoubtedly a very effective barrel cleanser and rust preventer, but it is not always available. At Army instruction ranges a supply is usually on hand

CANTING THE SIGHTS

Figure 35 will show how this curious result is brought about.

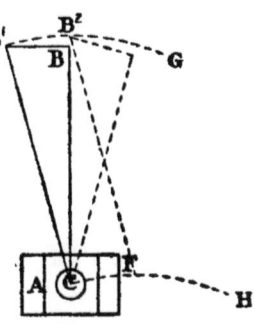

Fig. 35.—The effect of cant when the sight is adjusted for wind

A is the target at 800 yards. B is the point at which the barrel is directed when there is no wind allowance. But supposing there are ten minutes of wind allowance on the backsight, the barrel will point towards B¹, 7 feet to the left of B, and the bullet, when fired, will drift diagonally, as it were, to C. Now turn to Fig. 36, which represents the elevation and wind allowance on the backsight. From the position of zero, the line E shows the 800 yards elevation to the point O, which on a calm day would be the position of the aperture or notch of the backsight. But an allowance of ten minutes has been made for wind, and the notch has accordingly been moved to the point N. The position of N is now the correct position of the backsight notch relative to zero if the sights are held correctly, i.e. upright. Now cant the sights by pivoting them about zero until the notch N comes into the position N¹, and it will be seen that a higher elevation has been given. The effect of this on the barrel would be to point it to B² on Fig. 35. The bullet would fall 27 feet as before, and at the same time the wind would cause it to drift 7 feet to the right, the bullet striking at F. The dotted line B¹ B² G indicates successive points to which varying angles of cant would direct the barrel, and the line C F H the path of hits.

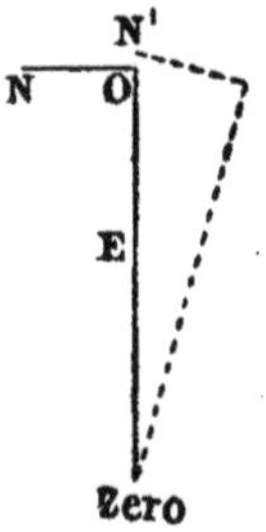

Fig. 36.—When the backsight is adjusted to make allowance for wind, the effect of cant against the wind is to throw the shot high

CHAPTER X

A Summary of the Conditions Necessary to Accurate Rifle Fire

ALL individual practice with the rifle is directed primarily to the attainment of accuracy, and accuracy is only attainable through uniformity. It is, of course, possible to successfully hit an object with a shot inaccurately delivered according to all the accepted canons of teaching, but such success can only be accidental, and cannot be termed accurate shooting. Let us assume that a rifleman attempts to hit an object at a known range for which his rifle is correctly sighted. In aligning his sights he sees the foresight to the left of the centre of the backsight notch and very much too high. Inadvertently he cants the rifle to the right. At the instant of releasing the trigger his point of aim owing to unsteady holding is much too low. Despite four serious errors on the part of the rifleman, the bullet lands exactly in the middle of the target. The explanation is, of course, simple and obvious. The error in aligning the foresight to the left of the backsight notch is corrected by the error of canting the rifle to the right, while the error in seeing the foresight too high in the notch is corrected by the unsteady hold causing a low point of aim.

Success in such circumstances is in the nature of a wild fluke, and cannot be called accuracy. Yet if the firer could reproduce exactly, shot after shot, these "errors" of aim and hold, success would not be accidental, and his fire would be "accurate."

At the risk of labouring the point a simile may be drawn by comparing three different brands of accurate ammunition. Take a .22 calibre ammunition test at 100 yards. The first brand gives a 2-in. group at the top of the target, and is passed

SEVEN ESSENTIALS FOR SHOOTING 275

as excellent. The second brand gives a similar group 2 in. to the right of the bull's-eye. This brand is also passed as extremely accurate ammunition. The third brand gives another 2-in. group at the bottom of the target, and is pronounced as of equal excellence to the others. Here, then, we have three brands of ammunition all reaching the highest known standard of accuracy. Now mix together three boxes of this excellent ammunition, one of each brand, and see what the result is on again testing it. The first shot hits the top of the target, the second is 2 in. to the right of the bull's-eye, and the third nearly misses the target low. The ammunition is no longer "accurate." It has lost its uniformity.

We will now lay down the essential points to be followed in firing one deliberate shot at a stationary target at known range. There are seven essentials, and these will be separately discussed in their proper order, starting from the assumption of the firing position until the shot is fired. In following the discussion the reader is asked to observe that all the details of firing are specially designed to afford the easiest means to acquire uniformity. Take, for example, the alignment of the foresight and backsight. The instruction given is to align the foresight in the centre of the backsight notch in such a way that the tip of the foresight is level with the shoulders of the notch. It is easier to exactly reproduce this alignment for each shot than it is to judge a less or greater amount of foresight, and manufacturers of military rifles are instructed to fix the line of sight accordingly. Similarly, although a slight cant would counteract drift, the instruction is to keep the sights upright, for it is easier to keep the sights upright than to judge a certain degree of cant.

The seven essentials are as follows:

1. *Correct Position.*—The assumption of a good and comfortable position is a necessary preliminary to the efficient handling of the rifle. Positions called military positions have been evolved by competent military experts as being most suitable to the average man, and these positions can be adopted with confidence for any class of rifle shooting. Any slight modification may be made to suit abnormal build without loss

of efficiency. Illustrations of the various firing positions appear elsewhere in this work.

2. *Firm Grip of the Rifle with* BOTH *Hands.*—The necessity for gripping the rifle firmly with the right or trigger hand as well as the left is not always apparent, especially to the exponent of target shooting. Many successful marksmen have been content to trust to the left-hand grip to control the rifle, the right hand being left in a semi-quiescent state on the small of the butt, the middle finger in some cases operating the trigger. The disadvantages of this one-handed grip do not make themselves felt to any great extent in deliberate target shooting, but in rapid fire and snap-shooting the handicap is serious. The left hand grips the rifle at or near the point of balance, forming a kind of pivot about which the rifle swings. The control obtainable from such a grip can only be small, hence it is necessary to utilise the right hand for the direction and control of the rifle. The grip of this hand should be confined to the thumb and three fingers round the small of the butt, the first or index finger being, as it were, entirely set aside for trigger pulling. An illustration of the right-hand grip will be found on Plate XLVII. A good exercise to develop the grip apart from the trigger finger is to hold the rifle out at arm's length pistol-wise with the right hand only, the trigger being at full cock and the trigger finger on the trigger. The rifle should be held out without releasing the trigger.

3. *Correctly Centre the Foresight in the Notch of the Backsight.*—This is the first preliminary to aiming, and may be described as finding the true line of sight. The rifle manufacturer adjusts this line of sight so that it will pass through the centre of the backsight notch level with the shoulders and the tip of the foresight, and intersect the trajectory at the required distance. If, therefore, the firer sees the tip of the foresight to the left of the centre of the notch, the true line of sight will pass through the centre of the notch, the tip of the foresight, and a point considerably to the left of any object upon which the foresight is aligned. As the trajectory would intersect the true line of sight at the known distance, the bullet would

accordingly pass through that point to the left of the target. The firer, therefore, to find the true line of sight, must see the foresight truly centred in the backsight notch and in such a position that the tip of the foresight is level with the shoulders of the notch.

In the case of aperture sights, the tip of the foresight should be seen in the centre of the aperture circle. When the aperture sight is so situated that the aperture is close up to the eye, the field of vision is very great. In centering the foresight in the aperture, the firer sees the whole foresight and a large portion of the rifle barrel. Indeed, to the uninitiated there appears to be no backsight at all, and each shot is accompanied with misgivings and doubts of it ever reaching the *vicinity* of the target. A little consideration of the matter will bring comfort. The aperture probably does not exceed .06 or six-hundredths of an inch in diameter. Consequently if the foresight were seen on the extreme edge of the aperture instead of the centre, the error would only be one of three-hundredths of an inch, perhaps not sufficient to cause a deviation of more than 3 in. per 100 yards of range. As it is easy to detect an error of a fifth part of the radius from the centre of the aperture, one can readily appreciate the accuracy of the aperture as a sighting medium.

4. *Sights must be kept upright.*—The effect of canting the sights when firing has been already fully dealt with. Incorrect alignment of sights has the effect of throwing the true line of sight out of the aim, whereas if the sights are canted, although the true line of sight may be retained, the effect is to twist the trajectory away from the line of sight in the direction of the cant.

5. *Correct Focus of Sights and Target.*—In aiming with open sights, the eye is asked to focus three separate objects at three different distances—namely, the backsight, the foresight, and the target. This is impossible of simultaneous accomplishment. An ordinary photographic camera affords a good illustration of this. A near object being focused, distant objects appear blurred or are unseen. Conversely distant objects being focused, near objects appear blurred. Similarly the human eye cannot focus objects at different distances

simultaneously, but its mechanism is so sensitive and active that the change of focus can be accomplished in an almost inappreciable time. Now, when shooting at targets of intense visibility where no difficulty is experienced in defining them, good shooting may be done even when the target is not in actual focus. Hence there is a tendency among many target-shots to be careless as to whether the target is in correct focus or not, attention being concentrated on a clear definition of the foresight in its relation with the backsight. In shooting at war targets or big game such a procedure is fatal. The objective is almost certain to be obscure, if not almost invisible, and, as is well known, nothing short of concentration of eyesight upon such a target will keep it in view.

At the instant of firing, therefore, the target must be in perfect focus. The firer first focuses the backsight, the objective and foresight being blurred. He then brings the blurred foresight into the clearly defined backsight. The focus is now shifted to the foresight, which is brought into its correct position in the centre of the notch. When this has been done, the eye should be concentrated on the mark or objective. If the right-hand grip of the rifle is maintained, the rifle pressed well into the shoulder, and the head rested by pressing the jawbone firmly against the stock, the rifle becomes almost a rigid part of the shooter, and the sights and the eye are held into their correct alignment, allowing the marksman to pick out his objective and complete his aim without losing his true line of sight. The various changes of focus are effected very rapidly, and the most deliberate aim at a stationary target should not exceed ten seconds.

6. *Steady Hold.*—The rifle should be steadied at the instant of firing. The word "steadied" is used in its practical and not its literal sense, for no man ever yet held a rifle without movement. Anyone who thinks he has may satisfy himself (or otherwise) by aiming through a telescopic sight! "Holding" has been already gone into very fully, so need not be enlarged upon here. It is, however, important to observe that in all rifle-shooting, whether snap-shooting or rapid firing, an effort must be made to steady the rifle before pressing the

PLATE LIV

Photo: Gale & Polden, Ltd.

THE BAZAAR LINES, BISLEY

Bisley's street of shops, which springs into being for a fortnight every year, is an institution which possibly brings more delight to the rifleman than profit to the trader. However, every important rifle-maker or seller has a tent in the Bazaar Lines, if only to afford him a chance of meeting with and talking to his customers

trigger. Occasion may arise when even comparative steadiness is impossible, as, for instance, in shooting in the standing position in a high wind, in which case one must depend on one's sense of touch to release the trigger at the psychological moment, but even in such conditions one does one's best to minimise the movement. In discussing "holding," it must not be forgotten that breathing plays an important part. To steady the rifle, breathing must be suspended, and in deliberate shooting it is best that this suspension should take place during exhalation, not at the beginning nor at the end, but about midway. In rapid firing this may not be possible, but it should be followed as nearly as circumstances and time permit.

7. *A Smooth "Let-off."*—To effect the release of the trigger without disturbance of the rifle is absolutely necessary to an accurate shot. All the care and attention to position, sight alignment, focus, and steady hold are thrown away if the "let-off" should disturb the rifle. The trigger release should be effected solely by the first or index finger of the right hand. The inside of the first joint should engage the trigger near its lower end so as to get the best leverage. If the trigger have a double pull, the first pressure will be applied while the sights are being aligned, the remaining pressure being the "let-off" with which we are presently concerned. The trigger finger alone must apply the pressure. Reference has already been made, in describing the right-hand grip, to the detaching of the forefinger from the control of the right hand, and too much insistence on this point cannot be made, for upon the work of the trigger finger in its most individual sense depends the fruition of all the care exercised in the preceding essential attributes of a shot.

In developing or educating the trigger finger, the trigger-pull or press should be applied slowly at first, the concentration of mind being bent upon learning the amount of power required, or in the popular technical phrase, the "weight of the trigger." As the mind becomes familiar with this "weight" the power can be applied with greater confidence, care being taken that the trigger release is effected exactly when intended. Some riflemen of repute advocate a slow and steady increase of power until the trigger goes off "accidentally," but this is obviously a doubtful habit acquired in target practice of the most deliberate kind.

Having now described in detail the essential points to be remembered in firing an accurate shot from a rifle, it remains but to give one other and very important essential to be carried out after the shot has been fired. It is this:

Nominate the position of the shot fired.

All shots are fired with *some* error. Even those shots which hit an objective have errors corrected or intensified by other errors, and these errors are greatest in beginners. Proficiency in shooting is only attained by correcting or minimising these errors, and the rifleman must therefore be constantly on the look out for his faults. As the accuracy or success of a shot depends entirely upon the position of the rifle in relation to the objective at the instant of discharge, it follows that the rifleman must *see* that relative position immediately *after* the trigger release. He must, in fact, have his eyes not only open, but concentrated on his aim until the recoil throws the rifle out of alignment, and he must retain in his mind's eye the impression of the aim at the instant of disturbance. Only by this means can he nominate the position of the shot or analyse faults shown by the strike of the bullet. For instance, a shot to the left of the target can be accountable to four or more causes: the foresight may have been seen to the left of the backsight notch, or the rifle may have been canted to the left, or the aim may through unsteady holding or other cause have been to the left, or wind may have caused the bullet to drift to the left. With these four potential causes of one error in direction it can readily be understood how impossible analysis would be if the rifleman's eye be closed at or before the trigger release. On the other hand, if he retained the impression of the sights on the discharge of the rifle, and could say with certainty that his sights were correctly aligned and aim taken at 6 o'clock, he could then, by referring to the weather conditions, form a reliable opinion as to which of the remaining causes accounted for his error.

In conclusion, it only remains to say that there is nothing

THE ROYAL ROAD TO SUCCESS

mysterious or wonderful in accurate rifle shooting. Given the necessary normal physical attributes, it remains but to apply one's mind to acquiring the ability to repeat with a minimum of variation the firing functions just described. Visual training, judging distance, trajectory shooting, and kindred branches of musketry provide the means of applying to a target accurate rifle fire, and without proficiency in these methods of application success is impossible in the field or the forest.

There is one royal road to success, and that is—Work. No amount of teaching or lecturing or reading will ever turn a man into an expert rifleman. He must take a rifle in his own hands and practice assiduously, making himself familiar with the rifle in every detail, and particularly with the appearance of the sights in the aiming position. Accuracy means uniformity, and uniformity depends on the ability of the rifleman to detect and correct the smallest variations in detail.

Proficiency can only be attained by observing and correcting errors. It is a curious fact that errors discourage beginners in almost every sphere of knowledge, whereas they ought to encourage the learner to further effort. For error is the progenitor of knowledge. It is commonly said that the man who never made a mistake never made anything. Nor did he learn anything. Errors are a necessity to the learner. A bull's-eye *teaches* nothing to the would-be marksman. An outer may teach a lot.

CHAPTER XI

The Care of the Rifle

NEXT in importance to having a rifle well made is to have it well cared for. The accuracy of a rifle can only be preserved by keeping it in a condition as nearly as possible to that in which the rifle performed its best work, namely, when it was new. As the accuracy of a rifle may be said to depend largely upon the accuracy of the barrel, so the preservation of that accuracy depends upon the preservation of the barrel. In these days of modern smokeless powders the chemical action of the deposit left in the barrel after combustion causes the almost immediate appearance of rust in a most violent form. The corrosive action begins immediately the rifle has been discharged, and, owing to the pressure set up in the barrel, some of the acid products of combustion may be said to be forced into the steel beneath the surface, or skin, making it impossible to free the bore entirely from this chemical fouling by the ordinary process of cleaning. It has been found necessary, in order to neutralise the effect of the corrosive acids, to employ a strong alkaline solution in the form of a cleaning oil, and after extensive experiments, covering a number of years, satisfactory preparations have been produced, several of which are in the market, the best known being Young's .303 Cleaner and Rifline, both of which are procurable through any gunmaker.

In addition to the bad effects of corrosion, the rifleman has to combat the disconcerting trouble of metallic fouling, commonly called "nickeling." Nickeling starts with the very first shot fired from a new rifle. It is true that the earliest shots leave very little metallic deposit in the barrel, and that for several hundreds of rounds no appreciable sign of metallic fouling will be observable, provided the rifle is looked after with reasonable care. In course of time, however, the bore of the rifle will become slightly roughened, causing increased friction with the bullet, and particles of the nickel envelope will be rubbed off, and will adhere to the lands. These particles of nickel will be found to have a firm hold on the steel, and will, in fact, appear to have been welded into the interior surface of the barrel. Each particle will enclose between itself and the surface of the barrel a minute portion of acid deposit, and this acid will, in course of time, cut into the steel. Even if the metallic fouling is then removed, a small pit mark or rust hole in the barrel will be exposed, and this in turn will collect nickel fouling from subsequent bullets.

Metallic fouling is one of the most prevalent causes of inaccuracy in a rifle, and it is only by the exercise of the greatest care in the early stages of the "life" of a barrel that metallic fouling can be guarded against. It may be said at once that metallic fouling cannot be altogether prevented, but its presence in the bore can be materially checked, and with reasonable care its effect upon accuracy may be almost entirely avoided until the rifle barrel has been worn out.

It has already been indicated that the barrel is least likely to accumulate metallic fouling when it is new, or, in other words, when the surface of the bore is clean and well polished. Consequently, the treatment which preserves the smooth skin of the rifle barrel is the best to prevent nickel fouling. As has been stated, the first shot through a new rifle leaves some slight, although almost infinitesimal, deposit of nickel fouling in the barrel. In order to preserve the smooth skin, therefore, it is necessary that the slight metal deposit be immediately removed. This can be done in two ways. One is to dissolve the nickel deposit by chemicals, and the other to remove it by the cruder method of abrasion. Both may be commended, but the latter is in our view preferable for one or two reasons. In the first place, the chemical process is not always ready to hand, and unless applied very shortly after shooting the destructive effect of the acid will have begun. Once the steel has been roughened by corrosion the chemical removal of the nickel deposit from the surface only prepares the way for an aggravation of the metallic trouble, and each succeeding chemical treatment leaves the barrel in a worse state than before; on the other hand, the use of an abrasive entails less trouble and time. Even in cases where the rifle can be immediately attended to after shooting, the good scrubbing out with a suitable abrasive will, if it does not entirely restore the barrel to its original condition, at least leave it in a reasonably polished state; and subsequent scrubbings will not leave it less so. The chemical preparations most in use are "K.N.S." and "Kysol," both of which are familiar to most rifle-makers.

The best abrasive preparations are "Motty," the invention of a well-known Australian rifleman, and the familiar household preparation, Brooke's Soap, "Monkey Brand." The former is a well-thought-out preparation, and contains as its chief abrasive pumice powder, which will grind copper (the chief component of the so-called nickel envelope), but which will not grind steel. On the other hand, Brooke's Soap, if properly applied, is one of the finest barrel polishers known, and has a reputation for keeping the "skin" of the rifling in perfect condition. The best way to apply it is as follows:

Wrap a piece of flannel of regulation size—that is, 4 in. by 2 in.—round the end of a steel cleaning-rod, dip the flannel into benzine or petrol, cut a groove about a quarter of an inch deep into the side or top of a cake of Brooke's Soap, and lay the petrol-soaked flannel in this groove, revolving the rod until a suitable quantity of the abrasive has been taken on the flannel. Insert the rod in the barrel from the breech end, and rub gently backwards and forwards. After a few applications the inside of the barrel will be found to have taken on a high polish and to be entirely free from nickel fouling. The rifle may then be thoroughly cleaned and oiled and put away.

It may be that a considerable quantity of nickel has adhered to the lands without being immediately observable to the unaided eye. To provide against the contingency of such a large quantity of nickel deposit being allowed to pass unnoticed, it is important that the rifleman provide himself with

PLATE LV

THE STICKLEDOWN BUTT, BISLEY

Photo: Gale & Polden, Ltd.

A beautiful view of the world-renowned long-range butt taken from the 1,200 yards firing point. There are 50 targets on the Stickledown Butt, and here the Final of the King's is shot, as well as such important team matches as the Elcho and Mackinnon. The 1914 Elcho match was in progress when this photograph was taken

a barrel gauge or gauges. These gauges are short cylindrical plugs of steel cut to the diameter of the bore of the barrel. By passing one of these plugs through the barrel the presence of a very small deposit of metallic fouling can be instantly detected. These gauges, or plugs, are made to a ten-thousandth part of an inch, hence, if a usually tight-fitting plug goes right through the barrel, any metallic deposit on the lands must be of a negligible quantity.

In all rifle cleaning, whether for sporting or military rifles, the best tool to use is a stout steel rod, preferably with a large wooden knob or handle. This handle may be swivelled or fixed, according to the taste of the user. It is a popular fallacy to suppose that wood-covered rods are preferable to solid steel on the ground that they are less likely to wear the inside of the barrel. It is only necessary to point out that wood will take up grit more readily than steel will, and that if such grit becomes embedded in the wood it may present a formidable cutting edge to the steel of the barrel. The steel rod should have the end so cut that flannel patches may be readily wrapped round it for cleaning and oiling purposes, and should also have the end screwed so as to take a bristle brush. The bristle brush is very necessary to efficient cleaning, and provides one of the best means for the even distribution of a liberal quantity of oil on all parts of the interior of the barrel.

The effective cleaning of a cordite rifle after shooting should be carried out somewhat on the following lines: Immediately after completing the shoot a pull-through should be used, fitted with an oily rag, the oil being one of the approved alkaline oils and liberally applied. On reaching the armoury or gun-room the rifle should be cleaned out with a steel rod and oily brush. In this and subsequent cleaning it is a great advantage if the rifle can be held in a bench vice. The bore being thoroughly brushed with an oily brush, the brush should be taken off the rod and replaced by a "jag," or "jag" brush, round which a flannel patch should be wrapped and inserted in the barrel. The barrel should be rubbed "rag clean." A correctly sized gauge or plug should then be passed through the barrel to see if there is any nickel deposit. If the rifle appears to be quite free of this, the barrel may then be thoroughly oiled with a clean rag soaked in oil, or a clean brush dipped in oil. It is, however, a good precautionary measure to scrub the barrel out with Motty Paste or "Monkey Brand" Brooke's Soap in the manner already suggested. If this be done, the barrel should be dry cleaned with flannel; then brushed through with the last oily brush; then dry cleaned with flannel again before being oiled and put away. If the gauge or plug discloses the presence of metallic fouling, the barrel should be scrubbed out very thoroughly with Motty Paste or Brooke's Soap until the metallic fouling is cleared out, the barrel-gauge being passed through after each scrubbing until the metallic fouling can no longer be detected. When satisfied that the nickel fouling has been removed, the barrel should be cleaned and oiled as above described.

The brushes used on all occasions should be good quality bristle brushes. Steel or brass brushes are not recommended, as they either wear badly or scratch the interior of the barrel. In certain circumstances one may use a barrel-scourer—a steel brush with the "bristles" pointing diagonally outwards towards the handle of the rod. This provides a very strong and effective agent for removing metallic fouling or other fouling in badly fouled or worn barrels. With a well-looked-after rifle, however, the steel barrel-scourer is not required, and consequently it can only be recommended as an appropriate tool for barrel cleaning in special cases.

What is known as the "boiling water" method of cleaning has been adopted by the British army, and where large boilers are provided in rifle ranges it is very effective as a rust preventer when special care is taken to dry and oil the barrel after the water has been poured down it. The method of cleaning is as follows: The bolt of the rifle is withdrawn and a specially made "filler" inserted in the breech. Boiling water is then poured down the barrel, the rifle being held muzzle downward. After the fouling is washed out, the barrel is dry cleaned with flannel, then thoroughly oiled (see Plate LIII.).

The user of a high-velocity sporting rifle seldom fires as many shots in a month as a target-shot will do in a day. As a

CLEANING THE ·220 RIFLE

consequence he is less concerned with metallic than with the acid fouling. Nevertheless, the user of the sporting rifle will do well to consider the method by which the Service rifle target-shot keeps his weapon in good order. The expensive paraphernalia of the armoury cannot possibly be taken into the wilds, but a rod and brushes and flannelette, with a good alkaline oil—not the Rangoon, so beloved of the country gunmaker—will, properly used, prolong the useful life of the rifle very considerably.

The small bore of miniature rifles requires even greater care and attention than the .303 Service rifle. Though the velocity of the bullet up the barrel is only about half that of the Service rifle, and the amount of powder used is extremely small, yet the bore of the .220 weapon has proved itself to be even more susceptible to corrosion than its full-charge brother. Metallic fouling it does not suffer from in the same form, but the lead should be cleared from lands and grooves at frequent intervals with the aid of a wire scratch-brush or barrel-scourer, and "Leadene," a mercury paste which has a strong affinity for the detritus of lead bullets. The recommendation as regards removing the acid fouling as soon as possible after shooting applies equally to the miniature as to the Service rifle. The cleaning kit should contain a steel rod, a plug and round flannelette patches, a loop and oblong patches, a bottle of Young's .303 oil or "Nackanack" paste, a couple of brushes, and a wire scourer.

So far we have dealt only with the bore; but though not so essential to accuracy, it is necessary that the rest of the weapon, particularly the bolt action-body and magazine, should be thoroughly well looked after. The bolt requires particular attention in two places; one is the face of the bolt-head, and the other is the business end of the striker. After every shot the flat face of the bolt-head, where it comes up against the cartridge, should be carefully wiped with the same alkaline oil which is used for the rifle barrel. There always seems to be a slight escape of gas from the cap, and as the fumes of the percussion composition are extremely acid, unless the slight deposit on the bolt-head is wiped away, a corroded ring is very quickly formed. A bad cap leakage, or a burst cap, will blow a considerable quantity of gas into the striker hole and on to the striker, so that every now and then it is advisable to unscrew the bolt-head and wipe the end of the striker, which is thus exposed, thoroughly with an oily rag. With the old pattern Lee-Enfield or Lee-Metford the bolt-cover will have to be removed before the bolt-head can be unscrewed. The bolt should be kept as free as possible from any heavy oils. Usually the amount of oil which a careful man will use on his weapon is ample to keep the inside of the bolt quite sufficiently lubricated; but if it should get dry a drop or two of machine oil applied with a camel's-hair brush or feather will be all that is required. The inside of the body should be kept thoroughly clean and free from grit, particular attention being given to the cam-shaped groove on the left-hand side of the body in which the locking-lug works. In rifles made on the Mauser or Mannlicher pattern, the particular place in the body which wants attention is the hood immediately behind the chamber where the lugs work and where the resistance pieces are. The trigger mechanism should be kept free from all foreign matter, and it is advisable that the scear and bent should be quite dry.

All woodwork on a high-class rifle is highly polished when it is sent out by the maker. This polish should be retained, as it is one of the best preventives of warping. Less well finished rifles will often repay a little trouble spent on the woodwork in the way of improving the polish and keeping the woodwork well oiled. All action screws should be tightly home. It will always repay a rifleman to keep the exterior of his rifle, as well as the interior of the barrel, in a condition as nearly as possible like that in which he obtained it from the maker.

Special circumstances have developed special methods of keeping rifles in good condition. Some of the most interesting are those in use in the big Bisley club houses. Here are stored throughout the summer many hundreds of private rifles which are used in most cases only on Saturdays. The owner, once he has cleaned and locked up his rifle, will not be able

PLATE LVI

Photo: Gale & Polden, Ltd.

THE FIRST STAGE OF "THE KING'S"

A view of the 600 yards range at Bisley during the firing of the first stage of "The King's." In the foreground Mr. A. P. Humphreys is seen speaking to one of the competitors. Well to the rear of the firing point the camp tramway can be discerned. The trees at the extreme left on the skyline are just behind the "Siberia" firing point

STORING THE RIFLE

to attend to it again until he takes it out of its locker the next Saturday. The Bisley man is, therefore, a very thorough cleaner, and he usually puts his rifle away full to the muzzle with a liquid alkaline oil which he keeps from leaking out by placing a thickly greased fired case in the chamber. The oil is used again and again.

Not the least important part of the care of a rifle is the provision which is made for storing it when it is not in use. If a rifle cupboard is not available, the weapon should always be kept in a case, and should be well smeared with grease before being put away. Dust is a great breeder of rust, and should not be allowed to collect on unprotected metal surfaces. It is a good rule never to put a rifle out of sight. If it is where it can be seen, it will get an occasional examination even when not in active use, and such occasional examinations are needful if rust, the great enemy, is to be prevented from getting a hold.

CHAPTER XII

Team Selection and Team Shooting

THE selection of a team is the most difficult problem the prospective captain has to face. Particularly is this so in the case of a team to go abroad. Where the teams are selected from a number of competitors at an open meeting to shoot a match on the same range within 24 hours of selection the task of selection is somewhat easier; but nevertheless they are sufficiently complex to give a big advantage to the team captain who knows his work. The captain who merely follows form—that is to say, who selects for his team the necessary number of highest scorers who are eligible for selection—is going to find trouble before his match is half over, for good individual rifle shots are not of necessity good team shots. Shooting in an important team match carries with it a much greater feeling of responsibility than shooting for oneself, and it is this extra "weight" which many men cannot carry and be sure of a high score. To others the feeling of responsibility brings them up to a high state of nerve tension, bringing out their highest and best efforts. The successful captain is he who can discriminate between these two classes.

There are other important traits in the desirable team shot. He should be unselfish, so that any sacrifice he personally can make for the benefit of the team as a whole should be unhesitatingly made. He should not be unduly vain of his personal prowess, for occasions arise where the complete sacrifice of one or more shots may be demanded of him in the interests of his team, the victim being relegated to a very low place in the team. He should be cheerful even in adversity, for the preservation of good spirits is essential to the production of a good finish. He should be well disciplined that he may take orders

THE CAPTAIN'S RESPONSIBILITY

from a captain or coach without hesitation or question, and above all he should be a good sportsman to take defeat like a man, and be generous in victory to the vanquished.

In team matches, such as are provided at Bisley, the team captain is concerned almost solely with

(1) Present form, and
(2) Whether his men are good team shots.

In match rifle competitions, such as that for the Elcho Shield, (1) will very largely depend upon the "form" of the barrels in use by the prospective members of the team. Here is an added responsibility to those already shouldered by the team organisers.

The selection of a team to go abroad, however, is one which entails much greater care and possibly greater knowledge of character. Many men who are eminently qualified as riflemen to take place in the most select team at Bisley are entirely unsuited for selection in a team to go abroad; for it must be remembered that the members of the team have to be together not for one day's shooting, but for possibly some months, continually in each other's society. The greatest harmony must exist at all times to ensure that the team as a whole will give its best work, and if there is any meanness or petty jealousies among the members, the best team work can never be realised. One discordant note may spoil the whole tune, and so one undesirable team member may spoil the whole team. Social position of itself is unimportant in the selection of a team, but the man without a big heart has no place in a travelling team, however high his position or shooting abilities may be.

The composition of almost every service rifle team since such team had to be selected has been adversely criticised, and the criticism has usually been hottest when the team has had to represent the country abroad. Usually the comment which has had the biggest vogue has been that "half the team could be replaced with better shots." That is often true, if one is to take men solely by individual performances. The critics forget the many and weighty considerations which we have attempted to indicate.

The value of such criticism was amply shown in a recent

international team which shot for the Mother Country at Bisley. Those not in the know could not understand the inclusion of a man who could certainly have been replaced, on paper, by at least a dozen eligible shots. The criticised member of that team, far from being a weak or broken reed, proved to be its strongest prop.

It is usual for a team that has travelled some distance to spend a few days on the range preparatory to a match, and in the interval between the arrival and the day of the match, it is the duty of the captain to make his men into a team. This may sound rather simple, but in point of fact it is a preparation of considerable perplexity and much difficulty. This making of a team has to be done whether the team is on its home ground or is travelling. The only difference is that, in a strange country on strange ranges, it is likely to be a little more difficult.

The object to be achieved is to score on the day of the match the highest aggregate number of marks, and this object should never be lost sight of. To accomplish this there must be mutual support among the members of the team to the entire exclusion of self. The suggestion made by one prominent rifleman that individual scores in a team match should not be published is a suggestion of one who thoroughly understands and appreciates this elimination of the individual.

The first step in the preparation is to bring each individual to a common ground or centre, and this is done by taking the team to a zero range—that is, a range not exceeding 50 yards—and there bringing all rifles to one common zero. It may be thought that, having attained this uniformity, little remains but to issue orders; but, indeed, this reduction to a common zero opens up a vista of endless trouble. If all sights on rifles were fitted by the makers in a perfectly upright position, and if the shooters invariably held their rifles in the upright position, zeroing rifles would put an end to half the troubles of the team captain or coach, but unfortunately manufacturers and shooters are not infallible. Consequently, the coach finds that, while Private Jones is getting bull's-eyes with the wind allowance called, Private Smith persistently requires two or three

PLATE LVII

Photo: Gale & Polden, Ltd.
THE "RUNNING DEER" FIRING POINT
The well-known sporting shot, Mr. Walter Winans, shooting at the "running deer"

Photo: Gale & Polden, Ltd.
THE "RUNNING DEER" BUTT
The "running deer" moves along a railway, down a short hill and up another. The "running deer" ranges are the prettiest part of the "common"

TEAM ZEROING

minutes more, even though at short range both their rifles agree perfectly. Nor is this all; for on going back to extreme range, Private Smith finds the coach's allowance correct, while Private Jones is now four minutes out. In fact, one-third of the team may seem to have "floating zeros." What between badly fitted sights and badly held rifles the zero is a perfect "will o' the wisp," and the first week spent in training a team is apparently thrown away upon finding zeros.

On this subject, the wag of a British Rifle Team shooting in Canada once perpetrated an amusing joke upon the rest of the team. After about the third day's practice he was seen, immediately after firing, wandering about behind the firing points searching intently in the grass. Presently a friend asked him if he had lost something, to which he replied "Yes," and continued his search. The friend joined in the search, and was followed afterwards by others, until presently some half-dozen people were searching intently among the grass to help our wag out of his trouble. Presently one of the search-party thought he had better find out exactly what the appearance of the object was, so he turned to the wag and asked what he had lost.

"Oh," came the reply, "I have only lost my zero."

It was only a due appreciation of the claims of the team to the services of a valuable rifleman that saved the zero hunter from just retribution.

The truth is that it is impossible to ensure that a rifle properly zeroed at ten yards and handled by a first-class target shot will maintain a true zero up to 1,000 yards. Nor will it always give similar results even in the hands of the same man. In the first place, the mechanical fault may be present in the fitting of the sight, and this may be sufficient to account for a defect in the zero at the longer ranges equal to several minutes of angle. Secondly, the liability of the shooting man to lean the sights of his rifle to one side or the other is ever present, and while he may in some circumstances fire a series of shots without material error in holding the sights upright, a change of position or a different slope of another firing point or a different slope of the line of targets may introduce into his holding an unconscious error of quite a considerable amount. It is within the knowledge of the writer that a well-known member of international rifle teams persistently held his rifle with a cant which necessitated a lateral allowance of fully eight minutes at 1,000 yards. He put it down to drift, but the cause was quite observable even to a novice from a position immediately behind his rifle.

This canting or leaning of the sights, whether from the fault of the manufacturer or the shooter, is thus a serious obstacle in bringing a team of riflemen to that uniform standard which is necessary to realise the full capacity of the team. The first thing to be done is to ascertain to what extent these deviations are present, and this can probably be done in some measure by agreeing on a common zero at ten yards and then taking the whole team to 1,000 yards. Those members of the team whose zeros remain unaltered at both these ranges may for the present stand aside so that attention may be devoted to those whose zeros appear to have altered.

If the captain of the team be fortunate enough to find that his whole team still agree at 1,000 yards as at ten yards, well and good; but if not, his next move should be to try to separate or isolate the two faults. In others words, suppose A should find his zero three minutes wrong at 1,000 yards, it is important to know whether the fault is mechanically in the sight or in the shooter, because if it be in the sight it can easily be rectified and the trouble removed.

A simple way of finding this out is to give the doubtful rifle to another member of the team whose rifle has been found to be correct at both ranges, and to ask him to zero it himself at the zero range and then shoot it at 1,000 yards.

If the defect is corroborated it can safely be put down to a mechanical fault; but if the zero be true at 1,000 yards the fault must be the original shooter's.

In the case of a rifle which appears to be very much out at 1,000 yards, there may be faults both in the fitting of the sights and the holding of the rifle, but these faults can be separated in the same manner as is above suggested.

Now, if the shooter uniformly cants his rifle, this fault can be corrected by mechanically leaning the sight in the opposite

MECHANICAL DIFFICULTIES

direction. At the same time the cause of his leaning the sights may be due to a badly fitted foresight. It frequently happens that, in fitting the military blade foresight on a rifle, a slight defect in construction may cause the blade to have an eyeable cant to one side. In aiming through the old tangent opensight, the guide to keeping the sights upright was the side of the leaf or the flat top of the backsight bar. In shooting through an aperture-sight, however, no such guide exists, and the shooter therefore learns to take the upright blade as his guide. If this blade has a slight cant in itself, holding it upright will cause a lean on the backsight, and this is very often the cause of shooters holding the rifle with a perpetual lean to one side. When it is ascertained that there is a mechanical fault in the sight, it is therefore better to make a close examination of the foresight before proceeding to alter the backsight, and that is one reason why it is better to separate the two most prevalent causes of alteration of zero.

Even where the fault has been definitely traced to the shooter and found to be due to an inherent defect in position, there may be objections to mechanically leaning the backsight in the opposite direction to the cant; but it is better that this should be done than that the captain or coach should attempt to operate with a conglomeration of floating zeroes.

So far we can deal with the mechanical adjustment of the team's lateral zero. But now we come to the purely personal error complicated by the liability of the weak action of the Lee-Enfield rifle to give way under the moderate pressure to which it is subjected.

It frequently happens that, despite every care taken in the adjustment of rifles, and the exact ascertainment of individual zeroes, a rifle in the course of practice, or even in an important match, will suddenly appear to change its zero at long range some 4 or 5 minutes of angle. Sometimes this apparent phenomenon is due to nothing else than an awkward position into which the firer has fallen, or to some unobserved slope at the target butts from which he takes his "plumb line." It may be, however, that grit or other fouling may have become seated between the bolt-lugs and the resisting shoulders of the action, causing an unequal pressure upon the one side. Or it may be that the case-hardening of one lug may have slightly given way, throwing the major pressure upon the opposite lug, and so altering the vibration or "flip" of the rifle. From whatever cause this may happen it is extremely disconcerting, not only to the man himself, but to the coach, and consequently to the rest of the team. It cannot be said that it is an incident which rarely happens, and allowance can only be made for it by instructing the firer to consider his zero as having permanently shifted, and to make due allowance for it in his subsequent shooting.

Having taken every precaution to see that the rifles and men have been brought to a common zero, it remains for the captain to draw up his programme for the system of practice. In drawing up the programme it is well to see that he is fully equipped in the necessary accessories for carrying out this practice. In the first place his coach, if he have only one, should be equipped with a tripod telescope of considerable power, certainly not less than 50 diameters, and having an object glass of not less than 4 in. So large a diameter of object glass is necessary for illumination, this being a most important feature in a good telescope for range work. Each member of the team should provide himself with a powerful telescope of not less than 20 diameters magnification, preferably more.

For the purpose of analysing scores and selecting the team and reserve, the captain should provide himself with a liberal supply of score cards of not less than 4 in. square, containing space for name, range, score, elevation, and wind allowance for each shot, and other necessary particulars, such as rifle number, time of shooting, weather conditions, etc., and also a fair-sized representation of the target itself, in order that a diagram may be kept thereon of the position of the shots to which the particulars refer. This may necessitate three or more different kinds of cards, but they are necessary for the efficient working of a team. Scoring books are of little use in team practice, because a score keeper cannot very well take more than two scores at one time, and if three targets were going

PLATE LVIII

THE TARGET PITS AT BISLEY

This view of the "Century butt" shows the target apparatus being used for holding class-firing targets. The apparatus is of iron, the target-frame being of wood and the targets themselves paper-faced canvas

Photo: Topical Press

HOW TO ZERO

at once it would necessitate three score books being simultaneously in use.

Coaching a team is perhaps the most thankless task of any in rifle shooting, although one of the most important. Every fault that is committed, every point that is dropped, seems to be piled upon the shoulders of the team coach, while the credit for any success or for any good performance is taken by the shooter, despite the fact that his real position is that of a part of the team mechanism. The success or failure of a coach may almost be said to depend upon the unity of a team, both as regards men and rifles. That is to say, the men must be animated by a desire to make whatever sacrifice may be called for to benefit the team as a whole, and their rifles must be calibrated or zeroed as one. Without such qualities in a team no coaching can be altogether satisfactory, nor can complete confidence exist between the team coach and the team members.

The reason for having properly zeroed rifles has already been indicated, but it is seldom appreciated except by an experienced team captain or coach. In most cases riflemen are content to determine the lateral zero of the rifle, without particular regard to the absolute zero of elevation. One of the best methods of zeroing a rifle is to shoot it at a very short range, say 10 or 20 yards, using as a target a square white card having a cross painted on it in lines about a quarter of an inch or half an inch thick. Aim being taken at the intersection of the two lines, the position of the shot hole will determine how far the zero requires adjustment, the correct position for a properly zeroed rifle being about an inch below the point of aim depending on the height of the foresight above the axis of the bore. If the zero range is 25 yards or more, the position of the shot hole below the point of aim should be equal to the height of the foresight above the axis of the bore plus the drop of the bullet for the range. If it is possible to measure exactly $12\frac{1}{2}$ yards from target to muzzle, such a range is convenient for zeroing with accurately scaled sights such as those of a match rifle, as at this range $\frac{1}{8}$ in. on the target equals one minute of angle on the backsight. (*See* Chapter XIII., Part I.)

If each member of the rifle team is armed with a rifle properly zeroed in accordance with these directions, the work of the team coach is very considerably lightened. On the contrary, if the rifles are not zeroed, no team coach can be certain whether errors in lateral allowance are attributable to his fault, to the fault of an unzeroed rifle, or to indifferent holding; and he is, therefore, at a loss what course to take to correct the fault in the next shot.

Records of all the practices should be carefully collected after firing, and examined and analysed in the endeavour to rectify any faults which may be capable of remedy. If the practices are carried out by a selected body of men which includes a team and reserves, the analysis of practice scores should be very thorough before the final selection of the team is made.

At the commencement of a match it is usual for the team captain or coach to select one member of the team to fire the first shot, particularly if the conditions of the match preclude the sighting shots. This precaution is advisable to prevent a wrong estimate of wind allowance being given to more than one man. Having ascertained or corroborated the correct wind allowance, the coach takes the whole team in hand, and calls the wind allowance as he reads it. It is an essential quality of a team coach that he should have decision of character. Nothing is so disconcerting to members of a team as uncertainty or indecision in a team coach.

Another quality of importance in team coaching is quick reading of atmospheric changes, and in this connection it is well to continuously repeat the reading until a change occurs. This continuous repetition conveys to the members of the team that the team coach's attention is continually fixed, and that no change in the wind will be likely to take the team unawares.

It is important, also, that the team coach on his part should have every assistance from the members of his team, and to this end it is necessary that each man, as he fires, should inform the team coach the exact wind allowance he has made. At first, the inexperienced team shot is inclined, for some

THE COACH'S RESPONSIBILITY

reason, whether nervousness or vanity it is difficult to say, to wait for the result of the shot before informing his coach what allowance he has made. This practice is very disheartening to the coach, and should be put down by the team captain with a firm hand. When, for any reason, a bad shot is made, it is to the team's advantage that the coach immediately accepts the responsibility. The position of the shot as it subsequently appears on the target may exonerate the coach from blame, as, for example, a shot which is high or low, but the benefit to the team of removing from the mind of the team shot the responsibility for making a bad hit is considerable.

CHAPTER XIII

The National Rifle Association

AMONG the many organisations which exist for the purpose of promoting and encouraging rifle shooting, the most important and influential is that Imperial body the National Rifle Association. This association was instituted in the year 1860, when, as the result of a petition which was presented to Her late Majesty Queen Victoria, bearing the signatures of the late Duke of Cambridge, the late Duke of Westminster, the late Earl of Wemyss, and others, a Charter was granted to the association by the Sovereign, creating the association and defining its purposes. The chief credit for the creation of this association undoubtedly belongs to the late Right Hon. Earl of Wemyss (then Lord Elcho), who was the leading spirit in the original movement which started shortly after the institution of the Volunteer Forces, now translated into the Territorial Forces. The present patron of the association is His Majesty King George V., and the list of Vice-Presidents contains such names as His Royal Highness the Duke of Connaught, the Duke of Hamilton, the Duke of Bedford, the Duke of Norfolk, the Marquis of Lansdowne, and many other distinguished personages. The membership of the National Rifle Association exceeds 3,000, including many Colonial and foreign members in almost all parts of the world, and its influence is extended to every part of the world where rifle shooting exists as a sport. The event of the year for which the National Rifle Association is chiefly famous is the holding of a very large rifle meeting at Bisley Ranges in the county of Surrey. Prior to the year 1890 the ranges of the National Rifle Association were situated at Wimbledon, but owing to the encroachment of building it was found no longer possible

BISLEY COMPETITIONS

to conduct a rifle meeting on Wimbledon Common with safety, and accordingly the present camp and ranges were acquired from the War Office. The extent of the ground actually occupied by the association property is 600 acres. The ranges extend outwards towards the north-west in a fan shape, and include facilities for almost all kinds of rifle and revolver shooting at distances from 25 yards to 1,200 yards; with the danger space behind the butts, which is under the control of the War Office, they occupy an area of ground reaching many thousands of acres.

The competitions provided at the Bisley meeting are many and various. Principal among these is the Service Rifle Section, embodying contests covering almost every conceivable form of service rifle shooting. There are competitions for teams and individuals, at bullseye and service targets, stationary, moving and disappearing targets, requiring all varieties of rapid and deliberate fire.

Chief in importance as well as in historic interest is the competition for the King's Prize, for which his Majesty presents a sum of £250. This money, in a lump, goes to the winner, and in addition the N.R.A. gives a large number of other money prizes, varying in extent from £50 down to £1. Needless to say, the Gold Medal which is presented to the winner is the most coveted shooting distinction of any that can be won.

The competition for the King's Prize starts at 200 yards at a service target, 500 yards at a service target, and 600 yards at a bull's-eye target, seven rounds at each range, the highest 300 competitors passing into the second stage. The conditions of this shoot, which are known as "King's Prize First Stage," have up to the present been the model upon which all short-range deliberate competitions are arranged in this country and very largely elsewhere in the Empire. The second stage consists of a ten-round shoot at 300 yards and ten rounds at 600 yards bull's-eye targets. The highest 100 scorers of the first and second stages pass into the third or final stage, commonly called the "King's Hundred," and for this each of the hundred receives a decoration to commemorate the feat. The final stage is shot on the last day of the meeting, and consists of fifteen shots at 900 yards and fifteen shots at 1,000 yards, the highest aggregate scorer of all three stages being adjudged the winner and the champion marksman for the year.

The final quarter of an hour at the last range is often a time of the tensest excitement, at any rate, amongst the spectators, a considerable portion of whom are themselves expert rifle shots. The scores are marked up on huge blackboards, which are believed to be the biggest portable blackboards in use anywhere. As the scores mount up, it is seen that the final contest will lie between two, or perhaps three or four men. They have each perhaps one or two shots to fire, and the slightest error in judging the changing wind, or the least trace of "nerves" will probably mean disaster. The crowd gathers in great clusters round the blackboards which tell the scores of the few prominent men, and runners bring news from group to group, telling that so and so "has got a miss," or, blessed sound, the favourite "has finished three bulls." Most likely it happens that one particular man finishes with such a score as is not likely to be beaten, or perhaps it is known that some of those still shooting can beat it. But sometimes the contest ends in a tie. That is what the enthusiastic crowd loves. It does not appeal to the competitors in quite the same way, for the shooting for any important competition is wearing on the nerves, and when the tie has to be shot "on the spot," as the N.R.A. regulation idiomatically puts it, the strain is great indeed. However, the ordeal has to be faced, and presently a great cheer proclaims the victor.

Then comes the romantic ceremony known as "chairing the winner." The champion has always been carried round the camp, but the chair dates only from 1883. The winner, rifle in hand, sits in the chair, which is hoisted up by comrades from his own regiment, and proceeded by a band playing the famous march of conquest from *Judas Maccabæus* is carried first of all to the N.R.A. offices, and then round the camp. The latter half of the ceremony takes place after the prize giving. The winner is welcomed at each of the clubs by the president or senior member, who offers him a loving-cup. He is

PLATE LIX

Photo: Topical Press

A SHORT-RANGE TARGET
The Army figure target used for instructional and standard test purposes

Photo: Topical Press

REPAIRING THE FRAMES
The picture of the Bisley 200 yards butt gives an excellent idea of the sound nature of the concrete head cover for the markers

MATCH RIFLE SHOOTING 303

then conducted into the club-house to receive the personal congratulations of the members.

In addition to Military Rifle competitions, there are competitions for sporting rifles, which are mostly conducted at a target representing a running deer. These competitions are well attended by many noted sportsmen, and have undoubtedly done much to help in the evolution of the modern small-bore high-velocity sporting rifle.

For purely long-range work a series of competitions are reserved for what are commonly called "Match Rifles." The type of rifle used for these competitions usually represents the most advanced form of Military High-power Rifle. The rifles are fitted with magnifying sights, specially arranged so that the competitors may fire from what is known as the "back position," a position lending itself to great steadiness and comfort in holding, and the shooting is conducted at ranges of 900, 1,000, 1,100 and 1,200 yards. The accuracy of this type of weapon is little short of marvellous, instances being known where the competitor has exceeded fifty consecutive bull's-eyes at 1,000 yards, the bull's-eye being 36 in. in diameter, while in 1913 one competitor made the astounding run of thirty-three consecutive bull's-eyes at 1,100 yards.

The object of this style of shooting is to develop the highest possibility of the military cartridge and rifle by eliminating as nearly as possible the human error, and it is perhaps not too much to say that the progress achieved in the development of modern military small arms owes more to the Match Rifle Shooting of the N.R.A. than to anything else.

Mr. Metford, about whose work so much has been said in the first part of this book, conducted much of his practical shooting with the Match Rifle, and in this he had the assistance and advice of his great friend, Sir Henry Halford, who shot almost exclusively with his rifles. In recent years it is only necessary to think of the work done by Captain Hardcastle and Mr. F. W. Jones, the one dealing with ballistics as affecting the projectile, and the other in the matter of powders, to realise that the work of the Match Rifle is by no means over. Every Bisley meeting teaches the manufacturer something—something, it is safe to say, that he might have been much longer in finding out had it not been for the insistent demands for improvements of the competitors in the Match Rifle events.

The principal prize in the Match Rifle competition is the "Hopton Cup," presented by Colonel J. D. Hopton in 1900. It is won by the competitor who scores the greatest aggregate in the six single-entry events, and comprises 170 shots, made up of 35 at 900 yards, 65 at 1,000 yards, and 70 at 1,100 yards.

Revolver and pistol shooting is well provided for by a formidable series of competitions, extending daily for a whole fortnight. These competitions are in considerable favour, particularly among naval competitors, who as a body are exceedingly efficient in the use of the small arm.

The miniature or "small-bore" rifle has a meeting all to itself during the first week of the Bisley fortnight, and is well attended by competitors from various parts of the country. This portion of the great Bisley meeting is absolutely self-contained, and is remarkable for the fact that in recent years the conduct of the meeting, the squadding and judging of the targets has been in the hands of volunteer members of the "Rifle Clubs Committee," well acquainted with the work and idiosyncrasies of the "small-bore" rifleman.

In describing the method by which Bisley competitions are conducted, it may be of interest to describe the targets and the method of scoring generally in use. In the military competitions the targets at 200 yards are of "Service" design and colour —that is to say, they represent the head and shoulders of a prone man in the act of firing. This figure is coloured brown on a green or grey background, and the bull's-eye is an invisible circle, 5 in. in diameter, placed at the base of the figure. The bull's-eye counts five points, and successive divisions of the target shown by larger rings count four, three, and two points respectively. The whole target is 4 ft. square. At 300 yards the target is circular, 4 ft. in diameter, and containing a black bull's-eye on a white ground, the bull's-eye being 8 in. in diameter. At 500 yards the target is somewhat similar to that at 200 yards, being, however, 6 ft. square. At 600 yards the target is 6 ft. in diameter, of the bull's-eye pattern. The diameter of the bull's-

BISLEY TARGETS

eye for 500 and 600 yards is 15 in. and 18 in. respectively. At ranges over 600 yards the targets are 10 ft. broad by 6 ft. high, the black bull's-eye being 36 in. in diameter. In 1914, because of the consistently high scoring in the Match Rifle competition, a "central" 24 in. in diameter was introduced into the long-range bull's-eye. It was signalled by a white "V" on the bull's-eye panel, and in Match Rifle competitions scored six marks. The rest of the target outside the bull was divided up into an "inner" 54 in. in diameter, a "magpie" 72 in. square, and an "outer," which comprised the rest of the target left and right of the "magpie."

The system of marking at Bisley is a very simple and effective one. The targets are of canvas in wooden frames, and are mounted upon movable iron-frame mechanism, oper-

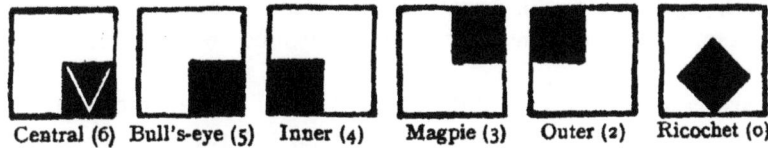

Central (6)   Bull's-eye (5)   Inner (4)   Magpie (3)   Outer (2)   Ricochet (0)

Fig. 37.—The Bisley marking panels

ated by chain and pulley in such a way that the target can be hoisted into the view of the shooter, or lowered into the target trench or pit at will. The iron frame holding the target is balanced by a dummy target, so that when the target is pulled down into the trench the dummy target is hoisted into view. On this dummy target, which is of the same dimensions as the target itself, a large square black panel is hung to denote the value of the hit, the position of the panel on the dummy indicating the division of the target struck.

An illustration is given, showing how these values are signalled. Immediately after the value of the hit is signalled the target is again raised for the next shot, the marker having inserted in the shot hole just signalled a small square "spotting disc" or card to show exactly the position of the shot. Upon the next shot being signalled, the spotting disc is removed from the last hole, which is then patched up with paper and paste. At the firing-point the score is recorded upon a small blackboard in full view of spectators, and also upon a competition card. The "register keeper," as he is called, is required to call out in a loud voice the name of the competitor and the value of the shot just signalled, recording these on the blackboard and the card at the same time. Any spectator or competitor is entitled to correct an error in the score, or to protest against incorrect scoring. When the competitor has concluded his shoot, the register keeper calls upon the officer appointed to take charge of the range, who thereupon checks the score on the card with that on the blackboard and signs the card. This officer then hands the card to an "orderly," who is usually on horseback, and whose business it is to convey completed cards to the Statistical Office. The staff in this office sort the tickets out into their respective positions in order of merit, and when the competition finishes and the results have been collected, the prize list is issued without further delay.

Nearly all the outside staff at the annual Bisley meeting—that is to say, the markers in the trenches, the register keepers, the range officers, and orderlies—are regular soldiers, drafted from adjacent commands by permission of the War Office, the National Rifle Association paying them for their work. The number employed during the Bisley fortnight is very large, but, as is to be expected from highly trained soldiers, the work is carried out with clock-like precision. This high standard of work seldom varies, but there is at least one instance when the markers employed during the Bisley meeting showed the exception which proves the rule. This was in the year 1900, when a large proportion of the troops were in South Africa. The only available regiments which the War Office could conveniently draw upon were composed of Royal Irish Militia, and, while they did their best, the incidents which accompanied their efforts provided considerable entertainment to the competitors.

One register keeper who seemed quite incapable of learning the different signals on the dummy target was nevertheless quick-witted enough to observe that, if he gave a magpie where a bull's-eye was signalled, he was sharply called to

PLATE LX

THE SCORING PANEL

The position of the black panel on the scoring frame tells the firer the value of his shot. In the picture the panel is about to be hung on the top right-hand corner, signifying a "magpie"

THE LONG-RANGE BISLEY TARGET

The N.R.A. long-range target looks big close at hand, but its 36-inch bull's-eye is none too large at the ranges of 900 yards and over at which it is used

A BISLEY STORY

account by the competitor, whereas if he shouted "bull's-eye" irrespective of the value shown no serious complaint was made. Fortunately no dishonest competitor turned up to take advantage of it, and so the register keeper's education was eventually completed before any serious harm was done.

But it was chiefly in the pronunciation of competitors' names that high comedy was really reached, and the ingenuity exhibited by "Pat" in getting out of difficulties was typical of the Irishman at his best. As an instance, one register keeper found himself with three register tickets, of which one bore a very uncommon name—that of Mr. Le Poidevin, of Guernsey. The first thing the register keeper has to do on receiving the cards is to call out the names in the order in which they have to lie down on the firing-point, this order being usually decided by the alphabetical order of the initial letters of the names. Pat looked long and earnestly at the curious name, trying to make up his mind how he would pronounce it. To give himself more time he thought it best to shout out the name of the right-hand man. So he called out loudly and confidently: "Gibson on the right." Next in alphabetical order was the puzzling name, and Pat scratched his head earnestly as he looked at it. Something had to be done, however, as time was getting on, and suddenly the solution flashed across his mind: "And Smith on the left!" he shouted, leaving Le Poidevin no option but to take his correct position. Still the difficulty had not been overcome, for Pat's instructions distinctly were to call out in a loud voice the competitor's name as each shot was fired. The right-hand man opened the firing with his first sighter, and Pat called out: "Gibson, Sighting Shot, an inner, 4." The Guernsey man then followed, and Pat, after much head-scratching, called out in a very subdued voice: "Jones, Sighting Shot, a bull's-eye, 5." "Jones" promptly looked round at the register keeper and the blackboard, but observing that the score was correctly recorded concluded he had not heard aright, and the incident passed unchallenged. Smith completed the first round, Gibson fired his first to count, and was followed by the Guernsey man. This time Pat was more confident. "Jones, First Shot to count, a bull's-eye, 5!"

cried Pat, but this was more than the Guernsey man could stand.

"Here, Corporal," he said, "my name is not Jones; it is Le Poidevin." Pat leaned forward in his chair, and delivered his explanation in his most apologetic and confidential tone: "Yis, sor; I know, sor; but I could not say that, sor, so I jist said Jones." And Jones it was to the end of the shoot.

The number of competitors attending the annual meeting at Bisley varies from year to year. At one time, about the year 1880, the numbers exceeded 2,000; but since then, from a variety of causes, all much discussed and more or less problematical, the number has shrunk until now it is usually about 1,200. These, however, come from all parts of the world. Representatives of Australia, New Zealand, Canada, United States, South Africa, Uganda, Egypt, Ceylon, India, Malay States, and various parts of continental Europe have at one time or other taken part in this historic meeting, and on various important occasions, such as for instance the late Queen Victoria's Diamond Jubilee, the King's Coronation, the Olympic games, etc., the assemblage of a very representative gathering has lent considerable piquancy and a deal of colour to the Bisley meeting.

The representatives from Canada have a permanent house in Bisley Camp, and enjoy all the comforts of a good club during their stay. Considerable numbers of other competitors find quarters in the substantial pavilions erected by various rifle clubs, and also in wooden huts rented from the National Rifle Association.

The bulk of the competitors, however, and all the temporary staff are under canvas. The competitors pay at the rate of about 15s. per week for tent accommodation, three in a tent; and in addition to this they have to find their own food, for which ample provision is made by the camp caterers.

The entrance fees for the various competitions vary from the sixpenny shot at egg-pool to the £1 12s. 6d. entrance fee for the Albert Match Rifle competition. If the competitor desires to enter for the principal single-entry Service Rifle competitions, he will require to spend a sum of about £7, so that, including living expenses, he must before coming to Bisley find a sum of at least £10 over and above his railway fare and travelling expenses. This may, in large measure, account for the falling off in entries, because the initial expenditure of such a sum can only be within the means of a comparatively limited class.

The daily programme during the Bisley meeting is a very full one, and the energetic competitor need never be at a loss for something to do. Shooting usually starts at 9 o'clock in the morning and, with an hour's interval for lunch, it continues until 7 o'clock in the evening. Competitions in every branch of rifle shooting proceed simultaneously each day, the majority of these being competitions in which the competitor is allowed to enter as often as he wills. In the case of a single-entry competition, competitors have to be at the firing-point at a pre-arranged time, and must proceed without delay to complete their firing. In all cases the methods of recording and collecting the results is that which has already been described. Competitions open to teams under Service conditions are more or less confined to two days of the meeting, and these afford an interesting variation to the sight-seeing visitor.

The commencement and cessation of firing each day is signalled by gun-fire, a mortar being fired from an eminence near the camp.

After gun-fire, at 7 o'clock, music is provided in the Umbrella Tent, or a concert is arranged by some regiment or club, who engage London concert artists for the occasion. The evenings are thus comfortably spent, and altogether very complete arrangements exist for making the competitor's visit to Bisley Camp a pleasant one. Despite the many attractions apart from the main shooting business, the keen rifleman undoubtedly derives his chief enjoyment from his intercourse with fellow competitors. There is a comradeship in rifle shooting of the most democratic character, and the delight of the new-comer is to meet and mix with veteran riflemen whose names have been as the names of the Prophets in his far-off little community. Many a youngster at Bisley for the first time has found himself taken in hand by a veteran who has been able to make all things clear. Many, too, are the life-long friendships that have begun at Wimbledon or Bisley.

Since the removal from Wimbledon to Bisley in 1890, the latter place has undergone something of a transformation. Within the camp enclosure quite a number of large and handsome buildings have been erected. Principal among these are the new offices of the National Rifle Association (used for the first time in 1902), a large and substantial brick building specially designed to suit the exigencies of its particular business. In the main office are on view many items of interest to the rifle-shot, including specimens of the rifles used by the armies of most of the great military Powers, and a unique collection of rifles and other objects of historic interest.

The Canadian Hut has already been mentioned. It stands on high ground near the entrance to the camp, and is built of Canadian woods specially brought over from Canada for the purpose. The building has a very handsome appearance, and contains many fine Canadian trophies of the chase.

Other important buildings are the London and Middlesex Rifle Association Pavilion, the North London Rifle Club House, the head-quarters of the most influential rifle club in England, the English Twenty Club House, the Council Club House, the Army Rifle Association Club House, the National Rifle Association Club House, the National Rifle Club of Scotland, the large Refreshment Pavilion, and the club houses of the East Surrey Regiment, the Honourable Artillery Company, and the Inns of Court. And last, only because it is the smallest, the hut of the English VIII. Club, the walls of which are adorned with pictures of every English VIII. since 1862, and where is kept that wonderful book in which is entered particulars of every shot fired in the Elcho Shield match by the members of each team from the very beginning. Besides these there are numerous lesser buildings, principally huts erected by members of the association for their own occupation during the meeting, and a large number of small huts belonging to the association which they rent to competitors.

The system of lighting at Bisley is by electricity, and most of the principal club houses have had this installed.

THE BISLEY "HUTS"

The catering during the meeting is carried out at the Refreshment Pavilion, which is open to the public; but, in addition, several of the clubs, notably the Canadian Hut, the London and Middlesex Association, the North London Rifle Club, and the Council Club, do their own catering in a very complete and efficient manner. The shooting man eats and drinks moderately, but what he has he likes to be good; besides, he often has to entertain friends during the meeting, and is keen for Bisley's reputation. The caterers, clubs, and associations do not have an easy task.

Such a large and efficient rifle range as Bisley could hardly be allowed to remain in a state of disuse, either before or after the Bisley fortnight, and in point of fact the ranges are very much in use during the off season—namely, between April and July, and August and October. Numerous regiments and clubs carry out a complete programme of competitions on Bisley ranges throughout the whole season, and it is no uncommon sight on a Saturday afternoon to see the whole of the Century Butts, comprising 100 targets, in use. The North London Rifle Club and the Middlesex Rifle Association each provide competitions on two days of every week, while many regiments and civilian rifle clubs in the London district, such as the Honourable Artillery Company, the London Scottish, the Stock Exchange Rifle Club, and others, have their own separate series.

These clubs and regiments hire the necessary target accommodation from the National Rifle Association, who thereby derive a considerable income from this source, besides enabling them to give permanent employment to a large and efficient staff. In 1914, after many years of agitation, the N.R.A. opened their ranges for Sunday shooting in the afternoons. A number of regiments carried out class firing, for which purpose the arrangement was formerly intended. The North London Club and the Middlesex Association had competition shoots every Sunday from April till July, but they were not extensively patronised.

If there ever existed any question as to the utility of the work done by the National Rifle Association, such questions have now been amply answered. By the agency of the National Rifle Association a corps of instructors, over 1,000 strong, has been created for teaching Lord Kitchener's new army and the new battalions of Territorial troops. It is difficult to imagine how the need for musketry instructors could have been filled had there been in this country at the outbreak of war no such body as the National Rifle Association.

When the 1914 Bisley meeting came to an end on July 25th, there was but a small cloud on the political horizon, so small a cloud that it is safe to say that not one of the crowd of spectators who witnessed the great tie shoot between Private Dewar and Private Fulton for the King's Prize had the faintest idea that within a week Europe would be plunged into the greatest war of history, and that within ten days the British Empire would also be embroiled. However, the end of the first week in August—a fortnight after the close of the Bisley meeting—saw signs of an activity which is not usual at Bisley during August. The National Rifle Association had placed all its resources absolutely at the disposal of the War Office, and already some of its best-known experts had offered their services as musketry instructors. It was soon decided that a corps of instructors was to be formed by the National Rifle Association, and invitations were sent out through the Press to all members of the National Rifle Association and competitors at Bisley who were over recruiting age to volunteer their services for that corps of instructors. At once responses to that invitation came pouring in, and a little band of voluntary workers, under the direction of Lieut.-Colonel Crosse, the secretary of the association, and Lieut.-Colonel Matthews, chief executive officer, began to classify the names sent in. Captain J. P. Somers, of the Inns of Court O.T.C., was made temporary head of the office operations under the two officers before mentioned, and the work went on often into the small hours of the morning. Two instructors from the Hythe School of Musketry arrived early on the scene, and started work at once with the Bisley men who were at hand. In those first few weeks there could be no doubt that Hythe and Bisley got to know more about one another than they had ever done before,

PLATE LXI

Photo: Gale & Polden, Ltd.

THE CENTURY BUTT, BISLEY

The famous Century Butt, which has one hundred targets and firing points at 200, 300, 500 and 600 yards. This butt used to be known as the "Ninety," but in 1903 an additional ten targets were added. All the important short-range competitions at the Bisley meeting are shot on this butt

and they found that, after all, despite many years of bickering, the Empire's need found them both ready.

Of course, the Hythe instructors found the crack shots with whom they had to deal were splendid material for their purpose. All that was necessary was to instruct them in the methods of teaching which have been developed for the better guidance of the British soldier. The target-shot has always said that if it was necessary for him to shoot quickly he could do so, and he proved it up to the hilt. Not only did he quickly prove his ability to shoot in the military way, but, what was far more important at the moment, he quickly learned to impart a knowledge of military shooting to others. It was not long before Bisley became a school of musketry, turning out expert instructors at a rate exceeding 100 a month, a truly splendid performance. Major-General Lord Cheylesmore is Commandant of this school of musketry which has arisen to meet the nation's need on the marksmen's well-loved common. Lieut.-Colonel C. R. Crosse is Staff Officer, and Colonel Barlow is Staff Paymaster. The Chief Instructor is that famous rifleman, Major P. W. Richardson, to whom rifle-shooting owes so much, and whose energy and ability made the success of the new School of Musketry a certainty.

The School of Musketry at Bisley was for the instruction of instructors, and naturally for this purpose not a large amount of range room was necessary. The splendid ranges were free for the benefit of units under training, and never has the firing point at the Century Butt been so crowded as during the winter of 1914-15. Up to the end of May, 1915, over 1,500 officers and non-commissioned officers attended the Bisley school, and of these 1,191 passed out as instructors. In the Machine Gun School 428 officers and men have been passed out.

This year (1915) will see the first break in the continuity of the National Rifle Association meetings since they started at Wimbledon fifty-five years ago. Through fair days and foul, in the face of a continuous diminution of interest on the part of a country rapidly forsaking the sterner sports of life for golf and football, the Council and the band of stalwarts who made up its membership have carried on—and it is impossible to place a value on the work they have done. As to the future—that is on the knees of the gods. When we, as a nation, have come out of this fight, with lean flanks and girded loins, maybe the man who is fit for war, "the man who can ride and shoot," will come to his own again, and the butts will know a prosperity such as has not been seen in our Island since the days of the longbow—when everybody shot because of the love he had of marksmanship, and because the law of the land fostered that love. Whatever is the future of the N.R.A., it can look back on fifty-five years of the best work any private association or citizen has ever done for a nation.

Miniature shooting, which owes its popularity in this country directly to the influence and preaching of the late Lord Roberts, has also played its part in the training of the new armies which Britain has raised in her hour of need. Almost without exception a very large part of the initial instruction which has been given has been done on the miniature range, and in this the clubs affiliated to the Society of Miniature Rifle Clubs have also played their part. Lord Roberts's foresight was the means of creating all up and down the country a large number of fully equipped miniature rifle clubs, and these have been to a very large extent available for the training of troops. Even when such clubs have not been partly or wholly taken over by the War Office, a very large number of men, keen to acquire that knowledge of the rifle which Lord Roberts said was nine-tenths of the making of a soldier, have availed themselves of the facilities for teaching or free practice, or instruction at the rifle clubs which has been offered them. So great was the activity in the miniature rifle clubs that in September, 1914, Lord Roberts himself addressed a personal letter of thanks to all the members of the clubs affiliated to the Society of Miniature Rifle Clubs. His ambition had been to see a rifle club in every village, and that ambition was not fulfilled, but there were many thousands of clubs in existence all over the country, and many more springing up every day. Lord Roberts wrote: "I am proud of my rifle clubs. I am proud of the Society that binds them together. I am proud of the unanimity with which all the clubs at this time of national

THE FASCINATION OF THE RIFLE 315

emergency are placing their ranges, the personal service of their members, and in many cases their arms and ammunition at the service of the Territorial Force, the National Reserve, and all others who either for practice or instruction desire to shoot."

The rifleman, then, has come into his own. For years he has gone on his way, sneered at as a pot-hunter, laughed at as a crank, snubbed oftentimes by those to whom he naturally looked for help and guidance. He has fought his own battles and gone his own way, not altogether unruffled and unperturbed, but knowing in his heart, as knew the prophet of old, that he who believeth shall not make haste. The target-shot has developed rifle shooting as a sport because it pleased him—perhaps. Without doubt the fascination of it gripped him, with always, behind the concentration of mind, the cleanly living, the control of body and nerves, the knowledge that perhaps one day his skill would be needed. That day has come, and the nation has cause indeed to bless the names of those who founded the National Rifle Association in 1860, and the other men who very many years later, urged by Lord Roberts, brought the Society of Miniature Rifle Clubs into existence.

CHAPTER XIV

Some Foreign and Colonial Rifle Associations. British Teams Abroad

MOST countries which maintain a standing army, and have therefore the interests of marksmanship more or less at heart, have some kind of association for the promotion and encouragement of rifle shooting. In the United States of America the parent body is called the National Rifle Association, and its objects are somewhat similar to those of our own N.R.A. Its principal meetings are held at Camp Perry and Sea Girt, and draw competitors from all parts of the United States.

Canada has its Dominion Rifle Association, with headquarters at Ottawa. The principal Canadian Rifle meeting is held at ranges near Ottawa, and this meeting, which usually takes place in August, draws a very large and representative body of Canadian riflemen, some of the competitors travelling as far as from Vancouver Island to attend, necessitating a journey of as much as six days.

A point of considerable difference between the English N.R.A. meeting at Bisley and the American and Canadian meetings is in the amount of entrance fees and prizes. At Bisley the prizes vary in value from £250 to £1; a very few years ago the lowest prize in single-entry competition at Bisley was £2. In America and Canada the highest prize does not exceed £50, and the lowest prize is $1.

The entrance fees for the respective meetings are somewhat in similar proportion, and this in spite of the fact that the cost of living, and therefore of income generally, is considerably higher in America than it is in England.

In Australia each State or Province has its rifle association, and each conducts its own meeting and has its own "King's

AUSTRALIAN RIFLE CLUBS 317

Prize." These meetings are held at Brisbane, Sydney, Melbourne, Adelaide, Hobart and Perth, and the dates are so arranged that competitors with the necessary means and the time may attend all. The highest prize is the King's Prize given at Sydney of £100, the rest of the prize lists having a somewhat similar substantial appearance to that which prevails at Bisley.

In Melbourne the principal prize carries with it the sum of £50 and a £50 trophy, the other prize lists being somewhat similar to those at Sydney.

The system of scoring throughout Australia varies materially from that at Bisley. Owing to the high cost of labour, and to there being no Regular Army from which to draw, the provision of markers and register keepers on the same scale as is provided at Bisley would entail an outlay out of all proportion to the money available as prizes. It has, therefore, been found necessary to institute a system which reduces the amount of paid labour to within reasonable bounds. Accordingly, while the markers are employed in the ordinary way and paid a daily wage, the keeping of the register or score is done by the competitors. In a squadded competition the competitors are assembled in front of the head-quarters or office, in similar formation to companies of soldiers in columns of sections. The roll of competitors is then called, to which each man answers his name. On completion of the roll call the whole body of competitors is marched off to the firing-point, each section being detailed to a particular target and taking up position at an appropriate point of the firing-line, there being usually about six men detailed to each target. No. 1 of each section takes up position ready to fire, while Nos. 5 and 6 keep the blackboard and register tickets respectively. The whole line being in readiness, the competition is started by bugle call, upon which the competitors commence firing, and continue in their own time until they have completed their rounds, or until the expiry of the time limit, previously fixed, which time limit usually works out at about ten minutes for each eight rounds. Each shot is separately signalled in the ordinary way. Upon No. 1 competitor finishing, he gives way to No. 2, and takes the place of No. 6 in keeping score. On No. 2 completing his shoot, he relieves No. 5, and so on.

This system of register keeping cannot be said to be a popular one, but in the case of Australia it is a necessity. It may be that, if in this country the War Office should throw over their support and decline to allow regular soldiers to act as score keepers at Bisley, a similar system would have to be adopted by the National Rifle Association, if target shooting in its present form is to be continued.

Australia is well provided with rifle ranges, due chiefly to the fact that the Government give every assistance in the way of grants of land and money towards the formation of rifle clubs. Most towns which boast of a few thousand inhabitants have their own rifle clubs, with a full-size range equipped with the latest system of target apparatus. In addition, each province or state has its central body or rifle association, with a large and well-equipped rifle range suitable for conducting a prize meeting on an extensive scale. The largest ranges are at Randwick, near Sydney, and Williamstown, near Melbourne.

In most European countries outdoor target shooting takes the form largely of standing shooting at 300 metres. The firing-points are covered in so as to minimise the effect of wind on "holding," while the rifles are of a special type adapted to this system of shooting. In particular, they are usually of abnormal weight, are fitted with special adjustments to facilitate steady holding in the standing position, such as a palm rest, which enables the firer to rest his elbow against the side of his body while supporting the rifle in the firing position. The rifle is also fitted with elaborate sights of an entirely unmilitary description. This particular style of shooting is not intended to be anything more than a specialised game, nor to be of any value as a military exercise. It is, nevertheless, an extremely interesting sport, and is deservedly popular in Switzerland, France, Germany, Belgium, Sweden, and other shooting countries. It must not be supposed from the above that attention is not given to shooting of a purely military character in those countries named. On the contrary, there is probably no country in the world which in proportion to population devotes more

PLATE LXII

THE SHORT-RANGE FIRING POINT, CAMP PERRY, U.S.A.
A view of the firing point and targets during "surprise firing," which is an individual sharpshooting event held during the National Rifle Association (U.S.A.) Annual Meeting

AMERICAN FIRING POINT ARRANGEMENTS
The convenient desks allotted to the score-keepers at Camp Perry are a model that all other Associations would do well to follow

SWITZERLAND AND SWEDEN   319

time and money to purely military shooting than does Switzerland. In Switzerland shooting is the national game, and to such an extent are the inhabitants imbued with the desire to perfect themselves in the art of shooting, that the adult male who is unable or unwilling to acquire proficiency in the use of a rifle is looked down upon, as a more or less useless member of the community, by his fellow men.

In Sweden, which has a population of less than six millions, there are 150,000 men who participate in the sport of rifle shooting. This is a very large percentage, and is perhaps explained by the financial encouragement given to shooting by the Swedish Government. For the upkeep of ranges and for prizes in shooting the Swedish Government gives a grant of something like £7,500, which is probably twice as much as the monetary value of the support given by the War Office to voluntary shooting in Great Britain.

In France, Germany, and other conscript countries, the need for supporting voluntary practice in military rifle shooting does not exist to the same extent as in other countries, as military shooting may be said to be compulsory.

In its efforts to encourage rifle shooting imperially the National Rifle Association has done good service, especially taking into account the very little support which it receives from public funds. Besides attracting yearly competitors from all parts of the British Empire, it has sent out two teams of riflemen to Canada and one to Australia. The first of these teams went to Canada in 1902 for the ostensible purpose of competing for the Palma trophy. The Palma trophy originated in America, and was more or less a standing challenge "to the riflemen of the world," to quote its own inscription. In 1901 a Canadian team visited the Sea Girt rifle range, and succeeded in capturing America's favourite trophy. By the conditions of the competition, this trophy has to be shot for in the country of the holders, and accordingly, in response to a pressing invitation from the Canadians, the National Rifle Association decided to send a team to Canada to participate in a three-cornered contest between America, Canada and Great Britain in 1902. The visit was a memorable one, and the team, under the captaincy of the Hon. T. F. Fremantle, gained a brilliant victory over the American and Canadian teams by the comparatively narrow margin of twelve points, the scores at the end of the match being Great Britain, 1,459; America, 1,447; Canada, 1,373.

In the following year America sent over a team to Bisley, and succeeded in winning back the trophy; but owing to a dispute as to the non-observance by the American team of certain rules of the competition, the trophy was returned to the N.R.A. at Bisley at the end of the same year. This was a most unfortunate end to a memorable match, for, it being the year of the Coronation of King Edward VII., there were present in this country, besides the American team, teams from Canada, Australia, Natal, Norway and France. The British team used a cartridge specially loaded by the King's Norton Metal Company, with a heavy charge and a 220-grain bullet. This ammunition attained a great reputation as the "Palma" cartridge.

In 1907 the National Rifle Association, responding to repeated invitations from the rifle associations of Australia, decided to send a team representing Great Britain to shoot a match against all Australia. To commemorate this match, and indeed to perpetuate it, the National Rifle Association of Australia gave a trophy, called the Empire trophy, to be held by the winning team. New Zealand also decided to send a team to compete in this match.

With the object of killing two birds with one stone the National Rifle Association sent their team via Canada to again compete for the Palma trophy. Meantime, an Australian team of riflemen were at Bisley, and they in turn decided to return to Australia by way of Canada, so that they, too, could participate in the contest for the Palma trophy. America and Canada were also represented, there being thus a four-cornered contest. After a memorable match the American team, armed with their new Springfield rifles, fitted with aperture sights, gained a sweeping victory, beating Canada by forty-one points, the totals of the competing teams at the end of the match being as follows: America, 1,712; Canada, 1,671; Australia, 1,653; Great Britain, 1,580.

After the match the British and Australian teams journeyed together via Vancouver and Honolulu to Brisbane. The British team took an active part in the rifle meeting at Toowong, the shooting head-quarters of the Queensland Rifle Association, situated a short tram ride out of Brisbane. From the point of view of disheartening or puzzling conditions, Toowong was quite the worst range in Australia. Wind indications by flags were quite useless, and before the British team had been there two days it was the common "tip" to make wind allowance in direct contradiction to the flags.

From Brisbane the team journeyed to Sydney, where they at once started active preparation for the Empire trophy match, which was to take place on Australia's chief range at Randwick.

At no period up to the day of the contest could the British team be said to have shown that harmony and confidence which bespeaks success, and even in the middle of the match itself the lack of harmony made itself felt with most disastrous consequences.

It was thought that the match would resolve itself into a contest between Great Britain and Australia, and the results at the first range appeared to justify the expectation. Half way through the 500 yards score the two teams were still "neck and neck," when suddenly a member of the British rifle team made the regrettable mistake of firing at the wrong target. But worse was to follow; the man on his left seeing his own target go down before he had fired, thought that *he* had just been about to fire at the wrong target, so he promptly switched on to the next one and fired. By the rules of the match both shots were disallowed, but the curious point was that the whole affair happened so quickly that the register keepers did not appear to notice it, and the two shots consisting of a bull's-eye and an inner were marked down in the ordinary way. Major P. W. Richardson, the British team captain, however, immediately reported the matter to the range official, and the nine points were, after consultation, deducted. The incident had a most embarrassing effect upon the team, but the chapter of accidents was not yet completed. After struggling manfully through the remainder of the 500 yards shoot, the teams repaired to 600 yards, and immediately after starting a third member of the British rifle team, to the horror and disgust of his companions, put yet another shot on the wrong target. Probably no more demoralising effect has ever been seen in a rifle match, for in the course of the next three rounds per man the British rifle team dropped some forty points further in the rear. At the end of the first day's shoot, which comprised only one-half of the match, the British rifle team were thirty-two points behind Australia and level with New Zealand; and although the second half of the match consisted of eight shots per man at 800, 900 and 1,000 yards, it was apparent that against a team of the shooting calibre of the Australians, nothing short of a miracle would enable the British rifle team to win.

In point of fact, the shooting in the second stage was fairly uniform, and Australia finished with a lead of forty-nine points over New Zealand, a weak finish by one member of the British rifle team reducing his team to third place by the narrow margin of three points.

Having unsuccessfully fulfilled its principal engagement, the British rifle team started upon a pilgrimage throughout Eastern and Southern Australia. Most of the principal rifle clubs in New South Wales, Victoria and Adelaide had made fixtures with the British rifle team, and these were shot on the home ranges of the various clubs. Curiously enough, as soon as the Empire match, in which the British rifle team could do nothing right, was finished, all their ill-luck seemed to desert them, and their progress throughout the remainder of their tour was something of the nature of a triumph. Bathurst, Bendigo, Wangarratta, Hamilton, Melbourne, Hobart, Adelaide were among the places visited, and at each of these places matches were shot against local teams, each of which was successively defeated by the British rifle team, which seemed now to have found its feet. Wherever they went the team acquitted itself admirably, both in matches and in open meetings, and as the tour neared its end the British rifle team achieved still higher flights. At Hobart, in Tasmania, nearly every first prize was captured by members of the British rifle team. At Melbourne the first prize and second prize in the

PLATE LXIII

THE SHOOTING HOUSE, CAMP PERRY, U.S.A.
A covered firing point on the Continental plan, used for firing international competitions

THE 300 YARDS FIRING POINT, CAMP PERRY, U.S.A.
A rapid fire match is in progress

AUSTRALIAN HOSPITALITY

King's were also secured, while in the last shoot of all, at Adelaide, in a match against a representative team of South Australia, the British rifle team wound up with the phenomenal score of 1,002 for ten men, making an average of no less than 100.2 per man.

The hospitality of the Australians towards the Home Country team was a thing to remember. Money, time, and trouble were at a discount, and each town, club or association vied with the other in dispensing hospitality. The most novel entertainment was given at Bathurst, when the team were invited to take part in a kangaroo and wallaby drive. The team were driven out to a farm about eighteen miles from Bathurst, and, having been mounted on horseback, they rode out to take up position a few miles out. Mounted beaters were meantime sent out at a gallop, enclosing a strip of country many thousands of acres in extent. Gradually the cordon closed in, and, amid loud "cooes" and cracking of stock whips, all the ground game, consisting chiefly of wallaby, were driven towards the firing-line. The first drive being over, the team again mounted, and made off to another selected position two or three miles farther on, and the operations were repeated. After three or four repetitions of this procedure the visitors made tracks for the farm, where a most generous fare was waiting. Afterwards the team were initiated into the mysteries of sheep farming, including shearing by electric clippers, an operation calling for great skill on the part of the shearer. At length the time of departure arrived, bringing to a close one of the most pleasant and instructive days of the tour.

At each place the team visited they were received by the chief municipal or state officials, and were fêted and banqueted in a most lavish fashion. In fact, of such importance was the visit of the British rifle team in the eyes of Australia that the Commonwealth Government voted £1,000 for entertainment.

In 1912 a team representing Great Britain visited Stockholm to take part in the Olympic Games; but, although nominally under the auspices of the National Rifle Association, the credit for sending the team must in a large measure rest with that enthusiastic and generous patron of rifle shooting, Major P. W.

Richardson, who captained the team and paid the bulk of the expenses, the rest being contributed by the British Olympic Association.

The visit was an instructive one in many ways. It demonstrated that in deliberate bull's-eye target-shooting the American Springfield is unsurpassed in accuracy. The attempt of the British team to make up for their handicap in rifles by using powerful match-rifle ammunition failed, the American team finishing first and winning the gold medals, Great Britain being second and winning the silver medals, while Sweden finished third.

The Olympic Contest between military teams for the Rifle-shooting Championship demonstrated another very important fact—namely, that the advantages of the military rifle of Great Britain will never be shown in a deliberate target-shoot. The military rifle of this country was designed for war, and as an active service weapon it is unsurpassed by any military rifle in the world. Its chief characteristics are speed and handiness in manipulation, to attain which necessitated sacrifices in certain qualities necessary in a purely target rifle. Hence to give a British military team the full advantage of their rifle, it is necessary that the conditions of any military rifle competition in which they take part should be modelled on active service lines throughout.

INDEX

A

ABEL, SIR FREDERICK, 106, 112
Acetic ether, its power to dissolve guncotton, 106
Action, Lee-Enfield, 295
Aiming, hints on, 239, 240 et seq., 274; time occupied in, 248-9
Air movement. (*See* Wind allowance)
Air resistance to projectiles, 10, 110, 160, 168, 208, 250 et seq., 262, 263
Alignment of sights, 239, 272 et seq.; correct, 276
America and the development of rapid-fire rifles, 92
American Civil War, the, 18, 19, 65, 67, 76; gun factories, 23, 24; rifle-making, 23
Ammunition, sporting rifle, 179 et seq.
Anderson, Mr., chief engineer of Woolwich Arsenal, 79
Aperture sight, the, 75, 239, 240, 242, 275
Archers, their desire for spin, 3
" Arms and Explosives " *cited*, 25, 182
Army musket, the, 19
Assegai-throwing, 3
Australia, scoring system in, 317
Australian ranges, 316
Austria adopts the solid-drawn case, 88
Austrian Government, the, and Volkmann's works, 107; straight-pull Mannlicher, the, 133
Auto-loading rifle, 177
Automatic rifle, the Browning, 177; rifles, 177

B

BACKSIGHTS, 239, 274; buckhorn, 75; peep, 75
Bacon, Roger, 28
Baker, Ezekiel, 20; rifle, the, 20, 36; Sir Samuel, 172
Balance, the " sense " of, 232
Ball, egg-shaped, 8; spherical, 34
Balle D projectile, the French, 162, 163
" Ballistic co-efficient," the, 210, 265 et seq.; pendulum, the, 31 et seq.
Ballistics, simple, 205 et seq.
Ballistite, 109, 112
Barlow, Colonel, 313
Barrels, cleaning, 280 et seq.; revolving, 4; rifling of, 4; unrifled, 5
Bashforth, 31, 163
Bashforth's standard projectile, 209
Bavaria, rifled matchlocks in, 14
Baza, the siege of, 29
Beaumont rifle, the, 90
Belgium, adoption of the Minié bullet in, 48
Berdan action, the, 74, 90
Bertie-Clay, Captain, 119
Bethel-Burton magazine, the, 145
Big game shooting, a good rifle for, 265-6; the Mannlicher rifle and, 265
Birmingham Small Arms Co., 193, 197; bolt-action miniature rifle, 193; ·220 high-power rifle, 184; ·220 rifle, 190

325

INDEX

Bisley, 61, 62, 128, 156, 165, 166; competitions, entrance fees for, 309; cordite at, 115, 116; marking, 305; ranges, 300; School of Musketry, 313; scoring, 304; Sunday shooting at, 311; target frame, 305; targets, 304; team matches, 291; the Mark IV. bullet at, 119; the Museum of the National Rifle Association at, 80–1; wind judging by telescope at, 257

Black powder sporting cartridges, 181
Bland's rook rifle, 175
Blasting gelatine, 109
Blenheim, the battle of, 19, 20
Block action, 90
Blunt-nose ammunition, 252
Boer War, the, 153
Bolt action, the, development of, 90 et seq.; cleaning the, 285
"Book of the Gun," Greener's, 14
Bore-fouling, 4
Boucher, Mr., 49, 51, 52–3, 62, 64
Boucher's disc bullet, 51
Boulangé, 31
Boulanger, General, 108
Boxer, Colonel, 85; cartridge, the, 86, 87
Boys, Professor, 161
Breech-loader, the, development of, 54 et seq.
Breech-loading firearms, 17; rifle, the first military, 65
Brendlin-Albini rifle, the, 74
British Army, marksmanship of, 220; cartridge, the, 153
"Brown Bess" musket, the, 19
Browning automatic rifle, 177
Brunswick ball, the, 172; rifle, the, 21, 39, 42, 55, 56, 172
Bullet, the, of the future, 167; patching the, 36; the elongated, 36 et seq., 43, 45; envelopes, metals for, 149 et seq.

Bullets, expanding or mushrooming, 43, 180; hollow base, 45; MV and sectional density $\left(\frac{w}{d^2}\right)$, table of, 170; pointed, 161 et seq., 265, 267; round-nosed, 265, 267; spherical, 2, 8, 9; the flight of, 161, 262; their velocities influenced by size of powder, 265; time of flight of, 263; trajectory of, 163; in flight, photographs of, 161

Butt magazine, the, 16

C

CALDWELL, Mr., 165
Cambridge Cup, the, 165
Camp Perry, 316
Canada, the flint-lock in, 25
Canadian Hut, the, 310; North-West Mounted Police, the, 146
Cant, the effect of, 271 et seq.
Canting the sights, 294
Carabine-à-tige, the, 39
Cartridge, the, earliest recorded use of, 78; Gibbs's ·505 sporting, 185; history of the, 78 et seq.; length of, 153; the "Ideal," 149, 152; the modern rifle, 149; the Palma, 320; ·220 high-power, 184; weight of, 153
Cartridge-case, the British, history of, 116 et seq.
Cartridge-cases, rubber, 69; solid-drawn, 34, 80, 87, 88
Cartridges, match rifle, 163; metal-based, 67; Minié, 48, 78; needle-gun, 83; Rubin, 179
Central-fire case for cartridges, 83
"Certus" rifle, the, 192
Chairing the King's Prize-winner, 302
Charger-loading, 99
Chassepot, the, 66, 71, 77, 84, 86, 90
Chasseurs-à-pied, the, 39
Chasseurs d'Afrique, the, 46

INDEX

Chaucer's reference to guns and gunpowder, 29
Cheylesmore, Major-General Lord, 313
Chinese, the, discovery of gunpowder wrongly attributed to, 27
Cleaning tools, 283
Clip-loading, 99
Coaching a team, 297
Co-efficient, ballistic, 210
Cogswell and Harrison, 192
"Collodin," 107
Colloid, 106, 109, 152
Colt, Colonel, and his revolving rifle, 92
Comber, A. J., wins first miniature rifle championship, 191
"Commission de Pyroxyle," the, 105
Continental muzzle-loading rifles prior to first breech-loader, 22
Converted Martini ·220 rifles, 193
Copper percussion cap, the, 21
Cordite, 112, 118; at Bisley, 115, 116; effect of increase of temperature on, 182; Express rifle, the, 265; expresses, early, 181; rifle, method of cleaning, 283; the stability of, 114; tubular, 152
Cotton powder, 105
Crimean War, the, 48, 55
Crossbows, 3; early German, 4
Crosse, Lieut.-Colonel C. R., 312, 313
Cupro-nickel envelopes, 150
Curtis and Harvey's gunpowder, 79
Cut-off, the, 100

D

DANISH rifle, the, 125, 138, 144
Davidson, Colonel, 45
Decimal target, the, 196
Delvigne, M., and long-shaped bullets, 45, 172; rifle, the 22, 38, 39, 45
Delvigne's bullet, 45, 46

Demondion's breech-loader and cartridge, 83
Deutsche Waffen und Munition Fabrik Aktiengesellschaft, 164, 166
Dewar, Private, 312
Digestion, its relation to good marksmanship, 226
Distance judging, 47, 242 *et seq.*, 266, 279; difficulties of, 244–5
Doyle, Mr., 161
Dreyse rifle, the, 65, 68, 69, 74, 83, 91
Drift, 5, 7, 273, 278; the theory of, 9
Driving bands, 87
Dum-Dum bullets, 119; in the Great War, 120
Dum Dum, ordnance works at, 79, 119
Dynamite, 108

E

EARLY cordite expresses, 181
Egg, Durst, 91
Egyptian War of 1888, the, 88
Elcho match, records of, in English VIII. Club, 310
Elephant rifles, 265
Elevation, angle of, 158, 168
Eley's ·280 match rifle cartridge, 151
Enfield bullet, the, 85; rifle, the, 49, 55, 59; rifle cartridge, the, 78; rifle used in the Crimea, 48 (footnote), 55; rifle *versus* Whitworth, 57; the Royal Small Arms factory at, 61, 71
English VIII. Club, 165, 311
Entrance fees for Bisley competitions, 308
Expanding bullet, the, 43 *et seq.*, 120, 180; bullets forbidden by The Hague Convention, 119
"Explosive" bullets, 154, 156
"Express Train," the, 173
Eye training and aiming, 238 *et seq.*

INDEX

F

FEATHERS as aids to spin, 3
Field, the, organises trials of sporting rifles, 174, 175
Fire, observation of, 247
Firearms, early, inaccuracy of, 6
Fireworks, 28, 29
Fish-tail wind, the, 253, 254
Flash-hole, the, 13
Flash-pan, the, 13; cover, the, 13
Flint-lock, the, 14, 15
Flint-locks, modern, 25
Florence, cannon-making in, 29
Focus of sights and target, 275
Foreign and Colonial Rifle Associations, 316 et seq.
Foresights, 239, 274; globe and pinhead, 75
Forsyth, Rev. Alexander J., 21, 25
Fosbery, Lieut.-Colonel, 111, 112
Fouling, 4, 5, 20, 35, 39, 48, 58, 60, 61, 81, 150, 151, 280 et seq.; metallic (See Nickeling)
France adopts the Minié bullet, 48; formation of a rifle corps in, 46
Francotte ·220 rifle, 192
Fremantle, the Hon. T. F., 320; on the Field rifle trials, 174-5
French military bullet, ballistic co-efficient of, 263; Rifle Brigade, the, 39
Fulton, Arthur, 312; sen., 192
Future of the National Rifle Association, 314

G

GAME shooting, 221; target practice for, 221; wind allowance in, 250
German bullet, ballistic co-efficient of, 263; crossbows, early, 4; School of Musketry, 221
Germans, the, and the wheel-lock, 13

Gibbs, Mr., of Bristol, 172, 173
Gibbs's ·505 sporting cartridge, 185
Gold medal of the N.R.A., 301
Græcus, Marcus, a manuscript of, 28
Gras, the, replaces the Chassepot in France, 90
Gravitation, terrestrial, 158
Great Britain and the Minié Musquet, 48
Great War, the, 120, 145, 147, 154
Greener, W. W., 14, 23, 24, 39 et seq., 44, 173, 174, 196
Greener ·220 rifle, 192
Greenhill, Sir George, on "drift," 9; and the problem of twist, 11, 12
Guedes single-loader, the, 104
Guilamôt, M., 110
Guncotton, Sir Frederick Abel's discoveries, 106
"Gunmakers, Lectures to Young," cited, 182
Gunpowder, Germany claims discovery of, 28; invention of, 27; its part in the velocity of bullets, 263; the ingredients of, 27 et seq.
Guns, the first authentic record of, 29
Gustavus Adolphus, King of Sweden, 78
Guttmann, Oscar, 104-5, 107
Gyroscopic stability, 11, 22, 59, 64, 155, 156, 162

H

HAGUE Convention, The, forbids use of expanding bullets, 119
Halford, Sir Henry, 61, 87, 115, 157, 303; wins the Duke of Cambridge prize, 88
Handling the rifle, 230, 249, 274
Hardcastle, Captain J. H., 9, 10, 12, 161, 162, 163, 164, 165, 168, 169, 270, 303
Harper's Ferry, the Remington factory at, 75
Hartig, Dr., 106

INDEX 329

Hebler, 110
Henry VIII.'s breech-loader in the Tower of London, 78
Henry, Mr., 59, 71; action, the, 66, 67
Henry's rifle, 93
High-power ·220 cartridge, 184
High-velocity bullets, 154
Higher velocities, the demand for, 102 et seq.
"History of the National Rifle Association," the, *cited*, 156
Holding the rifle, 232, 249, 274, 276
Holland and Holland's special sporting bullets, 184; express rifles, the, 175
Hollow base bullets, 45
Honourable Artillery Company at Bisley, the, 311
Honourable East India Company, the, 43, 49
Hopton, Colonel J. D., 304; Cup, 304
Horsley, Sir Victor, 154
Houiller and his pinfire cartridge, 83 84; and his rimfire cartridge, 83
Hythe, the 1862 contest at, 82; the School of Musketry at, 248

I

"IDEAL," ·220 rifle, Stevens', 189
Ignition, 12, 69; by percussion, 21; mechanisms, 13
Increase of temperature, effect of, on cordite, 182
Indian Mutiny, the, cause of, 79
Irish VIII., the, 165
Iron envelope bullets, 150

J

JACOB, General, his bullet, 49, 50, 157, 173; his four-groove rifle, 42-3, 49, 56
Jacob's shell, 50
Japanese pointed bullet, 211; rifle, the, 132
Jarman rifle, the, 93

Javelins, the spin of, 3
Jeffreys' special sporting bullets, 184
Jencks carbines, 76
Jones, Mr. F. W., 303
Jump, angle of, 206
"Jumping" the rifling, 11, 37, 59

K

KENTUCKY small-bore rifle, the, 171-2
Kerr, the bolt action of, 71
"Keyholing," 155, 156
King's Hundred, the, 301
King's Prize, the, 301; first stage, 301; winner, chairing the, 302; tie between Dewar and Fulton, 1914, 312
Krag-Jorgensen rifle, the, 74, 125, 138, 144
Kropatschek rifle, the, 93, 94
Kynoch, Messrs., 164

L

LANCASTER carbine, the, 59, 71, 72
Lebel rifle, the, 93, 95, 138, 140 *et seq.*
"Lectures to Young Gunmakers" *cited*, 182
Lee action, the, 77
Lee magazine, the, 98, 111, 175
Lee, Mr. James Paris, 100-1, 145
Lee-Burton rifle, the, 145
Lee-Enfield action, weak, 295; rifle, the, 116, 129, 138, 145, 146, 147, 148; Mark I. rifle, 146; Mark I.* rifle, the, 146; Mark III. magazine, the, 146
Lee-Metford Mark I. rifle, 145
Lefaucheux cartridge, the, 83
Lenk, General von, 106
Le Poidevin, Mr., 307
Let-off. (*See* Trigger-pulling)
Liége gun factory, the, 23
London and Middlesex Rifle Association, 311
London Scottish at Bisley, the, 311
London Small Arms Co., 193

Long-range shooting, rapidity of aim in, 250-1
Long-shaped bullets, 36, 43, 45
Lorentz, 110

M

MACH, Dr. Ernst, 161
Machine-made rifles, 23
Magazine gun, the earliest known example of, 15; rifles (cf. Repeating rifles), 93; weapons, 15; cleaning the, 285; development of, 90 et seq.
Magazines, loading of, 98 et seq.
Mannlicher, his first magazine, 96-7; rifle, the, 96, 133; charger-loading system a feature of, 99; its trigger mechanism, 236; the straight-pull, 133; turning-bolt action, the, 136, 138
Manton, Joe, 83
Manual exercises indispensable to good musketry, 231
"Manufacture of Explosives," the (Guttmann's), 104-5, 107
Mark I. magazine rifle, the, 145; I.* rifle, the, 145, 146; II. bullet, the, 118; II. rifle, the, 145; II.* rifle, the, 145; III. bullet, the, 118; III. magazine, the, 146; IV. bullet, the, 119; IV. rifle, the, 146; VI. bullet, the, and wind allowance, 254; VI. bullet, the, ballistic co-efficient of, 265; VII. bullet, the, 152, 165, 271; VII. bullet, ballistic co-efficient of the, 265
Marking at Bisley, 305
Marksmanship of the British Army, 220
Martini action, a defect in the, 71; cartridge, the, 88; principle the forerunner of the Peabody action, 67
Martini ·220 converted rifles, 193
Martini-Enfield rifle, the, 88, 146

Martini-Henry rifle, the, 59, 71, 87, 146; officially adopted by Great Britain, 72
Martini-Metford rifle, the, 146
Match rifle competitions, 303
Matchlock, invention of the, 13; musket, the, 19
Matchlocks, use of, in Bavaria, 14
Matthews, Lieut.-Colonel, 312
Mauser action, 90, 125; bolt, the, 127; Paul, 66, 72, 73, 87, 128; a Government bounty to, 73; rifle adopted by the German and Prussian Army, 73, 76, 87; rifle of Germany becomes a magazine arm, 93; rifle, the charger-loading system a feature of, 99; rifle, trigger mechanism of, 236; rifles, 73, 125 et seq.; Wilhelm, 73; a bounty from the Prussian Government, 73
Mauser-Verguiero rifle, the, 125
M.D. cordite, 116
Metal-based cartridge, the, 67, 84
Metallic cartridge case, Colt's, 92
Metals for bullet envelopes, 149 et seq.
Metford, Mr. W. E., 11, 49, 61, 64, 85, 86, 88, 157, 303; bullet, the, 50; his first rifle, 64; refuses the invitation of the 1867 Commission, 71; system, the popularity of, 61
Metford's explosive bullet, 119; solid-drawn case, 88
Midland Railway Rifle Club, 196
Military breech-loader, the development of the, 54 et seq.; magazine rifles, weights of, 125; rifle ammunition, modern, 149 et seq.; rifles, the essentials of, 122 et seq.; shooting, 219; shooting, suggested physical exercises to ensure fitness, 226 et seq.; wind judging, 255
Miniature ammunition, accuracy of modern, 202

INDEX 331

Miniature rifle, 186 *et seq.*; defined, 199
Miniature rifle clubs and the war, 314; first regulations of National Rifle Association for, 187; Society of, 186, 188
Minié bullet, the, 47–8, 51; Captain, 47; cartridge, the, 48, 78
"Mirage," 251, 257, 258, 259 *et seq.*
Modern military rifles, a critical examination of, 121 *et seq.*; rifle cartridge, the, 149; sporting rifle cartridges, 183
Montaigne's criticism of firearms, 6
Montpensier, Duc de, 46
Morris tube, the, 188; tube cartridge, the, 189
Moser cartridge, the, 83
Murata rifle, the Japanese, 93, 94
Muscular brain, the methods for educating, 229 *et seq.*; movement, 228
Mushrooming bullets, 180
Muzzle-loader, the perfecting of the, 54 *et seq.*
Muzzle-loading, difficulties of, 35; the usual methods of, 35

N

NAGANT rifle, the, 138, 142 *et seq.*
National Rifle Association, the, 54 *et seq.*, 71, 80–1, 83, 300 *et seq.*; and sale of converted rifles, 193; and the war, 312; and Sunday shooting, 311; first regulations of, for miniature rifle clubs, 187; future of the, 314; membership of, 300
National Rifle Association of U.S.A., 316
Needle-gun, the, 65, 66, 68, 71, 86, 91, 92
Newitt, E. J. D., 188, 195
Newton, Sir Isaac, experiments on air resistance, 207
Nickel-coated bullets, 264
Nickeling, 280 *et seq.*; abrasive preparations for its removal, 282; chemical preparations for removing, 282 (*See also* Fouling)

Nitro-cellulose powder, 108, 109, 112, 114
Nitro-glycerine, 108; explosives, 150
Nobel, Mr. Alfred, 108, 112
Norris, Mr., of the Remington Company, 73
North London Rifle Club, the, 310, 311
Norton, Captain, 43

O

OBERNDORF, the Royal rifle factory at, 72, 73
Olympic Games, 1913, British rifle teams at, 323
Open sights, 239, 240, 242, 275
Orthoptic sight, the. (*See* Aperture sight)
Owen-Jones rifle, the, 145

P

PACKET loading, 99
Palma Trophy, the, 319; cartridge, the, 320
Paper cartridge, the, 21; fulminate cap, the, 21
Patches, 36, 38, 51; the disadvantages of, 52–3
Pauly's cartridge, 82–83
Pea rifles, 171–2
Peabody action, the, 67
Peep sight. (*See* Aperture sight)
Peninsular War, the, 19
Percussion cap, the, 21; ignition, 21, 25
Physical condition in relation to rifle shooting, 226 *et seq.*
Pinfire cartridge, the, 83, 84
Plevna, the siege of, 93
"Point blank," 173
Pointed bullet, the, 155, 156; bullets, advantages of, 158; Captain Hardcastle on, 161–2; Japanese, 211
Pottet, M., and the pinfire cartridge, 84
Poncharra, Lieut.-Colonel, 38
Poncharra's saboted ball, 38–9
Pope, H., 198

Porta, Baptista, 30
Poudre A, 108
Poudre B, 108
Prince, sporting rifle action of, 69
Prince's action, 69; rifle, 81
Pritchett, Mr., 49; bullets, 49, 50, 57, 85
Projectiles, air resistance to, 10, 110, 160, 168, 250 *et seq.*, 262, 263; high-velocity, 102 *et seq.*; and propellants, the early history of, 27 *et seq.*
Prussian Army, the, supply of rifles, 76
Prussians adopt the Needle-gun, 65
Purdy, Mr., 180
Purdy's rifle, 56, 173

Q

QUEEN'S Prize competition, the, 56-7; the Hythe contest to determine rifle for, 82

R

RAMILLIES, the battle of, 19
Range-finders, 248-9; flags, 251-2, 257
Ranges, Australian, 316
Rapid-fire rifles, 92; shooting, 237; time occupied in aiming, 248-9
" Rauchschwaches pulver," 106
Recoil, 161, 235, 278
Reduction, co-efficient of, 209
Regulation Minié Musquet, the, 48
Reid, Mr. Walter, 108
Remington action, the, 66; Arms Company, the, 73, 74, 75; magazine rifles, 91; Samuel, an inauspicious cartridge and, 76; ·220 rifle, 189
Remington-Lee rifle, the, 77
" Repeaters," early, 15
Repeating arms, early forms of, 16; rifles, definition of, 93 (*cf.* Magazine rifles)
Resistance of air to projectile in flight, 208 (*See also* Air resistance)
Revolver, the, 16

Revolving magazine, the, 96
Richardson, Major P. W., 313, 321
Rider, John, 66
Rifle Brigade, the, 19, 20, 21, 36, 55; the French, 39
Rifle Clubs Committee, 304; Conference, the, 85; corps in France, formation of a, 46; elevations, nomograph for, 168 *et seq.*; fire, conditions necessary to, 274 *et seq.*; fire, the theory of, 240 *et seq.*; firing, observation of fire, 247, 279; practice, accuracy and uniformity in, 274-5, 281; shooting, the royal road to success, 281; shooting, theory and practice, 220 *et seq.*; sights, 239; the bolt-cleaning, 285; hints on handling and holding, 230 *et seq.*, 274-5, 278-9; metallic fouling of, 282 *et seq.*; movements for handling, 230 *et seq.*; storing the, 289; the care of, 282 *et seq.*; ·220-in. calibre, 186 *et seq.*; War Office miniature, 193
Rifled arms, the early history of, 1 *et seq.*
Rifles, cleaning the ·220 weapon, 287; cleaning tools for, 285; description of, 2; early cordite express, 181; shot and ball, 177; small-bore double, evolution of, 176
Rifling, definition of, 2; invention of, 3
Rigby, John, 60, 71, 180
Rimfire cartridges, 83
Roberts action, the, 74
Roberts, the late Lord, and rifle clubs, 186
Robins, Benjamin, 6, 7, 28 *et seq.*; invents the ballistic pendulum, 31 *et seq.*; on the usual method of loading, 35
" Roman candles," 28, 29
Ross, Sir Charles, 140, 150; rifle, the Canadian, 98, 138, 139
Ross's ·280 match rifle cartridge, 150

INDEX

333

Rostolan, General, 46
Rotatory projectiles, the origin and theory of, 1 et seq.
Round-nosed bullets, 154
Royal Small Arms Factory, Enfield, 61, 71
Rubin cartridges, 179; Major, 102 et seq., 110, 116
Russian rifle, the (Nagant), 138, 142 et seq.
Rust, prevention of, on rifles, 289

S

SALISBURY, the late Lord, and rifle clubs, 186
Savage magazine rifle, the, 96
Schmidt-Rubin rifle, the, 125, 138-9
Schœnauer revolving magazine, the, 96
Schönbein's cotton powder, 105, 106
School of Musketry at Bisley, 313; German, 221
Schultz, Captain, his excellent sporting powder, 106-7
Schwartz, Bertholdus, 28
"Science of Gunnery," Greener's, 23, 40
Scoring, Bisley, 304; system in Australia, 317
Sea Girt range, 316, 319
Sea Service rifle, the, 48 (footnote), 55
"Serpentine," the, 13
Service rifle bored for ·220 cartridge, 190
Shape, co-efficient of, 209
Sharp rifle, the, 80, 81
Sharp's carbines, 65, 67
Shooting, seven essentials for, 273 et seq.
Shot and ball rifles, 177
Sight, the line of, 240 et seq., 274
Sights, aligning the, 272 et seq.; aperture, 239, 242; canting the, 270-1,
275; open, 239, 240, 242; orthoptic, 240, 275; telescopic, 240, 242
Simple ballistics, 205 et seq.
Single-loading rifles and their action, 90
Sladen's formula, 210
Slings and their relation to spin, 3
"Small-bore" rifles, 186 et seq.
Smith, Gilbert, the action invented by, 69
Smoke-feeble powders, 106
Smokeless powder, 104, 111; an ideal, 113
Smokelessness, 113
Snap-shooting, 237; time occupied in aiming, 250
Snider cartridge, the, 86, 87; rifle, the, 65, 70, 77, 85
Society of Miniature Rifle Clubs, 186, 188; and rifle sights, 193; and sale of converted rifles, 193; first miniature club regulations, 194
Society of Working Men's Rifle Clubs, 191
Solid-drawn cartridge cases, 34, 80, 87, 88
Somers, Capt. J. P., 312
South African War, the, 146
Southfields Rifle Club, the, 195
Spearmen and the spin of their weapons, 3
Spencer rifle, the, 93
Spin, 5, 8, 9; axis of, 2; the attributes of, 3; the virtues of, 3
Spitzer bullet, the German, 163, 164
Sporting bullets, 264 et seq.; Holland and Holland's special, 184; Jeffreys' special, 184
Sporting cartridges, black powder, 181
Sporting rifle, the history and development of, 171 et seq.; ammunition, 179 et seq.; calibres, table

of, 178; cartridges, modern, 183; cleaning, 284-5; shooting, trajectory in, 264; trigger mechanism of, 236; varieties of bullets for, 264
Springfield action, the, 74; rifle, the, 74, 75, 131
Stag targets, 267-8
Standard projectile, Bashforth's, 209
Steel envelope bullets, 150
Stevens firm, the, 75
Stevens' "Ideal" ·220 rifle, 189; ·25 rifle, 192
"Stonehenge." (*See* Walsh)
Stopping power in military bullets, 153
Straight-grooved rifles, early, 4
Straight-pull rifles, 133
"Stripping," 11, 37, 59
Sunday shooting at Bisley, 311
Sweden, King Gustavus Adolphus of, 78
Swedish drill, 226
"Swift" bullet, the, 161, 164, 165
Swiss Government, the, and target-shooting, 12
Switzerland and the magazine rifle, 92; shooting in, 319

T

TABATIÈRE, 65
Table of sporting rifle calibres, 178
Tamisier, Captain, 59
Target frame, Bisley, 305
Target-shooting, 12, 222; the correction of error in, 257 *et seq.*, 274 *et seq.*; the "sighting shot," 254; time occupied in aiming, 250; wind allowance in, 250
Targets, Bisley, 304
Tartaglia and gunpowder, 30
Team selection, 290 *et seq.*; shooting, 290 *et seq.*; captain, duties of a, 291; coaching a, 297; matches, Bisley, 291; shot, traits of a desirable, 290; to go abroad, selection of a, 291
Telescope, the, wind judgment by, 257 *et seq.*
Telescopic sight, the, 240, 242
Terrestrial gravitation, 158
"Territorial Pattern" rifle, the, 146
Terry's action, 69; rifle, 81, 82, 86
"Text Book of Service Explosives," the, *cited*, 27
"Text Book of Small Arms," the, 78, 122, 140, 170
Thierry, M., 45
Thouvenin, Colonel, 39; rifle, the, 39, 45
Thun, the Swiss army laboratory at, 102
Times, the, on the Delvigne bullet, 46
Touch-hole, the, 13
Tower of London, the, 78
Trajectory, 207; curve, the, and its part in practical shooting, 264 *et seq.*; plotting a, 210, 213; the line of, 240 *et seq.*; and wind allowance, 250; shooting, 264 *et seq.*
Trigger exercises, 235 *et seq.*; finger, the, 279; pulling or "let-off," 234 *et seq.*, 279; "flinching," 235; "weight" of the, 279
Tube magazine rifles, 94
Tubular cordite, 152
Turks, the, use Winchester repeater at siege of Plevna, 93
Turning-bolt Mannlicher action, the, 136, 138
Tweedie bullet, the, 118, 119
Twist, 11, 22, 59, 63, 64
·220-in. calibre rifle, 186 *et seq.*
·220 cartridge, the, 200
·220 high-power cartridge, 184

INDEX 335

U

Umbrella tent, the, 309
United States Army, the service rifle of, 74, 131; the small arms of, 73, 74
Ure, Dr., 40, 41

V

Velocities of rifle bullets, 265 *et seq.*; and pressure curve, 208
Velocity, the first essential to flat trajectory, 264
Vetterli repeating rifle, the, 72, 90, 93
Vetterli-Vitali rifle, the, 91
Victoria, Queen, fires the first shot at Wimbledon, 55
Vielle, M., 108
Visual training, 243 *et seq.*, 279
Volkmann, Frederick, and collodin, 107
Volunteer movement, the, 55, 85, 86, 115
"Volunteer Rifleman and the Rifle," Boucher's, 62

W

Walsh, J. H. ("Stonehenge"), *cited*, 7, 8, 11, 174
War of Independence, the, 18, 19
Warfare, range-finders in, 246, 247; wind allowances in, 250; wounds in, 155
War Office Miniature Rifle, the, 193
Waterloo, the battle of, 19, 20
Weather conditions and wind judgment, 255
Wemyss, the late Earl of, 301
Werndl rifle, the, 88
Westley Richards, Messrs., 71, 72, 177

Wheel-lock, the, 13; a modification for smokers, 14; and sporting weapons, 14; invention of, 14
Whitworth hexagonal bullet, the, 50; rifle, the, 50, 56, 57, 59, 60; Queen Victoria's shot from, 55; *versus* Enfield, 57; Sir Joseph, 55, 57, 60, 61, 64, 71
Wilkinson, Mr. Henry, 27
Wimbledon ranges, 300; Remington-action rifles used at, 66; the National Rifle Association at, 54 *et seq.*, 71
Winchester autoloading rifle, the, 177; magazine rifle, 91, 93; Repeating Arms Company, the, 75; repeating rifle (illustration), 95, 146; ·220 musket, 189
Wind allowance, 250 *et seq.*; cross winds, 254; hints on acquiring good judgment, 252; unevenness of air movement, 253; analysis, usefulness of, 261; deflection, formula to work out, 211; judging with telescope, 257 *et seq.*
Windage, 35, 37
Woolwich Arsenal, 79; the Royal Small Arms Factory at, 71
Working Men's Rifle Clubs, Society of, 191
Wounding effect of bullets, 155

Y

Young's ·303 Cleaner and Rifline, 280

Z

Zeroing of a team's rifles, 292
Zundnädelgewehr, the Prussian, 84

www.ingramcontent.com/pod-product-compliance
Ingram Content Group UK Ltd.
Pitfield, Milton Keynes, MK11 3LW, UK
UKHW042006230426
12048UKWH00009B/594